Nicholas Bethell was educated at Pembroke College, Cambridge, where he read Arabic and Persian. In 1962 he joined the editorial staff of *The Times Literary Supplement*, and in 1964 he moved to the drama department of the BBC, where he wrote scripts for radio and television. His translations of the Polish playwright Slawomir Mrozek, including Tango, have been published and performed. Leaving the BBC in 1967 he wrote a biography of the Polish leader Wladyslaw Gomulka, published in 1969, and with David Burg he translated Alexander Solzhenitsyn's Nobel Prize-winning works *The Love Girl and the Innocent* and *Cancer Ward*. He was briefly a junior member of the 1970 Conservative Government.

By the same author

THE LAST SECRET

Nicholas Bethell

The War Hitler Won

September 1939

Futura Publications Limited
A Futura Book

A Futura Book

First published in Great Britain in 1972
by Allen Lane The Penguin Press
First Futura Publications edition 1976

ISBN 0 8600 7310 6

Printed in Great Britain by
Hazell Watson & Viney Ltd
Aylesbury, Bucks

Futura Publications Limited
110 Warner Road
Camberwell, London SE5

Contents

Preface

The Hitler sword bisects the Chamberlain umbrella. This drawing, a Nazi propaganda poster in 1939, sums the book up more neatly

than any Preface. Hitler's conquest of Poland and the Allies' betrayal is a tragic enough story, but one too well known to need detailed analysis today. A more interesting thought that emerges is how an act of pure cruelty invalidated morality and turned relations between countries upside down. Those few days of fighting showed that it is impossible to condemn the conqueror without also despising the posturing of his enemies and blaming them too for the tragedy that had come upon the world. 'Might equals right' was a principle that was going out of fashion, but by the end of 1939 millions were re-converted to it.

The umbrella was a symbol not only of Chamberlain, but also of the mood of Britain and France in 1939. Hitler preferred the sword, but it was not only brute force that won him the war of those months. Passion, eloquence and dedication combined to give him a charisma which far outmatched the respectability, complacency and liberalism of the British and French, and it is no wonder that in less than a year of war he came to dominate

Europe. The only thing that could oppose him was a counter-charisma, Churchill, the man who shook out the muddled bureaucracy and turned lethargy into energy and determination. It was not Churchill's morality or humanity that counted, or even his efficiency as an administrator. It was his genius, a lesser genius than Hitler's and therefore one less likely to inflate itself and explode.

This is a book of paradoxes. It describes only a few weeks, but in them Chamberlain, the man of peace, became an influence so dangerous as to threaten the civilized world with defeat and barbarism. Churchill, with his unreasonable whims, tactlessness, unreliability and bouts of depression became the ideal political leader. And Hitler the mass murderer became elevated not only in power, but also in morality, for his successful aggression made it that much easier to apologize for him and defend him from slander. So virtue became vice and vice became virtue.

1 The First Day

The Second World War began at 4.17 a.m. on 1 September 1939. German forces opened fire on Polish-occupied points in the Free City of Danzig.[1] At 4.45 a.m. the people were awakened by the sound of heavy guns. The German warship *Schleswig-Holstein*, in Danzig on a 'courtesy visit', was shelling Westerplatte, the small peninsula where according to a League of Nations resolution (9 December 1925) Poland was entitled to maintain a military depot and eighty-eight soldiers. Also at 4.45 a.m. German forces crossed the Polish frontier in a massive invasion of the country,[2] and German aircraft began bombing Polish airfields, railway junctions, munition dumps and communication centres — not only military objectives, but also, when no more attractive target could be found, the homes of the sleeping population.

The British acting Consul in Danzig, F. M. Shepherd, wrote in his report, 'In view of the strong possibility that Herr Forster's action would lead to war it seemed advisable to take the earliest opportunity of withdrawing.'[3] Forster was the Nazi Gauleiter who controlled Danzig's mainly German population. During the night copies of a poster had been pasted up all over the city. It was his proclamation: 'Men and women of Danzig, the hour for which you have been longing for twenty years has now come. This day Danzig is returned to the great German Reich. Our Führer, Adolf Hitler, has freed us.'[4]

Shepherd too had been up all night, and he knew there was something in the wind when an Associated Press journalist named Kidd told him at 2:15 a.m. that his German colleagues were all out and about, winding up their cine-cameras. At 5.15 a.m. a detachment of S A and S S troops occupied the railway station, the Polish officials there having been arrested beforehand on charges of smuggling arms to the Polish minority. The Polish Post Office on Heveliusplatz was the only place to offer any real resistance.[5] Its staff of fifty-one was well armed and refused to surrender in spite of armoured-car fire from the streets outside. First the Germans tried to break into the post office from a next-door building by blowing a hole in the wall. They were driven back by Polish machine-gun fire. German sappers then dug under the building, placed an explosive charge and blew up part of the structure. The Poles retreated to the cellar, which they continued to defend. The Germans then procured a motor pump and a hose, covered the building in petrol and set it ablaze from top to bottom. Only then did the Poles surrender. Four of them managed to escape, six were killed in the fighting, six died in hospital from their wounds and the rest, not being in uniform, were shot as *franc-tireurs*.

Within a few hours Carl Burckhardt, the Swiss empowered by the League of Nations as Head of State, was packed off together with his staff and the diplomatic corps through East Prussia to the neutral Baltic states, their presence being no longer required.

At 5.40 a.m. Hitler broadcast his proclamation to the German Army:

The Polish state has refused the peaceful settlement of relations which I desired and has appealed to arms. Germans in Poland are persecuted with bloody terror and driven from their homes. A series of violations of the frontier, intolerable to a great power, prove that Poland is no longer willing to respect the frontier of the Reich. In order to put an end to this lunacy I have no choice than to meet force with force; the German Army will fight for the honour and rights of a new-born Germany . . .[6]

The lie that it was Poland which had invaded Germany, that Germany was replying only in self-defence, was one so gross that only Hitler could have contrived it. Early in August he had personally ordered his intelligence chief Admiral Canaris to obtain 150 Polish uniforms, together with some Polish rifles and revolvers. On 31 August a squad of concentration-camp inmates were dressed in the uniforms, equipped with the arms and ordered to 'attack' a radio station at Gleiwitz, close to the border with Poland. Instead they were killed and their bodies brought to the scene of the attack as evidence of it. German SS troops dressed as Poles made their way to the station around 8 p.m., bound and gagged the porter, burst into the studio and overpowered the night-duty staff.[7]

The 'Polish soldiers' proceeded to take over the transmission and broadcast a statement that the city of Gleiwitz was in Polish hands. They claimed to represent a non-existent 'High Command of Polish Upper Silesia Hunter-Volunteers'. For four minutes they spoke, calling on the population to rise up against the Nazis, and ending with a few revolver shots, some cries of 'Long live Poland!' and other appropriate sound effects. They then departed leaving the dead prisoners, dressed as Poles, scattered about the building. Police cars arrived a few minutes later, supposedly alerted by amazed local radio listeners, and soon after that a group of foreign journalists who 'happened to be near by'. They were in time to witness the end of the masquerade and to watch the police drawing up their report of the 'invasion'.[8]

The incident was duly reported in several foreign newspapers on 1 September. The *New York Times*, for example, wrote: 'The police are said to have discovered that the attackers were assisted by regular Polish troops. The Gleiwitz incident is alleged here to have been the signal "for a general attack by Polish *franc-tireurs* on German territory".' The American reporter was being careful about committing himself, but obviously the manufactured invasion convinced some people.

Thus Josef Goebbels, Nazi Germany's Minister of Propaganda, was able to rely on the morality of power and make truth out of falsehood. The young Nazis who provided the backbone of Hitler's movement were ready to believe anything their Führer told them. They believed the lie, and their enthusiasm grew for the war that was to restore Germany to her rightful place in the world. Other Germans did not believe it, but they pretended to, feeling too weak to resist the inevitable. Most importantly, the lie confused the outside world, only briefly of course, but in a lightning war every hour counts. The British and French riposte, if it was to come, which Hitler thought unlikely but had to consider as a possibility, had to be delayed until Germany had established her initial gains.

It was Hitler's broadcast that gave the world the news that it was war. It was picked up by Havas, the French news agency, which telephoned Foreign Minister Georges Bonnet at 6 a.m.[9] At that time also a German note was delivered to the British Embassy in Berlin. A piece of remarkable impudence, it warned that the Bay of Danzig was closed to navigation because of the possibility of military operations 'against hostile attacks by Polish naval forces or by Polish aircraft'.[10] The Polish Ambassador in Paris, Juliusz Łukasiewicz, was rung and informed only at 7 a.m., by an American diplomat, C. Offy.[11] In Warsaw itself most diplomats had slept through the first air raid of the war, which was not severe, less violent than the *blitz* attacks on London a year later according to eye-witnesses of both events.

A more vicious air attack was made on Katowice, an important industrial town in Polish Silesia near the frontier with Germany. Clare Hollingworth, there as a young *Daily Telegraph* reporter, describes it: 'Slam! Slam! A noise like doors banging. I woke up. It could not be later than five in the morning . . . I grabbed the telephone, reached the *Telegraph* correspondent in Warsaw and told him my news. I heard later that he rang straight through to the Polish Foreign Office, who had had no word of the attack.'[12] (The telephone link between Katowice and Warsaw must have been efficient in 1939. Thirty years later it takes about an hour to get a connection between two Polish cities, and this even without an air raid.)

It was from Katowice too that the British Embassy in Warsaw heard of the attack, from John Thwaites, its Consul there. Frantic telephone calls roused the staff from their beds. The American Ambassador Drexel Biddle rang Clifford Norton, Counsellor in the British Embassy, from his villa at Konstancin, just outside town. 'They're attacking!' he shouted. The bombs were going off closer and closer, until finally one exploded in his garden. His voice by now was one of utter disbelief. 'They're attacking *me*!' he shouted down the telephone. While naturally worried for his colleague's safety, Norton was secretly pleased to hear that the Germans were attacking American property. It would help to bring the United States more quickly and actively onto the Allied side.

One is liable to forget that the actual attack was a surprise to most of the world's leaders. True, Hitler's aggressions had followed one another regularly, recently every six months. True, a massive military build-up along Germany's eastern border had been observed, for example by Colonel Szymański, the Polish Military Attaché in Berlin, who had been driving round the area noting the frantic activity,[13] and confirmed by reports which reached London and Paris.[14] But in both capitals the general view was that Hitler was bluffing. It had by now penetrated the minds of the appeasers how mistaken they had been in not resisting Hitler's early demands — for the Rhineland, for Austria, for the Sudetenland, for Bohemia. They had information that, if only they had then stood up to Hitler, his generals would have withdrawn their support from him and even overthrown him. They imagined now that they had only to call Hitler's bluff, to stand firm in the face of his demands or, if he did take military action, to declare war on him formally, and the German High Command would do their job for them. The war would be over and Hitler would be finished without the need for either Britain or France to fire a shot.

Hitler had originally planned to invade Poland on 26 August, but changed his mind after the signature of the Anglo-Polish treaty on 25 August and the Italian confession the next day that she was in no condition to conduct even a defensive war. The Chief of the German General Staff, Franz Halder, writes in his diary that Hitler was 'considerably shaken' by these two events.[15] In fact, Hitler soon recovered and the postponement was only for a week, but there were those in Berlin who imagined that the operation was totally cancelled. Tragically, it was this version which leaked out to the British and French diplomats and was believed.

Robert Coulondre, French Ambassador in Berlin, wrote to Premier Daladier a letter which was read to the French Cabinet at 5 p.m. on 31 August: 'I have learnt from a reliable source that for the past five days Hitler has been hesitating. Irresolution has gripped the heart of the Nazi Party. Reports indicate a growing discontent among the people . . . You are a fisherman, I believe. Well, the fish is hooked. It now has to be played with the required skill so as to land it without breaking the line . . .'[16]

Maurice Gamelin, the French Commander-in-Chief, expressed at the end of August his opinion that 'Hitler will collapse the day war is declared on Germany. Instead of defending the frontiers of the Reich, the German Army will be forced to march on Berlin to suppress the trouble that will immediately break out. The troops manning the Siegfried Line will offer little resistance. We shall go through Germany like a knife through butter'.[17]

In London Ivone Kirkpatrick, a senior Foreign Office official, minuted that according to his information 'the German Government is wobbling' and 'the signature of the Polish Pact had fallen as a bombshell'.[18] If, as seemed likely, Italy did not join Germany in war 'the moral effect on the German people would be tremendous'. He concluded that 'the latest indications are that we have an unexpectedly strong hand'. This mine of misinformation was shown to Lord Halifax who, alarmingly, said that he quite agreed with it. Other British reports implied that Hitler had had a nervous breakdown.[19] In Paris Paul Reynaud remarked, 'Hitler is being deflated hourly'.[20]

The Americans, though not directly involved, acted quickly. Roosevelt noted in his diary, 'Last Friday at ten minutes of three o'clock in the morning Ambassador Bullitt telephoned me from Paris the tragic news that hostilities had commenced in earnest, that bombs were falling on Polish cities . . . Lights were soon burning in many offices . . .' He telephoned his Secretary of State Cordell Hull. 'I said to the President,' Hull writes, 'I intended going to my office at once. After hastily dressing and telling Mrs Hull what had happened, I drove to the State Department and walked through the deserted corridors at about 3.30 a.m.'[21]

In Great Britain, with France the country most concerned with Poland's fate, there was no such unseemly haste. Hull writes, 'I telephoned to Bullitt in Paris and Kennedy in London . . . Kennedy said the British Government had not yet been advised of the German invasion and we had furnished the first news the British had received . . .' This is an exaggeration, since there is in the Foreign Office files a Reuter news agency report of Hitler's 5.40 a.m. broadcast, which reached London at 7.28 a.m.[22] There is also a telegram from the Ambassador in Warsaw announcing 'Frontier crossed by small German detachments' which arrived at 8.30 a.m.[23] But the confidential diary of Britain's Foreign Secretary, Lord Halifax, shows that the attack was not treated as a matter of *extreme* urgency. Halifax wrote: 'Alec [Cadogan] called for me at Eaton Square *about nine* and told me that he had heard *at seven* that Danzig had declared its incorporation in the Reich and a little later that the Germans had crossed the Polish frontier . . .'[24] (Author's italics.)

It was therefore at least four hours after the attack that the leaders of Britain, Poland's formal ally, began to address themselves to the situation. Alexander Cadogan, Halifax's Permanent Under-Secretary, had not thought it necessary to rouse his boss on receipt of the alarming news, but had waited two full hours before informing him; and this in spite of his country's obligation to afford Poland all possible help 'immediately'. In France, in these initial hours at least, things were moving more quickly. At 7.30 a.m. Bonnet spoke to his Prime Minister, Édouard Daladier.[25] They had agreed on general mobilization of the armed forces and the recall of the National Assembly, the body which alone could authorize France's entry into the war.

Nor was the Polish Ambassador in London, Edward Raczyński, any better informed. He writes, '*At about ten o'clock* I received from our embassy in Paris news of the German attack on Poland.'[26] He telephoned Halifax, was asked to come immediately to 10 Downing Street, and arrived at 10.30. He spent about fifteen minutes with Halifax, told him what he had heard from Paris, and concluded: 'The Polish Government considers this to be a case of aggression under Article One of the Anglo-Polish Treaty of Mutual Assistance.' He writes that Halifax replied, 'I have very little doubt of it.' Halifax confirms this. 'I said that I had no doubt we should take the same view,' he noted in his original report. But he must have felt that this was committing him too far, because subsequently he altered the note in his own hand to read, 'I said I had no doubt *on the facts as he had reported them that* we should take the same view.'

At 10 a.m. in the German Embassy in London the staff were listening to Hitler's speech to the Reichstag when an urgent telephone call summoned the Chargé d'Affaires, Theodor Kordt, to see Halifax.[27] Kordt writes that as he turned into Downing Street he caught a glimpse of Ambassador Raczyński leaving the Prime Minister's residence. Halifax received him at 10.50, shook hands with him and asked him for information about the reported attack on Poland. Kordt replied, accurately, that he had no information about this. (He had left the Embassy before Hitler's speech had mentioned the 'counter-attack'.) Halifax told him that the reports 'create a very serious situation', and that the Cabinet would meet shortly. Shortly after returning to his Embassy, Kordt telephoned Halifax with two pieces of information, both of them false. The first was a quotation from Hitler's speech that 'the Poles have been firing repeatedly across the frontier during the night, and since this morning we have been firing back'. The second was a denial that Warsaw and other Polish towns were being bombed.[28]

In Paris the Council of Ministers met at 10.30 a.m. and agreed to ask the National Assembly for a declaration of war and for a vote of funds to fight it. War could not be declared without the Assembly's concurrence. After this Bonnet saw the Polish Ambassador Juliusz Łukasiewicz and told him: 'France will fulfil all her obligations.' But Łukasiewicz writes, Bonnet 'could not inform me when and in what form this was likely to happen. He said it depended on the consultations going on between Paris and London.'[29] This was true as far as it went, but already there were vital facts which Bonnet was withholding from the Poles.

Whatever reassurances he had given the Polish Ambassador, Bonnet was determined to pause before plunging France into war. Amazingly, he had not yet given up hope that peace could be saved. He wrote in 1971: 'The conference proposed by Rome remains the only means by which peace can be restored. I have no doubt that the chances of this are small, but I wish to neglect nothing which might ensure success.'[30] Bonnet readily admits, 'I fought for peace as one fights to save a sick man while he has a breath left in him. I was convinced that it was not France alone but western civilization that was in peril.' Even in retrospect he remains 'proud of my fruitless efforts'.[31]

Bonnet's ideas, if not bold, were certainly consistent. The basis of his hesitation, as he told the author in 1971, was that 'I was very doubtful whether France could win the war. Unlike most, I did not believe that Hitler was bluffing and I was by no means sure that the French Army would be able to resist him. Our Air Force was too small. Our Army was equipped with out-of-date tanks and artillery.' Whatever promises France had made, Bonnet was determined to save the peace if he could. At such moments, he felt, promises count for less than the vital interests of one's own country.

Further confusion was being sown by Birger Dahlerus, a

Swedish businessman, a friend of Göring and of many influential men in Britain and Germany. For months he had been conducting a one-man diplomatic mission. As Henry Channon noted in his diary (28 August): 'A Balt named Mr D. and a Mr Spencer of mid-Beds have it appears been negotiating secretly here and pretend to come from Germany. According to them Göring is anxious to dethrone Hitler and set himself up as General Monk and restore the Hohenzollerns etc. I doubt the validity of the Walrus's [Dahlerus's] credentials, but he is taken seriously by Halifax . . .' Dahlerus claimed to be a neutral mediator, though how neutral he in fact was is doubtful, as will soon emerge.

At 9.50 a.m. he rang his friend Spencer from the British Embassy in Berlin and offered to come to London to discuss ending the conflict. It had only begun, he said, because the Poles had blown up the bridge at Dirschau (in Polish 'Tczew') on the border between Poland and the Free City of Danzig. Spencer asked him, 'How could hostilities be held up? Could you limit the hostilities until you have been to London?' Dahlerus's reply was to repeat what Göring had told him an hour or so earlier: 'The Poles are sabotaging everything . . . The Poles do not want to negotiate . . . they have never meant to attempt to negotiate with Germany and that has been a proof to Germany that nothing can be done.'[32] All this was of course untrue, but in the short term it helped to cloud the issue.

The British Cabinet did not meet until 11.30 a.m., by which time Poland had been under attack for seven hours. The British official historian Llewellyn Woodward explains that the Ministers spent the morning in 'departmental work' connected with the emergency.[33] But even when they met, and in spite of the violence of the first German onslaught, there was still doubt in the minds of some Cabinet Ministers about what exactly had happened. Prime Minister Chamberlain told his colleagues: 'The event against which we had fought so long and so earnestly had come upon us. But our consciences were clear, and there could be no possible question now where our duty lay.'[34] As Woodward notes perceptively, it is significant that Chamberlain's first reaction was to declare that the 'fight' was lost — the fight against war, that is. Clearly it was this fight which had occupied him in recent months, not the real fight against Nazi Germany. But to do him justice, now that war was forced upon him, he seemed resigned to the prospect and did not intend to run away from his obligations.

Active military aid to Poland was already overdue. The war was hours old, and the hard-pressed Poles needed help. Specifically they were relying on agreements reached three months earlier in talks between the Polish Chief of Staff, Brigadier Stachiewicz, his deputy, Colonel Jaklicz, and two British officers, Brigadier Clayton and Group-Captain Davidson. If Germany attacked Poland, said Clayton on 23 May, 'we would try to decrease the enemy forces by attacking his air bases and factories'. 'What if Germany bombs Polish villages but not British villages?' Stachiewicz asked. 'In that case,' said Clayton, 'we would bomb enemy objectives without restraint after consultation with our other allies.' Stachiewicz's vital question was as follows: 'Can we take it as decided that in case of Germany aggressing against Poland the British will bomb military objectives, and that in case of bombing of civilian objectives they will also bomb German civilian objectives?' According to the record, Clayton gave 'a completely affirmative reply after consultation'. Furthermore, according to the 25 August agreement, Britain was to provide this help 'immediately'.

But at 11.30 a.m. on 1 September the British Cabinet was thinking in terms of diplomatic approach rather than of military initiative. In spite of reports from news agencies, and of one from the British Ambassador which the Foreign Office received at 8.30 a.m., to the effect that Polish territory was being invaded and bombed,[35] the Cabinet refused to accept the bad news. The American Ambassador in Warsaw had reported the attack on his house, and this had been reported to Chamberlain by Ambassador Kennedy, but against this the Cabinet had Kordt's false but categorical denial. It seems that they preferred to believe the latter, for, according to the minutes, 'later in the meeting various messages were read out which appeared to indicate that reports of the bombing of Warsaw at any rate were premature'.

One Cabinet Minister (unidentified) pointed out that 'there was at present no very definite information as to what hostile action had taken place in Poland, and that it was desirable not to take any irrevocable action until we had some greater assurance on this point'. This view was supported by Lord Chatfield, Minister for Co-ordination of Defence, who said that 'the process of evacuation of the civil population had just started, and looking at the matter from that point of view it was obviously desirable that there should be a further delay before we sent a communication in the nature of an ultimatum? Halifax quoted Dahlerus's claim that the Poles had provoked the outbreak by blowing up a bridge, and that 'Herr Hitler had declared that he did not want to start a world war, and wanted direct negotiations with Great Britain'.[36] The Cabinet heard too that 'a telegram had also been received from Sir Nevile Henderson [British Ambassador in Berlin] indicating that after Herr Hitler's speech in the Reichstag there might be some further peace effort on Herr Hitler's part'. To sum up, the Cabinet was clearly in no mood to take any immediate or decisive action.

In Berlin five big anti-aircraft guns were mounted to protect Hitler as he drove to the Reichstag to deliver his 10 a.m. speech. Shirer noted that 'somehow he did not carry conviction and there was much less cheering in the Reichstag than on previous, less important occasions'.[37] Ulrich von Hassell describes the speech as 'weak'.[38] Perhaps the problem was that Hitler was still camouflaging, still playing the statesman in the hope that Britain and France would leave him to his devices. He felt impelled to speak movingly of his contribution to world peace, of his determination 'to change the relationship between Poland and Germany so as to ensure peaceful coexistence'.

Much of his speech was criticism of Poland and clearly designed to isolate her. Poland had sent ultimata to Danzig and had tried to strangle her economically. Poland had rejected the reasonable 31 August 'proposals' by declining to send a plenipotientiary to Berlin, and 'was not ready to settle the Corridor question in a reasonable way which would be equitable to both parties'. Instead she had launched a 'sudden general mobilization' and intensified the campaign of atrocities against the German minority. The previous night she had provoked fourteen frontier incidents 'of which three were quite serious', and in which 'for the first time Polish regular soldiers fired on our territory'. Hitler had therefore been forced to order that their fire be returned: 'From now on bombs will be met with bombs'.

There was the occasional outright lie: '. . . I have ordered my air force to restrict itself to attacks on military objectives . . .

Russia and Germany fought against one another in the World War. This shall and will not happen a second time . . .' But in one resolve he was speaking no more than the truth, in his promise that 'there will be no hardships for Germans to which I myself will not submit', and that he would die himself rather than surrender.[39]

The speech was in no way abusive of Britain and France, only of Poland, and clearly it was designed to make it as easy as possible for the Allies to escape from their obligations. Meeting at 11.30 a.m., the British Cabinet was still not quite convinced that war was inevitable — there was too much optimistic misinformation for that. The most they would agree was to order Henderson to deliver a 'severe warning' to Hitler and Foreign Minister Ribbentrop. *Five more hours elapsed* before this was telephoned to Henderson at 5.45 p.m. The Ambassador was told for his own information that the next stage would be an ultimatum with a time limit, or an immediate declaration of war, but there was no time limit in the warning itself. Henderson applied to the German Foreign Office for an interview promptly at 6 p.m., but had to apply twice more before finally being granted an interview with Ribbentrop at 9.30 p.m. The French Ambassador, Coulondre, saw Ribbentrop a few minutes later. Thus Germany was able to fight the first day of the war without receiving even a diplomatic approach from her enemy's powerful allies.

The delaying tactic was working well, and no wonder, for in spite of the crisis atmosphere of the past few days the attack had taken the British and French leaders unawares, and they were not ready to act. Maybe this sounds self-contradictory and illogical, but then so was their state of mind. The basis of the Allies' relations with Germany had been their policy of appeasement. But at other times the Allies had taken a firm line, for example when Chamberlain declared on 31 March 1939 that 'in the event of any action which clearly threatened Polish independence' the British 'would feel themselves bound at once to lend the Polish Government all support in their power'.[40] This guarantee was, of course, never designed to be implemented. It was designed to prevent the case from ever arising. Chamberlain felt sure, firstly, that the guarantee would convince Hitler he could not aggress again without involving Germany in world war, secondly, that the prospect of world war would deter Hitler from aggression. Chamberlain was mistaken in both assumptions. Hitler was never convinced of British and French resolve to fight for Poland, and even if he had been he would still have attacked.

The Allied leaders' other important weakness was their failure to work out Hitler's intentions. They seemed unaware of his plans for Germany as outlined in *Mein Kampf*, or at any rate, if they knew them, they imagined that Hitler did not mean them seriously. The world was to suffer wretchedly from its failure to face the unpleasant facts about Hitler. Looking back, it does seem gross dereliction of duty for leading democratic statesmen to have so neglected to inform themselves of Hitler's plans, for as William Shirer notes astutely, 'whatever other accusations can be made against Adolf Hitler, no one can accuse him of not putting down in writing exactly the kind of Germany he intended to make if ever he came to power, and the kind of world he meant to create by armed German conquest'.[41]

Mein Kampf (My Struggle), the book Hitler wrote in prison in the fortress of Landsberg during 1924, explains in terms which leave little room for doubt Hitler's belief that Germany needed, and was entitled to obtain, by force if necessary, more living-space (*Lebensraum*) for her people, and that this extra territory should be won at the expense of Russia and of the countries which lay between Russia and Germany. The following quotations from *Mein Kampf* illustrate the point:

Only an adequate large space on this earth can assure a nation of freedom of existence . . .[42] If land was desired in Europe, it could be obtained by and large only at the expense of Russia, and this meant that the new Reich must again set itself along the road of the Teutonic Knights of old . . .[43] And so we National Socialists . . . take up where we broke off six hundred years ago. We stop the endless German movement to the south and west, and turn our gaze towards the land in the East.[44]

From the beginning Hitler's position was strengthened and camouflaged by the Treaty of Versailles, which in 1918 had imposed such harsh terms on defeated Germany that instant and widespread popularity awaited any German leader who opposed it. Right up to 1939 Hitler had been able to disguise his aggressive plans as a campaign merely to restore to Germany what was rightly hers. The occupation of the Rhineland, the seizure of Austria and of the Sudetenland had all been condemned by western statesmen for the violent and unconstitutional way in which they had been carried out. But there were many who, however much they disapproved of Hitler's methods, felt that by reuniting Germans and Austrians with the Reich he was doing no more than his patriotic duty. However distasteful and worrying Frenchmen and Englishmen found the Nazi movement, they had to reckon with the grip it had on Germans, particularly young Germans, in Czechoslovakia, Poland, Austria, Danzig and France, as well as in Germany itself. The admitted injustices of Versailles moved them to take a charitable attitude to Hitlerism, to explain away its excesses by citing the genuine suffering that had been unfairly imposed on Germany in 1918. They did not want to believe that Hitler's basically just struggle against the consequences of the Versailles Treaty was only a stalking-horse for a future campaign of aggrandizement and enslavement.

In Munich in September 1938 Chamberlain had been taken in by Hitler, and had believed his assurance that the Sudetenland was to be his last territorial demand. Chamberlain's delight at the Munich agreement was genuine, as was his belief that the agreement would be a basis for a lasting peace. In retrospect his attitude seems very naive, but one must not forget that it was shared by a large majority in Britain and France, both in Parliament and in the population. Churchill's prophetic warnings were dismissed as old-fashioned sabre-rattling and political sour grapes. It was only in March 1939, when Hitler's armies marched into Prague and occupied Bohemia, that Chamberlain realized he had been deceived. The Czechs were not German, and this time Hitler could not claim to be reuniting his fellow-countrymen. The March 1939 move was seen for what it was — a piece of expansionism. Bitterly disappointed and disillusioned, Chamberlain published his guarantee of Poland, thinking that it would be enough to deter Hitler.

By what he wrote in *Mein Kampf* and by his occupation of Prague Hitler had, one would have thought, convinced even the most fervent appeaser of his plan to conquer, to enlarge Germany by a series of aggressive moves. But the appeasers lingered on. To be fair, Chamberlain was no longer one of them. He was now resolved that Hitler must be stopped, but he saw no logical reason why Hitler should persist in the face of British and French threats. And not all his colleagues had been so shocked by the March events. There were senior politicians in both Britain and France ready to make concessions to Hitler which would allow him to expand eastwards. There were many who still saw him as the only defence the West had against the encroachments of Bolshevik Russia. Few in Britain or France actually admired Hitler, but there were many who saw him as a necessary evil.

As German–Polish relations worsened during the summer of 1939, Hitler was again able to confuse the moral issue by pointing to justifiable German grievances. On the face of it, it *was* unfair that Germany should be divided in two, that there was no over-land communication between the two parts except through Polish territory, that the important German city of Danzig had become an artificial separate state with a non-German administration. As September approached, Hitler was able to build on the basis of these genuine complaints a mass of exaggerated and downright false accusations, designed to sow doubt in British and French minds as to whether they were right to be supporting Poland.

In 1940 a book called *Documents on the Events Preceding the Outbreak of the War* was published by the German Library of Information in New York. In wild, terrifying language it set out to show that during August 1939 the German minority in Poland had endured 'an unparalleled reign of terror', and that 'without the intervention of the Reich this minority would have suffered complete economic and cultural extinction'.[45] 'Hundreds of deposi-tions', it claimed, 'concerning frightful cruelties that had been inflicted indiscriminately upon the Germans in Poland – men, women and children; the healthy and the disabled; the young and the aged – were substantiated down to the minutest details by sworn testimony, eye-witness accounts, confessions, autopsies and examinations of bodies.'[46] The book reads like a parody of itself and is almost funny until one remembers that it was lies like these which justified and paved the way to the eventual Nazi extermina-tion of twenty per cent of the Polish population.

The book illustrates Nazi propaganda in its full crudity. A note at the end, advertising a companion volume, promised American readers 'photographs of murder and mutilation victims and the scenes of both individual and mass murders'.[47] And as if this were not enough, the preview continues, 'The American edition devotes only forty-eight pages to its pictorial supplement. The rest of the material – those photographs which depict the most gruesome horrors – too shocking for general circulation – appears separately in a special supplementary volume. The second volume is limited and is available to government officials, librarians, medical men, professors and students only, by application to the German Library of Information, 17 Battery Place, New York City.' One wonders what sort of Americans called at the library for their copies – presumably only those who had tastes, political or physical, in common with those of the book's Nazi authors, and who were therefore ripe for recruitment to the cause.

The extent to which the Poles did use violence against their German minority is impossible now to verify. That there were no such acts at all would be very hard to believe. The Germans in Poland were seen as a potential fifth column, and in the hectic atmosphere that preceded the outbreak of war there doubtless were instances of anti-German repression. What is equally certain, though, is that these incidents were exaggerated out of all proportion by Goebbels's propaganda machine. Fritz Hesse, who was a German official in London at the time, wrote in 1953 that 'when the German wireless played *Deutschland, Deutschland über alles* at midnight on 26 August, the German minorities in Poland regarded it as the signal, armed themselves and occupied certain strategic points'. The Polish authorities ordered the border area cleared of Germans. There was violence and local fighting in which, it was reported, probably with exaggeration, 4,850 Germans were killed. Hesse continues: 'This figure appeared in the German official publication of documents relating to Poland, only it was altered by order of Ribbentrop for reasons of propaganda. A nought was added, so that the figure 4,850 became 48,500, which in the official publication was rounded off to appear as 50,000.'[48]

The 'neutral' intermediary Dahlerus was another source of such stories. On the morning of 30 August he spoke to Chamberlain and Halifax by telephone from the British Embassy in Berlin. Dahlerus had seen Göring the previous evening, and was able to tell the British leaders of 'an incident which had just taken place in which five Germans had been shot while trying to cross a river.

This had been done under the eyes of a German officer in command of troops who, in deference to his express instructions, had refrained from intervening . . .' On 20 August the German Foreign Office had published a list of thirty-eight cases of ill-treatment of Germans in Poland. A sample case was that of the 'rustic labourer' Albert Krank who 'was attacked by two Poles who had disguised their faces. His penis and left testicle was so severely injured by stabs and blows that he had to be taken to the hospital . . .'[49] Very little attempt was made to make these claims sound even remotely plausible. There was no question of subtlety; it was just propaganda, a heavy blunt instrument, as if Germany was merely going through the motions of protesting, briefly playing the part of the persecuted helpless victim simply in order to build up a pretext. It was mainly for home consumption, to convice the waverers in Germany that their government was being forced to retaliate. Only those already prone to believing Dr Goebbels could ever have been taken in by such crude stories, but of course there were many such people, and not only in Germany.

These accusations were only one of many factors influencing the British and French away from a steadfast policy during the week that preceded war. Another consideration was the British delight at obtaining an assurance of Italian neutrality. At 1.30 p.m. on 23 August the British Ambassador in Rome, Percy Loraine, had a talk with the Italian Foreign Minister, Count Ciano, as a result of which he telegraphed home in great excitement at 2.50 p.m.:

I am now confident that Italy will not join with Germany if Herr Hitler makes war. It cannot be stressed too strongly that any suggestion in Parliament, press, radio, etc., that we have reached this conclusion is calculated to wreck everything. I am nevertheless of the opinion that our military authorities can now base their dispositions for a war forced on us by Germany on the assumption of the Italians' non-belligerency . . .'

The Italian decision was in fact the result of their realization that they were quite unprepared for war. But it was seen in London as a triumph and a diplomatic *coup*. Suddenly Mussolini was turned into an apostle of peace. His approaches to both sides and requests for concessions were to serve the German interest wholly, but in the new atmosphere they were, at first at least, kindly received in Paris and London.

On 23 August Ciano told Loraine that only a new fact could pacify Hitler and break the deadlock. This new fact could be Poland's recognition of the right of Danzig to return to Germany. Could Britain influence the Poles here? These ideas, Loraine noted, 'were clearly very important and I knew the Prime Minister and you [Halifax] would much appreciate Signor Mussolini's willing cooperation'. Mussolini's view as that 'without that card to play he could not intervene effectively. And meanwhile time pressed. We had maybe only to the end of the week.'

On this point at least Mussolini was well informed. The previous day (Tuesday 22 August) Hitler had held a conference at Obersalzberg at which he told his commanders-in-chief that 'the order for the start of hostilities will be given later, probably Saturday morning'.[50] This was confirmed by Halder who noted in his diary on 23 August, 'Y-day definitely set for the 26th (Saturday).'[51] So Mussolini's warning that a Polish concession, if it were to come, must come within a day or two was quite accurate. True, the attack was postponed for a week, but only because of the signature of the Anglo-Polish Treaty on the Friday, which made Hitler pause momentarily to review the situation. What the British and French did not know was that Hitler was resolved to invade Poland whatever they signed or whatever they did.

One effect of Mussolini's attitude was to make Britain and France more inclined to influence Poland to make concessions. His promise of neutrality was seen by the Allies as a triumph. His offer to intercede with Hitler was not to be rejected out of hand. The Allies felt, probably rightly, that the Italian offer was made in good faith and, certainly wrongly, that Mussolini's advice would carry weight with Hitler. If the cession of Danzig was the price of Mussolini's help, there were many in the West who thought it was a price which was worth paying. On 4 May a leading article headed 'Danzig is not worth a war' had appeared in *The Times*. More stalwart spirits realized that Danzig would not be the end of it, that it was only the thin end of a very cruel wedge. But there were others who took the simplistic view that Armageddon should not be risked for the sake of an unimportant city a thousand miles away which, since most of its people were German, naturally wished to rejoin Germany

One of these was clearly Percy Loraine, who again urged the cession of Danzig in a telegram from Rome just before noon on 31 August.[52] On this decision, he suggested, might depend not only the issue of peace or war, but also the attitude of Italy if war did in fact break out. He was wrong on both counts, since both the German decision to make war and the Italian decision to remain neutral were already taken in the light of what the leaders of both countries saw as their national interest. Neither decision was going to be influenced by the British or French attitude to Danzig.

Another influence against British firmness was their Ambassador in Berlin, Nevile Henderson. On 29 August he telegraphed Halifax urging him to influence the Poles to adopt a 'reasonable attitude'. He wrote: 'The question of exaggerated prestige and *amour propre* on the part of Poland must not be allowed to stand in the way of a fairly negotiated settlement.'[53] Again, a few hours later, he wrote: 'The situation is far too critical to stand on considerations of Polish prestige.'[54] That evening, 'fortified by half a bottle of champagne', he was called to see Hitler, after which he reported, 'I am not unhopeful that Hitler's answer may not be too unreasonable. It will probably demand too much, just as Poland will offer too little. In the end, if we remain firm with Germany, we shall have to be no less firm with the Poles.'[55]

The next evening (30 August) Henderson was summoned to see Ribbentrop, who read him a long note of 'proposals'[56] for ending the crisis, the gist of which included the holding of plebiscites in the disputed areas, and corridors for the country which lost the vote, to ensure for the Germans free communication between the two parts of the country, and for the Poles access to the sea at their newly built port of Gdynia. These ideas were, it is said, prepared by the German Foreign Office, rejected by Hitler as far too weak, but resurrected as a red herring to confuse the British and to convince the world of German moderation. Hitler knew that they would never be implemented, for within thirty-six hours they would be nullified by his military action, which was then definitely set for the morning of 1 September. Henderson described Ribbentrop's attitude as 'aping Herr Hitler at his worst'.[57] 'He kept jumping to his feet in a state of great excitement, folding his arms across his chest and asking if I had anything more to say.'[58] He refused even to give the Ambassador a copy of the proposals. They were invalid, he said, since no Polish plenipotentiary had yet arrived in Berlin to discuss them.

But the next day Henderson had a message from Göring, who was already being established as the 'nice guy' of the Nazi government, the counterbalance to Ribbentrop the 'heavy'. Like most dictators, Hitler believed in giving his adversaries treatment which was alternately sweet and sour. It confuses the reasoning mind. Göring had been present at Hitler's 22 August conference and knew there would be war. The message he gave the Ambassador was deliberately false and misleading: 'The German proposals, which he [Göring] described as very moderate and which in fact appeared so to me [Henderson] though I was not given the opportunity of studying them, would be still valid provided Polish plenipotentiary came at once to Berlin.' Optimistically preferring to believe this second-hand message to what Ribbentrop had told him the previous evening, Henderson proceeded throughout this last day of peace to tug at this last thread of hope. Only it could save his mission, which was peace. On this slender chance he staked not only his mission but also his reputation as an able senior administrator, only to lose both.

Henderson began to panic and, when the Poles showed themselves understandably reluctant to act on this nebulous offer, to accuse them of obstruction. 'I understand that the Polish Government is raising the question of procedure,' came a telegram from him at 11.33 a.m. 'The question of procedure should not be allowed to stand in the way.'[59] At 12.20 p.m. there was another telegram: 'I understand that the Polish Government is again hesitating to give him [Ambassador Lipski] instructions in view of procedure. Can procedure be allowed to stand in the way at such a moment? . . . Terms sound moderate to me and are certainly so in view of German desire for good relations with Great Britain [*sic*]. This is no Munich . . .'[60] In the Foreign Office files a note is added to this telegram that Halifax 'does not share view therein expressed as to obstructive attitude of Polish Government'.[61]

A more specific telegram from Henderson arrived that same evening: 'If there is to be genuine peace in future between Poland and her powerful neighbour, grievances of latter which are not of

Herr Hitler's making but national must be eliminated. In my opinion in order to achieve this end city of Danzig as distinct from port must revert to Germany. There must be direct and extra-territorial communication between Reich and East Prussia. And Germany minority in Poland must be got rid of by some exchange of population.'[62] It was Henderson's opinion, and here he was probably right, that even moderate Germans would regard this as fair.

There is a tendency for ambassadors to become sympathetic to the foreign policy of the country to which they are accredited. This is certainly illustrated by the attitudes of Henderson and of his colleague in Warsaw, Howard Kennard, whose view it was that Britain, Poland and France should not give way to Germany by one inch. Between these two stood Halifax and the mainstream of British policy. Halifax did not believe the Poles were being obstructive, but he did think they should make themselves more readily available for talks, and that at these talks, in return for proper guarantees, they should be ready to concede to Germany some areas of German-populated territory as well as Danzig. At 1.45 p.m. on 31 August he telegraphed to Kennard asking him to 'advise' the Polish Government to order Lipski to forward the German proposals to Warsaw 'so that they may at once consider them and make suggestions for early discussions'.[63]

Kennard's reply, received by the Foreign Office at 3.20 p.m., all but contradicted the Foreign Secretary. 'Do you wish me to insist', he asked, 'that the Polish Ambassador at Berlin be asked to accept such a document in spite of the danger of ultimatum in some form being attached thereto?'[64] That evening he again telegraphed: 'His Majesty's Ambassador at Berlin appears to consider German terms reasonable. I fear that I cannot agree with him from the point of view of Warsaw. While to the uninitiated they may appear plausible the Polish Government will certainly regard them as an attempt to strangle her under a cloak of legality.'[65]

Germany's call to discuss non-existent 'terms' was supported by her Italian ally, who launched a similar peace move around noon that same day. Both Halifax and Bonnet were telephoned from Rome with a proposal for a conference to begin on 5 September 'for the revision of the clauses of the Treaty of Versailles which are the cause of the present grave troubles in the life of Europe'.[66]

It was a matter of extreme urgency, Ciano explained. Unlike many British and French leaders, he did not believe that Hitler was bluffing. Doubtless he was better informed than they were. 'A clash between Germany and Poland might take place any minute,' he accurately reported.

This move was not German-inspired, but it might well have been, for it served the German interest exactly. It was to cloud the issue of peace and war, and it split the western allies. Bonnet's reaction to it was quite positive: 'Mussolini has made a valuable offer. It has not been done in collusion with Hitler. It is our last hope for peace.'[67] Chamberlain disagreed: 'His first reaction was that it was impossible to agree to a conference under the threat of mobilized armies.'[68] Percy Loraine, pro-Mussolini as usual, passed on the strange Italian idea that once Britain and France agreed to the conference, 'Hitler can hardly refuse'.[69]

Ciano had asked Loraine to support the idea and, he said, 'I do feel honestly able to do so.' This advice was not well received in London nor, it seemed at first, in Paris, for Eric Phipps (the British Ambassador) was told by French Premier Daladier that 'he [M. Daladier] will not accept Signor Mussolini's invitation to a second "Munich" in Italy on 5 September . . . he would rather resign than accept this invitation.'[70] But it would appear that later he talked to his Foreign Minister Bonnet and was convinced, for Bonnet told Phipps that France would not reject the Italian proposal offhand.[71] And subsequently, as a Polish historian justifiably complains, 'French diplomacy worked assiduously on the idea for three whole days . . . It was to absorb the attention of the Quai d'Orsay far more than any question of providing Poland with help.'[72]

Strangely, the German aggression the next morning seems to have softened rather than hardened the French Premier's determination. His Cabinet met, and at 10.15 a.m. a message was sent to Ciano that 'the Government associates itself with any initiative aimed at a friendly solution of the conflict which has broken out between Germany and Poland'.[73] They thanked the Italian Government for their efforts and for the proposal 'to which they give a favourable reply', provided that Poland were allowed to participate.

It was here that British and French policy began to diverge

seriously. At 11.20 a.m., an hour after Bonnet's 'favourable reply', the British wired Ciano in quite different terms. They too thanked him for his efforts, but continued, 'It would seem however from news now received that the action of the German Government has now rendered it impossible to proceed along those lines.' [74] 'A rupture!' comments Bonnet: 'I urge Corbin [Ambassador in London] to rally Lord Halifax to our text.'[75]

François-Poncet, French Ambassador in Rome, took Bonnet's message to Ciano and asked him to agree to Polish participation. Ciano agreed and asked the French to put the idea to the Poles. It must be emphasized that at this stage, the afternoon of 1 September, the Poles knew nothing whatever of the Italian idea, even though its aim was to buy Germany off at their expense with Danzig and some areas of Polish territory. The French Ambassador in Warsaw, Léon Noel, thus had the unenviable task of taking the message to Beck in the middle of an air raid. Beck, his gas mask slung over his shoulder, had come out of the Foreign Office shelter to receive him.[76]

One can imagine Beck's alarm and anger. Warsaw had been bombed several times that day. The Polish Army was resisting a massive assault along the length of the country's western borders. And here was Poland's ally proposing some vaguely defined conference without any assurance of what might be the result, or even of her support for the Polish cause. Given the circumstances Beck's reply was mild: 'We find ourselves in a situation of total war as a result of unprovoked aggression. We need not conferences but joint action, which our allies are bound to offer to resist this aggression. In any case this is the first I have heard of any Italian proposal.'[77] Because of communication difficulties this message reached Paris only at 3 p.m. the next day, 2 September.

Noel, it seems, was not happy about what he had been asked to do, for he took the unusual and irregular step of informing his British colleague Kennard of the exchange. He had no authority to do this, and he asked the British not to reveal that he had told them.[78] Kennard passed the message on to London, adding that 'every Pole is now asking how quickly and effectively we can implement the alliance'. This was one of many telegrams Kennard sent in an attempt to galvanize his government into action.

These fruitless ideas for impossible conferences were already bearing fruit for Hitler, granting him valuable hours to breach Poland's defences free of the fear of intervention in the West. Whether or not Mussolini wanted peace — which is probable — whether or not he believed Hitler would agree — which is improbable — his efforts were just what Hitler wanted. As for the Poles, they stood firm in the face of disaster. Their leaders have been accused of living in fool's paradise, or in fool's hell, and maybe they were, but their mistakes were those of earlier months. At this stage there was nothing they could do to avert the blow. Their concessions, had they offered any, would not have deterred Hitler, and they had more correctly analysed Hitler's murderous intent than many in the West who still thought Hitler was capable of being bought off.

For these were the questions Britain and France had to decide in the light of Mussolini's proposal. Was Hitler bluffing? In that case they had only to stand firm and he would collapse like a pricked balloon. Was Hitler resolved to take by force Danzig and Poland's formerly German-populated areas? In that case perhaps the Allies should not stand firm, but should make Hitler a reasonable offer, which he might well accept in preference to going to war. Or was Hitler resolved, come what may, upon a war of conquest, upon a German Reich that would extend to the Ural Mountains, upon enslavement and eventual extermination of the present inhabitants of these lands? This was the nightmare truth, implied certainly in *Mein Kampf* and in some of Hitler's private utterances, but believed by few in Germany and by hardly any in the West. The world was still nowhere near recognizing with what manner of man it was about to deal.

As 31 August drew to its close Halifax was wavering, faced with the most horrible decisions of his life, unable to make up his mind between the contradictory advice he was receiving from Paris, Berlin and Warsaw, let alone to coordinate it all with his own Government's policy. By 12.50 a.m. on 1 September he seemed to have changed his mind. Apparently he now believed the Poles *were* being obstructive, for he wired to Kennard: 'I do not see why the Polish Government should feel difficulty about authorizing Polish Ambassador to accept a document from the German Government . . . If the document did contain an ultimatum, the Polish Government would naturally refuse to discuss it until the ultimatum was withdrawn. On the other hand, a refusal by them to receive proposals would be gravely misunderstood by outside opinion . . . Please speak to M. Beck immediately in the above sense.' [79] A few minutes earlier Halifax had received a telegram from Henderson suggesting 'that the Polish Government be urged in unmistakable language' to send a plenipotentiary to Berlin. [80]

Four hours later the Germans invaded, thus making Halifax's diplomatic waverings out of date. He was unaware of Hitler's decision, taken in principle months earlier, to invade Poland not in order to redress just grievances, but to provide Germany with the living-space he thought his country needed and was entitled to take by force from countries whose people were racially inferior. The British and French ignorance is surprising because both countries had many friends and good intelligence contacts in Germany, particularly among the military leadership, who were continually urging a firm stand against Hitler and hinting that they would shortly remove him. The British service attachés in Berlin seem to have been quite free to talk to German officers and to gather information. [81] Considering that the two countries were on the brink of war, this is astonishing, and shows that the Nazi police system still did not fully dominate the German army. Stalin would never have allowed such a state of affairs. However, the generals stopped short of telling the Allies the one piece of information that might have galvanized them into action during the summer of 1939, and again during the last days of August — that Hitler had told them on 23 May of his decision 'to attack Poland at the first suitable opportunity', and on 22 August of his decision to attack in the next few days. [82]

Nor was the British Foreign Office any better informed on the probable consequences of the Nazi-Soviet pact. One of its most senior men, Moley Sargent, noted on 29 August: 'If Hitler intends to collaborate with Stalin in the complete suppression of Poland as an independent state, we must remember that a considerable time will be required for Germany to organize her collaboration with Russia, both militarily and economically. It is hardly possible that at the present moment such collaboration could be made to work.' [83] It is hard to find the reasoning behind Sargent's emphatic statement, which was so soon to be proved wrong.

On 24 August Gladwyn Jebb, Cadogan's secretary, minuted a

talk with a Czech journalist called Papirnik, who had letters from Ukrainian friends in Ruthenia. Apparently these had heard from their compatriots in the Soviet Union that on 15 August Commissar Andreyev had outlined Russia's plan: a Russo-German invasion, a residual Poland similar to the nineteenth-century 'Congress' Poland, absorption of the eastern lands into the USSR. Again, Charles Orde, British Minister in Riga, reported on 31 August 'that there was a secret understanding between the German and Soviet governments for a division of territory in Eastern Europe, which covered the Baltic States'. These very accurate reports were confirmed on 12 September by Reginald Hoare, the Minister in Bucharest, whose informant was the Rumanian President himself.[84] But it was not enough to convince the Foreign Office to draw any conclusion or make any plan. Frank Roberts noted that there were a lot of stories flying about on this, 'but we have no definite evidence of any kind'. After all, the Soviet Foreign Minister himself, Molotov, spoke on 31 August of 'those amateurs who read into the Pact more than is written in it' who had 'set on foot all kinds of insinuations and conjectures in order to cast discredit on the Pact in various countries'.[85] And Defence Commissar Voroshilov in an interview published in *Izvestiya* on 27 August had said that the Pact did not rule out a continuation of Soviet–Polish trade. Again, it was all camouflage behind which an aggressive move was being prepared, and most Allied statesmen were reluctant to believe that the worst was going to happen.

In theory at least the British Government machine was prepared for war down to the last detail. Over the years a 'War Book' – a list of things to be done immediately after the outbreak – had been compiled. Continuously revised and supplemented, it provided the administration with an essential framework for the many changes that were about to become necessary. Meeting on 1 September, the Cabinet ordered the 'precautionary stage' to be set in motion, and this was communicated at once to all government departments and to all British-ruled territories. The warning specified Germany and Italy as possible enemies, but emphasized that 'it is most important that no action should be taken which can be considered as provocative by Italy'. The bureaucratic machine allowed for a sub-committee to meet at once, and that same day various decisions were taken: to institute a Ministry of Home Security and a

Ministry of Information (for propaganda), to intensify air-raid precautions, to control radio messages and the movements of foreign residents, to prepare for food and fuel rationing, to decentralize the Smithfield meat market and the Billingsgate fish market and to fix maximum prices for some commodities. Whatever troubles the war might bring, the Civil Service was not going to be caught napping.

In Poland events were perforce moving with greater speed.[86] The Germans were throwing against Poland the whole of their armoured and motorized force, seven and eight divisions respectively, thus leaving the western front empty of tanks. Almost the whole of the German Air Force, about 2,000 aircraft in all, was in the East too. The Stuka dive-bombers were from the start particularly effective against infantry in the field, against Polish communications and generally at spreading confusion and panic among the population. Some came hunting in packs against specific military objectives, but others roamed the skies on their own, apparently with orders to shoot at anything that moved — trains, cars, horses or even pedestrians. General Władysław Anders, who commanded the Polish forces in Italy later in the war, wrote of the war's beginning:

Once I saw a group of small children being led by their teacher to the shelter of the woods. Suddenly there was the roar of an aeroplane. The pilot circled round, descending to a height of fifty metres. As he dropped his bombs and fired his machine guns, the children scattered like sparrows. The aeroplane disappeared as quickly as it had come, but on the field some crumpled and lifeless bundles of bright clothing remained. The nature of the new war was already clear.[87]

Against Göring's mighty Luftwaffe the Poles could muster only 771 aircraft, of which 350 were either in reserve, under repair or used for training purposes only.[88] The real need was for fighters, but of these there were only 170 ready for active service, old machines known as P-7 or P-11.[89] A senior Polish air force officer wrote after the war that these were 'unsuitable for military operations, since they cannot even keep pace with the enemy bombers, and in the face of enemy fighters are quite defenceless'. The Poles were due to have a consignment of new British fighters, fourteen Hurricanes and one Spitfire — hardly a war-winning supply, but it would have been something. Their departure kept being delayed, until eventually they were sent on the S.S. *Lassell* through the Mediterranean and the Black Sea for delivery through Rumania, around the end of September. But it was a voyage of several weeks, and the moment when these fighters were really needed was 1 September.

Numerically the German and Polish land armies were quite evenly matched. The German invaders, about eighty per cent of the Army's front-line divisions, numbered about a million and a half, and this was roughly the figure which the Polish High Command planned to mobilize in defence. But the British and French had exerted pressure to prevent full Polish mobilization until 30 August, frightened that Germany might view such a move as 'provocative'. The result was that a quarter of the Army never reached its units. The million or so defenders who did manage to report found themselves attacked a few hours after mobilization by an enemy who was better equipped, better prepared, and who had somehow mobilized fully in secret over a period of weeks the whole of his army, unknown to the British and French who were still busy restraining the Poles. German secrecy was so effective that at 9.30 on the evening of 1 September Ribbentrop was able to tell Henderson, and be briefly believed, that 'it was the Poles who had first mobilized and that yesterday it was Poland that had invaded Germany with troops of the regular army'.[90]

The two invading Army Groups, commanded by Field-Marshals Gerd von Runstedt and Fedor von Bock, were launched in a double pincer movement from south and north Poland, numbering 886,000 (thirty-five divisions) and 630,000 (seventeen divisions) respectively. These figures quoted by Halder are generally believed to be accurate. Churchill puts the total at fifty-six divisions, which may be accurate if one includes frontier guards, SS men and other special forces.[91] The piece of western Poland near Poznań (Posen) which bulged into Germany was, contrary to expectation, only held defensively, while the main thrusts came from the south through the 'Moravian Gate' towards the important industrial area of Silesia with the cities of Cracow and Katowice, from East Prussia in the north towards Warsaw only 100 miles from the frontier, and from east and west across the fifty-mile-wide corridor which was Poland's only link with the sea.

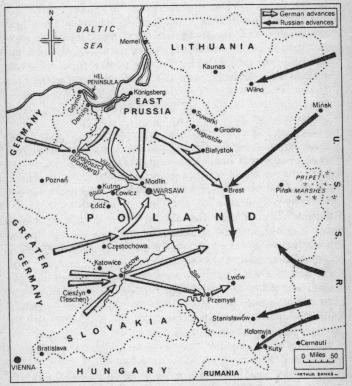

The German and Russian invasions of Poland, 1939

Not everything went well for Germany on the first day. The tactics of 'lightning war', conceived originally by the British strategist Liddell-Hart, were riskier than those of the First World War. They did not envisage a 'front line' in the conventional sense, so that in places the German frontier was defended thinly or not at all. On 1 September the Poles managed to invade and occupy a few points in East Prussia,[92] the Podlaska cavalry advancing to near Jansbork, the Suwalska cavalry into Margrabowa. It is reported that during these brief Polish successes 'the German population panicked easily'.[93] The German tank commander Heinz Guderian writes in similar vein in his book *Panzer Leader*.[94] On 1 September, it seems,

> there was a thick ground mist at first which prevented the air force from giving us any support ... Unfortunately the heavy artillery of the 3rd Panzer Division felt itself compelled to fire into the mist, despite having received precise orders not to do so. The first shell landed fifty yards in front of my command vehicle, the second fifty yards behind it. I reckoned the next one was bound to be a direct hit and ordered my driver to turn about and drive off. The unaccustomed noise had made him nervous, however, and he drove straight into a ditch at full speed.

Guderian refers on three occasions to his having to calm people down, successfully it seems, for on the next day 'the panic of the first day's fighting was past'. William Shirer too, wrote in his diary about the first air-raid warning at 7 p.m. on 1 September: 'The lights went out and all the German employees grabbed their gas masks and, not a little frightened, rushed for the shelter.' The cafés and beer-halls were packed with Berliners huddled together waiting for the bombs which never came. 'No raid tonight. Where are the Poles?' continues Shirer's diary.

But it is to the credit of German military skill that their *Blitzkrieg* took only a day to get into its stride. The Poles had little conception of what was about to hit them. On paper their thirty-one infantry divisions, plus six in reserve,[95] might have been a match for the invader, had it not been for the invention of this entirely new form of warfare. The fact that they possessed eleven cavalry brigades and only two armoured brigades was in itself bad enough, but what was worse was that it meant their strategists had no conception of the new role of the tank. Many of them felt that the tank was an overrated weapon, not so mobile or manœuvrable as the horse, and always liable to break down or get bogged down in the mud. Fuel for the horse is easy to find, they thought, it does not run out of petrol. They would not face the fact that central Poland, with hardly a hill, forest or river between Poznań and Warsaw, is ideal tank country, very difficult to defend. And while a horse can be stopped by a machine-gun bullet, a tank can not.

Psychologically too the Polish leaders were prejudiced in favour of the horse. It was with cavalry that they had fought in the First World War, as a result of which their country regained independence after a hundred years of foreign occupation. With horses too their hero Józef Piłsudski, who ruled Poland from 1926 to 1935, had entered the Ukraine in 1920 to fight the Red Army, had been forced to retreat almost to Warsaw but then, through the 'Miracle on the Vistula', had driven the Bolsheviks back into the Ukraine and Byelorussia, winning vast areas of territory at the ensuing peace treaty. Piłsudski's government, whose successors ruled the country in 1939, became caricatured as 'the colonels', a group of cavalry officers, fiercely proud, charging the enemy sabre in hand. Of course it was a distortion, but there was much of the old-fashioned cavalry officer in the mentality of Foreign Minister Józef Beck, of Marshal Rydz-Śmigły and of others. The horse had served them well, and in their September 1939 army there were a quarter of a million of them.[96]

There was also the matter of cost. In the years 1933–9 the Polish annual budget averaged between 2,000 and 2,500 million złoty, a total of 14,000 million złoty for the six years. Of this almost half (6,500 million złoty) was spent on defence, a huge proportion for such a poor country. But compared to the German contribution it was paltry. In the same six years, according to Hitler, the Germans spent 90,000 million marks (the equivalent of 36,000 million U.S. dollars or 200,000 million złoty) on defence,[97] i.e. thirty times more than the Poles.[98] British loans, promised after the 31 March guarantee, were still in the negotiating stage when Poland was attacked five months later, Britain insisting on devaluation of the złoty as a precondition to providing funds. Throughout most of 1939 Poland was actually *exporting* arms to Britain — 40-millimetre Bofors anti-aircraft guns manufactured in Silesia under Swedish licence. So when it came to war the Polish

Army had not even the most basic of equipment, not even a rifle for each infantryman.

The idea of constructing proper defences for Poland's borders, something along the lines of the Siegfried or Maginot lines, was to build castles in the air. Poland was an awkwardly shaped, almost land-locked country with more than 2,000 miles of frontier, of which the bulk was with Germany and Soviet Union, two potentially hostile countries. France, a far richer country, had managed to build a Maginot Line a mere 250 miles long, and even that did not protect her in 1940. During 1939 the British Military Attaché in Warsaw, Colonel 'Roly' Sword, was asked to prepare a report on the Polish frontier defences. 'I've done my report,' he told Clifford Norton. 'It consists of three words – "There aren't any".'

Earlier in 1939 the Poles too had been guilty of wishful thinking. It is difficult when dealing with a Hitler to think in any other way. Fortified with patriotic fervour, with the memory of their glorious imperial past but with little else, they did not realize how easily and quickly their twenty-one-year-old independence could be snuffed out. Military leaders made rousing speeches, a few even speaking of a Polish march on Berlin. Colonel Wenda said in a speech on 7 May, 'We are the people to whom the Prussians once gave homage.' If the Germans attacked, he went on, Polish fists would 'without a moment's hesitation fall on the head of the enemy and level him with the dust'. Rydz-Śmigły himself was more realistic. In an interview for the American press on 20 July he claimed that his army 'while not as great as the German Army, is still a good army'.[99] This did not mean, though, that the Poles would not fight to the last: 'We have learnt from experience what it means to live without freedom, and we are ready to die rather than lose it again.' The Poles were one of the few peoples for whom these were not idle words. Many millions were shortly to die in proving that particular truth.

Rydz-Śmigły also wrote in December (after the event, it is true, but probably truthfully): 'When the war began I fully realized that it was bound to be lost on the Polish front, which I regarded as just one sector of a great anti-German front. I began my fight under impossible conditions. I felt that the commander of a sector of the front which had to be sacrificed in order to give time and opportunity to others to organize and prepare themselves.' In his view Poland 'made the maximum possible effort in preparation for the war'.[100]

In their heart of hearts the Polish leaders probably realized their weakness, but they decided to stand firm rather than make concessions to Hitler and his threats. True, this policy lead them to disaster, and it is tempting to suggest that they might have got off more lightly if they had been ready to bend a little. One negative result of their stubbornness was to make them unpopular with their allies as well as with their enemies. It alienated the German liberals, von Hassell for instance, who wrote on 1 September that the Poles 'with Polish conceit and Slavic aimlessness, confident of English support, missed every remaining chance of avoiding war'.[101] What chance there was of avoiding war he does not explain, which is just as well, for so long as Hitler remained there was none. Hassell's remark illustrates that when it came to Poland the German 'liberals' were not very liberal. They were determined to undo the genuine injustices of the Treaty of Versailles, by force if necessary. Unlike Hitler they would not though have destroyed the Polish state but would have contented themselves with taking the German-inhabited areas.[102] By and large they thought the Poles an inefficient, feckless lot.

One might argue, though, that if these were the views of a German 'liberal', God alone could protect Poland from the fanatics who actually ruled Germany, that to make concessions would be merely to postpone the inevitable. Should not the Poles therefore fight now, with their territory intact and with help from Britain and France apparently assured? If they weakened in the slightest, if for example they agreed to yield to Hitler some German-inhabited areas, might not the British and French conclude that their ally was unwilling to fight and leap at the chance to duck out of their obligations? Even if Poland lost the initial campaign and was occupied, which the Marshal apparently foresaw, partisan warfare would continue and, provided that the Allies won, Poland would rise again. One would like to think that such ideas were at the back of the Polish leaders' minds as they faced the advancing hordes.

It is not certain exactly what in practice the Poles expected of their allies during these first hours of the war. They knew that the British Army was tiny, and that it would be days before it could be got across the Channel to France, let alone be ready for offensive action. The 'great anti-German front', if it came, would be almost entirely French at least for a number of weeks, or even months, for Britain was only in a position to supply sixteen divisions during the first year of war.[103] Had the western front lasted, this would have been a drop in the ocean. The British intention was summed up in the conclusion to a recent report by the Chiefs of Staff to the Committee of Imperial Defence, dated 28 July, which ran:

> If Germany attacks in the East and holds in the West, there is little that we ourselves can do either at sea or on land at the outset of the war to relieve the pressure on Poland, and therefore the problem resolves itself into what we can do in the air. As to this, we realize it would be impossible for His Majesty's Government to decide, in advance of the event, the precise manner in which our air forces should be employed . . . As a general point we should emphasize that the fate of Poland will depend on the ultimate outcome of the war, and that this in turn will depend upon our ability to bring about the eventual defeat of Germany, and not on our ability to relieve pressure on Poland at the outset.

This was from the Poles' point of view none too promising, and had they known about it they would doubtless have been less complacent, for it was less specific than the Polish military chiefs had a right to expect from the May conversations. In fact, it is hard not to conclude that the British misled the Poles, at least about bombing, since the above-quoted statement is quite different from what Davidson and Clayton had told General Stachiewicz. Nor were the Poles aware of the British conclusion, circulated in July, that their air action was unlikely 'to attract more than a few machines from the East', and that 'in the early stages we cannot rely on being able to relieve the pressure on Poland to any material extent'.[104] A different impression had been given in May.

The Poles did appreciate that the British Army would not be able to help them much, and that the Royal Navy was unlikely to be able to enter the Baltic, where Poland had her narrow stretch of sea. A channel only a few miles wide, flowing between Denmark and Sweden, was the only entrance warships could use, and it would be the easiest thing in the world for Germany to block it with minefields and submarine ambushes. Britain foresaw no naval operations in the Baltic unless a naval base there could be obtained, and none of the Baltic nations – Sweden, Finland, Denmark, the Baltic States or the Soviet Union – was likely to be so rash as to provide one.

But Poland *did* expect help in the air and in supplies. 'We have to last-out fourteen days', the Polish Marshal told Colonel Jaklicz, his Deputy Chief of Staff. He expected, Jaklicz told the author in 1971, considerable relief from British bombing of railway and road junctions near the eastern front, as well as of military objectives in the West. The conclusion that such bombing was unlikely to be effective is very difficult to understand except in the light of the decision, political not military, that such bombing was to be minimal or not at all. 'If we had had this help, we could have lasted out the fourteen days quite easily,' Jaklicz concludes. The Polish Army would then have been in a position to counter-attack when, as was also promised, the French Army launched its major offensive on 16 September.

French and British opinion was divided about the Polish Army. There were those who thought it should be written off from the start, that it could never become a significant military force. And there were those who thought it was a good army which could be relied upon to hold the Germans until the Western Allies were in a position to come to their aid. In the first case to help the Poles was a waste of time and resources. In the second case help was superfluous. Of course both were wrong. The Polish soldiers were brave and dedicated, but they did not have the equipment, the tools with which to begin their job, let alone finish it. Had they received them and had they been actively supported in the West the September Campaign might have gone differently.

Maurice Gamelin, the French Commander in Chief, and Edmund Ironside, the British Chief of the Imperial General Staff, were two of the optimists. On 27 August Gamelin, in conversation with Pierre-Étienne Flandin, pooh-poohed Hitler's startlingly accurate prediction that he would crush Poland in three weeks. 'I know the Polish Army quite well,' Gamelin is reported as saying: 'Their soldiers are excellent and their officers well up to their job . . . The Poles will hold out at least six months and we shall come to their aid through Rumania.' [105] On 4 September Ironside, addressing the Cabinet, 'expressed the personal view that the crushing of Poland by Germany in a few weeks was most improbable'. Also on 27 August Ironside gave Churchill 'most favourable' reports of the Polish Army, which he had viewed in July at the Poles' invitation. 'He had seen,' wrote Churchill, 'a divisional attack-exercise under a live barrage, not without casualties.'[106] 'We couldn't do that in England,' Ironside had confided to Embassy staff in Warsaw. 'We couldn't use live ammunition.' It was this touch of ruthlessness in the Polish approach which impressed him most.

Polish morale was high and Polish spirit willing, but this was not enough to defend their country against the newly invented war machine. By the end of 1 September it was already clear that Poland would soon be isolated from her allies. Her narrow neck of coastline was a battleground and Danzig was in German hands. There could be no question of sending supplies in that way. And already the Luftwaffe controlled the air, having bombed the main Polish airfields and put out of action much of their puny air force. Events were moving fast in the East, while in the West the British and French war machines were still only ticking over, warming up before they were ready to lurch slowly forward.

It seemed also, though, that Poland was not going to be left entirely in the lurch. The British and French *were* going to declare war. *The Times*'s first reaction to the aggression was that 'these pledges will of course be honoured immediately and without question'.[107] The previous evening at 6 p.m. Chamberlain told the House of Commons: 'The time has come when action rather than speech is required. Eighteen months ago in this House I prayed that the responsibility might not fall upon me to ask this country to accept the awful arbitrament of war. I fear that I may not be able to avoid that responsibility.'[108] That afternoon Chamberlain had asked Churchill to call on him. Churchill writes, 'He told me that he saw no hope of averting a war with Germany.'[109] Already he was thinking about his War Cabinet, and he invited Churchill to join it. His mind was made up, and he was slowly but surely going through the diplomatic preliminaries.

So strong were the Prime Minister's personal feelings, however, that in spite of his resolve to fight he was 'creeping like snail, unwillingly' into the conflict. At 2 p.m. a telegram had reached London from Kennard, who had just spoken to Polish Foreign Minister Beck.[110] Beck 'drew my attention to desirability of some military action from the air this afternoon'. On the face of it it was a reasonable request. Britain was bound to come to Poland's aid 'immediately', so why not that afternoon? Why not an immediate British and French declaration of war followed by an attack on Germany? Such suggestions presumably struck Chamberlain as naive, for they were not even considered by the Cabinet. There were still motions to be gone through and – who knows? – maybe some miracle would save the peace after all.

Bonnet's strenuous efforts can only have tempted Chamberlain to believe that this might happen. Making the most of the provision in the French Constitution that only the Assembly may declare war, he was able to resist any British or Polish demand for strong action on 1 September. At 5 p.m. Halifax suggested the withdrawal of the British and French Ambassadors in Berlin, to which Bonnet replied that 'a hope remains of saving the peace and I do not wish to destroy this hope'.[111] 'That evening,' Bonnet writes, 'our ambassadors lodged a first vigorous protest, in accordance with our treaty obligations . . .'[112] But the obligation was not to protest but to assist, immediately and with all available forces. Bonnet felt that Hitler might still avoid war by agreeing to the conference, 'and he was still in a position to do that because the main body of the invading army had not yet crossed the frontier at the end of that first of September.'[113] Bonnet clearly was badly misinformed, both about the speed of the German attack and about Hitler's potential willingness to end it.

Halifax did not share Bonnet's optimism, or even if he did a little, he still had to acquaint the Frenchman with the mood of his Government which was not one of compromise. 'Believing the Italian proposal may succeed,' he told Bonnet on the telephone, 'is like believing you can revive a hanged man by throwing holy water on him.' Bonnet replied, 'Peace stands with a rope round its neck, but it is not yet tied to the gibbet.'[116]

Ribbentrop received British Ambassador Henderson and at 10 p.m. French Ambassador Coulondre. He was presented with identical notes which threatened that unless German aggression ceased and German troops were withdrawn from Poland, Britain 'will without hesitation fulfil their obligations to Poland'.[115] Ribbentrop said he would have to show the note to Hitler, and added to both ambassadors the staggering lie that, far from Germany being guilty of aggression, it was Poland which had invaded Germany.[116] He told Coulondre that Poland 'had provoked Germany in unprecedented fashion, by cutting off Danzig economically, cruelly harrassing the German minority in Poland and continually violating the frontier'.[117] He promised Henderson 'an immediate answer',[118] but did not say when this would be, there being no time limit in the Allied note. To have included a time limit would have given the note the character of an ultimatum, which according to Bonnet would have been a violation of the French Constitution. At this stage Henderson had few illusions. He asked the American Chargé d'Affaires to take over his embassy if he was forced to leave, burnt all his ciphers and confidential documents, and moved all his staff either into the embassy or into the Adlon Hotel next door.[119] Bonnet felt slightly differently, for he writes, 'Nothing has been broken off irretrievably. A feeble hope still exists.'[120]

Bonnet was still resolved to 'sell' the conference, but for this he would have to convince not only Germany but also Britain. Surely the two sides were too far apart for such a happy outcome? Maybe, but Bonnet was determined to try, and at 6.30 p.m. he had a crumb of encouragement from Chamberlain. Speaking in the House of Commons the Prime Minister spoke of his 'satisfaction' that Mussolini 'has been doing his best to reach a solution'. Harold Nicolson noted that 'the Opposition mind very much his having brought in that friendly reference to Mussolini'. And indeed, one can imagine that it indicated to Bonnet that maybe Britain's rejection of the conference might be reconsidered.

Determined to push Britain as far in that direction as he could, Bonnet released that night to his official news agency Havas a statement that 'the French Government, like other governments, concerned itself yesterday (1 September) with an Italian proposal for solving the difficulties which have arisen in Europe. After considering the proposal, the French Government gave it a positive response.'[121] Mussolini's idea was rapidly becoming a *fait accompli*.

And so the first day of the war, one crammed with events, approached its end, leaving Poland's two allies on paths drawing ever more widely apart. On the British side it was by and large assumed that there would be war, only the preliminaries to it were being gone through slowly and meticulously in the hope of some miracle that would bring Germany to its senses. On the French side there was Georges Bonnet, resolved to prevent war if at all possible and ready to yield some of Poland's vital interests if that should be the only way. Events were moving quickly, the bureaucratic machine was being strained, and for the moment Bonnet was calling the tune. The one man in a hundred who believed that peace could be saved, Bonnet was nevertheless in a strong position in that everyone wanted to believe him right and themselves wrong. The longer any declaration of war could be postponed, the more ready the Allies would be to accept yet another deal with Hitler.

2 An Uneasy Lull

'No answer from Berlin, and the morning was occupied with making preparations for what now seemed inevitable. We drafted a statement for Parliament, which was to meet at the usual time. The great difficulty was the French . . .' [1] So began Halifax's diary entry for 2 September, a wretched and inglorious day for Great Britain and France. Poland had been under attack now for twenty-four hours by the cream of Hitler's armed forces. Her plan for survival was based on the 'immediate' help which her allies were bound by treaty to provide. But from London and Paris there came no word. The silence was terrifying to all who hated Hitler. It seemed to show that he would yet again escape scot-free.

By announcing the Italian proposal to the press the previous evening, Bonnet had foisted it upon his own and the British Government. They could now hardly reject it without previous discussion. Just before noon Halifax wired to Phipps: 'Delays in Paris and attitude of the French Government are causing some misgiving here. We shall be grateful for anything you can do to infuse courage and determination into M. Bonnet.' The British leaders' minds were made up. They drafted a statement to be read in Parliament at 2.45 that afternoon.[2] 'It is impossible to wait for more than a very limited time before resolving the present situation, and His Majesty's Government do not intend to do so,' the House of Commons was to be told.[3]

However, Chamberlain was conscious of the special problems of the French. Britain was an island, and difficult to invade, but France was Germany's neighbour and would receive the first blows of the attack. The French Army was huge in comparison with the British Army. It was they who would have to do the fighting. Britain was also less vulnerable to air attack. She was further away from Germany, and her air defences were better. In such circumstances it was dangerous for Britain to take too hard a line or to seem to be dragging her ally into war. The French might resent being led into the slaughter from behind.

A few days earlier Daladier had told Phipps that constitutionally the French Parliament had to be summoned and would have to debate the issue before war could be declared. Phipps was now telling Halifax that since Parliament had not met for a long time, 'Proceedings may be longer than anticipated. Moreover it must be remembered that every hour gained to enable the French general mobilization to proceed unhindered is precious.'[4] The session would not begin until the afternoon, which seemed to make a French declaration of war impossible before the evening. This meant the British could not act before then either, but the British statement planned for 2.45 p.m. would announce that as soon as the French Parliament had set their seal, the allies would 'jointly make their final communication'. It was important, thought Phipps, for both allies to declare war simultaneously, or else the French should declare first. It would look bad for the British to act, and for the French to seem to be following obediently behind them. There were many in France who felt London already had too much influence over French foreign policy.

It soon became clear that there was a second point of basic disagreement between the two allies. At 12.20 p.m. on 1 September Birger Dahlerus had spoken on the telephone to Alexander Cadogan, trying frantically to smooth over Hitler's invasion and suggesting talks between Britain and Germany.[5] An hour later he rang London again and was told there would certainly be war unless, firstly, the Germans suspended hostilities, and secondly, German forces were immediately withdrawn from Polish territory.[6] The problem was that this second condition had not been agreed with the French.

Bonnet agreed to the British idea of sending a 'final communication' after the French Parliament had sat, but trouble arose when Bonnet added that he assumed that the 'final communication' would be 'in terms suggested in your telegram No. 255'.[7] The point was that this telegram, dated 25 August, had been overtaken by events and no longer formed part of British policy.

Halifax had then suggested to the French, through Phipps, 'that we should now without further delay concert our procedure' in case Hitler should invade Poland: 'His Majesty's Government would propose in that event to demand that within a fixed time limit German Government should *halt their troops* and express their readiness to enter into negotiation.' [8] (Author's italics.) If the Germans refused there would be war. French agreement to this procedure was requested 'so that there may be no confusion or loss of time when situation presents itself'. The French duly approved this on the following day, 26 August.

But the agreed formula said nothing about German withdrawal. True, the Quai d'Orsay had slipped up badly the previous day by agreeing to serve identical warning notes which included this demand on the German Government, but by 2 September, when German withdrawal was essential to British agreement to the conference, the French were less sure that they would insist upon it. A cease-fire by itself would not have satisfied London, let alone Warsaw, but it might have satisfied Paris. As it was, Bonnet was able to back out of his Government's position, as expressed in the note Coulondre had handed Ribbentrop, by pointing to what the British had agreed on 25 August. Presumably neither side had expected the initial German attack to be so intense, for such gains to be achieved in the first twenty-four hours of war, since clearly to demand a cease-fire and not withdrawal is not to fulfil a guarantee of an allied country's territorial integrity. A cease-fire, say, at midnight on 2/3 September would have left Germany in control of Danzig, much of the Corridor and large parts of Silesia. Most of Hitler's aims, as announced to the world, would be accomplished. And so, belatedly, Britain resolved that she would not contemplate a conference which began with Germany already in a position of such strength. They probably thought that Hitler wanted only to absorb the German-populated areas, and that it was hardly possible to discuss these areas' future while Hitler was in military control of them. They still did not appreciate that they were but a drop in the ocean of Hitler's demands, mere camouflage, and that his real aim was to expand the living-space of his German Reich as far as the Ural Mountains.

Until the early afternoon it was assumed by most of the Allied leaders that that afternoon, after the French Parliament had debated the matter, simultaneous declarations of war, or at least ultimata with a time limit, would be handed over by Henderson and Coulondre in Berlin. A statement was prepared for John Simon, Chancellor of the Exchequer, to read to the House of Commons and the gist of it was telegraphed to Paris for French approval. Its message was that 'it is impossible to wait more than a very limited time before resolving the present situation, and His Majesty's Government do not intend to do so'. However, the British and French action should if possible be 'simultaneous and identical'. Since France could not declare war without Parliament's concurrence, neither side could act before later that afternoon, but 'as soon as the requirements of the French Constitution had been met, they would jointly make their final communication to the German Government'.

For forty-eight hours the Italian proposal for a conference had been a smouldering barrier in the way of any decisive Allied move, but then it suddenly burst into life to dominate the attention of politicians in London, Paris and Rome, leaving Berlin to continue its military progress. Ciano had not been idle that morning. At 9 a.m., although he had as yet received no reply to his idea from the Poles, he asked Bernardo Attolico, his Ambassador in Berlin, to put the idea before Ribbentrop, though in a form subtly different from the way he had presented it to Britain and France. 'There is still the possibility', he wrote, 'of obtaining the agreement of England, France and Poland to a conference.' The basis of this would be, firstly, a cease-fire *with the two armies to hold their positions*, secondly, a conference to take place within two or three days at San Remo, thirdly, a settlement of the German-Polish quarrel. 'Such a settlement', noted Ciano enticingly, 'would as things stand at present certainly turn out to be favourable to Germany.' [9]

Ribbentrop was in no hurry to receive the Italian and began by fobbing him off with his deputy, Ernst von Weizsaecker, with the excuse that he was unwell. Finally, after a quick recovery, he received him at 12.30 p.m. He had discussed the proposal with Hitler, he said, and was sceptical of its feasibility in the light of the two notes he had been handed by Henderson and Coulondre the previous evening, which seemed to have the character of ultimata. Attolico assured Ribbentrop, apparently on his own authority, that the notes were not ultimata. In fact he was correct. France could send no ultimatum without Parliament's approval. Attolico was also able to point to the 'favourable reply' announced by Bonnet the previous evening.[10] France fully supported the Italian proposal, he said, 'and England would follow'. Ribbentrop replied that 'some time would be necessary for the study and drafting of more precise proposals'.[11] He did not think a German answer would be ready before Sunday evening, 3 September. Meanwhile, he suggested to Attolico that he go and check the point about the ultimata.

Paul Schmidt, Hitler's interpreter, was present at the meeting and writes, 'I can still see Attolico, no longer in his first youth, running out of Ribbentrop's room and down the steps to consult Henderson and Coulondre.'[12] Henderson assured him that the note was not an ultimatum but a warning,[13] showing him his instruction from London that an ultimatum was to be 'the next stage'.[14] Coulondre did likewise. Schmidt writes, 'Half an hour later Attolico came running back, as breathless as when he had left.' There was no question of any ultimatum, Attolico told Ribbentrop. Indeed, had he been asked, Henderson would have told Ribbentrop as much last night.

The German Foreign Minister does not seem to have been very impressed by the Italian's valiant and genuine efforts to save the peace. He said that Hitler 'was examining the Duce's proposals' and 'would draft an answer in a day or two'.[15] This was ridiculous, as both men must have known, and shows that although ideally Germany hoped to keep Britain and France out of the conflict, she was not prepared to sacrifice her military initiative in Poland. Germany might be ready to provide a sop, but only a very small one. Attolico told Ribbentrop that it was essential to have an answer by that evening, and as a compromise Ribbentrop said that the answer would be ready by noon the next day (3 September).

Count Ciano, Mussolini's son-in-law and Italy's Foreign Minister, even after such small encouragement from Berlin, felt entitled to approach London and Paris and to sell them his scheme for saving the peace. At 2 p.m. he summoned the two Allied ambassadors, Loraine and François-Poncet, and told them of Attolico's Berlin conversations. (London and Paris already knew of them through their Berlin ambassadors.) Exaggerating Attolico's success and the German desire for compromise, Ciano told the two men 'that the Führer was not against the suggestion of an armistice to be immediately followed by an international conference'.[16] But, said Ciano, Hitler would not negotiate in the face of any ultimatum. Again he wanted to be assured that the British and French notes of the previous evening were only warnings. Apparently it did not occur to the Allies to wonder why Hitler should be so busy hair-splitting a single word, if not simply to confuse the issue and delay action. The British and French notes had been quite clear. He was entitled to assume that they meant exactly what they said.

Again copies of London's instructions to Henderson were produced to prove to Ciano that there was no ultimatum. But now the Italian had a second question: would Britain and France allow Hitler until noon the next day to consider the conference proposal in detail? It was beyond the ambassadors' competence to answer this, but they encouraged Ciano to take the unusual step of telephoning their foreign ministers direct.

Cleverly, he rang Bonnet first and was told that 'in his [Bonnet's] opinion the answer of the French Government to both points would be affirmative. He would however consult M. Daladier.'[17] Writing in 1971, Bonnet says that he undertook also to consult the British, a claim which is not supported by any of the official records. Anyway, his reply delighted Ciano and the two peacemonger ambassadors. François-Poncet wrote Bonnet the following moving account of the scene: 'Count Ciano spoke to you first and was so excellently and favourably received that we had the impression that the game was won, that peace was saved, and while we were waiting to be connected with London we were roughing out between us the plan for a San Remo conference.'[18]

Ciano then rang Halifax, getting through at 2.30 p.m. According to François-Poncet, Halifax's reaction 'was altogether different, really icy'.[19] Again Ciano was cleverly using Bonnet as leverage on Halifax. Over-simplifying Bonnet's already rash statement, Ciano told Halifax that 'the French Government's reply to both points was affirmative'. Halifax stood firmer than usual. He said he thought that *his* Government's position was 'that the first step must be the withdrawal of German troops from Polish soil'. It was a position which, if maintained, more or less shot down the whole

Italian idea. Ciano said 'he was afraid that this would be impossible' and that the maximum he thought he could obtain was an armistice with a conference the following day. He added 'with some emphasis that the Germans would never listen to a demand for the withdrawal of their troops from Polish territory'.[21] In his view 'such a request would be hardly reasonable in the existing circumstances'. Halifax replied that 'it would be very difficult for us to contemplate a conference with German troops on Polish soil'.[22] Still, he told Ciano he would ring him back later that afternoon, which indicates that for the moment the door was to be kept open.

Ciano, Loraine and François-Poncet 'dispersed to await the definitive replies from Paris and London, our recent enthusiasm dissipated'. The French Ambassador continues plaintively, 'It was the British attitude which brought to nothing the Italian offer — an offer which had been formulated only after Hitler had been sounded and to which you fully agreed (I was standing by the telephone in Ciano's office) subject to the Cabinet's approval.'[23] He and Bonnet agreed that the British were being too hasty. Bonnet disapproved of the British position that a conference was only possible after Poland had been evacuated. An hour and a half later Halifax told him that 'Poland had to be freed before midnight [2/3 September]. After that Britain would begin hostilities.'[24] Bonnet thought that this time limit was too short, that effort should still be made to avoid war. He did not approve of Hitler's agression, but he thought that to condone it, or at least part of it, was a lesser evil than to go to war. 'Victors and vanquished — who could prophesy?' he writes. 'Only one thing was certain. We had come to the situation I had foreseen and vainly tried to ward off — the end of traditional Europe.'[25] It was this that he feared above all.

But behind Halifax's icy, stubborn and (to Bonnet's mind) unreasonable reactions there lurked the beginnings of doubt and an inclination to withdraw from any hasty movement into war. As a result of his talk with Ciano he and Chamberlain decided on the spot to postpone the statements which were to be made in Parliament at 2.45. Halifax writes, 'I managed to rush over to the House of Commons to stop John Simon [Chancellor of the Exchequer] making the statement that had been prepared for 2.45 in order to

give time to get in touch with the French about the conference proposal and to synchronize with them any action we might decide to
take with Germany.' [26] Poor man, he was having to move frantically from place to place to fulfil his commitments. Simon told the
House that the Prime Minister himself would make a statement as
soon as possible, and it proceeded with its emergency legislation.
Halifax and his Under-Secretary R. A. Butler then walked across
to the House of Lords. Butler's Private Secretary Henry Channon
writes, 'I followed, trying to listen.' [27] At 3 p.m. Halifax told the
House of Lords that he had hoped to be able to make a statement,
but was unfortunately unable to do so. Chamberlain then called a
Cabinet meeting for 4.15 p.m. The members of parliament realized
something strange was in the wind, as senior ministers were seen
making their way towards 10 Downing Street. Channon writes,
'There was a *sauve qui peut* from the Front Bench.' It was apparent
to the members that the situation was becoming confused, and that
decisions were being reconsidered in haste. They began to be suspicious of what was being cooked up. The British leaders, en-
grossed in the crisis, did not appreciate this, or the danger they
were running by keeping Parliament in ignorance and suspense.
The House of Commons can be formidable when it is roused.

By 4 p.m. Halifax was back in the Foreign Office and speaking
on the telephone to Bonnet. The gap between the two sides was
becoming ever wider, and communication between the two foreign
ministers ever more difficult. But while Bonnet was resolved to do
all in his power to avert war, Halifax was less fixed in his determination. As Foreign Secretary, it was his job to understand and
to approach as closely as possible the point of view of his French
colleague. But as a member of the British Cabinet he was one of
a team, whose collective opinion was for the moment out of tune
with that of the allied government of France. So many forces were
pulling him and pushing him that he was in danger of being torn
apart.

The position was that Bonnet had agreed to allow Hitler until
noon the next day (3 September) to reply to the warning note.
Halifax had not agreed. Halifax had said that there could be no
conference while German troops remained on Polish soil. Bonnet,
having demanded this of Germany the previous evening, was now
reconsidering whether or not the demand was negotiable. And

even if France and Britain agreed to send their ultimatum, there was no agreement on how long the time limit should be.

Bonnet had, in the words of his Rome Ambassador, 'fully agreed' to the extension until noon the next day.[28] Loraine, the other witness to what was said, confirms that Bonnet agreed, adding only that he must consult his Prime Minister.[29] But at 4 p.m. Bonnet said nothing to Halifax about having agreed to the extension. He told Halifax only that 'he had said that he must discuss the matter with M. Daladier'. He had done this, he said, 'in order to gain time and to consult with His Majesty's Government'.[30] Halifax suspected that he was not being told the whole truth and that Bonnet 'had committed himself rather further than he was willing to admit to the conference'.[31] The feeling that Bonnet was trying to pull a fast one on him can have done nothing to help Halifax's composure.

Halifax repeated to Bonnet his view that a conference was impossible without German withdrawal. Like Ciano, Bonnet said he thought that this condition would be unacceptable to Hitler. The most he would say was that withdrawal was 'obviously desirable'. He thought that 'a conference might be contemplated provided that Poland was represented at it. That was the really essential point, and he put that to Count Ciano.' He urged Halifax to handle the conference proposal carefully. It was important, he added cleverly, to make it clear to French and British public opinion that everything possible had been done to avoid war.

The next surprise Halifax received was a request from Bonnet for a space of forty-eight hours from delivery of ultimatum to commencement of hostilities. Halifax replied meekly 'that this proposal had only just been put before us and would be considered immediately'.[32] He was not being strictly accurate since the Foreign Office had received the request at 1.30 p.m. from the Paris embassy,[33] but presumably what with everything Halifax had not had time to read and think about it. The French General Staff wanted this delay, said Phipps, 'to enable evacuation of big towns and general mobilization to take place unhindered'. Maurice Gamelin, the French Commander-in-Chief, was not the sort of man who likes to be asked to embark on an undertaking without receiving proper notice. He had told the French Cabinet that his armies would not be in position until 5 a.m. on Tuesday 5 September. 'I personally was opposed to the delay,' says Bonnet, 'but I was obliged to press for it.'

Again, the British view was quite different. Lord Chatfield, Minister for Co-ordination of Defence, said in Cabinet on 2 September: 'Once an ultimatum had been dispatched, immediate action might be taken by the potential enemy. In principle therefore the period between the dispatch and the expiry of the ultimatum, which was one of uncertainty, should be as short as possible.' He wisely feared a German surprise air attack while Britain's hands were still formally tied. Also it was the view of the Royal Navy, Britain's strongest weapon, that every moment's delay would allow submarines and raiders to escape from German ports, and would complicate the imposition of an effective blockade. Many people in Britain believed in this blockade. It would, they thought, make life miserable for the German people. They would lose all stomach for the war, rise up and overthrow Hitler. And so the war would be won.

The record shows that Halifax did little to acquaint Bonnet with the British side of these arguments. He merely listened and promised to put the various points before the British Cabinet, which was to meet in a few minutes. It was a dangerous tactic to adopt with a politician as forceful as the French Foreign Minister. Firstly, it gave Bonnet the impression that his requests were all worthy of consideration and that some at least of them would be met. Secondly, it put Halifax in the position of being the French Government's (or rather Bonnet's) advocate among the British Cabinet. Had he expressed his own views to Bonnet more strongly, while conceding that his Cabinet would have to take the final decision, he would have made Bonnet realize the extent of the gap between them, and perhaps avoided some of the misunderstandings which were shortly to erupt.

Meanwhile Łukasiewicz in Paris was trying frantically to persuade his country's allies to act. During the morning of 1 September Bonnet had told him he was sure that France would fulfil her obligations. After the 10.30 a.m. meeting of the French Cabinet Bonnet saw him again and confirmed this. However, the Ambassador writes, 'he was unable to inform me exactly when or in what form this would happen'. Bonnet and Łukasiewicz met for the third time at 9 a.m. on 2 September, by which time the Pole's patience was wearing thin. Bonnet writes that he was 'over-whelmed by the terrible news. His voice was full of anguish as he asked me, "When are you going to send an ultimatum to Hitler?" I replied, "Parliament meets this afternoon to authorize it." He insists that the French Army come rapidly to the help of his country. I am in full agreement with him.'[34] But he was not. He was still trying to keep France out of the war altogether, and to accomplish this was ready to make some concessions at the Poles' expense.

At the same meeting he told the Ambassador that even after the ultimatum was sent, there would be a delay of forty-eight hours before France went into action. When the Pole protested, Bonnet told him – quite incorrectly – that the delay was agreed two weeks earlier at the insistence of the British. Łukasiewicz protested officially at the length of the delay and told Bonnet that he hoped this 'ambiguous situation' would be ended before the day was out. He rang Raczyński, his colleague in London, who told him that any idea that Britain had insisted on the forty-eight-hour delay was 'completely out of the question'. On the contrary, Raczyński said, there was a feeling in Britain too that France was dragging her feet. In great distress, Łukasiewicz cast about for reasons for the French behaviour and concluded 'that there was either some new Italian attempt at mediation, or else some diplomatic diversion on the part of the Soviet Union'.[35] It was the former, and he should have known about it, for it had been announced by Bonnet the previous evening. But perhaps he can be forgiven such a lapse during the horror of those hours.

At noon Łukasiewicz saw Daladier, who told him that 'he personally was for quick action'. But on leaving the Premier's office he found himself besieged by journalists all asking him to confirm reports that the war was over, and there was a cease-fire on the Polish front. 'They were certain it was true,' the Ambassador writes. 'My categorical assertion that these rumours were being put about by German propaganda and were completely untrue shocked and alarmed them.' He was concerned that these reports had reached not only journalists, but also members of the Assembly, who were to sit at 3 p.m. They were bound to strengthen the case of the defeatists and weaken that of those who were for quick action. Again, the Germans were skilfully confusing the issue, and leaving every possible escape hatch open for those who favoured delay.

Łukasiewicz attended the Assembly meeting, and had his work cut out quelling the rumours. He was disappointed in Daladier's speech which, while resolute in tone, was imprecise in detail. 'Poland is our ally,' the Premier said. 'We have contracted engagements with her in 1921 and 1925. These engagements have been confirmed.' If France failed to meet them, he went on, 'we would only buy, at the price of our honour, a precarious and revocable peace. And when we have to fight tomorrow, we would have lost the esteem of our allies and of other nations. We would be nothing more than a wretched people doomed to defeat and servitude.'[36] Phipps reports that at this there was loud applause from the deputies, but there was loud applause too for the passage in which Daladier said that even now, were reason to prevail, France would be ready to work for peace.[37] Bonnet writes that 'the most loudly applauded part of Daladier's speech was his account of my efforts to save the peace'.[38]

Sitting next to Phipps in the diplomatic gallery, the Polish Ambassador complained bitterly about this passage. The speech itself was 'hesitant', he later wrote. 'It lacked any attempt to build up a mood for the war.' No doubt this was so, but whether this one speech could have done much to change the mood of the French people is doubtful. Phipps tried to console his colleague, pointing out how essential it was that the Premier show his people that every tiny chance of peace had been exhausted. 'It was better,' he said, 'to have an absolutely united country a few hours later than one even fractionally divided a few hours earlier.'[39] This was another piece of wishful thinking, for there was little chance of the French people uniting itself on this issue, or even of the French Government doing so, as long as Georges Bonnet remained Foreign Minister.

When the British Cabinet met at 4.15 p.m. they were in Halifax's words, 'in an extremely difficult mood', though one would not have thought so from the bland style of the minutes. Halifax reported his talk with Bonnet, and found himself in the embarrassing position of having by and large to support Bonnet's line, since he had not countered it effectively on the telephone an hour earlier and did not see much hope of Bonnet being talked out of it. He understood that the British Chiefs of Staff were opposed to further delay, but he had to tell the Cabinet that the French military leaders took the opposite view, and were pressing for a forty-eight-hour interval between the ultimatum and the declaration of war.

On the other important point Halifax supported Bonnet entirely: 'He [Halifax] thought that we might be prepared to consider an extension of the time limit from 12 noon tomorrow to 12 midnight on 3–4 September, if this would facilitate consideration of a conference.' It was the remark of a died-in-the-wool appeaser and it infuriated the majority of the Cabinet.

Malcolm MacDonald said, 'The Germans could make up their minds quickly enough on occasions, and had been known to ask other people to make up their minds in a very short time.' It was pointed out, contrary to the French view, that every hour's delay gave the Germans more and more advantage, and everyone agreed that talks were impossible so long as German troops remained on Polish soil. Hore-Belisha writes that both he and his naval and air colleagues were opposed to further delay.[40] In Halifax's words, the Cabinet was 'pretty unanimous' that a statement should be made to Parliament quickly, and that it should contain an ultimatum with a short time limit. Halifax's recorded objections to this would seem to have put him in a minority of one. 'I never remember spending a more miserable afternoon and evening,' he wrote.

Halifax tried to explain to the Cabinet that such action as was proposed could hardly be taken without French approval, and that they 'were certain to be difficult'. But he did not make clear the extent of the difference between the two countries. As Foreign Secretary he was responsible for relations with France, and probably he did not feel like admitting that communication with them on these vital issues had collapsed. He did not admit that on 25 August he had agreed with the French on a procedure for declaring war which envisaged no demand for a withdrawal of German troops. He was therefore now faced with a Cabinet which insisted on the withdrawal condition, and with an ally which regarded German withdrawal as merely 'desirable'. The result of all this was that the Cabinet decided on a course of action which could not possibly be fulfilled.

The Cabinet agreed 'that it was undesirable to allow Germany longer then until midnight 2–3 September to make up her mind'. It sounds a vague decision, but Cabinet Minutes as recorded are often vague. Hore-Belisha's diary note that 'unanimous decision was taken that ultimatum should end at midnight 2–3 September'[41] sounds more decisive and likely. The ultimatum was to be sent 'in cooperation with the French'. The only problem was, would the French cooperate? The Cabinet dispersed Halifax and the Foreign Office chiefs applied themselves once again to the telephone link with Paris. But not all the diplomatic skills in the two countries could achieve agreement in time.

At 5 p.m. Alexander Cadogan telephoned Bonnet about the three unresolved points: the time limit, the conference and the withdrawal condition.[42] If Hitler withdrew, Cadogan said, the British Government would agree to a conference, but if he did not agree by midnight that night there would be war. Bonnet replied that France had accepted Mussolini's idea two days earlier, before the German attack. This was incorrect. The French acceptance was actually sent to Rome at 10.15 a.m. on 1 September.[43]

The French Cabinet, said Bonnet, was going to deliberate (*va délibérer*) on whether German withdrawal was essential to a conference, and that 9 p.m., or perhaps 8 p.m., was the earliest time by which a decision might be expected. He added that it was 'firmly' his Government's view that a forty-eight-hour time limit was necessary. Cadogan repeated that *his* Government was resolved to act at midnight. Bonnet replied that if the British 'insisted on the midnight ultimatum, they would incur a grave responsibility *vis-à-vis* France, because French evacuation is incomplete and will take two days more to complete'. Bonnet quotes himself as having said: 'All our railway stations are swarming with passengers on their way to the front. There are women and children there, and we risk exposing them to a terrible carnage in the case of air attacks. Can we not wait a few hours for a war which Lord Halifax has told us will last five years?'[44] Bonnet is fond of quoting such conversations verbatim — a dangerous practice for a writer of memoirs, let alone for a historian. He writes that this conversation was with Halifax. In fact it was with Cadogan. After decades have elapsed such details are forgotten. He can hardly be blamed for that. But it does mean that the conversations he quotes word for word are also liable to be distorted by time. By contrast, the Foreign Office record is there in black and white and does not change.

It was 'impossible', Bonnet told Cadogan, for France to issue a midnight ultimatum. It was a blunt enough way of putting it, and it seems to have impressed Cadogan. Like Halifax, he acquiesced, saying that Britain 'would await the French verdict on the question'. He asked Bonnet whether the Poles had yet asked him for help on the ground that there was a big battle. Bonnet's astonishing reply was, 'Not yet.'

It was another example of Bonnet's ambivalent attitude. Only half an hour earlier, according to his own account, he had met Łukasiewicz who was 'in a furious temper, complaining that France was breaking her treaty obligations to provide her with "efficient and rapid" military assistance'. The Ambassador demanded immediate help from the French Army and Air Force. Bonnet continues, 'I invited him to apply to the Ministry of War.'[45]

However, writing in 1971, Bonnet was still unrepentant about the line he took: 'I did not hide from Lord Halifax [*sic*] the seriousness of the line Britain was taking. By its inflexibility it precluded any chance of peace.' It would appear that even now Bonnet refuses to accept that the war was unavoidable on that day.

Chamberlain and Halifax now realized the seriousness of their predicament. The minutes were ticking by. The House of Commons had been promised a statement by that evening. The Cabinet had agreed on a course of action which, because of Bonnet's numerous objections, was incapable of fulfilment. At 6 p.m. Halifax telephoned Phipps to tell him frankly that 'the position of the French Government was very embarrassing to His Majesty's Government'.[46] He told Phipps that the forty-eight-hour delay, which he had himself suggested to the Cabinet an hour and a half earlier, was 'impossible'. He had been told by his naval advisers that with such a delay the Germans would be able to make 'all kinds of dispositions'. Their merchant ships in British-controlled ports would be able to escape seizure, their warships to escape into the open sea to pillage and plunder, their minelayers to sow minefields in the North Sea. Would not Daladier agree to an ultimatum expiring at midnight? Phipps said this was 'impossible'. (The word 'impossible' was being liberally used.) The evacuation of French women and children was still in full swing, he told Halifax – an argument which would probably not have appealed to the women and children of Poland, France's ally, who had been bombed and machine-gunned by the German Air Force for thirty-six hours already.

Mussolini's conference idea was by now in its death-throes. At 6.38 p.m. Halifax rang Ciano again in what was to be his final attempt to avert the war.[47] He would accept a conference, he said, but German withdrawal was 'an essential condition'. Ciano said, as he had said earlier that afternoon, that he did not think Hitler would accept this. Halifax urged Ciano to try his best. Ciano was unwilling, but Halifax pressed him. But at last it was clear that there was an irreconcilable difference between the two sides. Halifax could not abandon this condition even if he wanted to. The Cabinet would not let him and the House of Commons certainly would not, while for his part Ciano knew that the condition would be unacceptable to Hitler. 'Nothing more could be done,' he wrote in his diary. 'It is not my business to give Hitler advice which he would reject decisively and maybe with contempt.'[48] But Halifax had now apparently swung to the side of Bonnet even more. If only his terms were put directly before Hitler and Göring, he thought, there was still a chance.

The British Ambassador in Rome too remained briefly hopeful. At 7 p.m. he telegraphed London referring to 'a peaceful solution of the German–Polish difficulties' – a very diplomatic way of describing what was happening in the East.[49] But a few minutes later he was rung by Ciano and his hopes too were dashed. The only action Ciano took was to ask his Ambassador in Berlin to pass on to Ribbentrop the gist of his talk with Halifax, with the demand for withdrawal from Danzig as well as from occupied Polish areas. According to the German records, 'the Foreign Minister received the communication from the Italian Ambassador without comment'.[50]

All this time the British Parliament had been kept waiting, not idly, for there was a mass of legislation to be rushed through, but impatiently and anxiously, so they were in a touchy mood when eventually at 7.44 p.m. Chamberlain stood up to make his statement – one of the most disastrous ever made by a Prime Minister to Parliament. According to Channon, some members had 'quenched their thirst in the Smoking Room, and when they returned to hear the P.M.'s statement, many of them were full of "Dutch Courage". One noticed their flushed faces . . .' But even he, a solid Chamberlain man, admits that 'a clumsy, or rather inartistic, document it was too'.[51] Harold Nicolson noted more cruelly, 'His voice betrays some emotion as if he were sickening for a cold.'[52]

It was a four-minute speech, worded in routine diplomatic jargon, with no mention of a declaration of war, and only the vaguest of any ultimatum or time limit. His explanations served only to increase the members' alarm. More than half the speech was about the almost defunct Italian proposal:

It may be that the delay is caused by consideration of a proposal which meanwhile had been put forward by the Italian Government . . . While appreciating the efforts of the Italian Government, His Majesty's Government for their part would find it impossible to take part in a conference while Poland is being subjected to invasion . . . If the German Government should be ready to withdraw their forces then His Majesty's Government would be willing to regard the position as the same as it was before the German forces crossed the Polish frontier. That is to say, the way would be open to discussion between the German and Polish Governments on the matters at issue between them . . .[53]

The Prime Minister sat down to be faced with a situation whose seriousness he had not even contemplated. The members had already been fobbed off once and they were furious at again being deprived of decisive information about the crisis. They had waited five hours and they wanted action, not some brief, routine statement. 'The House gasped for one moment in astonishment. Was there to be another Munich after all ?' wrote Nicolson. 'The House was oozing hostility,' wrote Edward Spears.[54] One Chamberlain supporter was in tears, he was told later, and two members vomited.

Arthur Greenwood, acting in Clement Attlee's absence as Leader of the Opposition, could well have brought the Government down if he had put the matter to a vote, but one of the virtues of the British system is that matters of such seriousness are usually kept outside party politics. 'Speak for England !' someone shouted as Greenwood rose to his feet. Some say it was Leo

Amery, others Bob Boothby. 'I think I started it,' Boothby told the author in 1970, 'but we were shouting together so quickly that it is difficult to be sure . . . within a split second, Leo Amery and I were chanting it in unison.' All in all, Greenwood had a difficult task. Hugh Dalton writes, 'He handled it wonderfully well.'[55] Spears writes that the speech 'was remarkable neither for eloquence nor for dramatic effect'.[56] Doubtless people's memories are dimmed by the emotion of the moment. The bald Hansard record reads haltingly and uninspiringly, but no printed page could convey the weight of such a speech in such a context. 'I am gravely disturbed,' Greenwood said:

> . . . I wonder how long we are prepared to vacillate at a time when Britain and all that Britain stands for, and human civilization, are at peril . . . I should have preferred the Prime Minister to have been able to say tonight definitely, 'It is either peace or war.' Tomorrow we meet at twelve. I hope the Prime Minister then — well, he must be in a position to make some further statement — (Hon. Members: 'Definite') — And I must put this point to him. Every minute's delay now means the loss of life, imperilling our national honour . . . The moment we look like weakening, at that moment dictatorship knows we are beaten. We are not beaten. We shall not be beaten. We cannot be beaten; but delay is dangerous . . .

Greenwood sat down to resounding cheers. Nicolson writes: 'Here were the P.M.'s most ardent supporters cheering his opponent with all their lungs. The front bench looked as if they had been struck in the face.' Indeed, for several Cabinet members it was a double blow, one from their back-bench supporters, another from their Prime Minister, who had just addressed the House in terms quite contrary to what the Cabinet had agreed two hours earlier.

The fact was that Chamberlain's speech was aimed not only, and perhaps not principally, at the House of Commons. At 8 p.m. a summary of the speech, emphasizing the possibility of peaceful settlement, was telegraphed by Halifax from the Foreign Office to Henderson in Berlin.[57] A few minutes later another telegram, referring to the summary, instructed Henderson: 'You need not communicate this to German Government, but in order that they may have as much time as possible to consider their reply you may think it well to pass it immediately to certain quarters.'[58] Halifax had in mind the Swede Birger Dahlerus. At 9 p.m., while Dahlerus was dining in Berlin, a messenger from Henderson handed him the speech.[59] Attached to it was Henderson's visiting card. The speech might interest him, Henderson had scribbled on the card, 'especially if you brought it to knowledge of a certain quarter'. This time the cryptic 'certain quarter' meant Dahlerus's friend Göring. In dire straits, the Foreign Office was conducting its vital diplomacy in a bizarre manner. In the event, Dahlerus decided not to interrupt his dinner to run the errand. He was going to see Göring at nine the next morning anyway.

It all gave the impression, in Hore-Belisha's words, 'that we were weakening on our undertaking to Poland, and that the French were ratting. The House was completely taken aback.'[60] True, Chamberlain had said, 'I should be horrified if the House thought for one moment that the statement that I have made to them betrayed the slightest weakening either of this Government or of the French Government.' But this served only to feed the flames of suspicion. Nicolson wrote, 'He [Chamberlain] must know very well that the better-informed among us already know about Georges Bonnet. He is not telling the truth, and we know it.'[61]

At about 8.30 p.m. rebellious Cabinet Ministers met in John Simon's room, and deputed Simon to go and see the Prime Minister and press for another meeting. Halifax was back at his home in Eaton Square. *His* statement in the House of Lords had gone quite well, and he was just going out to dinner with his wife when he was telephoned by Chamberlain and asked to go at once to 10 Downing Street. 'I had never heard the Prime Minister so disturbed,' he wrote.[62] Chamberlain gave him dinner and told him that unless the position could be cleared he did not believe that the Government would be able to maintain itself before Parliament the next day. He had seen a deputation of rebels, led by Simon, and had tried not very successfully to pacify them with the excuse that he had not seen any means of consulting the Cabinet in time about a change of policy made necessary by the French attitude. Churchill too was becoming restless. He had heard nothing from the Prime Minister all day, and he wrote to him complaining that 'entirely different ideas have ruled' from those of the previous day, and that 'the apparent weakening of our resolve' might damage national unity.[63]

Halifax's attitude to the drama was petulant and without grace.

For those whose feelings had run so high he had not one scrap of understanding or tolerance, and unlike his Prime Minister he was quite unrepentant about the 7.44 p.m. statement. There had never been the least ground, he wrote in his diary, for the widespread suspicions: 'The sole reason for the French delay was General Gamelin's desire to secure further time for completing mobilization. The whole thing, to my mind, showed democratic assemblies at their worst . . .'[64] There can be few who, in the light of history, will view this last sentence with anything but scorn. It seems he had forgotten that there was more than one reason for delay, that he himself at the 4.15 p.m. Cabinet meeting had under French pressure favoured delay 'if this would facilitate discussion of a conference'. For two days Bonnet had urged the conference by fair means and foul, keeping his Polish allies in ignorance of his true intentions. But none of this did Halifax see fit to mention, nor did *The Times*, which wrote in an article presumably based upon British Government information (4 September): '. . . for strictly technical reasons the French Government and their General Staff wished to delay the opening until yesterday, simply in order to complete their defences. This was the sole reason for the delay at this end.'

Halifax knew perfectly well that this was not true. For reasons of Allied solidarity he could not release the real reasons for the delay to the press, but there was no reason for such reticence (or was it self-deception?) in his confidential diary. What actually happened was that the French Cabinet, meeting at 7.30 p.m., agreed with Gamelin that more time was needed to complete mobilization and evacuation. From the purely French point of view it was a debatable point, but from the wider point of view it was clear that, in the words of the historian L. B. Namier, 'The terms of the military convention signed with the Poles on 19 May 1939, and the extremely grave exigencies of her situation, were being overlooked with something that can only be described as short-sighted selfishness.'[65]

Bonnet also made the point that he had given his word to Ciano to wait until noon the next day before sending an ultimatum. (He had done this without consultation with Britain or, it seems, with Daladier.) But what really counted with the Cabinet was the need to gain time. 'This reason suffices for me,' writes Jean

Zay, the Minister of Education. 'The entire Cabinet is agreed, except Mandel who thinks that our mobilization was decided upon too late, and that our action in support of Poland should have been immediate.'[66] (Georges Mandel was Minister of the Colonies, a Jew, and the most anti-Nazi of the members of Daladier's Cabinet. He was murdered by the Vichy French police in 1944.)

Someone remarked that it was a pity to have such disagreement and lack of synchronization at the very beginning of the war, to which Anatole de Monzie replied: 'If for once we are coming in later than England, we can well afford the luxury.'[67] De Monzie, Minister of Transport, was if anything more defeatist than Bonnet. Even at this stage he felt bound to resurrect the Italian proposal, which in view of Halifax's insistence on prior German withdrawal the French Cabinet had hardly discussed, for it was indeed a dead letter. De Monzie writes:

When we were leaving, I pressed Bonnet to disregard the British *non possumus*. To demand the withdrawal of German troops from Poland was an indefensible claim . . . Could there not be a third solution, somewhere between an effective withdrawal of troops and acceptance of the invasion as an accomplished fact? A symbolic withdrawal by a few miles? . . . It was agreed that while dining that evening with Guariglia [the Italian Ambassador] I would sound him out on this proposal, which was after all quite honourable.[68]

Charles Corbin, French Ambassador in London, was being besieged by journalists and politicians. He pointed out the effort that would be demanded of France and begged their understanding. Churchill rang and, in Paul Reynaud's words, 'his ear-splitting voice making the telephone vibrate', informed Corbin that if France ratted now, he who had always been a friend of France would become utterly indifferent to her fate.[69] Corbin said something about technical difficulties, and Churchill reportedly replied, 'Technical difficulties be damned! I suppose you would call it a technical difficulty for a Pole if a German bomb fell on his head.'[70]

In Poland, after two days of bombs and *Blitzkrieg*, there was little time for diplomacy. Earlier in the day in Warsaw Józef Beck had seen Kennard and Noel, the two allied ambassadors, and informed them that German air superiority was endangering the

Polish Army's struggle. Kennard wired, 'He very discreetly suggested it was essential that there should be some diversion as soon as possible in the West.'[71] Łukasiewicz received a similar message from Beck at 5 p.m. and once again presented himself to Bonnet. This time the niceties of diplomacy deserted him and he was in no way discreet. 'He was in the grip of extreme anger,' Bonnet writes. The Pole returned to his embassy, and wrote a formal protest to Prime Minister Daladier. According to Nicolson, he attached a memorandum headed, 'Herewith my record of my interview with your Foreign Secretary.'

Already Beck had told Noel that in the Polish Army there was talk of French 'betrayal'. Late in the evening the two men met again. Noel writes that the conversation 'was painful from start to finish. It was impossible for me not to understand their growing anxiety, and having no instructions and scarcely any information from Paris, I was in no position to reassure them.'[72] Telegrams were still reaching him, but only to raise technical matters or to inquire after French citizens caught in Poland.

Kennard too was bombarding his Ministry. Five telegrams from him reached London on 2 September, all urging some British air action which would take the heat off the Polish Army. Later that night his temper too began to wear thin, for he wrote, 'Delay in implementing the Anglo-Polish Treaty is difficult for the Poles to understand and is making my position and that of the Head of the Military Mission very awkward and unenviable.'[73]

Hitler's purpose was already far advanced. Having successfully seized Danzig within a few hours of the outbreak, German forces were now teeming across the Corridor, threatening to link the two parts of Germany. Gdynia, Poland's new and only port, was under air and artillery bombardment, as was the strongly defended Hel peninsula. At dawn on 2 September two German destroyers had attacked Hel unsuccessfully. However, as far as maintaining Poland's link with the sea was concerned, it was already clear by that evening that Hel and Gdynia would not be used to supply Poland with reinforcements. A mass of German warships and U-boats lay off Poland's forty miles of coastline. As a lifeline the Corridor was squeezed into uselessness.

Poland's main industrial centres lay in the south-west corner of the country. A vulnerable but key area, it was entrusted to the

Cracow Army, commanded by General Szylling. By noon on
2 September he realized that his army was being outflanked by the
German tanks and motorized infantry. Częstochowa, a large city
at the north of his command, was rapidly being surrounded. He
radioed headquarters in Warsaw and obtained permission to withdraw. Police and military pulled out of Katowice, and at 5 p.m. the
Polish defenders, numbering a division, abandoned Częstochowa,
but as they withdrew on foot they soon found themselves overtaken and surrounded by German motorized units near the town
of Janów. For two days they tried to fight their way out, but they
were destroyed. This early German success was to be the pattern
of the campaign.[74]

German air bombardment was still haphazard. Polish military
airfields had been pinpointed and were systematically attacked,
but most of the machines had been moved to smaller fields before
the outbreak and were saved.[75] Other attackers flew widely over
the country, dropping a few bombs on each town and creating an
atmosphere of terror. On the evening of 2 September Kennard
wired London that bombing was not confined to military objectives.[76] Villages and factories having nothing to do with the war
had been attacked, and there were heavy civilian losses. Kennard's
reports can have left little room for doubt in the mind of any open-
minded man that Hitler's air force was in breach of international
law.

At 6.30 p.m. the French Cabinet met and confirmed the decision
it had taken the previous day – but subject to Parliament's concurrence – to send Hitler an ultimatum with a time limit. The
question was, should the ultimatum be sent at midnight that night,
as Britain was urging, or at noon the next day, as Bonnet had
rashly promised Ciano? And should German withdrawal be a
precondition of any conference? On this last point France decided
to support the British line, but on the first point to accept Bonnet's
timing in order, as he writes, 'to give peace its last slender
chance'.[77] To his mind at least this was the reason for the delay,
but it was not the reason he gave in his talks with the British. With
them, as with Łukasiewicz, it was his policy to 'pass the buck' to
the Ministry of War.

At 9.50 p.m. there took place the ultimate in telephone calls, a
direct talk between the two heads of government. In those days

such a thing was most unusual. Prime Ministers communicated with each other through the usual channels, through their foreign ministers and ambassadors. Only when he was on the point of being overthrown and when, most people expected, British and French cities were about to suffer wholesale slaughter from the air, did Chamberlain feel compelled to pick up the telephone to speak to his opposite number in Paris. 'The situation here was very grave,' he explained. 'There had been an angry scene in the House of Commons . . . His colleagues in the Cabinet were also disturbed.'[78] He told Daladier that he appreciated that France would have to bear the brunt of the fighting as soon as war began, but he was convinced that the situation in Britain was such that some step had to be taken that evening. As a compromise he suggested that both ambassadors deliver ultimata at 8 a.m. the next day. There would be a short time limit, and war would be declared before Parliament met at noon. The Government would thus be safe.

One wonders whether Daladier felt that the need to save Chamberlain's political career was sufficient reason for plunging France, as he saw it, prematurely into war. He appreciated, as did the British, the need for compromise. For two allies to launch themselves upon such a desperate task, divided as they were, was absurd and dangerous. He had put the problem before Gamelin, who suggested that France might agree to the midnight ultimatum, but only on condition that Britain placed the Royal Air Force at the disposal of the French Army to defend it against German bombing attacks during mobilization. Bonnet writes: 'Gamelin knew in advance that they [Britain] would refuse, so we were covered.'[79] It was hardly a spirit of *entente cordiale*. Daladier duly told Chamberlain, 'Unless the British bombers were ready to act at once, it would be better for France to delay if possible for some hours attacks on the French armies.'[80] Chamberlain was unable to persuade him to send the French ultimatum any sooner.

The differences between Britain and France were degenerating from the political to the personal, and there was a danger that the war would begin in an atmosphere of inter-ally bitterness. France did not see why it should sacrifice its blood unnecessarily to prop up Chamberlain. Bonnet was unwilling even now to make the final jump into war, to break the last slender strand of communication with Berlin. 'Why this unseemly haste?' he asked Phipps at 10.30 p.m. Phipps told him of the crisis in Parliament and of the Admiralty's desire to go quickly into action. 'And what about your land army?' Bonnet asked Phipps, a question which Phipps could hardly answer.

On the other hand, the British leaders and members of parliament were suspicious that France was planning to leave them in the lurch. Charles Corbin, French Ambassador in London, was called to 10 Downing Street and made aware of this feeling. He reported to Bonnet, with colourful French turn of phrase, that France 'was being accused in the corridors of wishing to disrobe herself'.[81] Chamberlain told him that so far public opinion in Britain was united, but it would not be if there was much more vacillation.[82] As for the Italian proposal, 'no one wished to hear a word about it. It was considered as a trap designed to favour the advance of the German armies.' In a way they were right, for this was the effect that the proposal was having. But they were wrong in thinking that Mussolini was deliberately providing a smoke-screen for Hitler's aggression. The two men were momentarily on bad terms. Mussolini was not yet ready for war. He genuinely wished to avert it. And he was angry with Hitler for signing the treaty with the Soviet Union without consulting him.[83]

The British suspected that Bonnet was the fly in the ointment, and maybe Chamberlain thought that by by-passing him and talking direct with Daladier, he would get what he wanted. Unfortunately, he chose a time when Bonnet's view had already prevailed in the French Cabinet and so accomplished nothing. And so, at 10.30 p.m., Halifax and Bonnet spoke yet again.[84] But this time the British attitude had hardened and for once Halifax was being firm. An announcement this evening was 'essential', he said. It was 'impossible' for the British Government to wait until noon. If, as it seemed, joint action could not be agreed, the British would propose to act separately provided that the French promised to follow suit within twenty-four hours.

This was unsatisfactory of course for several reasons. The delay would look bad. It would show the world there had been argument and difference. And it would imply that Britain was dragging France unwillingly in, setting France up to do her fighting for her. Bonnet told Halifax it would be 'far preferable' if Henderson and Coulondre acted together, and he did not see that a matter of four hours made so very much difference. But finding Halifax an unusually steadfast negotiator, he had reluctantly to agree to the British plan. He could not accelerate French action, he explained, because of pressure from his military chiefs, but he would allow Britain to act earlier. He would accept, but it would have a bad effect on world opinion.

The Labour Party executive met too at 9.30 p.m. Dalton writes that 'some, including Tom Williams and Shinwell, inclined to the view that if France wouldn't fight, we shouldn't either, no matter what the terms of our treaty with the Poles might be'.[85] But the Party as a whole was solidly for action. Its National Executive had already promised that the Government's decision to resist Hitler 'receives the full support of the Labour movement in this country'.[86] There were by now only a few pacifists and appeasers holding out against the flood. Channon, for instance, took the same view as Halifax of the House of Commons's outburst that evening. It was 'insane', he wrote in his diary. 'Are we all mad?' he asked Alec Douglas-Home, then Chamberlain's Parliamentary Private Secretary. He begged David Margesson, the Government Chief Whip, to do something. 'It must be war, Chips, old boy,' was the reply, 'there's no other way out.'

Simultaneously with the negotiations and recriminations still continuing in 10 Downing Street, an extraordinary gathering of angry Cabinet ministers had collected in John Simon's room at the Palace of Westminster: John Anderson, Hore-Belisha, W. S. Morrison, Malcolm MacDonald and Reginald Dorman-Smith. They were understandably furious that the decision they had taken that afternoon to send an ultimatum at midnight was apparently overruled by Chamberlain and his clique without consultation. They were under strange leadership, for Simon was as deep-dyed an appeaser as Halifax. Channon explains Simon's defection, perhaps rightly, as a bid for power, a clear attempt to have Chamberlain thrown out of office by his own party. For it was clear that this would happen unless a decision was taken soon. 'My colleagues already there had decided that they would not leave that room until such time as war had been declared,' writes Dorman-Smith, then Minister of Agriculture. 'As we sat there and waited by the phone and nothing happened, I felt like a disembodied spirit. It didn't seem real. We were on strike.'[87]

All the time Chamberlain and Halifax were telephoning Paris they were aware of this room full of their senior colleagues, smouldering quietly for the moment but ready to explode unless a solution was soon found. Dorman-Smith continues: 'There was a feeling of great emotion. All of us were getting back to our natural selves. I became more Irish and Hore-Belisha more Jewish, talking of rights and indignities and so on . . . As we waited we got scruffier and sweatier. I don't remember that we had any food brought in.'

Meanwhile the last German attempt to keep Britain and France out of the war was launched upon Whitehall. All day Berlin had been trying to confuse the issue and prevent an early decision. Information direct from Poland was hard to come by. What little emerged from Polish sources was bound to be suspect in London and Paris, where it was assumed that the Poles would exaggerate the extent of the battle so as to enlist swifter and more active help from their allies. Conditions were thus good for the use of Goebbels's most effective weapon, the outright lie. That morning Ribbentrop had told Henderson that 'yesterday it was Poland that had invaded Germany with troops of the regular Army'. Through that day German agents had been spreading rumours around Paris that fighting had ceased and that the war was a non-starter. From Germany's point of view every hour was important. If Britain and France were to come in, it was essential that it should not be until they had broken the back of Polish resistance. They feared a war on two fronts, and to avoid this Hitler was ready to offer any number of false promises.

At 7 p.m. Ribbentrop telephoned London and spoke to Fritz Hesse, the correspondent of the official news agency Deutsches Nachrichten-Büro. The Foreign Minister did not announce himself but said 'in the deep voice no one could fail to recognize: "You know who is speaking. Please don't mention my name . . . Please go to your confidant (*Vertrauensmann*) – you know whom I mean – and tell him this: the Führer is ready to move out of Poland and to offer reparation for the damage done on condition that we receive Danzig and a road through the Corridor, if England will act as mediator in the German-Polish conflict."' Hesse duly asked to see Horace Wilson and was received by him at 11 Downing Street at about 10 p.m.

Hesse explained the proposition and, according to him, Wilson was 'visibly impressed'. But he did not believe that Hitler had changed his mind. Would Hitler be ready to make a public apology for the violence he had committed? Hesse replied that to ask for this would be a 'psychological error', that if there was to be war simply because Britain insisted upon an apology the world would say it was Britain's fault. But Wilson was clearly embarrassed at the idea of putting such a vague and unsubstantiated proposal before the Cabinet which was about to assemble. He realized that the members would be in no mood to listen to such honeyed words. He told Hesse that things had gone too far, that things had happened that made it impossible to consider the proposal. And so, Hesse writes, his mission failed.[88]

Horace Wilson gives quite a different version of this meeting in a note in the Foreign Office archives.[89] Wilson confirms Hesse's claim that Ribbentrop had telephoned London that evening, but according to him Hesse was instructed to ask 'whether His Majesty's Government would agree that I should be authorized to go to Berlin secretly to meet him and Hitler . . . to discuss the whole position heart to heart including Poland'. Wilson makes no mention of Hitler's offer to withdraw and to offer reparation.

In the published German archives the Hesse proposal itself is marked 'not found', but the wording of Hesse's report to Berlin after the meeting seems to confirm Wilson and to deny Hesse's story, which was of course written many years later. This report claims that Wilson 'received the proposal in a friendly but negative manner. He said that as long as German aggression into Poland continued, it was impossible for the British Government to enter into a conference. It followed therefore that conversations of any kind were impossible for him, Wilson. The *status quo* must first of all be fully restored by the withdrawal of German troops from Polish territory. After this the British Government would be prepared to let bygones be bygones and to start negotiations immediately.'[90]

Wilson's own version of his answer is by and large the same as this. At the end of it Cadogan scribbled a revealing little note: 'These indirect approaches rather reassure me. The Germans must be feeling the draught.' Once again it reveals the frantic optimism of senior British officials. In spite of the facts they insisted on believing that Hitler was bluffing. On 30 August Ambassador Kennedy reported the view of the British Cabinet that it 'had Hitler on the run'.[91] The British were still refusing to accept that in war it is armed forces that count, and Britain's army was tiny. In fact the boot was on the other foot. It was Britain who was bluffing. Hitler suspected as much and was acting accordingly.

Hitler's pacific noises were of course mere procrastination, and Chamberlain should really have faced this fact earlier. He, Halifax and Horace Wilson — the leading appeasers — have been rightly criticized for their refusal during the late 1930s to accept the bitter truth, to prepare properly for the probable future war and, when it came, to fight that war as if they meant to win it. One wonders though what some of the Prime Minister's critics would have done if they had been in his shoes that day, believing as he did that any future war would kill millions in the first few weeks, untold millions if it was allowed to continue for years. After all in the 1970s there are so many people, motivated by human feeling often to the point of idealism though not always by logical thought, who believe that if some force threatens to conquer the world, however evil it may be, war should not be contemplated as a means to oppose it. The price is too high, the slaughter too immense. It is better to submit. One must remember that there were those who felt this way in 1939 and Chamberlain was almost, though not quite, of their number.

When does a peace-lover become an appeaser, a weak fool, an unwitting danger to the peace he is trying to preserve? This is the question that has to be answered before one can judge Chamberlain. He was ready to bend over backwards to believe Hitler. Even after Hitler deceived him by seizing Prague in March 1939, he insisted on exploring every remote escape hole from what now seemed inevitable. But when it came to the crunch in September he would not be fooled again. The Devil tempted him with almost irresistible offers, but this time the Devil's words were not enough. He wanted Hitler to withdraw his invading army as a preliminary sign of good faith. To give the appeasers their due, they never budged from this demand. Their insistence on believing, even on 2 September, that Hitler might accept this demand betrayed ignorance and perhaps foolishness. The Government's message to Hitler that if he withdrew Britain would 'let bygones be bygones' sounds weak and scarcely fair to Poland. But once convinced that Hitler would not withdraw, Chamberlain did brace himself to do what came least naturally to him.

A cynic might claim that it was only the threat of dismissal by the House of Commons that made him take the plunge. This was Dalton's view. But the record shows that although the 'angry scene' may have accelerated the decision by a few hours, it did not alter the final outcome. Halifax was more inclined to delay even than Chamberlain, and his angry reaction to Parliament's outburst reflects no credit upon him. But even he at no time budged from the withdrawal demand, and given the fact that Hitler was not inclined to accept this demand, war was inevitable, even with Halifax and Bonnet as the two Foreign Ministers.

Soon after 11 p.m. the angry Cabinet Ministers, still in Simon's room at the House of Commons, received word to join the Prime Minister. By this time they were, in Dorman-Smith's words, 'really scruffy and smelly'. The meeting began with an incomplete Cabinet. Members were trickling in for several minutes during the opening discussions. The first thing Dorman-Smith noticed was that Halifax and Cadogan were in evening dress, while Chamberlain was not. 'The P.M. had evidently not changed for dinner,' he wrote, unaware that there was a simple explanation for this strange state of affairs: that Halifax and his wife had expected to dine out, not at 10 Downing Street, and so he had spent the early part of the evening preparing himself. It all emphasized the incongruity of such a gathering, some in tail coats, Samuel Hoare in a dinner jacket, others in crumpled daytime suits, some fed, some hungry, the Prime Minister like a stag at bay, his ministers crying for action and if necessary ready to destroy him.

Dorman-Smith continues: 'This was a plain *diktat* from the Cabinet . . . facing a Cabinet on a "sit-down strike" he had no alternative. The climax came most dramatically. The P.M. said quietly: "Right, gentlemen, this means war."' Dorman-Smith's account is here misleading, for Chamberlain had already decided that war must come. His only problem during the past couple of hours had been to try to coordinate British and French entry. What does cast some credit upon him is that he was at least ready to make a sort of apology to his colleagues for keeping them in the dark. There was no angry scene, and the Prime Minister showed none of Halifax's grumpiness and bitterness. He said 'he recognized the strength of feeling shown in the House of Commons' and 'it was clearly necessary that a fresh start be made to correct the position' which had arisen from the 'important departure in the statements they [the Government] had made from the line which the Cabinet had approved'.[92]

Chamberlain explained that the French had pressed for a joint ultimatum to be delivered at noon on 3 September with a declaration of war at 8 or 9 p.m. They would not agree to the British idea of an ultimatum at 8 a.m., giving time for a declaration of war before Parliament reassembled. Their differences had been irreconcilable and the only way out had been to agree to separate approaches to the German Government. The Cabinet approved this procedure. It would not be announced for the moment. All that would be said was that the Prime Minister would make a statement in the morning, by which time it was essential for the ultimatum to have expired. The ministers realized that a new Cabinet would have to be formed and agreed to put their resignations collectively in the Prime Minister's hands. The meeting ended at 12.15 a.m. and Ambassador Corbin was informed of the decision. Most accounts of the scene mention that during these last minutes a thunderstorm broke and torrential rain was falling. It was a fitting relief from the bright sun that perversely shone on Europe throughout September.

At about 1.30 a.m. Halifax walked across Downing Street to the Foreign Office and bumped into Dalton. They exchanged a few memorable words. According to Halifax's version Dalton said, 'Can you give me any hope?' Halifax said, 'If by "hope" you mean hope of being at war, I think I can give you sure hope for tomorrow.'[93] Dalton replied, 'Thank God!' Dalton's version is rather different.[94] He claims he said to Halifax, 'I hope you have brought the French into line now. I warn you that, if the House of Commons meets again without our pledge to Poland having been fulfilled, there will be such an explosion as you in the House of Lords may not be able to imagine. It may well blow up the Government altogether.' Halifax replied, 'I quite understand. It has been very difficult. But it will be all right tomorrow.' These two accounts of the same story are a good illustration of the fallibility of politicians as autobiographers. Memories are gilded by time. Every man likes to believe he came off best out of every little incident, and often he ends by convincing himself that this is the case. It does him and the casual reader no harm, but it can put the truth in danger, and it is history which suffers.

And so at last the leaders of France and Britain could go to bed, the great issue decided. For the Poles it had been a day of tragedy and disillusionment. For a second whole day they had fought the German invader single-handed, while their British and French allies remained neutral. Their Ambassador in Paris had been driven to distraction by the delaying tactics of Bonnet and Gamelin. Their Foreign Minister in Warsaw had been humiliated by calls to negotiation while his government was fighting a total war against unprovoked aggression. Their borders had been pierced by fast-moving columns of tanks, driving deep into Poland, carving out tracks for the advancing infantry which could then wheel and surround the Polish armies it had passed.

By allowing this to continue for more than forty-eight hours before formally declaring war on Poland, Britain and France must by any standard be considered to have broken their treaty with Poland, which obliged them to afford help 'immediately'. This delay, and the consequent military disadvantage with which the Allies eventually began the war, was caused by ignorance of Hitler's intention, by the British belief that Hitler was bluffing and would be deterred by strong words, by Bonnet's belief that Hitler's aim was limited to the seizure of what was, many thought, justly his. The problem of obtaining reliable information from Poland and the smokescreen of lies which Goebbels's men were spreading about the new war increased British and French irresolution.

'There was never any question of France not fulfilling her obligations,' Bonnet told the author in 1971. 'Even if a conference had been possible, France would only have agreed to it with the concurrence of Britain and Poland. If France had wished to accept the conference and Britain had not, then France would have had to observe the treaty and go to war in spite of her own wish.' Such words are some reassurance, I suppose, but still the nagging doubt remains: what if Hitler had agreed to a cease-fire though not to a withdrawal? What if he had called off the formal attack, had held on to the Polish territory already occupied on 1 and 2 September, and had continued by subjecting Poland to infiltration, subversion and armed raid? Would Britain really have been able to insist on total German withdrawal? Or would the Ribbentrop–Ciano–Bonnet–Halifax chain of communication and distorted information have kept the Allies talking to Germany in San Remo while Hitler's purpose was stealthily and inexorably accomplished? There were so many influential men in Britain and France ready to give Hitler the benefit of the doubt. If only Hitler's aggression had not been quite so blatant, might he not once again have obtained British and French acquiescence? One cannot know for sure, but the published records seem to indicate a mood in France and Britain that would not have allowed declarations of war in such a case. It does appear that Hitler could probably by a little more subtlety have kept Poland's allies out.

In spite of their dangerously weak reaction to Hitler's aggression, it is hard not to feel sorry for the British and French leaders who had to deal with the 2 September crisis. For Hitler had shattered not only their future, but also their unity. His sudden move had made the wheels of the government machine race at such a speed as nearly to seize the engine. In both countries diplomacy and the decision-making process had failed. They were on the pinnacle of a structure which that day had all but crumbled and fallen. In Britain the relationship between administration and legislature had been strained to breaking point, as had that between the British and French Governments. They were locked together by necessity, but with strategic and foreign policies which could hardly be reconciled.

Chamberlain wrote to his sister, 'The final long-drawn-out agonies that preceded the actual declaration of war were as nearly unendurable as could be.'[95] That night, having made the terrible decision, he felt as one imagines in modern times an American President or Soviet First Secretary would feel having just pressed the button to launch a nuclear attack. 'Our preparations had been for Armageddon,' wrote Samuel Hoare.[96] It cannot be easy to sleep having just taken a decision which could well mean the end of civilization.

3 A Tentative Beginning

A few minutes after midnight on 3 September telegrams from the British and French governments were on their way to their ambassadors in Berlin instructing them to present ultimata with time limits. Henderson was to present his at 9 a.m., Coulondre his at noon so that Bonnet's promise to Ciano would not be broken. So much was agreed between Halifax and Bonnet the previous evening at 10.30.[1] But in spite of this agreement Bonnet was still scheming to keep France out of the war. There was still de Monzie's idea of a 'symbolic withdrawal', which they had agreed to put before Ambassador Guariglia at 10.40 p.m., that is to say *after* the details of the ultimatum were agreed. 'Perhaps the British might have changed their decision,' writes Bonnet in 1971,[2] but it is hardly an adequate excuse for his action in making such a defeatist approach at such a time and without the knowledge of his British or Polish allies.

De Monzie writes that Guariglia found his idea quite acceptable but feared the British would reject it. There would then be a hopeless situation, since the conference could accomplish nothing unless the British took part in it. (Bonnet's original insistence that the Poles should also take part seems at this point to have weakened.) De Monzie reported Guariglia's reaction to Bonnet at 11.30 p.m.[3] The foreign Minister too thought there was little chance of selling the idea to London, but de Monzie reassured him, 'It will succeed if you speak to London strongly enough.' De Monzie had the impression that Halifax himself was showing 'good will' towards the French appeasers, but was under the baleful influence of the 'grumbling' House of Commons.

In spite of his reservations Guariglia went ahead and submitted the proposal to Rome, where Ciano was roused from his bed to consider it. It did not take him long. 'I throw the proposal in the waste-paper basket without informing the Duce,' he wrote in his diary, concluding only that 'this shows that France is moving towards the great test without enthusiasm and full of uncertainty'.[4] It was yet another indication of France's weakness and of Bonnet's scheming, justified in his eyes by the need to seize every chance however slight of avoiding the horrors of war.

But there was another point of view: that Hitler was resolved on a war of expansion and therefore the chance of peace was nil; that Britain's and France's only course of action was to oppose Hitler and to make war against Germany until Hitler was removed as Germany's leader. To those of this opinion Bonnet's unwillingness to fight and the tricks he employed to make his point of view prevail in Cabinet and with his British allies were little short of treachery.

All in all, Bonnet's character was a strange one, a phenomenon which de Monzie did his best to explain to Łukasiewicz: 'Bonnet is always like that, a decent, honest man, but possessed of some almost physical inability to tell the truth right to the end. In what he says there is always something vague or left unsaid, with the result that one never knows how much of what he says is true, or how much is being concealed. This applies not only to his talks with diplomats, but also to the reports he makes to the Council of Ministers.'[5]

The Foreign Office in London took a less charitable view. Throughout 2 September they had been made to look very foolish. Their carefully constructed good relationship with France had all but collapsed at the crucial moment, nearly dragging the Government down with it, and there were few in Whitehall with any doubts as to who should bear the blame. 'One cannot help thinking that M. Bonnet was the villain of the piece,' noted Moley Sargent. 'He is, we know, the rallying point of French *defaitisme*, and although he has been defeated in the present encounter, we must expect that he will continue to exert his baleful influence over the French Government and on French policy. He will, we must assume, intrigue whenever he can to get France out of the war, and failing that to limit her effort in the war to a minimum.'

Sargent continued with an astonishing accusation: 'He may well establish contacts for this purpose with the Germans and Italians.'[6]

Sargent wondered what could be done to get Bonnet removed from office, with the aim of 'ensuring that the Quai d'Orsay is placed in charge of an honest man'. These damning comments were endorsed by Cadogan, who found it 'astonishing that M. Bonnet should have clung to his office for so long. So far as we know his views are far apart from those of M. Daladier, and he has I think practically no following in France and can be of little good to M. Daladier. He is entirely untrustworthy, and we know that on occasions he has lied and misrepresented us.'

One seldom encounters language so violent in British official papers, and it reflects the Foreign Office's fury not only at Bonnet's policies, but also at the situation into which his manoeuvring had placed them *vis-à-vis* their Government. They passionately desired Bonnet's removal, and on 13 September Sargent noted: 'I think that Sir E. Phipps should get into the way of going direct to Daladier on all important questions. If he is asked why he is cold-shouldering Bonnet, he should say baldly that he has been so instructed from here, and leave it at that. This sort of boycotting may eventually have its effect.'[7]

The British were apparently unaware that Bonnet was also having his troubles with his colleagues in France. In 1971 he assured the author that once war was declared he used all his influence to secure an immediate French offensive against Germany. He writes, 'We did not declare war so as to take refuge behind the Maginot Line and watch passively while Poland was exterminated. We declared war to prevent this. At the War Council of 23 August Gamelin explained to us that Poland was essential for France's national defence.'[8] He lays at Gamelin's door France's failure to take any important offensive action against Germany. His theory is that Gamelin was gradually seduced away from this plan by his belief that Hitler would not invade Poland, that he was bluffing, and that even if he did do anything rash, the German generals would rebel and remove him.[9]

In contrast to Gamelin's timidity there was the diplomatic aggression of another French group: the President of the Republic, Albert Lebrun, the President of the Senate, Jules Jeanneney, and the Minister of the Colonies, Georges Mandel. Bonnet complains

that these 'warmongers', while ready enough to resign themselves
to the defeat of Poland, wanted to launch a preventive war
against Italy and Spain, which they believed were about to attack
France.[10] Spain was believed to be on the point of seizing the
International Zone of Tangier and interrupting France's communication with Morocco. Italy was said to have a plan to attack
France on 15 September.

On 11 September de Monzie noticed that a series of precautionary and repressive measures were in force against Italians and
their sympathizers. The French police were subjecting Italian
workers in France to administrative pinpricks. A friend of de
Monzie's found himself under observation by officers of the
deuxième bureau for no other reason than that he had sometimes
dined with Ambassador Guariglia. 'The unfortunate Lady A.,
guilty of loving a handsome Italian who also by the way loves
France, is issued by the police with a deportation order,' de Monzie
adds.[11] The militant Mandel, who told him on 1 September that
'France needs to *declare* war in order to get herself in a fit state to
make war', authorized sanctions against the Italian residents of
Jibouti, a French colony surrounded by Italian-ruled Abyssinia.[12]

It soon emerged what all this was leading up to. Lebrun and
Jeanneney suggested sending Italy an ultimatum demanding
neutralization of two of her ports under French control and the
dispatch of her fleet from the Mediterranean to the Atlantic. Italy
would doubtless have refused such a demand, and the way would
have been open for a French invasion overland, a task more
realistic than any invasion of Germany and more within the
French Army's compass.

In this matter for once Bonnet had support from the British, and
he says that he discussed the matter daily with Ambassador Phipps,
finally persuading London to support his point of view and to help
stop the preventive war. Britain still had high hopes of detaching
Italy from her alliance with Germany. Her ambassador in Rome
was sending home exaggerated reports of the success of his mission, apparently convincing some people that Italy was under-
going a real change of heart, not merely shirking the fight temporarily for selfish reasons.

Even Chamberlain was thus impressed, for he wrote to his sister,
'I place my hope, and indeed my confidence, on the attitude of the

Italian King, Church and people.'[13] But what of the Duce? The British Prime Minister would finally have to reckon with Mussolini's dictatorial need to indulge in military conquest. 'Why should Hitler have all the victories?' the Italian fascists were asking themselves surlily as they observed Germany's triumph. Halifax wrote to Lothian of his hope that 'we may prove to Italy that neutrality pays — an argument that makes, I suspect, a more direct appeal to the Italian mind than considerations of higher morality'.[14] Such outright xenophobia was indulged in all too frequently by British leaders of the 1930s. Cadogan in his diary actually referred to the Italians as 'ice-creamers'.

Halifax was of course missing the point. Mussolini's reluctance to fight was based on his deep suspicion of Soviet Russia, his anger at not being informed in advance of the Pact with Stalin, his vague sympathy with Catholic Poland, but above all on the practical point that his armed forces were not yet ready for real war. True, they had routed the spear-brandishing warriors of Abyssinia, but they would not succeed against a modern European army.

Bonnet's opposition to the Italian adventure, wise though it may have been in this case, served only to bring him more enemies and to confirm his reputation as a defeatist. 'Georges Bonnet is going to be sacrificed,' noted de Monzie in his diary as early as 7 September. 'Sacrificed to the literature of the Anglo-Saxons who denounce peace as treason.'[15] In Paris as well as in London, it seemed, his position as Foreign Minister was seen as inconsistent with a policy of war. And soon there would be the peace offensive. Hitler would conquer Poland and propose 'generous' terms for a settlement. So much was foreseen. Bonnet would have been ready to consider such terms. 'I would not have rejected them outright,' he told the author in 1971. In the circumstances he had to go.

Thus, after a few days of war, Bonnet found himself politically bankrupt. He had succeeded in annoying almost everyone who had influence with his Prime Minister: the British who saw him as little better than a traitor, Gamelin and the French High Command who disliked his reckless idea of an immediate offensive against Germany, Mandel and the anti-Nazi 'hard-liners' who thought he was an appeaser of Hitler. The sum total of these pressures forced Daladier to act. On 13 September, the same day that Sargent proposed the British 'boycott' of Bonnet, Daladier summoned Bonnet and told him that he wanted to take the Ministry of Foreign Affairs under his own control. Bonnet was afraid that the Prime Minister would find himself overburdened with work, to which Daladier apparently replied, 'Yes, I know that I am taking on a grave responsibility. I'll do it, even though there's a risk that the house will collapse on my head.' [16] It was not much of a reassurance, nor even much of an excuse. Bonnet could only take comfort in the fact that Daladier remained personally loyal to him, keeping him in the Government as Minister of Justice, a harmless but prestigious post. The change brought many sighs of relief from those who ruled Britain and France.

Bonnet did his best to justify his past policies and to work for an end to the war, but it was hard for him to do this in his new job. During the autumn the French were preparing a *Yellow Book*, containing the main diplomatic documents of the 1–2 September crisis, and Bonnet was insisting upon a full revelation to show the world how nearly he had managed to save the peace. The projected volume caused consternation in London, since it was bound to reveal inconsistencies in British and French policy which would be exploited by German propaganda. For instance, there was Bonnet's message of 10.20 a.m. on 1 September with his 'favourable reply' to Mussolini's offer to intervene.[17] Frank Roberts saw the book in proof and noted (6 December): 'Insomuch as this account suggests that the French Government were rather less particular than His Majesty's Government about their treaty obligations to Poland, and that they were readier to consider a conference after the Germans had actually walked into Poland, it is discreditable to the French Government rather than to His Majesty's Government.' [18]

But this was not the point. The problem was to preserve the semblance of Allied unity and if necessary to conceal anything that showed the contrary. On 8 December Cadogan and the French Ambassador examined the proofs together. 'We considered what amendments might be proposed,' Cadogan noted. 'It would be difficult simply to omit the 10.20 message, as some of the following messages depended upon it. I pointed out that it might be sufficient to omit the word "favourable" and M. Corbin thought that possibly this might be the solution.' He thought that this was one of those times when history must be falsified so as

to serve a greater interest. But he was playing with fire. The doc-
tored text could so easily have been revealed for what it was, for
instance by the Italians who first received it, and then Goebbels's
men would really have exploited the lie. Bonnet too, one may
assume, would not have stood idly by while his telegram was falsified. In the end the correct text was used, which doubtless caused
some embarrassment at the time, but nothing so terrible that it
was worth committing forgery to avoid it.

As 3 September dawned in London the Government machine
was ready with a mass of work to be put in hand as soon as war
was declared. Some measures had already been ordered as part of
the 'Precautionary Stage'. Barrage balloons, huge, strangely
beautiful, egg-shaped, with cables ready to slice off a dive-
bomber's wing, were in place over London and other vulnerable
points by noon on 1 September, and since 4 p.m. the Central War
Room had been fully manned. An air search for minelayers and
destroyers had been ordered and strict controls and searches were
imposed at Liverpool and Milford Haven.

At 11.30 a.m. on 2 September there had been a meeting of
Permanent Secretaries at 6 Richmond Terrace to coordinate final
plans. There were 'Seizure' and 'Days of Grace' telegrams ready
to be sent to all British ports at home and abroad. The Secretaries
decided there would be no days of grace, that German ships would
be seized as soon as war was declared. They decided to send out
parties to requisition buildings for the occupation of government
departments which were to be evacuated from London forthwith.
The American Government was to be asked to take charge of
British interests in enemy countries. Action to intern enemy aliens
was to be put into effect, not on a wholesale scale but bit by bit.
A national register of all residents would be compiled as soon as
possible.[20]

At 9.30 a.m. on 3 September there was a meeting of the 'Sub-
Committee on Coordination', which consisted of a member of
every department. Edward Bridges, Secretary to the Cabinet,
asked everyone to go away and assemble an hour later at 6 Richmond Terrace 'to enable them if necessary to take immediate steps
to put the war stage of the Government War Book into operation'.

One man still not resigned to the inevitable was Birger Dahlerus,
who had learnt of the ultimatum from his friend Forbes in the

British Embassy in Berlin, and by 8.40 a.m. was at Göring's head-quarters.[21] Dahlerus says that he urged his German friends to make their reply 'courteous and obliging' and to emphasize 'the points which Göring solemnly vowed were the cornerstone of German policy, namely the desire to come to an understanding'.[22]

At 10.15 a.m. Dahlerus telephoned London and spoke to Frank Roberts. 'He had done his damnedest to endeavour to overcome the difficulties regarding the withdrawal of troops,' he told Roberts. 'These were however unsurmountable.'[23] Göring had told him that 'never in the history of the world had a victorious army been compelled to withdraw before negotiations had started'. He 'definitely confirmed' (it is not clear on what basis) that a German reply was on its way and urged the British to con-sider it in the most favourable light, since if a conference could be arranged 'there would be a good chance of world peace'. He rang again at 10.50 a.m. to say that the German reply was on its way, and to propose his plan, to which Hitler had apparently agreed, that Göring fly to London at once with a delegation. 'Rats!' was Cadogan's reaction to this suggestion. ('Rats!' in those days meant 'nonsense'.) London had had enough of that sort of thing. 'Got to the Foreign Office about 10 o'clock, but there was nothing to do,' was the amazing beginning to Halifax's 3 September diary. True, he had had a late night, but then it was going to be a busy day. He wrote, '. . . I did not see that there was any good in Göring coming here.' There was now no point in anyone deluding himself ten minutes before the war that it was not going to happen.

At 11.13 a.m. Edward Bridges informed his Sub-Committee that no answer had been received to the ultimatum, and that therefore the War Book instructions were to be put into effect. A letter dated '11.15 a.m. 3 September' and signed by the Secretary to the Sub-Committee William Elliot was sent to twenty-nine government departments and to the King (George VI). It began, 'Sir, I am directed to inform you that a state of war exists between the UK and Germany . . .'[24] Also at 11.15 a.m. Chamberlain announced to the world by radio that it was war — a moving but rather pathetic speech, again emphasizing the personal grief of the speaker. Harold Nicolson found this note 'shocking', adding that 'after last night's demonstration he cannot possibly lead us into a great war'. Anthony Eden wrote, 'It seemed rather the lament

Any further communication on this
subject should be addressed to:—

THE SECRETARY,
Offices of the Cabinet
and Committee of Imperial Defence,
Richmond Terrace, S.W.1.
and the following number quoted.

19/1/3. (War Book.)

MOST IMMEDIATE.

OFFICES OF THE CABINET
AND COMMITTEE OF IMPERIAL DEFENCE,
Richmond Terrace,
London, S.W.1.

Date 3rd September, 1939.

Time of Despatch 11.15 a.m.

SECRET.

INSTITUTION OF WAR STAGE.

Sir,

I AM directed by the Prime Minister to inform you that a state of war
exists between the United Kingdom and Germany.
~~that His Majesty's Government have decided to declare war against~~
~~that war has broken out between His Majesty's Government and~~

with effect from 11 a.m. 3rd September, 1939.

2. I am to request that the arrangements laid down in the War Book
for the War Stage may be put into operation ~~with effect from~~ forthwith.

3. Please acknowledge the receipt of this letter immediately.

I am,

Sir,

Your obedient Servant,

William Elliot.

The actual document ordering British government departments to begin
the war. (Crown Copyright. Public Record Office. FO 371/23404 f 387)

of a man deploring his own failure than the call of a nation to
arms.' [25]

It was fitting that the false climax of Chamberlain's speech
should be followed by the bathos of an air-raid that never was.
Scores of writers recall how the sirens began to wail just as
millions of Britons were switching off their radio sets after the
announcement. Churchill's wife 'commented favourably upon

the German promptitude and precision'.[26] John Slessor wondered 'whether this was in fact the knock-out blow to which we had given so much thought in the past two years'.[27] Herd instinct drew many famous men to the House of Commons. Edward Spears picked up several colleagues in his car.[28] 'I sit on [Leo] Amery's knee and Anthony [Eden] sits on mine,' noted Harold Nicolson. They rushed for shelter in the building and stood out on the terrace listening for danger, until Spears told them that if there was a bomb aimed at them, they would not hear it, or indeed anything ever again. 'My audience noticeably thinned out after this.'[29]

The official papers record: '11.35, H.Q. Fighter Command issues "Yellow" warning of an air raid approaching England. "Red" warning issued and sirens sounded in London and other areas in error. Later it transpired that "raids" were friendly aircraft." It was, in fact, the assistant French Military Attaché, Captain de Brantes, returning from a visit to Paris at a very awkward moment.[30] The comedy was only spoilt by the fact that two British fighters, sent up to engage the attacking Luftwaffe, collided over London and a pilot was killed – the first British casualty of the war. (De Brantes was tortured to death by the Gestapo in 1943.)

A few hours earlier a thirty-man British military mission crossed into Poland from Rumania. Led by two intelligence officers, Carton de Wiart and Colin Gubbins, they had made their way by cruiser to Alexandria during August, thinly disguised as an 'agricultural mission' and possessed of false passports. It was the sort of set-up that the British Foreign Office does not like. 'The journey was carried out in the face of considerable diplomatic difficulties,' de Wiart wrote in his report.[31] To be precise, the British Embassies on their route through Egypt, Lebanon, Greece and Rumania would have nothing to do with them, so they had to appeal to the Poles, who provided them in Lebanon with an aeroplane and a pilot named Onoszko. They were by now becoming notorious, and over Salonika the Greeks ordered them to land, but they flew on, muttering something over the radio about the undercarriage having gone. By 2 September they had landed in Rumania and were at Cernauti, near the Polish border, having decided to abandon their aeroplane because of the reported state of Polish airfields after German bombing.

The Rumanians eventually allowed them and their quantities of 'agricultural equipment', to cross into Poland, doubtless glad to see the back of them. Rumania was frightened of being drawn into the conflict. The country swarmed with German agents and was subject to German influence. Gubbins noticed, for example, that German newspapers were on sale in Bucharest the day after publication, while *The Times* was a week old. On the other side of the river the Poles were waiting for them with open arms, and during the morning of 3 September they were whisked by train to Lwów and into buses for the drive to Warsaw.

About midday they stopped in Lublin for lunch, heard that Britain was at war and changed into uniform. After lunch they went out into the street to find that a cheering crowd had gathered. Their buses were covered in flowers, and they were hugged and kissed on the cheeks by Poles who assumed they were the vanguard of the British Army. Their hearts were touched, all the more so as they realized what was about to happen to Poland and that the Poles' gratitude and trust were completely misplaced.

In Cracow Clare Hollingworth realized Britain was at war when she heard a radio playing *God Save the King*. A Polish porter ran forward and kissed her hands. 'For me it was the worst moment of the war', she writes. '. . . I felt a little sick and recollected that neither Britain nor France could prevent all these people falling into German hands.' [32] In Warsaw demonstrations lasted all day. Beck came to the British Embassy and thanked Kennard from the bottom of his heart. Kennard opened a bottle of champagne. They drank, and Kennard made the rather tasteless suggestion that they both go out onto the balcony and toast the crowd. Beck thought that champagne was hardly appropriate in view of the suffering that was to come, but they did go out and wave in response to the crowd's shouts of 'Long live Great Britain! Long live the fight for liberty!' Noel [33] describes how, 'saluted with vivats', Beck called for silence and told the crowd, 'We never doubted that Great Britain and France would fight.' [34]

The French Embassy was likewise besieged with well-wishers. Noel remembered the Munich crisis a year earlier, when Poland had joined Hitler in seizing part of Czechoslovakia and Polish officials had tried to provoke *hostile* demonstrations by the French Embassy. [35] It seemed an eternity away. Noel received Beck in a small room because in the main rooms they were taking down the tapestries to save them from bombs and fire. News of French entry into the war arrived. 'What a relief for my conscience, but what anguish for my heart!' Noel remarks. As he escorted Beck to his car a delirious crowd shouted 'Vive Beck' and 'Vive la France'.

In Berlin William Shirer was standing in the Wilhelmplatz when the loudspeakers gave the news. 'Some 250 people were standing there in the sun,' he writes. 'They listened attentively to the announcement. When it was finished there was not a murmur. They just stood as they were before. Stunned.' [36] According to Hitler's interpreter Paul Schmidt, the Nazi leaders were similarly stunned. Hitler 'sat immobile, gazing before him'. Göring said, 'If we lose this war, then God have mercy upon us!', while Goebbels 'stood in a corner by himself, downcast and self-absorbed'.

At exactly this time in Bydgoszcz (in German 'Bromberg') heavy fighting was taking place between Polish forces and local German residents who were rising in support of their Führer. Bydgoszcz lay just to the south of the Corridor, an important railway junction through which thousands of retreating Polish soldiers would have to pass. It was the ideal spot for fifth-column activity, and during the morning of 3 September several hundred of them seized strong points in the city and began sniping at the retreating Poles. [37] According to Polish reports 238 Poles and 223 fifth-columnists were killed in the fighting, after which a Polish military court sentenced 260 fifth-columnists to death. They were summarily shot. [38]

What other repressive measures were taken by the Polish authorities or by the Polish civilians who had helped put down the revolt it is impossible to verify or even guess. After such an incident it would be strange if the Poles had not reacted violently, and of course not everywhere did the police and army have control. Individual Germans may well have been murdered, though certainly not on the scale that was afterwards claimed by Hitler as justification for his cruel revenge on the Polish nation. Clare Hollingworth saw a group of swastika-armbanded Germans being marched to execution, [39] and there was a similar report in *The Times* on 4 September. A modern German historian, Hans Roos, puts the number of German civilians killed in the first days of war at 7,000 — probably an exaggeration but one can never be sure of facts on such an emotive matter. Göring was even to aver in his own defence at Nuremburg that 'Bloody Sunday' was one of the reasons for the invasion of Poland two days earlier. He was confused, of course, but it shows how the incident must have been impressed upon him and how it stuck in his mind.

The Poles expected the French and British to take action immediately in their support. 'Is it true you've bombed Munich?' Clifford Norton was asked several times. Rumours flared up of a sudden French attack on Germany, and there were even reports in the Polish press that they had broken the Siegfried Line. As day followed day and nothing happened in the West, the Poles at first were impatient, then incredulous and then bitterly resentful. They had no idea how long it was going to take the Allied war machine to grind into action.

A. J. P. Taylor has aptly described this British machine as 'an expensive motor-car beautifully polished, complete in every detail, except that there was no petrol in the tank'.[40] Indeed, the huge administrative measures planned for the outbreak were carried out effectively. Cinemas, theatres and places of entertainment were closed. Football matches were banned, indeed any function which entailed the assembly of large numbers of people, with the exception of church services. Prisoners were released who had less than three months to serve, though not Irish terrorists. Enemy aliens, which for the moment meant Austrians and Czechs as well as Germans, were given until 9 September to leave the country, failing which they were required to register with the police and submit to severe restrictions. The dangerous animals in Regent's Park zoo were moved out of London for fear that a bomb might set them free to terrorize the city. The poisonous snakes and scorpions were destroyed.

Since the Munich crisis attempts had been made to instruct the British people in how they would be affected by the three major inconveniences of a future war: blackout, evacuation and air-raid precaution. A total of six leaflets had been pushed through the letter box of every house in the country, so in theory everyone knew what an air-raid warning was – a 'changing warbling note', or 'short whistle blasts' – and that football-match-style hand rattles meant a gas attack. Mothers were told: 'Make sure that you and every member of your household, especially children able to run

Moscow's view of the British electoral truce – the Labour Party 'lackey' shaking hands with the Conservative boss while his carriage runs over 'workers' demands' (*Pravda*, 31 October 1939). (Copyright British Museum)

about, have on them names and addresses clearly written. Do this either on an envelope or something like a luggage label, not an odd piece of paper which might get lost.'[41] Whitehall had dreamed up many such ideas which were seldom obeyed, unenforceable, and did little to help matters when the crunch came. For instance, hardly anyone knew what a warbling note sounded like.

'Carry your gas mask always' was another one, but even in the first few days of the war only about three quarters of the population obeyed it, and this figure was to fall alarmingly as the weeks passed and no bombs dropped. 38,000,000 masks were ready for 3 September, the children's ones coloured to make them look like Mickey Mouse, the babies' ones all-enveloping and worked by a hand pump. Chamberlain and his men set a good example and were duly photographed with their little cardboard boxes slung over their shoulders. *Völkische Beobachter* (13 September) published one such picture, captioning it with ponderous irony: 'The gas mask is not the only mask that Chamberlain wears.' At Eton College the decision was taken, never to be reversed, that boys need no longer wear black top hats with their tail coats. A spokesman for the school explained sensibly, 'One may wear a top hat, or one may wear a gas mask, but one may not wear both.'[42]

Another Moscow view: the British Houses of Parliament turned into a funeral parlour, with undertakers carrying 'freedom of speech' and 'freedom of the press' to burial (*Pravda*, 7 November 1939). (Copyright British Museum)

Mass Observation asked a number of people what they would do if they came across a burning incendiary bomb. A few said 'Run like hell', but most said they would throw water on it, in spite of a clear instruction in one of the leaflets: 'If you throw a bucket of water on a burning incendiary bomb, it will explode and throw burning fragments in all directions.'[43] The problem was that successive crises — the *Anschluss*, Munich, the seizure of Prague — had brought people to a pitch of excitement and then left them with feelings of anti-climax. For two years there had been these cries of 'Wolf!' and prophecies of disaster, until people found themselves perversely longing for action, even for the misery of war, if only it would put them out of their agony. As one man told a *Mass Observation* reporter, 'We keep listening to the wireless news, hoping, I am afraid, for something sensational.'[44] George Orwell had the same strange, self-destructive feeling when serving in the front line during the Spanish Civil War. He describes in *Homage to Catalonia* how he watched his own side being shelled, how the shells kept missing, and how he found himself secretly hoping that one would score a bull's eye.

The black-out did transform conditions of life overnight. Suddenly there was no light from cars, street lights or house windows, and moving from place to place after dark became a difficult and dangerous exercise. Traffic accidents rose by a hundred per cent during the month, and a Gallup Poll showed that twenty per cent suffered some injury, usually minor, as a result of not being able to see where they were going. Until mid October even hand torches were banned, and then the demand was such that they were unavailable. To begin with almost everyone stayed at home, but soon they got used to the dark and there were those who found it beautiful or even amusing. When the dance-halls reopened behind tightly sealed windows, a new popular dance was the 'black-out stroll'. You would be dancing, suddenly the lights would be switched off, and a few seconds later you would be dancing with someone else.[44]

In the first three days of September about 1,500,000 people were evacuated from the cities of Britain to safe areas in the countryside,[45] which by the end of the scheme had absorbed a little less than half of Britain's city schoolchildren. For millions it was a traumatic experience, not only for the hosts but also for the children and their mothers who found themselves suddenly in other people's homes, living cheek by jowl with strangers of quite different social background. By and large it was the poorer children who were billeted, the richer families being able to make their own arrangements. Nice, middle-class country families were shocked and discomfited by the state of the slum children they had to accommodate who were, they complained, insanitary, dirty, lousy and dishonest. The fact that no bombing took place seemed to increase the irritation, for it made the inconvenience seem unnecessary, and soon the children were beginning to drift back to the cities.[46]

Both Britain and France took immediate steps to deal with enemy aliens. The French reaction was strict. All male Germans, Austrians and Czechs between the ages of seventeen and fifty had to report to an 'assembly camp', the main one being the Colombes Stadium near Paris. They were allowed to bring a small quantity of belongings, but had to hand in all knives and razors, and any money in excess of 50 francs. The Czechs were released after a few days, but almost all the others were interned in what the French press innocently called *camps de concentration*.[47] Their only alternative was to enlist for five years with the Foreign

Legion, which struck many as highly unfair, since five years was a period longer than they imagined the war would last.

Chaim Weizmann, who visited France early in October, reported to the Foreign Office that 'the refugee situation was chaotic; the French had been interning all Germans without any selection or examination, and were only now beginning to consider the possibility of discriminating'.[48] Of course many of those interned were Jews, refugees from Nazi terror, who though officially labelled as enemy aliens were implacable opponents of the German regime, but such regimes have a habit of exploiting a refugee situation and infiltrating their own agents. The French felt in the beginning that they could not take risks with any German. It was impossible to be certain about anyone. He might be a plant, or even if he was not he probably had friends and relatives living under Nazi rule, and so would be liable to blackmail. It seemed wretched that those who had already suffered so much under the Nazis should again lose their liberty. The Foreign Office was soon to be embarrassed by a sea of protest mail from friends of refugees, begging Britain to intercede with the French for their release.

The British did not have the immediate threat of an enemy army on their borders, so could afford to be more liberal. Only about 350 enemy aliens were arrested, most of those with Nazi sympathies having departed within a day or two of the outbreak. This left 74,000 Austrians and Germans in the United Kingdom, 50,000 of whom were refugees. They were not interned but were at once put under restriction, not allowed to change their residence without permission from the police, or to travel more than five miles from their residence without permission, or to possess without permission any motor vehicle, boat, aircraft, camera, nautical chart or large-scale map. At once one hundred tribunals were set up all over the country to examine each case individually, and within two months 19,300 were considered, of which 15,140 were released from any restriction, 3,920 were kept under restriction and 230 were interned.[49]

It was in ancillary matters like these that the British administration had prepared well for war. Civil servants had spent years planning for the contingency, and when war came it was simply a question of looking up the rules and following them. Considering the extent of the upheaval, the transition was smooth, and though it was aided by the non-appearance of the expected mass air raids, it was hindered by despondency and truculence of millions who came to feel that their lives had been unnecessarily disrupted. Chamberlain felt it necessary to refer to this feeling in a broadcast on 26 November, pointing out that 'if they [the air raids] had come, as everyone had expected, and had found us unprepared, you would rightly have blamed the Government for its neglect'.[50] He wrote to his sister (23 September): 'One can already see how this twilight war is trying people's nerves. Without the strong centripetal force of mortal danger all the injustices, inconveniences, hardships and uncertainties of wartime are resented more and more because they are felt to be unnecessary.'[51] A year later the Government was to find that bombing has its compensations. Only then was there visible evidence of the real external threat. By providing a hate substitute for the sins of bureaucracy, Hitler's bombs reduced criticism of authority, induced into people a sense of urgency and made the war generally easier to run.

It was with such internal problems that the British War Book served the country best of all, but when it came to fighting and winning the war preparation was rather less advanced. The forces of pacifism, appeasement and plain imprudence had resisted expansion of the British and French armed forces. Only in April 1939 was conscription introduced in a very limited form in Britain, and when it was there was fierce opposition from anti-Government forces. The Labour Party leader Clement Attlee said in the House of Commons on 27 April: 'This country provides the greatest fleet in the world. It has a rapidly growing air force. It has to provide munitions for them . . . It cannot in addition to that provide a continental army.' Although conscription was passed the increase in the Army had been too small and came too late to make any real difference to the balance of power. By September Britain had only four or five divisions ready for action, which was miniscule compared to the French and German armies, which each numbered about 100 divisions. In the light of this, the British policy for the outbreak of war had been considered by the Chiefs of Staff, and on 28 July 1939 they submitted a report to the Committee of Imperial Defence (the body now superseded by the War Cabinet) which contained the following passage: 'If Germany holds in the West and attacks in the East, there is little that we ourselves can do either at sea or on land at the outset of the war to relieve the pressure on Poland, and therefore the problem resolves itself into a question of what we can do in the air.'[52]

British policy was also influenced by another passage in this report: 'As a general point, we would emphasize that the fate of Poland will depend on the ultimate outcome of the war, and that this in turn will depend on our ability to bring about the eventual defeat of Germany, and not on our ability to relieve pressure on Poland at the outset. This must therefore be the over-riding consideration which governs our course of action.'

Another point which was to bedevil the Allied war effort was the 'time is on our side' theory, first propounded in the Report on the first stage of the Anglo-French Staff Conversations. This report, agreed with General Gamelin and approved by the Committee of Imperial Defence, suggested that the time factor

> will work in favour of the Allies, who will be able to count on increasing British strength, and possibly the assistance of American industry. On the other hand time is against Germany and Italy, whose reserve stocks will in due course become exhausted, and who will then be faced with serious difficulties of supply, which should affect the morale both of the armed forces and of the civil population. Anglo-French strategy should therefore be adapted to a long war, implying (i) a defensive strategy at the outset, at least on the Continent, while executing the greatest measure of economic pressure, (ii) the building up of our military strength to a point at which we can adopt an offensive strategy.

Nevertheless, Britain was obliged by Chamberlain's 30 March 'guarantee' and by her 25 August treaty to support Poland 'immediately' and by all means in her power. But this turned out to be not specific enough for the situation. As one cynic pointed out, it obliged Britain to do nothing at all, since it was not in her power to give any support. But any such idea was grossly unfair to Poland, who had no reason to believe that Britain's treaty was an empty gesture. The main problem was that the above-quoted reports were not known to the Poles, who remained in a false paradise, believing they would be assisted certainly in the air and possibly by sea.

The French–Polish agreement was more specific, though even it was incomplete, depending on the signature of a political agreement which was not in fact signed until 4 September. According to the understanding of the Polish delegation, lead by the War Minister Tadeusz Kasprzycki, General Gamelin had promised during talks in Paris in May to launch an offensive against German territory 'with the bulk of his forces' on the sixteenth day after mobilization.[53] On this assumption the Polish Army had resolved to withdraw from Western Poland when attacked, and to make a stand on the line of the rivers Vistula and San, by which time the French would be ready with their attack, would draw off much of the German Army from the East to the West and make possible a Polish counter-attack. Land support was what the Poles expected from France, air and sea support from Britain.

Three specific requests, contained in a telegram from Józef Beck, were put before the French Government by Łukasiewicz on 6 September: air attacks on German military objectives, a breach of the Siegfried Line, and a small seaborne landing on the German coast. It was Beck's contention that the German nation had no enthusiasm for the war, and that this was Hitler's weak point, and that it should be immediately exploited. He wrote: 'The experience of a couple of our patrols which succeeded in invading German territory indicates that the civilian population is easily prone to panic.' Air attacks, he said, 'would convince people that the Allies are waging active warfare' while a land attack breaking the Siegfried Line in a couple of places 'would destroy the myth that this is impossible, and that the Line is in itself sufficient protection against France'.[54]

Of course Beck needed all the help he could get, and it was in his interest to exaggerate the low state of German morale in the hope of spurring his Allies on. His use of the word 'panic' is probably misleading. Maybe the German civilians in a few border villages *had* run for their lives when the Polish cavalry came charging in at high speed, sabres drawn and at the ready. It would be surprising if they did not. But this did not mean that the whole nation would fall apart once the bombs started falling. The last months of the war were to show that the Germans could be resilient in defeat as well as furious in victory.

Still, many British leaders approved Beck's thesis. John Slessor, a senior member of the Air Staff, felt that although Britain was weaker in the air than Germany, it might still be in her interest to take the initiative now. 'We are now at war with a nation that possesses an imposing facade of armed might, but which behind that facade is politically rotten, weak in financial and economic resources, and already heavily engaged on another front,' he wrote on 7 September. '. . . If we lose [the initiative] by waiting we shall probably lose far more than we gain.'[55]

The French, too, partly for political reasons, were anxious for Britain to begin bombing. For months French diplomats had hammered away at Britain to increase her army. This, Cadogan noted on 2 February 1939, 'will continue to be their best retort so long as they are so hopeless in the air'.[56] British land weakness and French air weakness had become a bone of contention between the two Allies, so naturally as Gamelin was hastily mobilizing his army, he expected the British to be equally busy. The British War Cabinet, meeting for the first time at 5 p.m. on 3 September, had for consideration a telegram from Gamelin urging 'that our British comrades should commence air activity by tonight at the latest', sent presumably before France had declared war.[57] It revealed another serious case of misunderstanding and lack of coordination, for apparently Gamelin did not know how narrow was the range of air action foreseen by Britain's leaders.

The background of Britain's air policy, which is an important part of the history of this period, will be investigated in detail in a following chapter. Suffice it to say that the Cabinet's reaction to Gamelin's idea was alarmed and negative. Not only did they themselves decline to attack, but they also, believing perhaps wrongly that the French were preparing to attack that night, sought to dissuade them as well. The Cabinet thought it important 'that any air action undertaken by the French should be within the bombardment policy which we had laid down, and that it would be desirable to take steps to restrain the French from taking precipitate action in this matter'. Newall was asked to tell Gamelin and Corbin of the British decision 'that we should not commence bombing that might mean attacking in ways involving civilian population. Such bombing would be contrary to undertakings we have given (as the French have given) in reply to the American President. The risk is especially great at night, and His

Majesty's Government wish most strongly to urge the French not to proceed with their proposed plan tonight . . .'

The first Cabinet meeting of the war made two decisions, both along the lines of a prearranged plan: to bomb the German fleet at Wilhelmshaven and to drop propaganda leaflets. They believed 'that these leaflets would have an important effect on German public opinion. Moreover the Germans would realize that British aircraft were flying over their territory.' The raid on Wilhelmshaven was launched at 5.45 p.m., immediately after the Cabinet's decision. But the six squadrons of Hampden bombers failed to find their objective and returned still carrying their bombs. An attack by twenty-seven Blenheim and nine Wellington bombers was ordered for the next day.[58]

The German leaders were disappointed at their failure to keep Britain and France out of the war but it would be an exaggeration to say that they were shattered by the bad news. Schmidt's account of their receipt of the ultimatum, like many accounts written by Germans involved in the events, was at pains to emphasize Hitler's erratic behaviour, and to imply that he saw the beginning of world war as a major miscalculation and disaster. The truth is that while he would have *preferred* to isolate Poland and to maintain his policy of destroying those he attacked one by one, he had nevertheless planned for the contingency of having to fight Britain and France as well. By 11.20 a.m. Ribbentrop was ready with a long propagandist reply to Britain's ultimatum, and by the same afternoon was ready with his 'Directive No. 2 for the Conduct of War'.[59]

The German reply, handed over a few minutes after war had begun, was clearly designed for internal and neutral consumption, and represented an abandonment of diplomacy with Britain.[60] It began with a list of the injustices Germany had suffered from the Treaty of Versailles, of which Germany desired merely a 'peaceful revision', which Britain had prevented. Britain had given Poland *carte blanche* to resist Germany's just requests, and to mount a campaign of terror against Germans who lived in Poland. A state of civil war had existed for months on the German–Polish border, the document claimed, and it was only in reply to this intolerable situation that the German Army had acted. The style of the piece can be seen from its conclusion: 'The German people and its

Government do not, like Great Britain, intend to dominate the world, but they are determined to defend their own liberty, their independence and above all their life.'

Hitler's 'Directive No. 2' was a cautious document, emphasizing the need to conquer Poland before embarking on any active warfare in the West. It is interesting to note that from the beginning Hitler ordered a more aggressive approach to Britain than to France, permitting offensive naval operations against Britain unconditionally, but against France only if France began hostilities first. As for air action, Hitler's orders were more cautious still. All-out attacks on London, Paris and other cities had been expected and planned for. Ambassador Henderson had actually reported by telegraph the day before that they would happen 'during light at height of 8,000 metres combined with dive-bombing attacks'.[61] But he was misinformed. All Hitler ordered was attacks on ships and troop transports, and this only if Britain or France made the first move. In fact Britain *did* make the first move with her air attacks on Wilhelmshaven, but even so it was several weeks before Hitler ordered retaliation.

In Berlin too there was the black-out, and people expected raids from east as well as from west. 'No raid tonight. Where are the Poles?' Shirer noted on 2 September. As soon as war broke out German income tax was increased by 50 per cent, and heavy taxes were imposed on spirits, beer and tobacco. 'German beer is 20 per cent thinner, spirits 40 per cent dearer than a few days ago,' *The Times* reported on 7 September. On 25 September new weekly rations were laid down: one pound of meat, five pounds of bread, three quarters of a pound of fats, three quarters of a pound of sugar, a pound of *ersatz* coffee made from roasted barley seeds. These were generous amounts compared to the shortages Britain had to endure during the war and even years after it was over. German heavy labourers received double rations and, cunningly, foreign correspondents in Berlin were included in this privileged category. The only real embarrassment Shirer mentions was a shortage of soap. He mentioned in a broadcast that he was restricted to one tube of shaving cream or one piece of shaving soap for the next four months, and that he would have to grow a beard. But this was not necessary as his sympathetic listeners sent him bars of the stuff from America.[62]

By the end of September almost everything in Germany was rationed except for vegetables, fruit, skim milk and fish. In one respect the Germans were better prepared than the British. Luminous buttons were available and were compulsory wearing for pedestrians during the black-out. In London walkers bumped into trees, lightless lamp-posts and each other, but the Berliners could see each other coming. Less pleasant for them was a new penal code imposing the death penalty on almost any offence against German security. 'Convicted men will be shot by firing squads of ten at a distance of five paces,' said the precise announcement. For convicted women there was a more traditionally Nordic method of execution – beheading.[63]

Hitler's guess that Britain and France would not declare war in support of Poland turned out incorrect, but he had staked much on his second guess: that if the Allies declared war, it would be a formal gesture unaccompanied by much in the way of action. He knew there were forces in both Britain and France who wanted to sneak out of their obligations, and he was ready to make it easy for them. He did not know, though he may have suspected, that Britain's strategy was based on the 'time is on our side' theory, that Britain's war planners wished to start slowly and build up to a climax in a couple of years' time. For the moment this suited Hitler's book exactly. Heavily committed in the east, with all his armoured units and almost all his air force in the throes of *Blitzkrieg*, he wanted nothing but quiet on the western front.

Conscious that he had launched an aggressive war (but, he believed, a just war) and that many of his military leaders opposed this war, Hitler wanted a quick and convincing victory against Poland which would turn his generals' fury away from himself and into the war effort. Such a victory would play a necessary part in building up his own prestige. He knew he was running a risk, but it was a calculated one. His generals had told him the risk was unjustifiable. Erich Raeder, Commander-in-Chief of the German Navy, wrote in his diary that he had been assured by Hitler there would be no war before 1944, and that his Navy was not ready for the struggle. Hitler thought his generals disloyal, weak and out of date. He overruled them. The next few weeks would prove him right and take the steam out of the engines of these old men.[64]

All he needed was for the British and French to allow him breathing space while his fine young Panzer and Luftwaffe commanders tested their mettle, their up-to-date equipment and their up-to-date tactics against a brave but doomed opponent. The Poles were just what he needed at such a moment. A matador prefers a *brave* bull. It may seem frightening to the uninitiated, but he knows that its lumbering attacks are easily avoided, that they will only exhaust it and make it easy meat for his steel sword. Then when he has won, his confidence will be boosted and the onlookers will be impressed. 'Woe to the conquered!' was the rule which guided Hitler's movement – a primitive chant, but one which was to dominate Germany and to captivate the millions who threw in their lot with him. Ruled by a violent ideology, they had come to the point where they needed violence and conquest to justify their obedience and their beliefs. In September 1939 Hitler had the ideal opportunity to provide this necessary test for his war machine, and while he wanted to keep Britain and France out of the battle, he was determined that it should take place. 'My only fear is that some bastard will propose a peace conference,' he said in a moment of truth. He wanted not only the fruits of war, but also war itself. This was available in the East in just the right measure.

4 The Fall of Poland

The imminent Polish collapse was still a secret from the world. The military correspondent of *The Times* wrote on 5 September that although many people had imagined the German advance was going to be very rapid, this had not in fact happened: 'In some cases indeed Polish counter-attacks appear to have been successful, as at Leszno and Rawicz . . .' Poor man, he had little information to go on apart from the two sides' communiqués, and naturally he preferred to believe his Polish allies. Equally optimistic was Patrick Maitland, *The Times*'s man in Warsaw, quaintly styled 'Balkan and Danubian Correspondent' and quaintly dressed in riding breeches and short fur jacket with an armband proclaiming 'The Times, Londyn'. He informed London on 5 September that 'the Poles are carefully withdrawing within their country's natural defences — namely, the rivers Vistula and Bug'. He added, as generals often do when they are forced to retreat, that it was all with the aim of 'lengthening the enemy communications in hostile territory'. 'Their [the Poles'] cavalry is probably the finest in Europe and the terrain offers the finest opportunity for its use,' he wrote. This was true in a way, but quite misleading, since the plain of Poland is also ideal tank country (until the rain sets in and turns the whole place into a marsh) and in spite of what many senior Polish officers maintained right up to September 1939, the horse is no match for the tank.

During September Europe was gripped by a heat-wave, weather which the Poles described afterwards as 'positively Hitlerite'. It left the skies blue and clear, so that the Stukas could observe and bomb everything that moved, the ground firm and hard, so that anti-tank ditches were difficult to dig while the tanks themselves could sail across country at high speed, the rivers shallow and fordable. Rain was very much in the thoughts and prayers of the Polish leaders, and the prospect of it made every extra day they could hold out important and worth fighting for. September was late in the campaigning season. If only they could defend for a month or two, winter would arrive and freeze the German advance, while the Polish army built an impregnable defence line along the big rivers and the administration reestablished itself deep in the western Ukraine. The Allies would send supplies through Rumania and Russia and continue the major offensive against the industrial heart of Germany which, Gamelin had promised, would begin on 16 September. Germany would be forced into a war on two fronts. The British fleet controlled the approaches to the Baltic and the two entrances to the Mediterranean — the Straits of Gibraltar and the Suez Canal. The Allied blockade could therefore starve Germany of raw materials and oil, eventually making it impossible for her to carry on the war.

Thus did the Poles optimistically forecast a limited withdrawal, followed by German collapse and a Polish victorious advance on Berlin. Their army was large, and its prowess had been demonstrated to many Englishmen and Frenchmen during the summer. Hugh Greene writes in 1969, 'I remember spending a day with a Polish cavalry regiment at their headquarters outside Warsaw, and one saw the most marvellous demonstrations of horsemanship. But somehow I knew enough about military affairs to realize how sad that was. This was an old-fashioned army.'[1] This was astute of Greene, especially as there were men like Edmund Ironside who should have known about military affairs, but who were impressed by the Poles' potential and thought they would do well against the Germans.

When war came it was difficult to accept that Poland was doomed. Her allies felt duty bound to radiate confidence, in spite of daily arrivals of bad news. Patrick Maitland wrote in *The Times*: 'Students of Napoleonic history will not need to be reminded of the deadly qualities of Polish mud.' Their cavalry could not defeat the tanks but maybe their mud could, Maitland seemed to be implying: 'It will be recalled that during the [Napoleonic] Polish campaign there were many cases of a stout-hearted soldier taking off his right boot, putting the muzzle of his musket into his mouth, and pulling the trigger with his toe rather than endure his agony any longer.'[2]

For the Poles it was a tantalizing thought, but one which can hardly have bothered the Germans as, safe inside their bullet-proof shells, they rolled across the dry Polish fields in wedge formation, piercing the sparse defences along a length of about two miles. Storm troops would be ready to hold the breach, while more tanks drove through and fanned out to widen it. This was the theory, but the Polish defence was weak and sometimes non-existent, so that often the tanks could advance in depth and prepare the way for the infantry which followed ten miles behind. Thus, for example the German Tenth and Fourteenth Armies took only three or four days to pierce deep into Poland on either side of Kraków, until on 5 September the Polish 'Kraków' Army was obliged to leave the city to avoid being surrounded.

That same day Hitler visited the front and, together with tank commander Heinz Guderian, drove across the Corridor to East Prussia. It was a moment of pride for the two men, for Hitler whose journey was a symbolic proof to his people of how he had united the two portions of Germany, for Guderian who was able to point out to his Leader that this was achieved by the tank. Four German divisions had won the Corridor, and the German casualties numbered only 150 dead and 700 wounded. Guderian writes, 'He [Hitler] was amazed at the smallness of these figures and contrasted them with the casualties of his own old regiment, the List Regiment, during the First World War.'[3] Guderian was delighted to explain that tanks were 'the life-saving weapon' which had preserved his men. When Hitler saw the ruins of some Polish buildings and enquired naturally, 'Our dive-bombers did that?', Guderian was likewise able to announce, 'No, our Panzers!' On 27 October Hitler presented him with the Iron Cross, which Guderian saw as 'a vindication of my long struggle for the creation of the new armoured force'.[4]

That evening the German radio made much of Hitler's adventure, and told of the rapturous welcome he had received from the civilian population, emerging from their hiding places now that the fighting was over to cheer and bring him flowers. Only a Hitler,

Goebbels's men proclaimed, would risk his life by visiting the battlefield at such a moment, and meanwhile, the British soldier might well ask, 'Where is Mr Winston Churchill? Where is Mr Eden? Where is Mr Duff Cooper? Where is Colonel Amery?'[5]

On 3 September the Poles had cheered outside their allies' embassies, but as the days passed they found themselves wondering, 'Where are the British and French?' By 4 September German penetration from Silesia and East Prussia was threatening to surround the Polish Poznań Army, positioned in the western bulge of the country. German attacks had been light in the Poznań area, leaving the Polish forces with a sense of false security and in imminent danger of being cut off. De Wiart reported that the Poles 'were always twenty-four to forty-eight hours late in ordering retirements' and that 'eight divisions in the Poznań salient were eventually cut off, whereas they could easily have escaped if a decision had been made in time'.[6]

It became clear that it was only a matter of a few days before the German tanks would be at the gates of Warsaw. On 4 September the Polish Parliament and the bulk of the government departments were ordered to evacuate the capital and to set themselves up at various points in south-east Poland. The offices were scattered in order to make bombing attacks more difficult, but of course the immediate effect of the dispersal was to strain Polish communications beyond the point of rupture. According to de Wiart, 'The "Hughes" tele-writer system often broke down. Wireless failed because of capture of codes by enemy and difficulty of issuing new ones.'[7]

This problem became critical when the Polish General Headquarters was also compelled to evacuate. It stayed in Warsaw until 6 September, two days longer than the other ministries, in a special shelter in the cellar of an unfinished building in Rakowiecka Street. But during the night of 6–7 September, as the German tanks approached Raszyn, Rydz-Śmigły and his GHQ moved 125 miles due east to Brześć (Brest-Litovsk).[8] The plan then, as Jaklicz told Colin Gubbins, was to withdraw to a line along the three rivers Narew, Vistula and San, keeping a bridgehead at Warsaw. The eight divisions caught in the Poznań salient would have to be given up for lost, as would the ten divisions which had not managed to mobilize before the German attack. The following day

Jaklicz told Gubbins that his men had not been able to hold the line of the Narew and were withdrawing to the Bug.

The staff of Warsaw's foreign embassies spent much of the first week of September packing up their valuables and loading up their cars, ready for evacuation they knew not where. The Poles for obvious reasons were unwilling to tell the diplomats where they would be going until the last moment. They assumed it would be somewhere east of the Vistula, the river on which the Poles were to stand fast, perhaps in the Pripet Marshes. Spending the winter there was a dismal prospect, and during the summer Clifford Norton's wife had hidden a cache of skis and flour somewhere in the mountains of southern Poland, ready for a possible escape through the snow. A woman of some resource, she also bought a lorry for £500 and eventually took over the evacuation of the British Embassy, after the task proved too much for the man the Ambassador had originally chosen for the job, his butler Whittington.

On the morning of 7 September the Foreign Ministry told diplomats that their new home was to be in Nałęczów, a pleasant eighteenth-century spa eighty-five miles south-east of Warsaw, and that they must be ready to leave by noon, since the bridges across the Vistula were about to be blown up. The British Military Mission had been presented with ten cases of champagne by their French colleagues, and these figured largely in the British 'train' — the lorry and a few cars — which lumbered out of the capital in the nick of time. In Nałęczów the foreigners found facilities rudimentary: no electricity and only camp beds. But they made the best of it and with the help of the champagne passed a pleasant if fitful night.

The diplomats did not even have time to unpack, for the next morning Beck informed the ambassadors that there were Germans only ten miles away, so they must move to Krzemieniec, 200 miles further to the south-east and not far from the then Soviet border. Discussing the matter with Ambassador Kennard, Beck then came to an embarrassing problem. What was to be done with the British journalists who had joined the embassy 'train' in the evacuation? Everyone had been caught napping by the speed of the German advance, and the move to Krzemieniec was an act of near-desperation. Could the journalists be trusted to keep quiet about it? It would not do at all if they started reporting to their head offices that the Polish Government was in headlong flight. Might it not be safer to leave them behind when the train moved on, and perhaps safer still *not to inform them that the Germans were so near*?

Kennard saw Beck's point and readily agreed to leave his countrymen behind to take their chance of falling into German hands. But luckily for them all Hugh Greene happened to call at the temporary 'embassy' where he was told by Mrs Norton — quite against the rules — of the plot to abandon him and his colleagues.[9] They were able to extricate themselves and join the hasty retreat into the bottom right-hand corner of Poland, where there were borders with still-neutral Russia, sympathetic Hungary and friendly Rumania.

Thousands of people were now gravitating into this hundred-mile-wide funnel: ministers, civil servants, diplomats, soldiers, indeed anyone rich enough to own a car. For the moment the peasants were not moving, so the roads were not clogged with refugees on foot or with horse-drawn carts. The speed of events had been too quick to allow a spontaneous mass exodus of the poorer people. The Poles were still putting out hopeful communiqués and promising to stabilize their lines of defence. People did not believe that within a week their country would collapse totally.

There were frequent cases of 'order — counter-order — disorder', the most serious of which concerned the defence of Warsaw. On 6 and 7 September Warsaw Radio appealed to all men capable of bearing arms to cross the Vistula before the bridges were blown, to make their way east and join in the new lines of defence. Many obeyed, but within a couple of days the Mayor of Warsaw, Stefan Starzyński, was calling for just the opposite, for every man to stay in the city and defend it to the last. Hardly any of the volunteers who left found any fighting unit which could accept them, and thousands spent days or even weeks wandering about the country fruitlessly and tragically.[10] Had they stayed in Warsaw they could have helped in the battles which were to come. As it was, most of them by the end of the month found themselves cut off from home, friends and possessions, under Soviet occupation and therefore easy prey for the suspicious Soviet security forces. Thousands of them were deported to die in the indescribable conditions of Stalin's corrective labour camps.

The privileged few suffered inconvenience but not tragedy. Surprisingly, petrol was not a major problem. Generally stocks lasted until the country collapsed, and even where there was a shortage, those escaping were usually rich enough to be able to persuade someone to part with a few gallons. They had to keep their eyes open for dive-bombers and fighters which buzzed about like bees in groups of two or three. The American Ambassador Biddle thought there must be about 5,000 of them. Like everyone else he over-estimated German air strength: 'It seemed impossible to get away from them,' he said in a press conference after he was safely out. 'My own car on the way to the Rumanian frontier was bombed fifteen times and machine-gunned four, forcing me to take refuge in a roadside ditch.'[11] He had a large 'stars and stripes' tied to his car's roof, but he found that it provided no protection and just attracted attention, so he took it off. By 10 September most of the diplomats were in Krzemieniec.

But the evacuation left Poland headless and in chaos. The administrators had to decide suddenly whether to go or stay, and it appears that all too often they acted on impulse, joining the headlong flight without thinking that perhaps they might do a more valuable job by staying at their posts. True, for some there were compelling arguments for leaving. It would be a pity if the able-bodied men fell into German hands. They were needed to fight the invader, either on Polish soil or, if Poland was to be defeated, in a new Polish Army based in France. The central government and administration obviously had to leave, but this assumed that they would find means of carrying on their functions in some safer place, and be able to *communicate* their decisions to the parts of the country they still controlled. Once government became impossible, the rulers would be mere passengers of the Army, sheer dead weight. The President himself was valuable as a symbol of Poland and as a provider of political continuity, but the rest were merely an embarrassment to the valiant efforts of the defenders.

Those who should not have left, but often did, were the local leaders. The historian Pobóg-Malinowski, a supporter of the pre-war Polish Government, calls this 'one of the cardinal mistakes of the campaign'. He writes, 'It was wrong to leave the population without leadership both in the capital and in the heart of the country. Provincial governors and especially district leaders should have stayed at their posts without exception, irrespective of the fate which may have awaited them. And at least two ministers should have stayed in Warsaw.'[12] Certainly the leaders' flight was open to misinterpretation, and sure enough after the war the communists attributed it to the cowardice and general moral degradation of the Polish ruling classes.

The point was that Polish strategy allowed only for a *brief* withdrawal, lasting a few months at the most, after which Britain and France would attack in the West and Poland would counter-attack in the East. The idea that the people would have to endure five years of German occupation was not foreseen. So as the local governors and mayors withdrew, they took with them the resources of the areas they controlled: money, works of art, fire engines, factory machines and even cattle. It was foreseen that the richer western half of the country might be occupied, so naturally its wealth must be moved to the eastern half where the country was going to be reconstituted and where the population was going to spend the winter in preparation for the big spring offensive.

What in fact happened was that the decision to evacuate each area was made always at the last moment in conditions approaching chaos. The German Army would be just a few miles away. The local Germans would have donned their swastika armbands and be roaming the streets in armed revolt. There would be no communication with the next town, let alone with Warsaw. Shells would be bursting and bombs would be dropping. It all added to the universal atmosphere of *sauve qui peut* which was demoralizing to the Army. By now uncoded radio messages were instructing all units to make their way as best they could to the south-east. De Wiart reported, 'The despairing character of these orders is obvious from the fact that they entailed a retreat for the Northern Army of some 200 miles across the heads of advancing German columns, a race against time that would undoubtedly have been lost.' Plan after plan had been overtaken by events. It is hard to see how any Polish officer managed to keep his sanity, let alone control over his men.

The British Cabinet received its first intimation of what was about to happen on 6 September, when Ironside informed them that the situation in Poland 'had deteriorated very rapidly. Information was very meagre, but the Polish Army still appeared to be intact.' A headline in *The Times* that same day told of 'Poland's gallant fight against the odds' — the first public hint that all was not well — and on 7 September of a 'Danger to Warsaw'. At the 8 September Cabinet meeting Hore-Belisha had a message from de Wiart that the situation was 'very serious', but Ironside was still maintaining that 'the Polish Army was fighting well and had not been broken'. Having announced on 4 September that a quick German victory was 'most improbable' he was doubtless concerned to protect his reputation as a military expert.

On 11 September Ironside told the Cabinet that 'the Poles were putting up a good fight and were defending Warsaw vigorously. Their main Army was still intact.' He gave the same impression to Cadogan who noted on 12 September : 'Ironside says they are not broken (but in a pretty bad way!). It has begun to rain in Poland (drizzle here). May it *pour*!' But in his diary Ironside recorded his real thoughts which were far more pessimistic : 'It is realized now that nothing can save the Poles, and that the only way of restoring them is to win the war.' [13] He had word that the Poles' only hope was to hold the line of the Vistula, but the river was fordable in many places, and there was a gap where the Third Army should have been. His information, presumably from de Wiart, was several days out of date, for the Vistula was already abandoned.

Ironside was committing that cardinal sin of military commanders, keeping bad news from his civilian superiors in the War Cabinet. He was forced to face the fact that he had badly misjudged the course that the Polish campaign would take. He had told the Cabinet that the Poles would be able to defend themselves for a long time, and as it became clear that they were on the point of collapse he was nursing the bad news and keeping the Cabinet in a fool's paradise. No one likes to be shown up in front of his superiors. Ironside did not want to admit he had made a mistake.

Such behaviour, however understandable on the personal level, was inexcusable in the circumstances and symptomatic of Ironside's failure as the link-man between the British Army and Government. His appointment, in the words of the official historian, 'failed to prove a satisfactory one'.[14] This is perhaps the understatement of the war. Before September he had been Inspector-General of Overseas Forces, and he expected that if war came he would be put in command of the expeditionary force to France. In fact he went around telling everyone that the job would be his, so much so that when the time came and he was proved wrong his bitterness and humiliation were all the worse.

He blamed his Secretary of State, Hore-Belisha, for landing him with the less glamorous job of Chief of the Imperial General Staff, and justly so, for it was Belisha who had engineered the rapid promotion of Lord Gort and finally presented him with the job Ironside considered his by right. 'I have a Secretary of State who knows nothing about military matters whatsoever,' he wrote in his diary on 7 September. This perhaps was not unjust. But his later references to him as 'that bloody Jew', (censored of course from the published version) show not so much his anti-semitism as his extreme dislike of the man who had done him down.

But it was not just Belisha. The French too thought Ironside inefficient and silly. That June Gamelin had come to England for the Ascot races, which were good cover for strategic talks at Aldershot. During the visit General Lelong, military attaché at the French Embassy, sought out Beaumont-Nesbitt, then Deputy Director of Military Intelligence, and gave him to understand that France would not favour Ironside as commander of any expeditionary force. Beaumont-Nesbitt passed this on to his boss Henry Pownall, who was in a position to influence the decision.

Stories abound of the indiscretions of Ironside, known to his friends as 'Tiny' because he was six foot five inches tall. Of course he lost no opportunity of saying what a bad general Lord Gort was. In early 1940 he gave broad hints to Americans at a private party that Britain was about to invade Norway. The real dynamite he tried to keep for his diary, but even this turned sour when an official photographer took a picture of him sitting at his desk writing it. Just before the photograph was released to the press someone noticed that the two open pages were quite legible.

Security was lax in Ironside's suite in the War Office. Ralph Arnold, his personal assistant, told the author in 1970: 'There was hardly anything for us to do. I remember we used to sit in armchairs reading yesterday's Cabinet minutes to stop ourselves getting bored. Even that didn't work sometimes. It worried me a bit because the only security check I had was a five-minute interview.

I suppose they thought it was all right because I was Ironside's cousin.' Several times Arnold had the job of telephoning Gort on the Maginot Line to give him orders from the Cabinet. 'It was difficult to get through,' he says. 'It took about an hour and then it was often a wrong number.'

Hore-Belisha's biographer describes Ironside as 'in his manner deferential and even obsequious' but 'quite inadequate in his dealings with the other services on the Chiefs of Staff Committee',[15] and this opinion seems to be shared by most of those who worked with him. But Belisha too was unpopular: for his personal vanity and supercilious manner, for his habit of calling everyone 'my dear boy', even men years his senior, for bringing new men into the War Office and placing them above the time-servers. Ironside writes: 'I find Belisha cannot take in anything from reading it . . . He can only take a thing in orally, and he will talk and argue over a subject with the idea of getting his own ideas in order and maybe convincing himself.'[16] All in all the two men loathed each other, and what really suffered as a result was the British war effort.

Ironside also complained that Belisha 'is very jealous of Winston's interference', which was probably true enough but hardly significant since almost everyone in Whitehall was suffering under a barrage of memoranda from Churchill. During his years out of office Churchill was a good friend of Ironside's, but once he was back in the Cabinet he began to treat the CIGS in what the latter considered a cavalier fashion. He was at his best during the small hours of the morning and would rouse Ironside from his bed whenever he needed his advice. Ironside would have to get dressed and make his way to the corner turret room at Admiralty House where Churchill worked to answer questions from a minister who had nothing whatever to do with his department. To make matters worse the question would often be a piffling one, like 'How many Bren guns are there in an infantry platoon?' Ironside told Churchill he would bring his batman along to answer points of detail. Their friendship collapsed, and soon after he became Prime Minister (May 1940) Churchill dismissed him.

Even at this stage Churchill was more than a mere Cabinet Minister. He was an alternative government. Not only was he a key figure in Chamberlain's administration, but he also had the means of destroying Chamberlain by rallying opposition to the

Prime Minister among his supporters in both Conservative and Labour parties. It was not yet time for a palace revolution. Mistrust of Churchill's erratic and volatile temperament were too strong to allow that. But by opposing Chamberlain he could have thrown British politics into such confusion that nothing would have been excluded.

Though currently colleagues in arms, the two men were bitter political enemies. Henry Channon wrote in his diary: 'He [Churchill] is behaving well, but their deep mutual antagonism must sooner or later flare up and make cooperation impossible. Then we shall all be sacked and we shall have a "glamorous" central government, reinforced by extreme left Conservatives and some Socialists who are already saying that while they have refused to serve under Neville they would agree to under Winston. I see it coming.' [17]

Churchill first interfered over the composition of the War Cabinet. A lesser man would have been content to know that he at least was to be in it, but for Churchill it was but the first step to higher things. 'Aren't we a very old team?' he wrote to Chamberlain on 2 September, pointing out that the average age of the War Cabinet members was sixty-four, only one year short of the old-age pension. [18] He suggested including Anthony Eden who was only forty-two, and incidentally a close ally of his. He wrote to Halifax, 'I hope you will not mind my drawing your attention from time to time to points which strike me in the Foreign Office telegrams.' [19] One can imagine the look of horror and irritation that crossed Halifax's face as he read this presumptuous note. But he dared do nothing about it.

Churchill writes that he felt bound to 'take a general view' and 'to subordinate my own departmental requirements for the Admiralty to the main design'. [20] He was aware that some of his supporters were against his accepting an arduous job that might clip his wings politically. On 7 September he wrote to the P.M., 'It seems most necessary to drill the civil population in completely putting out their private lights . . .' His suggestions about blackout regulations concluded with the sentence: 'Unless you have any objection, I would like to circulate this to our colleagues.' On 10 September he wrote, 'I hope you will not mind my sending you a few points privately,' and continued with remarks about bombing policy, artillery and supply. The next day he wrote, 'Everyone says there ought to be a Ministry of Shipping . . .', and on 15 September, 'As I shall be away until Monday, I give you my present thought on the main situation . . . I hope you will consider carefully what I write to you. I do so only in my desire to aid you in your responsibilities and discharge my own.' [21]

Not all his ideas were bad, and one must remember that he had been a senior minister in the First World War and so had a special right to influence the situation which for him was not new. But it was not so much what he said but the way that he said it. He addressed his chief in a tone of complete equality, almost of condescension. Chamberlain was not known for his tolerance of opposition, rather for his irritability in the face of it, but his letters show that he accepted Churchill's unnatural role philosophically. Privately he complained that Churchill took up too much time in Cabinet, holding forth sometimes 'not very relevantly' and keeping people up late at night until 'they are worn out in arguing with him', but he consoled himself with the thought 'that this is just the price we have to pay for the asset we have in his personality and popularity'.[22]

He wrote to Churchill on 16 September, 'All your letters are carefully read and considered by me, and if I have not replied to them it is only because I am seeing you every day, and moreover, because as far as I have been able to observe your views and mine have very closely coincided.' [23] It was true that now that there was war the differences between the two men had lessened. Their conclusions on policy almost always agreed, Chamberlain remarked, 'though we haven't always arrived at them by the same road'.[24]

In fact what had happened on the really crucial issues was that Chamberlain had come round to Churchill's point of view. For instance, Churchill had held all along that Hitler was an evil man and not to be trusted, and that if necessary Britain must ally herself with Soviet Russia to fight him. Chamberlain had just convinced himself of the first fact, but was only on his way to acceptance of the second. On 26 March he wrote, 'I must confess to the most profound distrust of Russia. I have no belief whatever in her ability to maintain an effective offensive, even if she wanted to. And I distrust her motives which seem to me to have little connection with our ideas of liberty, and to be concerned only with getting everyone else by the ears.'[25] In May he actually told Cadogan he would resign rather than sign an alliance with Russia.[26] He was strangely unwilling to face certain axioms of *Realpolitik* — that it is better to fight one enemy than two, that one must decide not which enemy is the more evil but which enemy is the more dangerous, and that when a Hitler is on the rampage it may become necessary to join forces with a Stalin.

Churchill did not take the hint from his chief's 16 September note. He continued his letter-writing, on 18 September about air-craft production, on 21 September about occasional meetings of the War Cabinet alone without secretaries. On 24 September he wrote to the Chancellor of the Exchequer: 'I am thinking a great deal about you and your problem, as one who has been through the Exchequer mill. I look forward to a severe budget based on the broad masses of the well-to-do. But I think you ought to couple with this a strong anti-waste campaign . . . An effort should be made to tell people the things they ought to try to avoid doing . . . Envelopes should be pasted up and redirected again and again . . .'[27]

On 1 October he wrote to Chamberlain again: 'This week-end I venture to write to you about several large issues. (1) When the peace offensive opens upon us it will be necessary to sustain the French . . .' The other issues ranged from the Regular Army to the Air Force ('The disparity at the present time with Germany is shocking'), and then to the need to review air-raid precautions. He concluded typically, 'There is really no reason why orders to this effect should not be given during the coming week.'[28]

Churchill's memoirs say nothing of it, but this time Chamberlain's patience did wear thin. He sent for Churchill the next day (2 October) and told him politely that his letters must cease. If he had any criticism of government policy, the proper course was to raise it with the minister of that department, or else to write a paper for the War Cabinet so that the matter could be discussed and settled there. Horace Wilson says that the talk was 'friendly throughout' and at the end of it Churchill promised to write no more letters. He assured Chamberlain that he was wholeheartedly behind him and wanted no extended powers himself. 'I believe all this was quite genuine,' the Prime Minister noted. '. . . To me personally Winston is absolutely loyal and I am constantly hearing from others of the admiration he expresses for the P.M.'[29]

Churchill confirms that relations were better than might be expected: 'Although at first he [Chamberlain] gave me the impression of being very much on his guard, yet I am glad to say that month by month his confidence and goodwill seemed to grow.' [30] On 13 November Chamberlain and his wife dined with the Churchills at Admiralty House. It was a success. Three times during dinner news was brought in that a German U-boat was sunk. In this mood of growing euphoria (false euphoria, for the reports were untrue) Chamberlain was telling stories about a little-known aspect of his life, his five years as a hard-bitten pioneer, unsuccessfully trying to grow sisal on a remote Caribbean island. Churchill recalls vividly how Chamberlain warmed to this conversation, the only intimate talk they had in twenty years of politics together. [31]

But these remarks show only one side of their relationship. Momentarily it was in the interest of both men to become friends, in Churchill's because only through office could he have real influence on events as well as a chance at the Premiership if it fell vacant, in Chamberlain's because he badly needed Churchill's popularity as an ingredient of his own team. Only by including him could he restrain the protests of the two pro-Churchill clubs, the December Group and the Eden Group: Cooper, Amery, Boothby, Bracken, Sandys, Nicolson, Cranborne, Spears, Macmillan and others. Nevertheless the Group, 'the glamour boys' in Channon's sarcastic phrase, continued to meet and to work for a clear aim, the replacement of Chamberlain by Churchill. Nicolson describes such a discussion at such a meeting at the Carlton Club on 3 October – 'The question is how and when' – and on 26 September Channon noted: 'Already today I noted signs of the "glamour boys" beginning to intrigue again. We must watch out.' [32]

Chamberlain hoped by appointing Churchill and Eden to behead the movement whose article of faith it was that the Prime Minister was, however well-meaning, an incompetent and inappropriate war leader. Eden notes in his diary (4 October): 'Chamberlain showed a flash of his old vindictiveness when Leo Amery's name was suggested for a job. I had passed it up on a slip of paper . . . Neville pushed it away with an irritated snort . . . [Then Halifax] had the bright idea of adding Duff [Cooper]'s name to the list. Neville Chamberlain at once said vehemently that he thought neither of them would be at all suitable. It was a revealing little explosion.' [33] Even more revealing of Chamberlain's determination to hang on to power was his telephone call to Amery on 9 May, the day after he had taken part in the revolt against Chamberlain that finally removed him from office. 'Would you now like to join the Government?' Chamberlain asked.[34] After this there was very little respect indeed left for the Prime Minister, who resigned on 10 May 1940.

It showed that from the beginning of the war, however deeply Chamberlain may have convinced himself that he commanded the full loyalty of all his ministers, there were many on the sidelines relying on Churchill to oppose the appeasement policies which, they believed, Chamberlain and his old friends – Simon, Hoare and Burgin – were still following. It showed too that although the war had brought the main political forces in Britain close to unity, much energy was still being spent on intrigue and political in-fighting. Likewise the War Office was split by personal feuds and resentments, embarrassed by the revelation of its puny resources when compared to those of France, let alone of Germany, and furious at the prospect of playing third fiddle to the Navy and the Air Force in future development. All in all the British Army was in no condition to put much hindrance in the way of the German Army as it drove its way into Poland at high speed.

'8 September. At 7.15 p.m. radio broadcasts High Command announcement that at 5.15 p.m. German troops reached Warsaw. Strange indifference of the people to this big news.' This entry in Shirer's *Berlin Diary* was premature. The German Fourth Panzer Division had reached Ochota, a district in suburban Warsaw, only to be greeted by heavy fire from the city's defenders and forced to retire. Still, the Nazis seem to have been confident that the city would fall quickly. That evening saboteurs put Warsaw's Praskie Radio out of action, whereupon Germans began broadcasting in Polish from Katowice on the same wavelength announcing that Warsaw had fallen. Other broadcasts in Polish called upon Poles to form groups and to disarm 'all stragglers of the defeated Polish Army'. Just before midnight broadcasts in English were picked up on the Warsaw wavelength, the voices being interrupted by loud and convincing sound effects – screeching bombs, crashing glass and the rattle of machine guns. Then Chopin's funeral march was played and the station went dead. Little was left to the foreign listeners' imagination. The important thing was to convince them that the defence of Warsaw had collapsed.

That evening too Molotov telephoned Schulenburg, the German Ambassador in Moscow, and gave him a note which was sent on to Berlin at 12.56 a.m. on 9 September. It was a shameful, notorious message: 'I have received your communication regarding the entry of German troops into Warsaw. Please convey my congratulations and greetings to the German Reich Government. Molotov.' [35]

During 9 September the German tanks made a second more determined attempt to enter Warsaw. Ochota was 'softened up' with artillery fire, after which tanks advanced along Grójecka Street. Polish anti-tank guns destroyed several of them and they withdrew to direct more artillery fire onto the barricades. It became clear that Warsaw was not going to collapse but would have to be conquered, and that for this the Germans would require far greater force than was at present available.

Furthermore on 8 September the Polish Army launched a strong counter-offensive from a town on the River Bzura called Kutno, seventy miles west of Warsaw. The Poznań Army under General Kutrzeba and the Pomerania Army under General Bortnowski struck eastwards to reach the capital, and initially they took the German forces which were in their way by surprise. The result was the 'Battle on the Bzura', a week of vicious ground fighting which was the biggest battle of the campaign, unsurpassed until the big battles with the Red Army. The German tanks were ordered to cease their probing attacks on Warsaw and make their way to the real fighting, leaving only a thin screen round the city. Thus valuable days were won allowing the population of the capital, organized by their heroic mayor Stefan Starzyński, to prepare defences.

The Polish infantry supported by cavalry advanced on a thirty-mile front southwards against German-held positions south of Kutno. By 12 September they had driven the Germans back about ten miles towards Stryków, their main objective, and their 16th Infantry Division, whose initial task was only to provide cover for the main offensive, had captured the town of Łowicz, just south of the River Bzura. Not only the Germans were surprised. The Polish High Command too was hesitating between ordering the armies to exploit these gains and the decision to pull them back to Warsaw, which they hoped to make into a bridgehead, but which was soon to become a besieged island of resistance amid the sea of German-occupied territory. Eventually the decision was made, and by 14 September the two armies were withdrawing eastwards to Warsaw.

Meanwhile the Polish Military Mission led by General Norwid-Neugebauer, which arrived in London on 8 September,[36] was having a hard time obtaining satisfaction. On 9 September the Polish general was received by Ironside who asked blandly what Britain could do to help. Ironside knew by now that Poland was in dire straits, and he may like many have half believed the German claims to have occupied Warsaw. The Polish account of the talks complains that not only did Ironside have no plan whatever for helping his allies, but he was also completely ignorant of the state of the campaign. The first complaint is true and valid, the second true but hardly Ironside's fault. The Polish generals were not keeping their allied embassies or military missions well informed of the situation. Indeed, it was so fluid that they themselves were seldom aware of it.

Ironside can hardly have been other than embarrassed by the Polish requests, which he knew he had little opportunity and no intention of implementing. The best he could suggest was that Poland buy arms from neutral countries, from the Baltic States and Sweden. Otherwise he would have to consult the War Cabinet. This he did, and the next day (10 September) he told Norwid-Neugebauer (though there is no record of this in the minutes) that he had urged 'the necessity of special action by the British Air Force against the Reich'.[37] The decision would be made soon. He also told him of the supplies dispatched to Poland in the S.S. *Lassell* via Constanza, though the Pole seems to have got the impression that the ship had already arrived, and post-war Polish historians have accused Ironside unjustly of lying.[38] Norwid-Neugebauer then asked if a hundred Hurricane fighters could not be flown to Poland from bases in France. (Where they were supposed to land is a mystery.) Ironside said he thought this was a good idea, but he would have to consult the Air Ministry. Like

Bonnet, he was becoming adept in making sympathetic noises and in passing the responsibility to others.

The purpose of this account is not to fix blame but to demonstrate the two allies' alarming lack of coordination and mutual understanding. Norwid-Neugebauer spoke of the British 'replacing by their machines the losses which the Poles had suffered in battle and by natural consumption of equipment'. But this idea was anathema to Britain, which saw its Air Force primarily as an investment in the future, and which had announced only a day or two earlier (9 September) that its plans were based on the assumption that the war would last for three years.

George Turner, who was then a senior official in the Ministry of Supply, explained to the author in 1971 that the munitions planners had not foreseen a war beginning before 1940, and that from his point of view it was impossible to fight the war seriously in 1939. The small British Army was well equipped initially, but not enough small-arms ammunition was being produced to feed the rifles even of such a force as this. 'Our trousers were well down, and we were pulling them up,' Turner says.

This explains why on 15 September Norwid-Neugebauer was called to the War Office and told regretfully that for the moment Britain could spare only a few thousand old rifles and a few million rounds of ammunition, and that it would be five or six months before she could think of supplying tanks, anti-tank guns, anti-aircraft guns, fighters or uniforms. Again he was advised to apply for arms to the neutral countries, Spain and Belgium. Britain would help in raising the necessary finance. But this sound advice did not appeal to the Pole, who hoped for quicker deliveries than would be allowed for under a time-table involving negotiation, contract, signature, payment and then the problems of delivery. Such slow, businesslike procedures were hardly suited to the situation of his country, whose territory was largely overrun, whose army was divided into three and whose administration was being driven from pillar to post, few departments knowing where the others were, let alone what orders they were issuing. He told Ironside frankly that 'England has to date not fulfilled her obligations, since for fourteen days we have been left entirely on our own'.

On 12 September, while the Battle on the Bzura was in full swing, the Anglo-French Supreme War Council met in the Salon de la Sous-Préfecture in Abbeville in northern France. The chief delegates were Daladier, Gamelin, Chamberlain and Lord Chatfield, British Minister for Co-ordination of Defence. The record of their talks shows that they had already given Poland up for lost. The subject of supplies did crop up, but Chamberlain explained how difficult it would be to send anything to Poland: 'There was only a single railway through Bucharest to the Polish frontier, dividing into two just before crossing the border, and much of the line was only single-track. It was true that there were roads as well, but these were in bad condition, and when the weather changed, as must be anticipated, they would serve little useful purpose. The easiest way to supply Poland was through Odessa; but he was afraid that it was not possible to count on this. He agreed in principle with the desirability of doing everything possible to help, but was not hopeful that very much could be done.'[39]

Nor did Gamelin offer the Poles much consolation. Chatfield asked him whether, if Poland managed to hold out longer than was anticipated, the French would take a more aggressive line on the western front. Gamelin's answer was a categorical 'no'. Anything the Poles were able to do, he said, 'would only give Great Britain and France more valuable time to prepare, and prevent the Germans withdrawing forces from their eastern to their western front'. It is this sentence which demonstrates how cruelly the Poles were deceived. They were fighting the Germans to the last man and the last round, believing that this first battle of the war would be decisive, that their allies would shortly mount an offensive to prevent their country from being conquered. But this life-or-death struggle was to Gamelin no more than a useful diversion which might provide a breathing space for his and the British forces.

Daladier was worried that 'Germany would make even greater efforts to divide Great Britain and France. This was evident from their wireless propaganda and from placards displayed in the front line to the effect that Germany desired the friendship of France. He added that French troops had not hesitated to fire on these placards.' Well, firing on German placards was at any rate a start. Daladier explained that his forces were 'steadily and methodically approaching the Siegfried Line. No spectacular success was anticipated, but it was possible that the attack might develop into a large-scale operation.' This statement, though self-contradictory, was in line with what Gamelin told Ironside on 4 September, that he would begin to 'lean against' the Siegfried Line around 20 September and test whether any breach might be made. But other remarks Gamelin made indicate that any 'large-scale operation' was far from his mind. He told the Council that 'he did not envisage casualties on a large scale . . . His offensive was confined to activities in no-man's-land, and he had no intention of throwing his army against the German main defences. He had in fact issued strict instructions forbidding anything of the kind.'

Chamberlain too seemed to conclude from Daladier's and Gamelin's remarks that there would be no large-scale operation, and he was very relieved. 'In his view there was no hurry as time was on our side,' are the exact words of the official report. One wonders what the Polish soldiers who were at that very moment fighting for Łowicz would have said if they could have overheard this simple statement of faith. He went on to explain to the Frenchmen the gist of his policy: 'The Allies required time to build up their full resources, and in the meantime it might well be that the morale of Germany would crumble.' But what if it did not? It was a prospect which the Prime Minister did not care to contemplate.

Gamelin told the Council that his troops' limited advance 'was to help Poland by distracting the attention of Germany', and no doubt this is true. He was prepared to make a feint, to pretend he was going to hit the Germans, but not actually to hit them. But of course it was not a matter merely of Gamelin's inclination, it was a matter of treaty. He was treaty bound to attack Germany 'with the main bodies of his forces (*avec les gros de ses forces*)', and whatever this meant in terms of actual numbers, it certainly meant more than the local attacks along a front of a few miles near the top of the Franco-German frontier which began during the night of 6–7 September. (See map on page 402.)

On 9 September a French communiqué announced: 'A brilliant attack by one of our divisions has won for us an important piece of territory.' It went on to proclaim that the forest of Warndt, a three-mile-square area just across the border in Germany, was now in French hands.[40] It was found to be full of landmines and traps of all kinds. The following communiqué (No. 12) declared that 'the enemy is resisting along the whole front . . .', while No. 13 declared that 'German forces have counter-attacked at numerous points along our front . . .'

Shirer noted in his diary (14 September): 'It is obvious from the broadcasts of Ed and Tom from London and Paris that the Allies are exaggerating their action on the western front.' The problem was that Gamelin's feint was unconvincing, designed to deceive not so much his German enemies as his Polish allies. On 6 September Marshal Rydz-Śmigły sent his attaché in Paris Colonel Fyda a telegram demanding 'implementation of our agreement, especially French air activity to ease the air situation in Poland' as well as 'an explanation of why the agreement has not been observed'.[41] It was handed in to Gamelin's headquarters that night. On 9 September, the day the French announced their success in the Warndt forest, Fyda handed Gamelin another telegram from Rydz-Śmigły: 'Has the French Air Force yet gone into action against the German Air Force and German territory? I have not noticed any lessening of German air activity on the Polish front.' The next day Fyda repeated this request and asked for 'action to be generally speeded up'.[42] He requested an answer which he could transmit to his Marshal.

It is always embarrassing to be put into the position of having to break one's word, and Gamelin was acutely aware of the agreement he had signed with the Polish General Kasprzycki on 19 May 1939. Point Three of this agreement promised that 'as soon as the main German effort against Poland begins, France will launch an offensive against Germany with the main bodies of her forces, beginning on the fifteenth day from the first day of Polish general mobilization'.[43] In his memoirs Gamelin complains that Fyda 'would not stop pestering us' and that Ambassador Łukasiewicz 'spoke unjustly about our Army'.[44]

His solution was to write to Fyda on 10 September in terms which, if not exactly false, can only have given a false impression:

More than half of our active divisions in the North-East are engaged in combat. Ever since we crossed our frontier the Germans have offered us vigorous resistance. None the less we have made progress. But we find ourselves engaged in a war of position against an organized adversary, and I do not yet have at my disposal the necessary artillery . . . we can claim with justice to be keeping on our front a large part of the German Air Force. I have therefore exceeded my promise that I would mount an offensive with the main bodies of my forces by the fifteenth day after the first day of Polish mobilization. There is nothing more that I could have done. Gamelin.

At the bottom of the letter he added in his own hand, 'With all my heart I share your anguish and have faith in the tenacity of your resistance.'[45] Words of sympathy he was ready enough to offer.

But however much Gamelin shared the Poles' anguish he shared very little of their fight against Germany. His claim to have engaged 'half of our active divisions in the North-East' was playing with words. What is an active division? Nor was there on the western front 'a large part' of the German Air Force. And as for the German 'vigorous resistance' – Gamelin himself admits elsewhere in his memoirs that his advance 'met no serious resistance'.[46] In fact the Germans had withdrawn their forces from the area between the frontier and the Siegfried Line and evacuated the civilian population from the twenty-odd villages there. True, they had sown the area with booby-traps, with both anti-tank and anti-personnel mines, and the French were obliged to sweep the ground first for infantry, then for tanks, then for artillery. But they were able to do this at their leisure and without being fired upon.

A more accurate description of 'occupied Germany' was given by a reporter from *The Times*, who wrote: 'In a deserted village on the edge of the Warndt Forest salient not a bomb has been dropped, and into it no shell has been fired. The silent houses are undisturbed. Pots of geraniums still flower in window-boxes, but there is no one to tend them.'[47] Charles Morice, military correspondent of *Le Petit Parisien*, wrote in *The Times* on 3 October that French troops were in occupation of 100,000 acres of German territory. It sounded a lot like that, though 100,000 acres is only about twenty-one square miles. Morice deduced that this gave the French a double advantage in that it put the Maginot Line out of range of the German artillery, while the French could bring up their artillery to batter away at the Siegfried Line. However, as Gamelin wrote ominously to Fyda on 10 September, 'Prisoners we have taken indicate that the Germans are reinforcing their battle front with important new units.' Once the Siegfried Line became reinforced and manned in strength, the position of the French in no-man's-land would hardly be tenable.

Meanwhile German propaganda was hard at work trying to convince the French that they were fighting a useless battle, and that their leaders were slaves of the uncivilized Poles and of the arrogant British. As French soldiers began to patrol the frontier on 5 September they were able to read huge placards which the Germans were holding up on the other side, with slogans like 'Let us avoid bloodshed,' 'We won't shoot first,' and 'Let us not kill one another on England's orders.' The radio transmitter at Stuttgart, not far from the French border, was broadcasting interviews with some of the few soldiers who had fallen into German hands, mentioning their names and addresses, and emphasizing that they were being well treated. Leaflets were being dropped from aeroplanes and by balloon. Loudspeakers were set up along the German front line to shout propaganda in French at anyone of the enemy who was in earshot. The arguments could be made to sound quite reasonable: that Germany wanted nothing from France so the war was unnecessary; that Germany wanted only to reunite her people, to put an end to the Treaty of Versailles, that unjust *diktat* now damned by almost everyone; that war would bring victory to no one and suffering to everyone; that it was only being fought on England's orders as part of her plan to dominate Europe.

The same line was pursued by Göring when on 9 September he addressed the workers of a Berlin armaments factory. After calling Poland 'a little state which has been inflated during the past few years as one blows up ridiculous little rubber figures', he made his point. 'We do not want to kill Frenchmen, we do not want to conquer the French or the British. We know that British motto: "We shall fight to the last Frenchman."' Such words were effective propaganda among Frenchmen who knew that, while their own casualties were small, the British casualties were zero. It was only in December that the first British soldier of the war was killed in action.

Nor were the French thrilled by the British announcement, on the same day as Göring's speech, that plans were being made for a three-year war. Chamberlain hoped by saying this to sap morale in Germany and to quicken the 'collapse of the German home front' on which he had staked so much.[48] Ironside recalls how it was discussed at the Cabinet Meeting of 9 September: 'When it was decided to dish this out to the papers the Prime Minister put his forehead down on the table and kept it there for nearly ten minutes. When he eventually looked up he looked more than ghastly.' His announcement seems only to have sapped the morale of his French allies, of his own people and of himself.

Another terrible matter which Chamberlain had to discuss on 9 September was whether the Royal Air Force should bomb Germany. A man of peace, he dreaded having to order air raids on Germany almost as much as he feared that Hitler might bomb London. When Roosevelt appealed on 1 September to all belligerents 'publicly to affirm its determination that its armed forces shall in no event and under no circumstances undertake bombardment from the air of civilian populations', the British and French agreed with alacrity to obey and to prohibit the bombing 'of any except strictly military objectives in the narrowest sense of the word'.[49] This was done on 2 September, before the Allies entered the war. Hitler too was ready enough to promise the same thing. In his speech to the Reichstag on the morning of 1 September he said, 'I have ordered my air force to restrict itself to attacks on military objectives.'[50] His reply to Roosevelt was merely a confirmation of this promise.

Chamberlain's deep relief at this agreement mitigated his horror at having to declare war, and as the days passed and no bombs dropped on Britain, even in reply to the attacks on German shipping and the leaflet 'raids', his determination to prevent bombing attacks communicated itself to the British decision-makers and permeated their minds.

The problem was that Hitler's promise was a lie. When his forces were invading Poland his air force bombed mainly military objectives. It was in its interest to do so. But it was also in its interest to create an atmosphere of panic throughout the country, which would disrupt Polish administration and communications. German aircraft were launching sudden 'terror raids' on towns and villages, bombing and machine-gunning the population.

Hitler was making little attempt to disguise his lie. Eye-witnesses of the invasion, both Polish and foreign, saw the terror attacks and reported them to the outside world as soon as they could. Ambassador Kennard did this on 2 September.[51] Members of his staff had themselves actually seen the haphazard bombing of Warsaw from the roof of the Embassy. The British press confirmed this unequivocally. *The Times* reported on 2 September that 'the capital was attacked from the air with incendiary and explosive bombs', and on 4 September that 'the Germans bombed the following "open" cities', appending a list. Colonel Beck had informed his allies of '1,000 civilian casualties as a result of air bombardment'.

The Royal Air Force did not begin the war well. On 4 September its aircraft did little damage to the German fleet, while its losses were serious. Then on 6 September the War Cabinet was presented with an alarming report:

Air raid warning (red) was received at 0640 on 6th and later unconfirmed reports of 28 hostile aircraft near Hornchurch. RDF [Radar] and observer reports indicated a massed attack on London and the Thames Estuary. Fighters were sent to intercept. Hurricane fighters were engaged by our own guns. Spitfires then attacked Hurricanes. Two Hurricanes were shot down by Spitfires and one Spitfire crashed . . . British submarine Seahorse, returning from patrol, was attacked and damaged by an Anson aircraft . . .[52]

British policy, in the words of the official historian, was that 'Bomber Command in 1939 was above all an investment in the future'. Its early performance can hardly have encouraged the Cabinet to let it off the leash.

But there was the treaty with Poland, something which the British and French were finding more and more embarrassing as the days passed and they, making decisions in their own national interest, as most countries do especially in time of war, did little or nothing to fulfil its terms. Polish diplomats and military envoys spent the early days of September in London and Paris offices begging for air action to relieve German pressure on their country. They looked chiefly to Britain, and rightly so, for the main part of their bargain with France was to be fulfilled by a *land* offensive. Britain could do nothing on land and, as her military leaders admitted in July, air action was the only action Britain was in a position to take in the war's early days. On 25 August the British leaders had promised to afford Poland, if Germany attacked her, immediately all the help and support in their power, and they were worried that, in envisaging R A F attacks only on German military objectives in the narrowest sense, they might be in breach of this agreement. It was only in the light of Roosevelt's appeal for restraint in the air and Hitler's acceptance of it that the War Cabinet could approve such severe limitation of air action, and at the same time maintain anything like a clear conscience towards Poland.

The British official historian writes: 'Up to 12 September it did not appear to them [the Chiefs of Staff], on the available evidence, that the Germans had adopted a policy of disregarding the accepted principles [on air warfare].'[53] On 6 September R. A. Butler, a junior minister in the Foreign Office, was asked in the House of Commons about press reports that Polish open towns had been bombed. He replied that the evidence in his hands was 'not conclusive' but that it 'tends to show that bombing by German aircraft has been generally against objectives serving military purpose and not indiscriminately against the civilian population'. He promised to try to obtain fuller and more definite information, but in the meantime no change of British policy was called for.

What it was that indicated that Germany was obeying the rules is difficult to discover. Even by 6 September the evidence of press report and diplomatic dispatch was overwhelmingly the other way. It was true that there was then in London no reliable British eye-witness to the raids, no one who could say positively, 'I saw German aircraft attacking civilians.' But then a day or two later even this gap was filled by the arrival of Captain 'Tommy' Davies, sent home early from the British military mission to Poland. He had actually seen the way the Luftwaffe bombed, and he reported accordingly.

Chief of Air Staff Cyril Newall told the War Cabinet of Davies's report at its 9 September meeting, and spoke of 'greatly extending the scope of British air action'. At this point Chamberlain, according to Ironside, 'shook his head in a dull way as if it were too much to consider'.[54] Newall said that on the basis of Davies's information it was clear that the German Air Force had not confined its attacks to purely military targets. There had been attacks on Polish industry and power installations. Newall told the Cabinet that in his view the RAF should launch a similar attack against Germany within the next few days. He was aware of Britain's relative inferiority in the air, and he recognized that the Luftwaffe would be bound to retaliate against British factories. They might also attack the British Expeditionary Force, which was then on its way to France. Neutral opinion might be alarmed by the British attack, so it would be necessary to prepare the way by revealing what the Nazis had perpetrated in Poland.

The Cabinet decided to refer this important matter to the Chiefs of Staff Committee and meanwhile to give publicity to 'the wide range of targets' which the Luftwaffe had been attacking. The British were still being over-cautious, of course, for Hitler's air force had been attacking not 'a wide range of targets' but anything at all that was thought worth the cost of the ammunition. Davies had, for instance, told of an attack on the purely residential area of Otwock near Warsaw, of bombs dropped on and around the villa of the American Ambassador, and of an attack on a refugee train full of women and children, many of whom were killed.

Others too were pressing for action in the air. Leo Amery went to see Kingsley Wood, the Air Minister, on 5 September with a suggestion to drop incendiary bombs on the Black Forest which was full of munitions for the German Army. It had been a dry summer and the woods would burn like tinder. To Amery's amazement Wood told him that the Forest could not be bombed as it was 'private property',[55] nor could even such purely military targets as the munition works at Essen or the German lines of communication. To do so would alienate American public opinion, Wood claimed.

Edward Spears, another member of parliament of the Churchill school of thought, resolved to raise the matter in the House of Commons with the support of many Labour Party members. After Butler's announcement that the German Air Force was probably obeying the rules, Ambassador Raczyński came to him with a list of open towns which had been bombed and begged him to use his influence to get some action. Spears agreed that pamphlet raids were not enough, and that 'the only thing we could be certain about was the use to which the Germans would put this paper'. He told Wood what he planned to do but was implored by the Air Minister to reconsider: 'Owing, he [Wood] said, to our unfortunate democratic system, questions of strategy could be discussed publicly in the House, and this was most dangerous.'

'It was ignominious,' Spears replied, 'to stage a confetti war against an utterly ruthless enemy who was meanwhile destroying a whole nation, and to pretend that we were thereby fulfilling our obligations. We were covering ourselves with ridicule by organizing this kind of carnival. It was as futile as reading a lesson on deportment to a homicidal maniac at the height of his fury.'[56] But of course he was restrained by Wood's warning that if he spoke he might damage the national interest.

This argument is one which senior administrators are apt to use when cornered by parliamentarians or journalists. Information need not be supplied in its support, which is why the latter seldom find it satisfactory and often suspect a plan to cover up official embarrassment. But it is not an appeal which can ever be lightly rejected. It *may* be genuine, in which case the sceptic who lets the cat out of the bag will have done a terrible thing. Spears recognized that to disobey his well-informed bosses in time of war would be very dangerous. 'I did not dare run the risk,' he wrote in 1954, adding, 'Today I regret that I kept silence.' It would not have made much difference, but at least it would have let the Poles know that someone cared about them.

On 9 September the Chiefs of Staff – Ironside, Newall and Dudley Pound (for the Navy) – set themselves to the consideration of the problem and the evidence, and two days later they were ready with a report for the War Cabinet. It must be one of the most misleading documents ever to have influenced a crucial military decision. Newall had completely changed his mind. He and his co-authors reported that new evidence 'appeared to confirm the view that the Germans were making an honest effort to restrict their bombing to military objectives. The fact that they may have made mistakes was in the nature of the hazards of air warfare.'[57]

The evidence gave the appearance of having been analysed piece by piece. The Committee had twelve reports of German bombing in which civilians had been killed, five of them from Captain Davies. They concluded, apparently on the basis of broad assumption and nothing else, that the bombs dropped on the American Ambassador's villa were 'probably released by accident', that the bombed refugee train was 'presumably mistaken for a military train' and that each of Davies's other reports was 'an instance of casualties due to normal inaccuracy of bombing'. It all went to show that 'the deliberate bombardment of the [Polish] enemy as such has not been pursued as a policy' and that the Germans had not broken the relevant international law, the Draft Hague Rules of Aerial Warfare of 1923. Furthermore, apart from the sinking without warning of the S.S. *Athenia* and the invasion of Poland itself, Germany was 'probably not in violation of the generally accepted principles of war, which His Majesty's Government would propose to follow themselves'.[58]

The Chiefs of Staff claimed that 'the Polish mission now in this country corroborated our view that the Germans were trying to abide by the rules'. This is untrue. Raczyński said exactly the opposite. They then reminded the Cabinet that they had promised President Roosevelt to restrain the Royal Air Force, just as both Hitler and Göring had promised to restrict the Luftwaffe, and that 'we have no definite or reliable proof that in fact they have not done so in Poland – though possibly on a somewhat elastic interpretation'. The Air Minister agreed that for this reason 'it was unthinkable that we should initiate unrestricted air attack on Germany'. He was worried about the effect on neutral, especially American, opinion if Britain had used her air force 'in such a manner as might expose us to criticism'.[59]

In the context of what was currently happening in Poland, such fine feelings were pure hypocrisy, even obscene hypocrisy. Britain had guaranteed Poland and made an alliance with her, and on such foundations Poland had formed her foreign policy. Britain was now deciding that for her own tactical reasons she would dishonour this agreement and leave Poland in the lurch, even in the air, the one area where she was in a position to help.

This was immoral enough, but in the circumstances probably forgivable. When their vital interests are threatened, especially in wartime, countries are liable to break treaties. This is a fact of life. During the invasion of France the following summer Churchill decided quite deliberately, in spite of the agreements that bound the two countries, to withhold units of the Royal Air Force which he thought vital for the defence of his own country. It was a cruel decision, but one which subsequent events have shown as clearly correct. Where Britain poured salt into the Poles' wounds was in breaking the treaty and then pretending that they were not, in satisfying their consciences with a report on the 'legality' of

German attacks which was nothing more than a piece of trumped-up nonsense.

Then there were the tactical considerations. Here too the Chiefs of Staff were at sea, though they were to beach themselves on firmer ground as they reached their conclusions. They began with one quite unjustified assumption: 'The Germans had virtually wiped out the Polish Air Force and the Polish aircraft industry and they need not maintain any material proportion of their total air force on their eastern front. Consequently nothing that we can do in the air in the western theatre would have any effect of relieving pressure on Poland.' These words were written on 11 September, when the Germans and Poles were in the throes of a great battle in which German air supremacy played an important part. The Polish Army had still a lot of fight left in it, but its attempts to build a line of defence were being thwarted by the disruption and chaos caused by German bombing. As late as 17 September *The Times* reported that 'every day the smallest concentration of Polish troops was spotted by enemy aircraft and strafed mercilessly'. The Germans were broadcasting in Polish from radio stations in captured towns. 'We know where you are,' was their constant message to the retreating Polish administration, and sure enough they seemed to have excellent information. Again and again German bombers would strike a town only hours after the arrival of Polish leaders. These attacks kept them constantly on the move. In the end, though their enemies knew where they were, their Polish subordinates did not. British and French air action in the West would have relieved some of this terrible pressure.

Another important reason for restraint, the Chiefs of Staff felt, was that 'the French Army are shortly to stage a large-scale operation against the Siegfried Line'. They should not assume, they wrote, that this attack would achieve immediate or spectacular success, but the whole French Army was going to be involved, and it might well develop into a combined Allied effort – the French Army supported by the Royal Air Force. Therefore Britain should not, they concluded, embark on 'independent air operations which might result in reducing our capacity to support the French offensive effectively should it achieve unexpected success'.

Again the Chiefs of Staff were working on a false premise.

There was going to be no 'large-scale operation against the Sieg-fried Line'. On 4 September Gamelin had told Ironside of his plan to 'lean against' the Line to test its strength, adding that he had no intention of wasting his best divisions by flinging them headlong into battle. Slessor felt that Gamelin 'looked on this offensive as little more than a gesture'.[60] The French General had, after all, promised the Poles a major offensive, and though he had little intention of carrying this out, he had to envisage it as a contingency. Only thus could he satisfy his conscience and the frantic entreaties of the Poles.

From the accounts of the 4 September meeting it is hard to believe that Ironside really thought Gamelin might attack the German line. Slessor certainly did not. And the next day (12 September), although Gamelin again mumbled something to Chamberlain about 'a large-scale operation', he also stated that he would not throw his army against the main German defences, and that he had forbidden any such attack. Anyway, this great assault did not take place, and it was unrealistic, perhaps even dishonest, for the British Chiefs of Staff on 11 September to base their decision on the possibility that it might.

But there were other more valid tactical considerations. Both Britain and France were wickedly unprepared for the war which had erupted. The German war machine was in top gear while the Allies were still at a standstill, warming up the engine. They would clearly gain more from a lull before the storm than would Germany. The Chiefs of Staff pointed out that the German Air Force was far superior to the British and French Forces combined, that Britain was 'dangerously short of reserves' and that 'successful attack on five main aircraft factories would at least seriously cripple our production of fighters and gravely prejudice our production of aircraft in general'.

They recognized how dangerous it was to leave the Germans as conquerors of Poland without experiencing any of the horrors of war. German morale was sure to rise as a result. German public opinion was known to be split and the people far from united behind the Nazis. They recalled how the bombing of the Rhineland in the spring of 1918 had led to a clamour by the Germans for limiting bombing to the battlefield. Would not bombs have more effect than leaflets? The question was a very important one, especially since 'a collapse on the German home front' was the Prime Minister's only recipe for winning a quick war.

Against this there was the immense relief felt by all Britons and Frenchmen that the outbreak of war had not brought with it the massacre of millions, that rain of death which had so terrified Chamberlain and lead him to believe that war was hardly to be contemplated. Was it really right to provoke this deadly exchange in fulfilment of a paper treaty, and in the vague hope that it might make the Germans throw the Nazis out? Who would take upon himself the responsibility of such a gamble? And if at the end of it all the stronger air force won, as was likely, where would Britain and France be then, their skies naked to the ravages of the Stukas and the Messerschmidts? The Chiefs of Staff decided that such a risk was not worth taking.

Britain's weak leadership, in spite of its 9 September announcement of a probable three-year war, did not yet see this as inevitable, was not yet resigned to future sacrifice and horror, did not yet have the stomach for a *real* fight. It was still thinking in terms of peacetime diplomacy, concerned to show itself as *morally* better than the Nazis. It is almost laughable now to think of so much time and energy being spent in such a superfluous exercise. Chamberlain did not appreciate that a war God is more often on the side of the big batallions than on the side of right. He wanted to tell the world of the justice of his cause, not of his resolution to win. And a flamboyant gesture, even a cruel gesture, may well have been what was needed to spotlight that resolution. Had he remained as Prime Minister he would not, for instance, have destroyed the French fleet at Oran. It took a Churchill to do that, killing hundreds of innocent Frenchmen but demonstrating Britain's will to win the war and winning admiration and allies from those who truly understood the motives and issues involved.

No sooner was this report approved by the War Cabinet when information finally arrived from Poland putting it beyond all doubt that the Luftwaffe had bombed illegally and that Hitler had lied. The diplomatic corps in Krzemieniec was eye-witness and victim of a vicious attack. 'This place, a defenceless open village, was bombed at 11 a.m. today.' reported the American Ambassador Biddle on 12 September. There seemed no reason for the attack. The Polish Government was not there, only the diplomats who had arrived a day or two earlier, causing consternation to the local Mayor who had nowhere to accommodate so many distinguished guests. The French and British were given a combined 'embassy' in a village inn, with nowhere near enough beds to go round. 'We dashed into the rooms putting hats on beds,' Clifford Norton recalls.

Many bombs fell in the market-place, killing about fifty Poles and provoking the fury of the diplomats who immediately held an 'indignation meeting' under the chairmanship of Ambassador Biddle. With the exception of the Swiss, whose first anxiety was of course to show how neutral they were, the heads of mission agreed to send protest telegrams to their governments about the bombing of civilian populations, and these were dispatched from the village post office. 'This became the *bombardement célèbre* of the war,' Clare Hollingworth writes. 'It was one of Hitler's affronts to the world, meant to daze and stun, to kill incipient opposition by a blow in the face. The poor diplomats did not understand; but the method has been known to drinkshop bullies for centuries.'[61] Nor did the British diplomats understand when a reply to their telegram came back from London, quick as a flash, 'Can you prove that Krzemieniec is not a railway centre?' There was a railway, a rickety single-track affair, but a poor excuse for such a massacre. But for the British any excuse was better than none. Anything was better than facing the bitter truth about Nazi bombing, or the obligations that this imposed.

The Nazis and the Allies were playing the game according to quite different rules. On 1 September Hitler had undertaken to restrict his air force, but this did not mean that he would actually do so. His job was to further his own country's interest, not to impress already hostile foreigners with his honesty. And now that his victory was nearly won, he did not feel obliged even to lie any more. On 13 September a German communiqué announced piously that 'German artillery and air men have shown excessive consideration for open towns, villages and hamlets', but that this was 'dependent on the condition that these places were not made by the enemy into a war zone'. Polish civilians were now being mobilized as defenders and therefore 'the German Air Force, in cooperation with heavy artillery, will take all suitable measures to make clear the uselessness of resistance'.[62] The British and French would not accept that Hitler did not care what the world thought. Lulled into a sense of false security by his inaction in the West, they still preferred to give him the benefit of the doubt.

On 14 September, two days after the attack on Krzemieniec, the Chiefs of Staff, obliged by the flood of telegrams to revise their report, admitted that the position 'may have changed', but saw difficulty in the fact that 'all the evidence we have received so far emanates from interested parties in Poland and would not therefore carry universal conviction'. The best they could suggest was a request to Roosevelt to 'establish the facts' and 'inform us accordingly'. This Roosevelt did on the basis of reports from Ambassador Biddle, who was taking great pains to inform his government of the horrible truth. But even after he knew the facts Roosevelt still did not feel able to criticize Germany by name. On 18 September he wired Polish President Mościcki of his hopes that the world would be spared aerial bombardment. 'I have been deeply shocked therefore,' he wrote, 'by the statements contained in your telegram as well as by reports received from other sources including officials of this Government in Poland.' He asked belligerent countries to 'renew their orders' restraining their air forces.[63] As a neutral he felt this was as far as he could go.

In London Polish Ambassador Raczyński told Lord Lloyd that he was 'in despair' over what was happening. Lloyd wrote to Lord Hankey, a Cabinet Minister: 'He [Raczyński] had asked at the Foreign Office for greater aerial diversion on the western front to relieve the terrible weight of German air attack on Poland, and had got a most discouraging reply to send to Beck.' Hankey replied to Lloyd with an interesting letter (14 September): 'I remember from the last war how heart-rending such appeals are. Unfortunately, however, the British nation in its wisdom, or unwisdom, never provides more at the outset of a war than a covering force acting as a shield under which we can mobilize our full strength.' It would be a mistake, he wrote, for Britain to 'fritter away her strength' while she was still unprepared. 'On the whole I would rather you destroyed this letter,'[64] he concluded. No wonder, for they were words of alarming truth. It was all very well heaping blame on Chamberlain for Britain's lack of manpower and supplies. But a country gets the government it deserves. A politician who during the early and mid 1930s had urged the necessary expenditure on rearmament would not have been voted into office, either by his party or by the country. Unless and until the world is in ferment and war is near, foreign affairs seem far away to the average man who has to earn a living and support a family. Foreign dangers go almost unnoticed until the bombs begin to drop.

As the second week of the war drew to its close the Polish Army was split and confused but by no means beaten. The Battle on the Bzura was still in full swing. On 14 September the Polish 16th Infantry Division, previously ordered to withdraw across the river from Łowicz, was again ordered to attack the town, and with the support of other units they captured it that evening. But they were outnumbered and outflanked. Street fighting made their hold on Łowicz tenuous. Already they were reduced to one third of their normal complement. The Polish Command finally realized that the only way the battle could be won or at least salvaged was for the two armies, the Poznań and the Pomerania, to join the garrison in Warsaw fifty miles to the East. The 16th Infantry Division again abandoned Łowicz and crossed the river to cover the main force's retreat. By 16 September the Poznań Army under General Tadeusz Kutrzeba was approaching Sochaczew, half way to Warsaw.

In the capital there was a lull as the German Army on the western bank of the Vistula concentrated its attention on the un-expected attack from the two north-western armies. But soon the city was threatened from across the river. The Third German Army had fought its way south from East Prussia, and by 14 September it was a 'left hook' menacing the Warsaw suburb of Praga, just across the Vistula. At the same time another 'left hook', the outer stream of the German pincer movement, was threatening the large town of Brześć (Brest-Litovsk), 120 miles east of Warsaw. By 15 September the town was surrounded, and a surprise attack on the famous Brześć 'fortress' only failed because the Poles had parked an old Renault tank across the entrance. General Guderian took part in this attack, during which his aide-de-camp was shot dead by a sniper.[65]

A few thousand Polish defenders still held out along the coast-line. Gdynia remained in Polish hands for a week after the Corridor was cut. On 12 September the Poles had endured such heavy casualties from German bombs and artillery that they decided to evacuate Gdynia itself, but to carry on their defence from a place nearby called Kępa Oksywska, where they remained until 19 September. Westerplatte, the mile-long Polish-occupied strip in Danzig harbour, surrendered on 7 September after a battle which the German press called their 'little Verdun' (*kleines Verdun*), and in which several hundred Germans were killed. On the Hel peninsula, a strange jut of land just north of Gdynia twenty miles long and a mile or so wide, a 3,000-strong Polish garrison was still in action. On 10 September bloody battles were fought for the small town of Wielka Wieś at the base of the point. It changed hands several times before falling to the invader. Because of its narrow neck the peninsula was easy to defend from frontal assault, but also an easy target for the concentrated fire of German artillery, aircraft and even ships of war. For days this tiny strip of Polish-held land was blasted by explosions which the Poles were somehow able to endure until 2 October when they surrendered.

Apart from these doomed, isolated strongpoints, there were the remnants of the two armies fighting on the Bzura towards Warsaw and the Warsaw garrison itself, busy making preparations for the ordeal that was to come. Thousands of Polish soldiers still roamed the occupied west of the country, surrounded by swift-moving columns of Germans, hopelessly cut off from any friendly unit of any size, reduced to the status of stragglers and soon to be rounded up. All this left the Polish High Command with little to rely on but its 'Rumanian bridgehead'. On 14 September Colin Gubbins visited the Polish Headquarters, then at Mlynów, to be told of this plan. He found no proper headquarters operating, little communication with what forces remained, and frantic preparations for yet another move south. 'The Staff at Mlynów were obviously exhausted by their ordeal of the previous fortnight and were lying fully dressed on the available beds, snatching what rest they could.'[66] He was told that 'the new front was to be a bridgehead extending from the Rumanian frontier west of Zaleszczyki along the course of the rivers Dniestr and Stryj to the Hungarian frontier. The garrisons of Warsaw, Brześć, Lublin and Lwów were, however, to fight out to the end and contain what German forces they could in order to assist the retreat.'

The previous day he had visited Lwów to find that a German

armoured division was already there and trying to enter the city. General Langner was in command of the defence, and his forces were able to last out the day, while women and children were mobilized to erect barricades across the streets. At one point Gubbins found his car hemmed in by barricades, and he was only just able to extricate himself before the city was completely cut off. He was warned too that another danger to beware of was rebellious Ukrainians. The areas the Poles still held were ethnically the least Polish of the whole country. Lwów was a Polish-inhabited island in a sea of Ukrainian-farmed land. Only a few of these inhabitants were 'polonized' and loyal to the state which had ruled them for twenty years. A few were inclined to communism, wanting these areas to join the main part of the Ukraine which formed part of the Soviet Union; others were purely nationalist, resentful against both the Poles and the Russians who over the centuries had taken turns in ruling them. In either case they were unlikely to weep many tears at the prospect of Poland's imminent collapse.

After they invaded the Soviet Union in June 1941 the Germans made efficient use of anti-Russian Ukrainians, hundreds of thousands of whom served Germany faithfully for several years. In September 1939 too German–Ukrainian cooperation played its part, though on a much smaller scale. German intelligence was in contact with Ukrainian nationalists, and after the invasion German agents were parachuted into places where they lived to stir up anti-Polish feeling. A 600-strong Ukrainian unit under a Colonel Roman Sushko, formed in Germany, took part in the invasion on Hitler's side and was disbanded only after the area was handed over to Russia.[67]

By 14 September armed Ukrainians were causing trouble for the Poles in Lwów and Stanisławów where there was occasional street fighting.[68] The 'bandits' numbered probably no more than a thousand, but they were able to attack small sections or individual soldiers of the Polish Army, and to raid Polish-owned manor houses, administrative buildings and supply trains retreating from the north and west. One source claims that Ukrainian nationalists actually proclaimed an independent republic in Stanisławów on 17 September.[69] They were only a drop in the ocean of trouble which the Poles had to face, but of course legally their action was treason. The Polish historian Pobóg-Malinowski admits that Polish troops took certain reprisals, burning the Ukrainian village of Piaseczno as well as part of Mikołajow and shooting a few 'bandits' whom they caught red-handed.[70]

These Ukrainian aspirations – one of the world's great lost causes – lasted of course only three or four days before the Soviet–German vice clamped shut. When an area changes hands in wartime there is often a moment of chaos during which its true character is able briefly to emerge. But at such times historical information tends to be scanty and unreliable, so these last days of the Polish Ukraine can hardly be documented with any precision. Pobóg-Malinowski admits charmingly that his information is based on 'documents which I happened to find lying in the road on 17 September somewhere between Kuty and Załucz'.[71]

France and Britain had by now given up Poland for lost. In a report dated 16 September the British Chiefs of Staff wrote that 'it is apparent that the military defeat of Poland may be accomplished in the very near future' and proceeded to outline the possible future course of a war in which Poland played no part. *The Times* told its readers that 'the Polish military situation, which a week ago was described in this correspondence as an orderly retreat with the Army intact, has now become the exact opposite'. On 14 September the British Embassy was moved from bomb-blasted Krzemieniec to Zaleszczyki, a few miles from the Rumanian border, where it was allotted a dormitory in a local hospital. 'The Embassy consists of eight iron bedsteads, one enamel washstand, one table with an oilcloth covering, several chairs and no telephone,' wrote Patrick Maitland for *The Times*.[72]

The British and French – diplomats, journalists and soldiers – were finding their position more and more uncomfortable as they retreated alongside their Polish allies. They were short of food, sleep, petrol and especially of information. The British military mission had impressive wireless equipment, but it was never even set up, such was the confusion of the retreat and the persistency of the bombing. The French Ambassador Noel decided to cross the border into Rumania and to establish himself at Cernauti, visiting Poland every day. Many journalists did likewise, for at least from Rumania they could telephone their stories to the outside world. The British Ambassador Kennard took a different view. He was accredited to the Polish Government, and so long as that Government existed on Polish soil he was determined to stay. With a skeleton staff he found accommodation in a dentist's house in Kuty, half a mile from the frontier. There was nothing for them to do except be a symbol of Allied support and stamp visas into the passports of Polish refugees. 'We played cards for matches,' Clifford Norton recalls. Clare Hollingworth crossed from Rumania to visit them on 16 September and was able to give them a newspaper, which thrilled them. 'Their knowledge of events in Europe was less than that of the suburban citizen over his tea-pot and marmalade,' she writes.[73]

In some ways the situation was now ripe for Polish counter-attack. The Poles were exhausted, but so were the Germans, having driven hundreds of miles over hostile country with little time for rest. The Polish Army was cut into pieces, while its main body was being driven into a bottleneck. But the German Army now had dangerously long lines of communication. They had travelled so far and so fast that their supplies had not yet caught up with them. Their tanks were running out of fuel. On 14 September eight Polish aircraft bombed German tanks near Rawa Ruska, and it became clear that some of the armoured columns were immobilized, sitting targets even for the most makeshift air force. On 15 September Rydz-Śmigły told Beck that 'German pressure was tending to weaken'.[74]

So effective had been the initial German attack on the Polish Air Force that after 8 September no more than ten Polish bombers were able to go into action every day.[75] On 16 September two Panzer divisions ran out of fuel near Siedlce, between Warsaw and Brześć, but by then the Poles possessed hardly a landing-strip fit for use and could not exploit the position.[76] On the evening of 15 September the Polish Headquarters was moved yet again to Kołomyia for the final organization of the 'Rumanian bridgehead'. 'I had the impression,' writes Jaklicz, 'that in spite of the seriousness of the situation the Commander-in-Chief would be able to get control of the situation and defend the bridgehead *until the results of Gamelin's offensive became effective*.'[77] (Author's italics.) The Poles still believed that they would be saved by their French allies who had promised in May an offensive fifteen days after mobilization. This date was 16 September. The Polish generals wished it could have been earlier, but since it was to be 16 September they would make the best of it and hold their position until they were able to advance and reconquer their country.

On 15–16 September fierce battles were also being fought near Sochaczew as the survivors of the Battle on the Bzura tried to force their way across the river to join the defenders of Warsaw. By 16 September part of the force, under General Kutrzeba, succeeded in crossing the Bzura north of Sochaczew and reaching the Puszcza Kampinoska woods, north-west of the capital. On the same day General Kazimierz Sosnkowski, having flown sixty miles east of Lwów to Przemyśl, launched a surprise attack on the Germans, capturing a quantity of equipment which he destroyed. He fought his way back to the outskirts of Lwów successfully.[78] That evening General Jaklicz heard on the radio of Sosnkowski's 'victory' and concluded that 'the situation had improved considerably'.[79] A British officer told Clare Hollingworth that Polish morale was much better. Best of all, it had started to rain. She met an Under-Secretary of the Polish Foreign Office who was 'tremendously' excited over the Polish victories and the rainfall.[80]

This brief spasm of euphoria made the Poles' gloom all the blacker when early on the morning of 17 September they found themselves invaded by the Red Army. (These events are described in detail in Chapter 8.) No longer was there now the slightest hope of maintaining the 'Rumanian bridgehead' or of establishing any line of defence whatever. Within a few hours what remained of the Polish Army in the East had disintegrated. The two invading armies were left with a mopping-up job which took them only a few days.

Only the Warsaw garrison was now left to resist the German Army on any organized, significant scale. The first German attempt to take the city by assault on 8 and 9 September had failed. German forces had withdrawn to meet the Polish counter-offensive on the Bzura, so giving the defenders valuable days to prepare themselves. During the week of 10 to 17 September air and artillery attacks on the capital were not heavy and what action there was affected mainly the Praga suburbs on the east bank of the Vistula, which were now threatened by the German Third Army. A light screen of German forces still surrounded the city, but for the moment this did not inhibit the defenders. Indeed on occasion it provided them with targets for effective sorties.

By 19 September, when the German Army was able to give its main attention to the capture of Warsaw, the city had effectively been turned into a fortress. The attacking tanks were unable to penetrate, and it became clear to the German command that only at the expense of heavy casualties would they be able to take the city by assault. That same day too the defenders were reinforced by the arrival of units which had fought in the Battle on the Bzura. For three days the soldiers poured in, about 30,000 in all, giving the morale of the people of Warsaw an unimaginable boost.[81] Their position was quite hopeless of course, but such were their emotions and so strong was their solidarity that they would not accept this fact.

The reinforcements were not a great help, for the new arrivals were quite exhausted after days of vicious battles and forced marches. In order to reach Warsaw at all they had been forced to abandon much of their equipment, and in the besieged city there was none to replace it. Meanwhile the attackers were dragging up their artillery and alerting their air force. The simplest way out of their problem would be to pound the city into submission.

The bombardment built up to a crescendo, until by 25 September life in the city was more or less at a standstill. The electricity, gas and telephone services no longer operated. Water mains were broken so that, apart from other inconveniences, the fire services were unable to do much about the hundreds of burning buildings. A German eye-witness describes the scene vividly:

The greatest results were achieved by our 30·5 cm. mortars, the noise of which for many days was the voice of Warsaw. The mortars spoke incessantly, one battery after another, showering a hot rain of metal over Poland's capital, bursting in windows and tearing out window-frames and doors. Watching by night we saw curves of coloured fire flashing gracefully towards Warsaw. The earth quivered and our eardrums seemed about to split. Looking to Warsaw we saw columns of smoke soaring languidly, as if from mighty cigars. In all directions long smoky tongues of fire spurted up every second. In the heavens the clouds were as red as blood.[82]

With no essential services and communication within the city all but impossible, the hospitals were unable to do much for the wounded, who were beginning to overflow into the hotels and cafés. During the evening of 26 September it was suggested to

General Rommel, commander of the defence forces, that further resistance was useless and would only lead to more loss of life. Stefan Starzyński, the Mayor of Warsaw, was in favour of fighting on nevertheless, but it was put to him that the defenders' ammunition was nearly exhausted and that, apart from the matter of civilian casualties, resistance was bound soon to fade away for lack of resources. Early on the morning of 27 September Polish envoys accordingly made contact with the German headquarters of General Blaskowitz. The surrender of Warsaw was signed at 1.15 p.m. the following day. About 2,000 soldiers and 10,000 civilians had been killed in the siege, and about twelve per cent of the city's buildings were destroyed.[83]

The German Government was then in a position to administer its share of Poland and to carry out its policy there. On 23 May Hitler had told his military chiefs in the Berlin Chancellery: 'Danzig is not the nub of the problem at all. It is a question of expanding our living space in the East, of securing our food supplies.' On 22 August he again addressed his generals:

The destruction of Poland has priority. The aim is to eliminate active forces, not to reach a definite line. Even if war breaks out in the West, the destruction of Poland remains the primary objective. A quick decision in view of the season. I shall provide a propaganda reason for starting the war – never mind whether it is plausible or not. The victor will not be asked afterwards whether or not he told the truth. In starting and waging war it is not right that matters but victory. Close your hearts to pity! Act brutally! Eighty million people must obtain their due.[84]

We know now what he meant by this last sentence: that the Aryan race by virtue of its innate superiority had the right to seize lands inhabited by Slavs or Jews and to use the local people as it thought fit. When he went on to speak in praise of Genghis Khan 'who had millions of women and children killed by his own will and with a gay heart', and to suggest killing 'without mercy all men, women and children of Polish race or language',[85] some of his audience thought he was speaking in metaphor. When a man says such things it is hard to believe that he means every word. But Hitler did.

The war against Poland was won, and in Wheeler-Bennett's vivid words 'back came the Wehrmacht from their Polish conquests, their cheeks bloodied, their swords fleshed, the laurel of the victor on their brows. It had been a "quick war", "right out of the book", and the Polish resistance had been just sufficient to add that welcome degree of danger and adventure that differentiates a blood-sport from a *Blumenkorso*.'[86] It was Hitler's view that the war was essential. He said to Albert Speer, 'Do you think it would have been good fortune for our troops if we had taken Poland without a fight, after obtaining Austria and Czechoslovakia without fighting? Believe me, not even the best army can stand that sort of thing. Victories without loss of blood are demoralizing.'[87] He told his generals on 22 August: 'I am only afraid that some bastard (*Schweinhund*) will make a proposal for peace.'

It takes facts and documents like this to reveal in their full uselessness the frantic efforts of men like Halifax and Bonnet to avert Hitler's invasion, and after it had begun to end it without declaring war. Hitler could never have been bought off, he was not in the market. The flights of diplomacy during the summer, the talk of extra-territorial *autobahnen* and of plebiscites were mere window-dressing to appease the appeasers, to make them believe what he and they both wanted to believe, that he was no more than a patriotic German trying to secure his country's rights. His enemies became his allies by allowing themselves to be deluded and delayed from military preparation, so that when war actually came there was little they could do to help their real ally.

It was too much to expect men who for years had struggled to keep the peace suddenly to jump to a policy of total war. Psychologically it was hard enough for them to find themselves going through the *motions* of war, which is all they were doing. They believed that time was on their side, but then so in the short term did Hitler, for protected in the West by his mighty army and in the East by his brilliant new treaty he was well placed for further advances as soon as the campaigning season returned.

Now that war had come Hitler was freed from the tiresome need to sham and play the gentleman. He could now offer himself to his people in his true role as conqueror and fade the reasonable, statesmanlike image he had previously cultivated for foreign consumption. The diplomatic game was over. Now the real game was upon him, a game for real men played with live ammunition. And he had begun well. Already he had won large areas of living-space in the East, with Danzig and the Corridor thrown in as incidentals.

What is more, he had kept up the momentum of his movement. 'Man has become great through perpetual struggle. In perpetual peace his greatness must decline,' he had written in *Mein Kampf.*[88] His victory gave him the chance to come to grips with his dissident generals, those prophets of doom who believed that his warmongering would lead Germany to disaster and were only waiting for the chaos of war to strike and remove him. 3 September was their moment. Germany was full of gloom and apprehension about the war. But in only two weeks Hitler the rash aggressor had become Hitler the victor. Nothing succeeds like success. Germany felt the momentary, false elation of a shot in the arm. But it was real enough to kill the generals' plans. They were too slow and victory defeated them. They had hardly time to get under way before the wind was taken from their sails by the success of their subordinates.

So long as there was a chance that the Allies would 'listen to reason' and make peace, Hitler was content to hold his hand in the West and endure the phoney war. But in Poland he could behave naturally. The Allies had protested against his aggression but done little to prevent it. They were hardly likely to do any more if he took steps to consolidate what he thought was rightly his. For one thing Poland was now a closed area without foreign journalists, and even diplomats were removed within a few months. News of what was happening there would take time to reach the outside, and when it did it would be in the form of garbled, third-hand information, exaggerated and distorted by emotion. To be sure, it was not long before stories started to appear in the world's press, but circumstances were such that they could not be confirmed, and they were very often dismissed as unreliable by shrewd observers who do not easily accept hearsay evidence of unspeakable horrors. Generally it was assumed that Hitler was treating the Poles harshly, but the full enormity of what he had authorized was not known, and even if it had been it probably would not have been believed. It is hard to credit the incredible.

Hitler felt a particular hatred for the Poles, the 'sub-human' people who, unlike the others of Eastern Europe, had defied his threats and fought his army. For weeks German propaganda had been painting a horrible picture of Polish ill-treatment of the *Volksdeutsche*. 'German families flee' read a headline in the *Berliner Zeitung*, and 'In the Corridor many German farmhouses are in flames' read another in *12-Uhr Blatt* on 26 August. 'Chaos in Upper Silesia' claimed *Völkischer Beobachter* on 27 August. According to Hitler's press, hundreds of Germans were fleeing Poland to escape a wave of atrocities.

Naturally this propaganda was stepped up after the invasion began. The 1 September *Völkischer Beobachter* carried a long article whose headline declared, 'The evil of Poland is irresponsibility, disorder and laziness.' Everywhere the Poles were murdering Germans, it went on, and while the Polish Army was massing on the German frontier, thousands of other Poles were moving in panic from Upper Silesia deeper into the country. They had stolen money from Germans and — horrors! — left hundreds of unpaid debts. In the next few days the press was full of accounts of acts of bestial cruelty committed by Poles, especially about 'Bloody Sunday' in Bydgoszcz (Bromberg) where, apparently, 'an old woman of more than seventy was captured, her left breast cut off, her heart taken out and placed in a bowl of blood'.[89] The next day photographs in the press (mostly false, one must conclude) gave Germany vivid 'proof' of the viciousness of the Polish character. 'How completely isolated a world the German people live in,' William Shirer wrote in his diary.[90] Many of them were ready to accept the propaganda, and such was Hitler's psychology that he may well himself have come to believe some of the lies he concocted.

On 12 September, with the campaign still at its height, the German Government saw fit to complain publicly of 'breaches of international law' by Polish civilians who were fighting the invader while out of uniform. The Army announced that henceforward the death penalty would be imposed on civilians who committed acts of violence against them, or who were caught in possession of arms or ammunition. That same day Ribbentrop handed to Keitel instructions from Hitler on how the Polish problem was to be solved. Admiral Canaris was there, and when he complained to Keitel about brutality in Poland, Keitel told him simply that Hitler himself had decided the matter. Canaris pointed out the danger involved in Hitler's policy. He knew, for example, that it involved the extermination of Poland's leaders, the nobility and the clergy. It was not so much that he objected to this in principle, but he wanted to avoid responsibility. Keitel replied that if the Army was unwilling to do the work it would have to accept SS and Gestapo 'commissars' in each unit to do it for them. Canaris felt he had no alternative but to agree, but he did remark prophetically, 'The day will come when the world will hold the Wehrmacht, under whose eyes these events occurred, responsible for them.'[91]

Even he may not have been fully aware of the extent of the massacres that were about to take place, and which were planned as soon as Poland was in Hitler's hands. On 7 October Hitler issued a decree 'on the strengthening of Germanhood' which referred to 'the elimination of the harmful influence of nationally alien populations, which constitute a danger to the Reich and the German community'.[92] His plan was to use Poland simply as a cheap supply of 'living space' for German settlers and of labour for German industry. Such policies would naturally be unacceptable to the Poles, who might be expected to try to overthrow German rule by force. The only way to prevent this, in Hitler's thinking, was to 'behead' Poland of that class of people which generally leads a violent revolt, and this meant her intelligentsia. Nor would it be enough to kill merely a few political leaders and aristocrats. The term 'intelligentsia' was deemed to include 'priests, teachers (including university lecturers), doctors, dentists, veterinary surgeons, officers, executives, businessmen, landowners, writers, journalists, and anyone who has received a higher or secondary education'.[93] Millions of Poles were thus earmarked for the attention of Hitler's bullies.

But of course enemy number one was the Jew, and as far as they were concerned as early as 21 September Reinhard Heydrich outlined his plans in terms which can have left no doubt in the mind of any intelligent administrator that what was planned was extermination. The 'final solution' of his plan, he said, would take some years to achieve.[94] It was one of the earliest uses of this most terrible of Nazi euphemisms. The death camps did not in fact begin operation for a couple of years, and in the meantime the idea of them was kept a close secret. To reveal it might really have provoked the anger of the neutrals, forcing off the fence and towards outright sympathy with the Allies millions of isolationist

Americans. It might also have risked an initial outbreak of violence from the conquered Poles who were still in the process of laying down their arms, believing that they would be treated correctly by the occupying army. Had they known that millions of them were doomed, they might have decided to fight on to the last man.

The first step towards Heydrich's goal was to herd the Jews into small areas, to identify them and separate them from the Poles so that they could more easily be disposed of when the time came. Many of them owned shops or small businesses, and at once these were confiscated and put in the hands of Aryan 'trustees'. One account claims that 'every shop name in Katowice changed overnight'.[95] Jews were thus thrown out of work by the thousand. During October the German authorities got into the habit of combing Jewish-inhabited streets for labour. The men were put to work clearing rubble, then released in the evening. Starvation-level rationing was imposed, allowing Jews only 200 calories a day, Poles 400 and Germans 1,600. In many cities the Jews lived only in certain areas, so it was easy to enclose these streets and create a ghetto.

By another of his bizarre conjuring tricks Hitler was able to camouflage his murderous intentions as a conciliatory gesture. In the course of his peace mission to Berlin, Dahlerus told Hitler that 'the British were considering where the Jews were to stay', whereupon Hitler replied 'that if he should reorganize the Polish state, an asylum could also be created for the Jews'.[96] He gave Dahlerus to understand that it was only out of a sense of duty that he was involving himself in Poland, since 'someone had to see that there was order in the East'. He spoke vividly of the 'awful impressions' he had gained from his recent visits to Poland and of the absurdity that 'for this wretched country millions of Englishmen and Germans were to lay down their lives'.

Dahlerus passed the gist of this interview on to Alexander Cadogan in London. He always did his best to moderate Hitler's language and to put the best possible interpretation on his ideas. Even so Cadogan noted that what Hitler planned was not an 'asylum' but 'settlement of the Jewish question by using Poland as a sink in which to empty the Jews' – an unattractive idea which makes all the more strange Cadogan's reaction to this and other points in the Nazi 'peace plan': 'All of this, or some of it, may be very nice, but we cannot trust the word or the assurance or the signature of the present rulers of Germany.'[97]

However equivocal was Cadogan's attitude to Nazi treatment of the Poles and Jews, there was in the event no chance of Britain making peace at their allies' expense. Hitler was not going to resign simply to open the way to a peace conference. And what the Nazis planned was not an asylum but a condemned cell. Briefly they kept up the façade and went ahead with plans to 'resettle' Jews in Poland's south-eastern corner. A French Government report had second-hand information from a German official of the plan to create a 'reserve' where the Jewish population of Germany, Austria, the Protectorate and Poland would be concentrated: 'It consists of an area of 800 to 1,000 square kilometres south-east of Lublin. Its natural frontiers are, in the West, the San and the Vistula, and in the East the Russian frontier. The German Government will apparently soon produce a map on which this area will be marked with the name of Judaea.'[98] The Zionist leader Chaim Weizmann confirmed in October 'that the proposal for a Jewish State (or concentration camp) in the Lublin District was apparently to be taken seriously. Representatives of the Vienna Jewish community had already been sent to Lublin to investigate.'

Within a few weeks tens of thousands of Jews were dumped in the Lublin area by train. The first to go were the Jews from the Incorporated Territories, the plan being to 'purify' the new Germany of their presence, but soon Jews from Vienna, Prague and Germany itself were being deported, forced to walk from place to place carrying their few belongings before they could find somewhere to stay. The local people took them in and shared their meagre rations with them, until Lublin and the smaller towns teemed with Jews on the verge of starvation. In a few cases the deportees were provided with a site, tools and building materials, and told to construct living accommodation which, as soon as it was ready, the Nazis promptly surrounded with barbed wire. Many died but more were sent, and in 1941 it was in this area that it was thought most convenient to build the extermination camp of Majdanek. A few managed to escape across the frontier to the Soviet Union, but even then their troubles were not over. Coming from Germany they were the subject of suspicion, and in such

cases the NKVD took the view that it is better to be safe than
sorry, better to imprison than to allow a 'socially unreliable
element' to run loose. Most of those whom the NKVD did not
touch and who were allowed to stay in the Ukraine or Byelorussia
were caught in the German advance into Russia in the summer of
1941. Rare indeed was the Polish Jew who survived the Nazi
Occupation.

The non-Jewish Poles were a little better off, but not much, for
by Hitler's secret decree they too were destined for eventual
liquidation. In the beginning some effort was made to placate them
and dull their fears. On 1 September the German Commander-in-
Chief von Brauchitsch promised that 'all the rulings of international law will be observed'. On 26 October Hans Frank,
appointed Governor-General by Hitler's decree of 12 October,[99]
addressed the Polish people: 'You will be able to lead your own
lives according to your established traditions. You will be allowed
to keep your Polish national individuality in all activities . . .
Everyone willing to obey the just measures of our Reich, which will
be in full conformity with your habits of life, will be able to work
in peace.'[100] On 7 November he made a solemn entry into Cracow,
which was to replace Warsaw as the capital and addressed his
subordinates: 'We come into this country not in any wild fury of
conquest, but as guarantors of work, ordered and conducted in
German fashion.' He prayed God to put an end to all the Polish
hatred which for centuries had been directed against Germany
from the historic Wawel Castle where he was speaking.

Privately he noted in his diary: 'The Poles will be the slaves of
the German Reich.'[101] And to confirm this Franz Halder wrote
in *his* diary in quiet disapproval: 'A low standard of living must
be preserved. Cheap slaves . . . The Reich will give the Governor-
General the means to carry out this devilish plan.' Frank was a
remarkable example of the intellectual gangster, a brilliant lawyer
who was at the same time a devotee of the arts and a ruthless
killer. His empire was smaller than pre-war Poland. The eastern
half of the country now belonged to Russia and in the West a
broad strip of land – to include Danzig, Toruń (Thorn), Poznań
(Posen) and Katowice (Kattowitz) – was annexed to the Reich
outright. What was left was about 100,000 square kilometres and
about 12 million Poles, two or three million of whom were Jews

and none of whom could expect much mercy from the man Hitler had put in charge of them.

On 31 October, a few days after Hans Frank formally took Poland over from military rule, he proclaimed a decree 'on combating acts of violence in the Government General', which provided the death penalty for a whole list of offences : disobedience to the German authorities, damaging the property of a German, refusal to report anyone found committing any such offence or in possession of arms. Such offenders could be tried before special S S courts, and according to the decree it was necessary only to record the names of the accused, the judges and witnesses, and the dates of sentence and execution. No rules were laid down about conducting any investigation or about the prisoner's right to a defence. In practice the death sentence was pronounced without hearing the accused, and usually in his absence.[102]

On 21 October the occupation regime's Polish-language newspaper *Nowy Kurier Warszawski* began a series of announcements of death sentences imposed on Poles for such offences. Six days later the Mayor of Warsaw Stefan Starzyński, whose broadcasts had so inspired the people of Warsaw during the siege, was arrested and taken to the prison in Daniłowiczowska Street. On 23 December he was deported to Dachau concentration camp where he died on 17 November 1943. In Bromberg (Bydgoszcz) the Mayor Leon Barciszewski was one of a large number, Pobóg-Malinowski says it was 20,000,[103] shot as a reprisal for 'Bloody Sunday'.

A notice dated 3 November and posted in prominent places in Warsaw announced that a girl student called Elżbieta Zahorska had been sentenced to death for 'sabotage'. What she had actually done was to tear down a German propaganda poster, one famous at that time, which showed Chamberlain standing against a background of ruined Warsaw.[104] 'This is your work, England,' ran the caption. (It meant that, by encouraging Warsaw's defenders to resist, Britain had made herself responsible for the destruction.) On 16 November another notice showed that seven Poles had been shot, this time for such crimes as 'failure to surrender Army property' and 'refusal to perform a job'. Such events happened all over Poland in the first weeks of the occupation. In each town ten or twenty Poles were shot or hanged in public, sometimes for some real anti-German act but sometimes simply to warn the population in general what would happen if they were so unwise as to attempt any such thing.

Paragraph 6 of Frank's 31 October decree laid down that 'any man who incites a crime or acts as accomplice will be punished in the same way as the one who commits it'. A very broad interpretation of this formed the basis for the Nazi law of 'collective responsibility', whereby the community at large was held accountable for any crime committed by any of its members. An early example of this was when a Polish policeman in German service was killed by a Polish Jewish 'criminal' named Pinkus Zylberryng on 13 November. The residents of the building where the killing took place, in all fifty-three people, were arrested and shot.[105] Then on 27 December in the Warsaw suburb of Wawer two German NCOs were shot in a bar by two local Poles. The owner of the bar was hanged in the street outside it, and some 120 local men were arrested and shot, their only offence being that they happened to live near where the crime took place.[106]

There were not yet any extermination camps. Rome was not built in a day, and even to destroy takes time and planning. 'I could not eliminate all lice and Jews in one year,' confessed Frank to the amusement of his audience and subordinates on 7 October 1940.[107] But he was able to reassure them. 'In the course of time, and if you help me, this end will be attained.' Meanwhile Jews and Poles were required to get in the harvest, to tidy the country up after the war and to man the essential services. They received wages, though on a far lower scale than that of equivalent workers in Germany. The Poles did not need such high wages, it was explained. The cost of living there was lower, and anyway 'their requirements were not so great'.[108] For the moment they were allowed to live in the Polish *Heimstatte*, the 'reserve' that Hitler had assigned for their accommodation, and provided that they were submissive, of little education, and did not have the bad luck to be Jewish, to be taken as hostages or used as reprisals, they would be permitted to survive for several years.

In the 'Incorporated Territories' of western Poland there was a policy of swift germanization, and mass deportations from there to the Government General began during October in Gdynia and other towns of the former Corridor. Fleets of lorries would de-

Jeichnung: Heincke (nach R. Ströbel)

Das Weichselmündungsland
in den ersten Jahrhunderten unserer Zeit-
rechnung. Ptolemäus hat uns die Namen
der germanischen Stämme überliefert und
zahllose Bodenfunde ergaben die alten
Gaugrenzen in germanischer Zeit vor
2000 Jahren

Hitler's *Völkischer Beobachter* explains on 24 September 1939 why
Poland's new port of Gdynia can be renamed 'Gotenhafen'. The
German text reads, 'German settlements in the first centuries of our
era. Ptolemy gave us the names of German tribes and countless
archaeological finds show the old frontiers of German habitation 2,000
years ago.' (Copyright British Museum)

scend upon a place, the Poles would be given just a few minutes to
pack their things, then taken to trains and transported into central
Poland, where often they were dumped in the country at night
several miles from any habitation. From then on they had to fend
for themselves, relying on the sale of any valuables they had been
able to salvage, or on the charity of the local people. In six months
about 400,000 mainly middle-class Poles were thus torn from
their homes.[109]

The deportees had to leave behind most of their property, and
this of course was confiscated by the German State, then distributed to Germans from all over Europe: the Austrian Tyrol,
Hungary, Rumania, and especially the Baltic States from which
the entire German community was evacuated as part of the
Ribbentrop–Molotov Pact.[110] On 14 October the first shipload of
Germans left Riga (the capital of Latvia) for Gdynia, and in the
next weeks 4,000 Reich Germans and 55,000 Latvians of German

Map in *Völkischer Beobachter* (27 October 1939) showing the repatriation of Germans from the Baltic States. (Copyright British Museum)

origin were thus resettled.[111] They were not allowed to live in Germany proper, their function being to repopulate the conquered territories. Arthur Greiser, Gauleiter of the Posen (Poznań) area, said on 26 October 1940, the first anniversary of his appointment, 'In this area the German is the master, the Pole the menial . . . Polish elements must be kept at the greatest possible distance. We must put an end to all forms of sentimental soppiness, which is quite out of place.'[112]

With amazing speed these areas were stripped of all trace of their twenty years of Polish habitation. Place names were changed, Gdynia to Gotenhafen, Łódź to Litzmannstadt. Often a name had to be invented, for there was no previous German equivalent. Everywhere Polish emblems were removed, Polish libraries looted and the contents publicly burned. The Polish language was banned even in the churches, and those heard speaking it were sometimes arrested and subjected to public humiliation. Education for Poles stopped except for a few elementary schools where pupils were taught to read, write and count up to ten. Inscriptions in Polish were even erased from tombstones. The Poles who were not deported stayed as a cheap labour force, housed in barracks on low rations. Their only chance of a decent life was to achieve assimilation as German citizens on the basis of family background. Such is the mixture of nationalities in Central Europe that many Poles were able to do this, but some could not, and many others would not as a matter of principle, even in order to provide the necessities of life for themselves and their families.

In the Government General the Polish language was used and it was recognized that Poles had a right to a separate cultural existence. But it was to be 'culture' at its most debased and primitive. The policy was to ignore the taste of the educated Pole, for he was a danger to the Reich and due for swift elimination, and to cater only for that of a population of sub-humans. The rigour and detail with which this policy was worked out, the exactness with which it was applied are if anything more horrific than the pure animal cruelty of Dr Frank's regime. Barbarism is unpleasant enough to endure, but when it is combined with clever efficiency and the imagination of fanaticism it becomes the ultimate evil.

The Nazis' policy was to crush the Poles morally as well as physically. As part of their plan to 'behead' the nation, petty rules were introduced to stamp out all vestiges of an intellectual or middle class. For instance, no Pole was allowed to carry a stick or an attaché case, to wear a fur coat or a felt hat, to use a telephone box or make a long-distance call, to ride in a taxi, to take part in athletics or to have his teeth filled with gold. He could not enter a railway station waiting room, or a public park, or use a park bench. 'The street belongs to the victors, not to the vanquished,' read one notice posted on street corners, and whenever a Pole met a German in uniform, he was obliged to step off the pavement, take off his cap and bow as he went past.

Later on more sophisticated methods were used to try to soften the Polish character. While the price of food went up and up, the price of vodka was reduced, and sometimes workers would be paid in bottles rather than in money. Late in 1940 a gambling casino was opened in Warsaw. In any society, however harsh, there are a few who rise to the surface, and Poles with money to burn were allowed to play there late into the night, receiving special permission to break curfew. Erotic magazines were printed in large numbers, and these were all the more widely read since most serious books in Polish had been confiscated and none were now being printed.

In the spring of 1940 a circular was sent to German administrators outlining cultural policy, the enormity of which is illustrated by the following extracts:

It is a matter of course that no German Service office should advance Polish 'culture' in any way. On the other hand, there is today no longer any reason for entirely denying the Poles a certain cultural subsistence. The *Kreishauptmann* is to permit the Poles cultural activity in so far as it serves the primitive need of amusement and diversion . . . The appearance of German and Polish artists together is forbidden on principle. German artists may not act in front of Poles . . . Jews are not allowed to undertake any cultural activities . . . Operettas, revues and light comedy may be played by Polish actors in front of Poles . . . Presentation of serious drama or opera for Poles is forbidden . . . In programmes executed by Polish artists there is no objection to a lowering of standards or to an erotic flavour. Any production which portrays Polish national characteristics is forbidden . . . Care will be taken that only shallow novels for amusement, short stories and suchlike should be passed . . .[113]

The Warsaw press had somehow kept itself alive during the siege, in spite of the destruction of many editorial offices and the eventual breakdown of the electricity supply on 23 September. The Polish Press House (the Dom Prasy Polskiej) had its own generator, and a few newspapers made use of it, turning out frequent small editions full of latest news bulletins. Distribution was of course impossible and would have been useless, since the streets were all but deserted. All the editors could really do was to paste each edition as it was printed outside their offices and in a few other prominent places.

On 27 September it became clear that Warsaw was about to surrender. The leading journalists decided to pool their resources and publish a news-sheet to be called *Joint Newspaper* (*Gazeta Wspólna*). For more than a week this was printed on a hand press in editions of about 1,000. The issue of 2 October carried the following appeal: 'Destruction and misery are boundless. We have not the elementary necessities of life. There is hunger . . . The whole strength of Poland must be alive to master these. We must show an unbreakable will, enduring effort, stubborn perseverance and patience. These are the needs of the immediate future.' Care was taken not to provoke the German military authorities who were busy consolidating their control of the city.

On 7 October electricity was partially restored and the presses could run. For two days several newspapers were able to appear in editions of about 10,000. But on 9 October the editors were told that their activities must cease at once, since the German authorities planned to set up their own press. Newspaper offices were searched, presses sealed and a few journalists detained for questioning. On 11 October the first edition appeared of the *New Warsaw Courier* (*Nowy Kurier Warszawski*), which was got up to look like a continuation of the old *Warsaw Courier*, founded in 1821. The first page carried a picture of Hitler reviewing German troops in Warsaw, and quoted with approval parts of George Bernard Shaw's notorious 7 October article in the London *New Statesman*, which is quoted in the following chapter.

This newspaper was published in Polish six times a week throughout most of the occupation, and for want of a better was widely read. Its contents were of course carefully controlled to serve the interest of German propaganda, to make the Poles resigned to their lot as underdog and content to work dutifully for their masters. It poured particular scorn on the 'intellectual clique' which had ruled Poland before September 1939, and which was responsible for the war and Poland's defeat. The aim was to drive a wedge between the intelligentsia and the working people. Also attacked were those who still harboured hopes of an Allied victory and of the restoration of Polish independence.

Its leading articles tried to convince the Poles that they were really much better off under German rule, that they should be grateful to the Nazis for bringing discipline and efficiency and for graciously consenting to put the Polish house in order. 'We understand perfectly well,' ran one leader, 'that any Polish Government of any kind will be influenced by world politics and therefore under Jewish influence. This means that it would have to tolerate the supremacy of Jews. We prefer to share our fate with you [Germans] and without Jews, rather than to have an illusion of independence linked to overwhelming Jewish influence. We prefer to live joined to an equal partner, to the German, for we should try to get rid of our many national defects and come to resemble you. We should learn to respect the law and acquire the many useful characteristics of your people.'[114]

On 12 November two German-language newspapers began to

appear for the benefit of the new German population. In his first leading article, headed 'Our Task', the editor of *Krakauer Zeitung* explained that the war had been caused by

> the arrogant megalomania and crazy blindness of a clique of [Polish] intellectuals . . . a war accompanied by the most bestial cruelties and inhuman atrocities against local German civilians and soldiers of our Reich . . . Under these conditions there can of course be no question of any sentimental fraternization with a people capable of such crimes . . . The German is only too prone to let sentimental mildness take the place of unrelenting severity. To all those who run the risk of becoming soft our paper is to be a constant and impressive admonition.

The editor pointed out: 'Only German interests exist for us. We have not come to clean out the Poles' pigsty for them.'

It was only in this matter that the German-controlled press differed in emphasis, whether it was Germany's task to restore order to Poland and to look after her 'inferior' people in the most humane way compatible with Germany's vital interest, or whether the policy was to use the Poles as beasts of burden, to tame them from their wild state, to put them to work, feeding them only as much as would keep them tolerably efficient, until they were no further use to Nazi Germany and could be destroyed.

The press in Poland had two tasks, one of which was in conflict with the other. The German readership had to be spurred on to greater efforts in controlling the Poles and extracting the largest amount of work possible from them. Human beings are accustomed to treating one another with sympathy, so the Nazi authorities were afraid of their subordinates treating the Poles thus. They felt the need to inspire their men with the spirit of the New Order, the brutality of Hitlerism. On the other hand the Poles had to be pacified and to some extent reassured, for it was rightly assumed that they would not take vicious treatment lying down. To lull them into a sense of security was clearly impossible as starvation mounted and more and more were arrested and shot. But the Nazis believed that the Poles were degenerate and would in a few months resign themselves to the hopelessness of their situation. After all, it was in their interest to be subservient, for the longer they made themselves useful to their masters, the longer they would be allowed to live.

It was here that the Nazis badly miscalculated, for the Poles never despaired. As they endured the first weeks of those five terrible years, the humiliations, restrictions and fears, the closing of their schools and universities, the uprootings, deportations and public executions, they kept themselves going with exaggerated estimates of the strength of the Allies, of their own Polish Army now reconstituting itself in France, of the British Fleet busy blockading Germany and starving her of essential supplies, of the French Army about to fling itself through the Siegfried Line and on to Berlin. They were convinced that sooner or later someone would save them.

On 18 October Lord Chatfield broadcast to Poland a message that can have given little reassurance: 'You shook the morale of the Germans by forcing them to realize that their infantry could not advance without tank support against your defensive positions.'[115] Any Pole who fought knew that the German Army had not *tried* to advance without tank support. Tanks had been the reason for the Germans' lightning success. And as for German morale, it was in a state of victorious euphoria. The Allied war effort, Chatfield went on, 'was none the less solid for being relatively unobtrusive'. Well, that was one way of putting it, but luckily for the Poles they still did not know the full extent of British and French military unobtrusiveness or its almost total ineffectiveness. If they had their morale really would have suffered. Four days later Dr Otto, the Reichskommissar for Warsaw, decreed that all radio sets should be handed in within ten days. It was a blow for the Poles, but at least they would no longer have to endure such naive and patronizing propaganda from the Allies who had done so little to save them from their predicament.

The Polish optimism, both before and after the defeat, was of course unjustified in the short term. They did not apparently foresee what they were about to endure, and how could they? It was beyond the bounds of imagination. But in one respect they did sense correctly. Poles who lived through these weeks have told the author how unshakeable was their conviction that Hitler's Reich could not possibly last, that it contained within itself the germ of its own destruction. Hitler was a cyclist racing along a narrow path, a cliff-edge in front, a chasm on either side. To halt was impossible, for in that case the result would be not stability but collapse. He had to go on, faster and faster, with conquest after conquest needed to keep the movement alive, for without this it would be like a plant deprived of its natural manure. What would destroy him was the likelihood that as soon as he became too great the rest of the world would finally weave itself into an alliance against him. Enemy would sit down with enemy out of sheer desperation to preserve themselves from the all-devouring Hitler.

It was this thought that enabled the Poles to remain a nation in spite of the crushing defeat of September, 1939, and to survive the cruelty of the Nazi occupation.

5 Exchanges of Harsh Words

On 3 September a Polish communiqué announced: 'This morning Polish aeroplanes destroyed two out of three motorized columns near Częstochowa in Silesia, the Polish losses being five aeroplanes.'[1] In fact the Germans had by that evening captured Częstochowa and forced the Poles to withdraw many miles to the north-west. On 4 September there were mass executions in the town – an early indication of what Poland was to suffer for the next five years.

'Polish cavalry counter-attacked in the sector Rawicz-Leszno on the Poznanian front and drove the enemy into Germany and are hotly pursuing them,' the communiqué went on, but this is not confirmed by subsequent Polish histories of the war. Another 3 September communiqué claimed that sixty-four German aircraft were shot down during 2 September, while the Poles lost only eleven machines. A German communiqué of the same day claimed that the Luftwaffe had lost only twenty-one machines during 1 and 2 September, while they had destroyed 120 Polish machines. One expects both sides to exaggerate at the beginning of a war, but in this case there was little need for the Germans to do so. They won control of the air so quickly that propaganda was superfluous.

But at this stage the British were relying on propaganda. On 4 September *The Times* announced proudly that six million leaflets had been dropped on Germany the previous night, and another three million were dropped during the night of 4–5 September. 'On this and the previous occasion all our aircraft returned safely,'[2] it was announced falsely, for Newall revealed to the Cabinet at 11.30 a.m. on 4 September that one aircraft was missing.[3] These nine Whitley bombers, Newall went on, 'had encountered no fighters and only ineffective anti-aircraft fire', which again conflicts with a statement in *The Times* (7 September) that the flights 'have been absolutely unopposed'.

Not knowing the circumstances of Gamelin's request for air action, Newall told the Cabinet of his concern:

He was opposed to any such action at a time when the French Army was not undertaking active operations. It was important to conserve the resources of the Air Striking Force so that it would be ready to meet any emergency, such as heavy air attack on this country, or an attempted break-through in France . . . the French should be assured that we were more than willing to cooperate with our air forces in the co-ordinated plan, but that we did not propose to undertake sporadic bombing which would lead to no permanent military result, but would cause unnecessary loss of aircraft. The French should be asked to conform and not to employ their air force in the manner which they had suggested to Chief of Air Staff until a plan had been agreed.

To agree this plan Newall and Ironside arranged to fly that afternoon from Hendon to Le Bourget (Paris) and to visit Gamelin in his war room at Vincennes. Ironside had informed the Cabinet of 'his personal view that the crushing of Poland by Germany in a few weeks was most improbable'.

Churchill too urged the Cabinet to take urgent steps to relieve the pressure on Poland: 'This could be done by operations against the Siegfried Line, which was at present thinly held. The burden of such operations would fall on the French Army and our air force.' But by the time he came to write his memoirs Churchill had changed his mind:

A French offensive from their eastern frontier would have denuded their far more vital northern front. Even if an initial success had been gained by the French armies at the outset, within a month they would have had extreme difficulty in maintaining their conquests in the east and would have been exposed to the whole force of the German counter-stroke in the north. This is the answer to the question, 'Why remain passive till Poland was destroyed?'[4]

John Slessor, who was present at the meeting in Vincennes, describes Newall as 'a great fisherman and an erstwhile whipper-in to the Quetta and Peshawar Vale hounds . . . when times were at their worst I would come out of his office feeling as though I had just had a stiff whisky and soda'.[5] He describes Ironside as 'huge and burly, an excellent man for African adventure and for a job like the command of North Russia in 1919, but with an apparent self-confidence in himself as CIGS which later turned out to be unjustified'.[6] Gamelin's 'little army brains trust' was a room bright with Moroccan furnishings with a huge map of the western front along one wall. Slessor 'could not help liking old Gamelin and feeling immensely sorry for him. I remember in particular being fascinated by his enormous detachable metal plaque of multi-coloured medal ribbons . . . He was a nice old gentleman, not remotely equal to his enormous job.'[7] Ironside calls him 'a small, dapper little man with dyed hair'.[8]

French troops had gone into action at 5 a.m. that morning, twelve hours after the declaration of war. The first war communiqué announced, 'Operations have been begun by the whole of the land, sea and air forces.' It sounded grand, but it meant little for Gamelin was still slowly but surely mobilizing his army and dragging his artillery towards the front line. It would be two weeks before it was in position, a fact which moved Gamelin to write in his memoirs, 'We could not undertake to breach the Siegfried Line until the twentieth day, beginning 20 September at the earliest.'[9] This was unfortunate in view of his promise to the Poles to mount a major offensive by 16 September, and one wonders whether he really had to move with *quite* such plodding method.

Gamelin shared the British view that the only real way of helping Poland was by defeating Germany in the war, and not necessarily by relieving the pressure of the initial invasion. 'The war will be a long one,' he explained to the two Englishmen: 'Poland will have to survive terrible defeats. But she will rise again just as Belgium, Serbia, Czechoslovakia and Poland appeared or reappeared after our last victory. Whatever happens, it is essential that the Great Britain, France, North Africa group remain an untouchable bloc . . . It would serve no purpose, rather the contrary, if we were to "break our tools" in initial battles, insufficiently prepared or too hastily conducted.'[10] Gamelin told Ironside of his plan to advance immediately into the no-man's-land between the Maginot and Siegfried lines. He would have his men and artillery in position facing the German line by about 17 September, after which he would 'lean against' the line to test its strength. 'All very steady and calm,' Ironside noted.[11] 'It's an experiment — isn't that right? — an experiment,' Slessor remembers Gamelin saying. ('*C'est une essai — n'est-ce pas? — une essai.*') Slessor got the impression that he 'looked on this offensive as little more than a gesture'.[12]

After this it was no surprise to the Englishmen when Gamelin refrained from pressing his request for British air action. 'French politicians were urging their generals to make some empty gesture which would be strategically unsound, without helping the Poles in any real way,' Slessor writes. It was this pressure that had forced Gamelin to send his 3 September message. Slessor did feel, though, that his air force should 'do something, if only as a gesture, to sustain their [the Poles'] morale and "show willing".'[13] In other words, he wanted a gesture but not an empty gesture, an attack on something vital to the German war effort just to show that Britain meant business. After all, it was already decided that in the short term the only help Britain could afford Poland was in the air. If Britain did nothing in the air, Hitler could be forgiven for concluding that Britain's declaration of war was a sham.

It transpired that Gamelin was against any sort of air attack. His argument was the one he had used since 1 September to delay France's entry into the war: he wanted to complete his concentrations. This showed his purist, defensive approach to the problem, and is hard to justify in the light of what Poland was presently suffering and of the temporary German weakness on the western front. More reasonable was Gamelin's concern for the cities and factories of France, which were badly equipped with anti-aircraft defence. Slessor was not impressed 'by the one, solitary rather dejected-looking balloon swaying at the end of a not-very-long cable which we had passed on our way from Le Bourget to Vincennes — we having left Hendon with a respectable forest of balloons gleaming in the September sunshine over London'. Nor did he think much of the Paris black-out, which he called a 'washy-blue dim-out'.

Both sides were relieved by the other's reluctance to act, and both Gamelin and Slessor in their subsequent accounts of the talks blame the other side for the joint decision. It was just as well that Gamelin took this view, because the British air policy had already been decided in London. If Gamelin had either wished or been persuaded to persist in his request for British action, there would have been another serious *impasse* in relations between the Allies. 'I hope myself we shall not start to bomb their [the Germans'] munition centres and objectives in towns, unless they begin it,' Chamberlain wrote to his sister on 10 September.[14] Even if the French had demanded it, and even if the Chiefs of Staff had recommended it, Chamberlain would have opposed strongly any British air attack which put German civilians at risk.

His justification – that the Germans had not yet begun it – was however false in that it ignored what had been happening since 1 September in Poland. From the beginning the Luftwaffe had bombed military objectives in Polish towns and one might have thought that as Poland's ally Chamberlain was entitled, indeed obliged, to retaliate in kind. The Luftwaffe was also terror-bombing Polish open towns, residential areas, non-military transport and refugees on foot. This, in spite of eye-witness evidence, the British were still refusing to accept. But even on the basis of what the British did accept there was every justification for British bombing of German military objectives.

Both policy and practicality determined that in these early days air action was the only string to the British bow, so it is worth investigating in detail how this important decision was arrived at. On 31 August a report had been submitted to the Cabinet envisaging two possibilities: that Germany would launch unrestricted air action from the outset of hostilities, and that she would confine her attacks to military objectives.[15] In the second instance it was proposed, rather illogically, to 'launch an attack on the German fleet at Wilhelmshaven unless we have certain information that it is not there', also to attack warships at sea, to drop propaganda at night and 'conserve our resources'.[16] This was approved by the War Cabinet at its first meeting on 3 September.

At 11 p.m. on 2 September, in spite of several reports from Kennard as well as from Polish sources that the German air force was bombing and shooting at everything in sight, Halifax telegraphed him, 'In the meantime it is accepted Germans are attacking only military objectives.' Immediately war was declared, therefore, the second instance became operative and the bombers were sent over Germany with their bundles of leaflets. British intelligence reported that six of Germany's most important ships were in Wilhelmshaven: the *Scharnhorst*, *Gneisenau*, *Deutschland*, *Scheer*, *Emden* and *Graf Spee*. The RAF had failed to find them on 3 September, but at about 6 p.m. on 4 September two squadrons of Wellingtons and two of Blenheims, twenty-nine aircraft in all, attacked them in the open roadsteads of the bases, attacks on the dockyards themselves being forbidden by the code. The Wellingtons attacked first. One aircraft aimed bombs at the *Scharnhorst* and *Gneisenau* but missed. The Blenheims then attacked the cruiser *Emden* and caused her superficial damage with splinters of two bombs that exploded near her, one against a lock by the entrance to the Kiel Canal.[17] Two 500-pound bombs hit the pocket battleship *Scheer* but they did not explode, being dropped from too low a height to work off the safety device on the fuses.

The British Cabinet was told merely that the bombs had hit, which was misleading but probably not intentionally so, since then no one could know for sure what happened to the bombs.[18] But the communiqué issued by the newly founded Ministry of Information that evening was a gross concoction of half-truths and false impressions. Of the attack on the *Scheer* it was announced that 'several direct hits with heavy bombs were registered . . . which resulted in severe damage'. In fact there were only the two hits, and the unexploded bombs put the *Scheer* out of action only until 10 October. The statement went on to call the cruiser *Emden* a battleship and to claim that it too had suffered 'heavy damage'.[19] In fact it took the Germans only twelve days to repair the *Emden* completely.[20] The statement declared that the attack was 'successful', although 'some casualties' were suffered, whereas it was by any standard a failure. Captain Roskill, the official British historian, wrote in 1954 that 'the results achieved were not commensurate with the losses suffered'.

Goebbels's propaganda machine was at pains to deny the British claims and to discredit the Ministry of Information, which it called from then on 'The World Lies Centre' (*Weltluegenzentral*). One must admit that in this particular instance Goebbels had a point. His counter-communiqué claimed that five British aeroplanes were shot down by anti-aircraft fire, and that part of the damage to the *Emden* was caused by an aircraft which crashed into her.[21] Roskill confirms that this was in fact the case, and indeed the Cabinet was told that *seven* British aircraft had failed to return – one machine in four – a higher number even than the German claim.

The British public and Britain's allies were reassured to hear that the Royal Air Force had gone into action. Raczyński, the Polish Ambassador, told Churchill he was relieved to read of the attack on the German fleet 'and to learn that the spell of "all quiet on the western front" is broken at last', but he also passed on a request for R A F attacks on German aerodromes and industrial areas. Shirer noted that it was in these areas that the Germans made the bombs and shells that were so effectively devastating Poland. He asked himself some of the questions that the German people were asking: 'The British, it is true, sent over twenty-five 'planes to bomb Wilhelmshaven. But if it is war, why only twenty-five? . . . not a bomb has fallen on a Rhineland factory. "Is that war?" they ask.'[22] In 1962 the Polish leader Władysław Gomułka declared in an important speech: 'During September 1939 not one single bomb was dropped [on Germany]. The intention was quite transparent. Hitler was to march across the corpse of Poland towards the East, against the Soviet Union.'[23] Gomułka was wrong, both about the bomb and about the intention, and the figures he quotes about French, British and German strength on the western front are mistaken, but his statement that 'the great strength of Britain and France watched in stoical silence while Poland perished under the Nazi blows' is quite true.

Most of the world's strategists saw the British 4 September bombing as a puny, half-hearted effort, small indication of Allied resolution to win the war. But to Chamberlain it was a horrible personal experience. He wrote to the Archbishop of Canterbury on 5 September: 'I simply cannot bear to think of those gallant fellows who lost their lives last night in the R A F attack, and of their families who have first been called upon to pay the price. Indeed I must put such thought out of my mind if I am not to be unnerved altogether.'[24] The thought that he had sent these few men to their deaths tormented him. One is tempted to wonder though whether his feeling was a noble compassion or merely a self-indulgence of grief. It was certainly inconsistent, for it seems that it did not extend to the many thousands who had already died in Poland, fighting for their country on the basis of a guarantee offered by Chamberlain himself in March. His humanity and hatred of war, feelings which in the 1970s it is difficult to criticize, were quite out of place in September 1939 and selective to the point of hypocrisy. He almost admitted this himself, for he wrote to his sister on 10 September, 'While war was still averted, I felt I was indispensable, for no one else could take my place . . .',[25] and again six weeks later, 'I was never meant to be a war minister.' His biographer Iain Macleod states baldly, 'He should have resigned on the outbreak of war.'[26] And indeed he should, for in war especially a leader's feelings are infectious. The warriors who were later to be inspired by Churchill were dominated in 1939 by Chamberlain's defensive approach, which for years had trickled corrosively down the chain of command.

The British air raids had failed and were discontinued. On 4 September advance parties of the British Expeditionary Force, which was to form the army in France, sailed from Portsmouth to Cherbourg in destroyers. The British wanted to transport their men across the shortest part of the Channel to Calais, Boulogne and Dieppe, but the French feared air attack and diverted the British to ports in eastern France – Cherbourg, Nantes and Saint Nazaire. It was doubtless a good safety-first policy, but it meant a far longer journey from England to the western front. In these first days of war the only British soldiers in action were the couple of dozen members of the Military Mission to Poland.

Carton de Wiart and his deputy Colin Gubbins were invited on 4 September for talks with the Polish munitions chief General Rayski, and told that German air action had already put most of her armaments industry out of action.[27] He might have added that part of it, around Katowice in Poland's south-west corner, was already in German hands, and quite undamaged, plans to sabotage it before withdrawal having been forestalled by local Germans. Clare Hollingworth writes that in one such factory the workers prevented destruction by means of a sit-down strike. 'Invasion is simplified when one has such good friends in the country invaded,' she wrote.[23] Rayski gave the Englishmen a long list of immediate requirements, but neither he nor the other senior Polish officers they saw would give much information about the state of the war, perhaps because they did not know too much about it themselves. Some of the British officers wanted to 'inspect the front', but this was not allowed either, perhaps because there was no front.

Captain 'Tommy' Davies, a junior officer with the mission, was almost immediately ordered to make his way back to London with documents and reports, some composed by de Wiart and Gubbins, others by Marshal Rydz-Śmigły. He travelled alone northeastwards to the border with Lithuania, then through Lithuania to Riga, the capital of Latvia. Davies arrived at the British Legation clutching his vital papers to be told that the Minister, Charles Orde, was unable to see him. Orde dined in his dinner jacket, as was his wont, received Davies at 10.30 p.m. and told him that his position as a serving officer of a belligerent nation in a neutral country was contrary to international law, and that he ought to be interned. Davies protested that he had important dispatches for London, to which Orde replied that as an accredited diplomat it would be most improper for him to have anything to do with 'spy material'. Davies asked Orde for a bed for the night, which Orde refused. Davies did what his superior officers had done more than once during the journey from England to Poland, and had recourse to the Polish Legation, whose Minister J. Kłopotowski was only too pleased to put Davies up and to help him find transport, an aeroplane to Stockholm from which he was able to fly to London quite easily. Only later did Davies learn that Orde had telegraphed Edmund Monson, the British Minister in Stockholm, to warn him that a British subject was arriving with 'spy documents'. The telegram was sent *en clair* and it was lucky for Davies no Latvian or Swedish counter-espionage official happened to pick it up.

Davies was able to provide London with its first eye-witness account of the German onslaught. He had actually stood on the roof of the British Embassy in Warsaw and watched the German aeroplanes circling and diving, bombing and strafing. During debriefing sessions he delivered an impassioned plea for aid to the Poles, but he soon realized that his words were falling on deaf ears and that his requests were an embarrassment. The only man in London with an eye-witness account of what had happened, he may well have expected his superiors to show some interest in his tale. If so he was disappointed. He had not appreciated that the Polish campaign was foreseen by the Allied planners merely as an incident in a war which would last several years.

This is not to say that the British and French were unwilling to provide Poland with supplies, so long as it helped the general war effort. But how could such material be delivered? Poland's corridor to the sea was cut off, and anyway the Baltic was dominated by the German Navy — the only part of the high seas which was. Her airfields were bombed and, if not unusable, at best a risky landing-ground, especially as the pilot would have to fly hundreds of miles from France over unfriendly territory. The only way to reach Poland now would be overland through a neutral country. Of these Lithuania was too weak and too close to East Prussia, while Hungary had definite links with Germany and was under pressure to provide *her* with transit facilities.[29]

The only countries which might help were Rumania and the Soviet Union. The S.S. *Lassell* was on its way to Constanza, Rumania's main port, with such supplies: fifteen modern fighters (fourteen Hurricanes and one Spitfire), seven bombers, 6,000 tons of bombs, 112 Browning machine guns for fighters, 2,750,000 rounds of ammunition.[30] A railway, part of it single track, joined Constanza with Cernauti on the Polish border and Stanisławów in Poland. But it was a long way round from England or France, and the *Lassell* was only one ship. Two others, the S.S. *Clan Menzies* and S.S. *Robur VIII*, were not due to leave England until 17·and 20 September.

During May there had been talks between senior French and Polish officers on what help France could afford in the event of German attack, and on 25–6 May General Mendigal for France and Lt.-Col. Karpiński for Poland had discussed air policy and agreed a plan to send three squadrons of Amiot 143s to Poland.[31] But the sudden success of the German air onslaught, together with the sixty-hour delay in declaring war, had scotched the idea. Gamelin writes that the speed of the German advance into Poland made it impossible to deliver the aircraft. The confusion and lack of communication were such that the French never knew what territory was or was not occupied. The Amiot 143 aircraft had a limited range, so that airfields in *western* Poland were needed. But naturally these were the first to be hit and overrun. All of this led Gamelin to pat himself on the back. 'How right I was,' he wrote, 'during our talks with the Polish War Minister in May to limit as far as possible the promises we made regarding air support.'[32]

The idea of transit through the Soviet Union at first seemed promising. On 1 September Sharonov, the Soviet Ambassador in Warsaw, asked Beck why Poland had not requested from Russia deliveries of military and raw materials, pointing to Voroshilov's statement in a press conference on 26 August that such supplies would be purely a matter of trade and quite separate from any pact or convention.[33] Kennard reported this in the small hours of 2 September with the comment, 'What may be behind this suggestion I cannot of course judge.'[34] Nor can we, even thirty years later. Probably Sharonov was not yet informed of the intentions of his government. Another theory is that the Russians were frightened the Poles might cave in without a fight, so they wanted to give them some encouragement.[35] But Stalin knew the Poles. It is unlikely that he or his government would conceive such an idea. Soviet cooperation would have been valuable to Poland in these early days, since it was becoming more and more doubtful whether Rumania, in spite of her pact with Poland, would be able to allow transit. Rumania was full of German agents and diplomatic pressure on her was increasing every day. Odessa is 200 miles up the Black Sea from Constanza and would have been a safer delivery point for Allied supplies.

But when Grzybowski, the Polish Ambassador in Moscow, followed up Sharonov's suggestion with Molotov, he was met with a blank refusal. The whole situation had changed, Molotov said, as a result of British and French entry into the war.[36] 'Poland has now become for us a synonym for England,' he explained, and Voroshilov could not have foreseen this development when he said what he did. The transit of war materials would now be contrary to the German–Soviet pact. A threat to this pact was a threat to the Soviet Union's security and therefore could not be permitted.

With both Britain and France unwilling to bomb Germany, and with supplies to Poland becoming more and more difficult to deliver, the question remained of what could be done on land. The feasibility of a large-scale French attack against the German

West Wall has been much discussed and is one of the great 'might have beens' of history. Wildly various estimates of German strength, or rather weakness, on the western front have been adduced in support of the argument that with a little daring and initiative the Allies could have won in September 1939. German generals, anxious to minimize the part they played in Hitler's conquests as well as to justify themselves professionally for having lost the war, have been at pains to emphasize how impracticable and irresponsible were Hitler's orders. Their distorted guesses have been seized on by Polish historians, anxious to show how blatantly and needlessly the British and French betrayed them, as well as by Soviet historians, determined to prove their silly theory, expounded in their official history of the war, that Hitler invaded Poland 'with the clear connivance of the British and French governments'.[37]

General Hans Jodl, Chief of Wehrmacht Operations, said in evidence at Nuremburg that 'if in 1939 we were not defeated, it was only because about 110 French and English divisions, which during our war against Poland faced twenty-three divisions in the West, remained completely inactive'.[38] This statement, often quoted in Soviet and Polish histories, is a distortion on two counts. Firstly, there were not twenty-three but thirty-three German divisions in the West on 3 September.[39] Secondly, although the French army consisted of 110 divisions, mobilization had been ordered only on 1 September and it was several weeks before all these were ready. Also ten of the French divisions were deployed along the border with Italy — a necessary precaution since Italian neutrality, while promised by Rome, had been unexpected and could not be relied upon to last. Another fifteen were manning the French possessions in North Africa. This left eighty-five divisions to face Germany, but of these only forty were to man the hundred-mile front with Germany.[40] The rest would defend the borders with Belgium and Luxemburg, and here they would have no Maginot Line to help them, though equally if the French were to *attack* through Belgium there would be no Siegfried Line.

Various figures have been quoted for German strength on the western front. Firstly, there is the doubt about what is a division. A unit of the Home Guard (Landwehr) or of the reserve might contain the same number of men as a unit of the regular army, but its usefulness as a fighting force would be much less. Also after the first week of war reinforcements began to arrive from the East, freed for action elsewhere by the rapid successes in Poland. The British official historian, who had access to all the papers, says categorically that there were thirty-three German divisions in the West on 3 September, and this is borne out by General Westphal, who puts the force at eight top-class divisions and twenty-five of lower quality.[41] British intelligence at the time underestimated the strength, putting it at twenty-four divisions on 7 September,[42] while French intelligence reported an almost exactly similar overestimate: forty-three divisions on 9 September.[43] Political considerations may have played a part in arriving at these figures, which appear to be the result of guesswork rather than of informed analysis. The French were naturally anxious to justify to themselves and to their allies their contention that a major land offensive during September was impossible.

Similarly the British, expected by her French and Polish allies to bear the brunt of the battle in the air, overestimated German air strength, somehow arriving at a figure of 1,750 long-range bombers,[44] when in fact there were only 1,200 in existence and 1,000 serviceable.[45] In all, the British estimated, Germany possessed 4,320 first-line aircraft as well as 1,000 troop transport aircraft. The true figures were 3,600 first-line aircraft and 550 transport aircraft.[46] 'The reserves of modern aircraft behind the first-line units are estimated at 100 per cent,' the British report went on. This was another serious exaggeration. The position during the early days of September was that 2,600 of Germany's first-line machines were engaged in Poland, leaving 1,000 in the West to face a combined British and French force of 3,195 first-line aircraft, including 2,241 bombers and fighters.

On the western front there was hardly a single German tank, all the Panzer units being needed for the assault on Poland.[47] The French had 3,286 tanks, a few hundred of which were obsolete,[48] and 1,600 guns against 300 German.[49] In fact it is indisputable that during the early days of September France had an impressive superiority both of men and of equipment on its front with Germany. Several German generals – Keitel. Westphal, Manstein, Jodl and Witzleben – have written and spoken of their amazement that France did not take advantage of this brief but vital opportunity. Hans Gisevius has written that Hitler's September victory was nothing but gambler's luck.[50] Jon Kimche has written that a massive Allied counter-offensive 'was possible and would almost certainly have been successful'.[51]

But this is to over-simplify an argument which decades after the event can never be exactly solved, depending as it does on so many imponderables. What is certain is that the Allies would have had to attack within a week from the outbreak of war in order to catch Germany with a serious war on two fronts as well as to forestall the reinforcement of the West. Could this have been done in the available time? Gamelin clearly thought not, and so on sober reflection did Churchill. It is true, as Kimche points out, that Gamelin began to assemble his forces before the actual day of mobilization, 1 September, but to what extent? Gamelin told Hore-Belisha on 21 August that he had recalled men from leave, ordered units in camp back to their garrisons and called up about 55,000.[52] But 55,000 is a flea-bite in terms of world war. On the evidence of a book by Ulrich Liss, Chief of German intelligence on the Western front,[53] Kimche concludes that 72 of metropolitan France's 100 divisions were mobilized by 26 August and in position by 7 September.[54] If this is true, then indeed France could have done something significant. An assault on one section of the Siegfried Line perhaps? In September it was by no means complete and at Nuremburg Jodl was to claim that it was 'little better than a large building site'.[55] Westphal called it 'a Potemkin village',[56] an impressive façade. But to mount such an offensive a day or two after the outbreak of war was beyond France's power, given the defensive approach of Gamelin and his political masters. Had there been a plan for such an onslaught ready for execution as soon as Hitler went east, then perhaps France could have breached the West Wall. As it was Gamelin spent the crucial days dragging up his guns and digging in his men.

The French Army could also perhaps have attacked Germany through Luxemburg and southern Belgium, thus outflanking the Siegried Line. The problem was that this would have meant violating Belgian neutrality. Of course as the war progressed country after country was to have its neutrality violated. Was it then so unthinkable for the Allies to move their armies through Belgium in 1939? Churchill apparently thought so, for he writes,

'An advance through Belgium without Belgian consent was excluded on grounds of international morality.'[57] One is surprised at his fine feelings on the subject at a moment when his enemy was violating every moral rule in the book. Nor did Churchill later on show himself averse to the British invasions of Iceland (10 May 1940), Syria (May 1941) and Iran (25 August 1941). Here was a chance to get at a thinly defended part of the German frontier, within easy striking distance of the Ruhr, Germany's industrial region and Achilles' heel. But the Belgians were enforcing a policy of strict neutrality, refusing even to form contingency plans with the Allies for a German invasion of their country, or to allow Allied officers to reconnoitre. In Cabinet on 12 September Churchill with his usual ebullience declared the Belgian attitude 'indefensible', adding that 'the Belgians owed everything to us, and their retention of their colonial empire would entirely depend on our victory'. The Belgian Government was believed to favour the Allies, but they were opposed by King Leopold who was, if not pro-Nazi, at least appreciative of German military strength and unwilling to antagonize Hitler. As Churchill points out, if British and French policy had been of a manly and resolute character, Belgium might perhaps have remained true to the old alliance of the First World War. But like Rumania she was more frightened of the Nazis than of the Allies, and therefore anxious to listen to the German side of the argument.

Churchill's moral objection to a move through Belgium was inadequate, but there were more cogent, practical reasons against such an act: the possibility of Belgian resistance, the effect on neutral countries and particularly on American public opinion. Most important of all, the bureaucracy would not allow it. The war had not been unexpected, and thousands of civil servants in London and Paris had spent months working out policies and contingency plans which precluded any great offensive either on land or in the air, foreseeing rather a war of attrition which would force Germany into economic difficulty, diplomatic isolation and internal collapse. The British and French leaders were not of any great strength, and they could not overturn months of planning on the basis of some sudden inspiration.

Had the Allied armed forces been controlled by a man of Hitler's calibre, who can say what might have been accomplished on or around 9 September? What if the cream of France's armoured units had been ordered to *Blitzkrieg* its way through Belgium and into the Ruhr, supported by the combined British and French air forces? The German forces along their frontier with Belgium were weak. Would they not have collapsed at the sudden appearance of the French tanks, leaving them a clear run to Dusseldorf and Essen? Softened up by the air raids and generally unenthusiastic for the war, would the German population of this area not have panicked and surrendered? And would this sudden stroke not have tipped the scale with the German General Staff? Might they not have arrested their Führer and sued for a just peace? Stunned by the shock of near disaster, Europe would have pulled itself together, agreeing fair frontiers and perhaps certain redistributions of population. The war would have been over in a week, and how many people would have been saved from death? Six million Poles (including 5,500,000 civilians), 397,000 Frenchmen (including 152,000 civilians), 520,000 Americans, 3,800,000 Germans (including 800,000 civilians), 463,000 Britons (including 60,000 civilians). These figures are quite accurate.[58] But how many Russians? Ten million? Twenty million?

There are those who have given precise answers to these questions, but when dealing with such imponderables precision is the child of emotion. To reach a real conclusion a historian would need more information. Too much of his data is unmeasured or unmeasurable. No one can ever exactly describe the state of German morale when war started. Most eye-witnesses agree that people were stunned and depressed, but this attitude cannot be computed in military terms. One may speculate, as Colonel Beck did, on the panic which might have been caused by bombing of the Ruhr, but this leads one to wonder also what would have been the effect of German bombing of Paris and the almost undefended industrial centres of France. One may look back upon the horrors of the Second World War, which one knows well, and conclude that the Allies had nothing to lose by making a bold gambler's stroke which at least stood a chance of averting the catastrophe. But this is to put the cart before the horse, since the massacres which followed September, while foreseeable, were not inevitable. Germany *might* have collapsed from within, the generals *might* have got rid of Hitler. To be sure it was an unlikely possibility to one who knew all the facts. But Chamberlain and Daladier did not know all the facts, trying to lead two weak, peace-loving nations to victory against a strong, warlike nation. Their position was wretched whatever they decided. It could hardly get worse, they thought wrongly, so they resolved to defend and to hope that time would heal their wounds. To do this would be less dangerous in the short term. The decision smacked of weak leadership, and maybe it was wrong, maybe a Hitler or a Churchill would have fought differently, but given the character of the Allied leadership it could not have been otherwise.

So it was that the first weeks of war brought massacre and destruction to the Poles but only inconvenience to the French, British and Germans. True, it was hard to find many ordinary people in the warring countries who greeted the war with any enthusiasm. In August 1914 there had been mass rejoicing, delirious crowds in the capital cities of Europe, since people then believed in the glory and excitement of war, but four years and millions of deaths later their joy had become the anguish of injury and bereavement. After the experience of 1914–18 it was only the very hard-hearted who could see war as anything but disaster. Maybe it had been colourful and exhilarating once, especially if waged by small, professional forces a long way from Europe, but now the killing had gone beyond all proportion. The weapons were now so efficient and could be launched from such a distance that even the politicians at home in the capital cities were in danger. Politicians were beginning to believe that war is wrong.

During the late 1930s Europeans became almost bored with crisis. Again and again the dictators made their demands and aggressions. Again and again the democratic leaders brought their people to the brink, only to withdraw in the face of the impending climax. By September 1939 the British and French were behaving like two inexperienced girls, unwilling to repeat the adventure of 1914 to which they had looked forward but which had turned out to be horrible. They were determined not to let it happen again and so they survived crisis after crisis, but by now their fear was diluted by a natural frustration. One more little push and they would be ready to take the plunge.

A public opinion survey taken on 2 September showed the British people heavily divided about what should be done to meet

Hitler's aggression.[59] Only two per cent said they would definitely be glad if there was war, and thirty-four per cent said that anything was better than war. But about half the sample were resigned to the inevitable. They were fed up with the recurring crises and wanted some action, if only to put an end to the general feeling of uncertainty. 'Let's get it over with,' was their attitude. Nerves were tense and an outlet was needed.

This was another important problem the Allied governments had to face. Most of their people were prepared to go to war, but only reluctantly. They would do what they were told, but without enthusiasm, and if the sacrifices they were called upon to make became too great they perhaps might not be counted on. Further-more there was a large minority which did not want to go to war, the thirty-four per cent who thought that there was nothing worse. Once war began, most of these accepted the fact, but a few did not. It was these whom Chamberlain called the 'peace at any price' people. The 'stop the war' movement was one of the weirdest Britain has ever known: a shapeless, ununited mass of fascists, communists, pacifists, defeatists, cowards and idealists who for reasons sometimes but seldom honourable believed that Britain and France had no business in a war against Hitler.

Apart from the few actual traitors, the most vicious group con-sisted of right-wing extremists, anti-semitic and sympathetic to Hitler's ideas. One of these was the Duke of Westminster – charm-ing, much-married, a brilliant womanizer, very rich, friend of the most powerful and the most exalted. His views were notorious, as well as loudly and widely expressed. On 1 September Winston Churchill was dining at the Savoy Grill with his daughter Mary, Duncan Sandys and the Duff Coopers. (Both Sandys and Cooper were to be ministers in Churchill's government.) After dinner they bumped into the Duke. Diana Cooper describes how, on 1 Sep-tember of all nights, 'he started by abusing the Jewish race, a red-rag subject where Duff was concerned'. He then plunged 'into praise of the Germans, rejoicing that we were not yet at war'. The next day he told a friend 'that if there were a war it would be entirely due to the Jews and Duff Cooper'.[60]

Had the Duke confined his prejudices to after-dinner outbursts, it would have been a matter of small importance. But he did not. On 12 September he assembled an impressively titled group and read them a pro-Nazi memorandum. Among his audience were Lord Arnold, Lord Rushcliffe, and the Duke of Buccleuch, all of whom were known to favour good relations with Nazi Germany. The tone of the document can be gauged by the following quotation from the first paragraph: 'The newspapers – especially those controlled by the Left and the Jews – take the line that no peace is possible until Nazism has been destroyed root and branch . . . thus the two races which are the most akin and most disciplined in the world will continue hostilities until both are bled almost to death.'[61]

The Prime Minister was soon informed of the meeting, and that the manifesto's extreme views 'were generally approved by those present'. It alarmed him to find that a group of such influential men were ready to do business with Hitler and to support him by and large. For they were not mere vapid aristocrats. Lord Arnold was active in the House of Lords. The Duke of Buccleuch held a Buckingham Palace appointment – Lord Steward of the Household. Buccleuch knew most of Britain's political leaders well, and was to bombard them with letters which became more and more abusive. On 20 February 1940, he wrote to Halifax: '. . . you did practically nothing to help a solution . . . Surely you are greatly in error to have made out that the Poles were almost 100 per cent in the right and Germany 100 per cent in the wrong. Fifty-fifty would be much nearer . . . You throw difficulties and create complications in the way of any sensible suggestion . . .'[62]

Lord Ponsonby, not present at the meeting but later identified as a sympathizer, had been a Cabinet Minister in 1931 and was the author of a book called *Falsehood in Wartime* about faked German atrocities in the First World War. Men such as these were the gilded tip of the iceberg. Lurking below there were many thousands of right-wingers in England, as in other countries, who had been captivated by Hitler and his New Order. Even now, after the outbreak of war, they were ready to give him their support.

The document the Duke read was written not by him but by Henry Drummond-Wolff, a former Conservative member of parliament who, like others in the group, had visited and been charmed by Herman Göring. A copy of it soon reached Chamberlain and was at once handed by him to a senior officer in British

Counter-Intelligence, Joseph Ball, who on 16 September reported to the Prime Minister through Horace Wilson as follows: 'It is, in fact, a very short summary – modified by recent events – of the document he [Drummond-Wolff] drew up after his last interview with Göring. Göring, as you know, has consistently suggested, through various friends of his, that provided the German Government were allowed to have Danzig, and that no obstacles were put in the way of their economic expansion in south-eastern Europe, they would be completely satisfied.'

Of course there were those who had doubted Göring's assurances, and to them the Duke next addressed himself: 'Surely, they [the doubters] ask, if Mittel-Europe were left to Germany as a sphere of influence, it would be our turn next? The answer is easy. For Germany to destroy the Empire she would, clearly, have to attack it. In war the attacker's military power must, for success, enormously outstrip that of the defences. Germany, even if she entertains the ambition, hopelessly lacks the power (actual or potential) to destroy the Empire.'

These ideas, which a few months later emerged as naive to the point of treachery, while not acceptable to Chamberlain in such a crude form, were close to his thesis of 'convincing the Germans they cannot win' because 'time is on our side'. Nor, as we have seen, was the Prime Minister opposed in principle to German repossession of Danzig, or to a limited German expansion in eastern Europe. A significant passage in Joseph Ball's letter to Horace Wilson reveals the official attitude to such ideas – guarded but not unsympathetic:

It would be highly dangerous for the Government to give the slightest indication at the present time to listen to any such proposals [as those of the manifesto]; and if the group really desire to see that anything of the kind should happen, they have been extremely foolish in allowing their views to transpire at the present juncture. If, as I understand is the case, Winston [Churchill] has heard of them, he will I imagine press hard for their immediate and categorical rejection; and should he do so, it is difficult to see how the P.M. can avoid giving him some assurance.

The Prime Minister did not contemplate doing a deal with Hitler, but he wished to have his hands free to allow German expansion towards the East. This seems to be the alarming implication behind Ball's note.

In other words there were men close to Chamberlain, Joseph Ball and Horace Wilson, who were worried by the Duke's manifesto not because of its outrageous racism and defeatism, but because it brought into the open ideas which, while not acceptable at present, might have to be considered at some future date. Interestingly, too, the manifesto mirrored two of Chamberlain's most dangerous mistakes: his belief that aerial warfare would kill by the million, and his belief that Hitler, while unable to defeat Britain, could not be defeated by her either. The British Prime Minister was probably not entirely out of sympathy with the conclusion of the Duke's manifesto: 'If, when the conquest of Poland is a *fait accompli*, we refuse to talk peace with Germany, what are we going to do. Go on with the war? How are we to set about that? Germany is impregnable on the ground, both in the east and the west. At sea the blockade will not affect her much. There remains only aerial warfare, with all its beastliness. There Germany will have the advantage. For London is, terribly, the best aerial target on the face of the earth.'

However tolerant may have been Chamberlain's attitude to such defeatist talk, Churchill's was quite different. Of the six-man War Cabinet he was the only one without responsibility for the previous policy which had tried and failed to appease Hitler. When he heard of the Duke of Westminster's group he was in a difficult position. The Duke was a close friend, but his views represented everything that Churchill hated. On 13 September he wrote the Duke a letter, characteristically frank and brilliantly phrased:

My dear Bennie

Several of the Cabinet were speaking to me this morning about the statement you read out at your private meeting yesterday, which has been sent to the Prime Minister among others. It seems to me on reading it that there are some very serious and bad things in it, the full bearing of which I feel you could not possibly have apprehended. It gave me great distress to read it, being one of your oldest friends. I am sure that pursuance of this line will lead you into measureless odium and vexation. When a country is fighting a war of this kind, very hard experiences lie before those who preach defeatism and set themselves up against the main will of the nation. Ramsay MacDonald went through it all in the last war, and rose again when it was over. Labouchere and Dr Clarke went through it in the little Boer War. But I wonder whether you have really counted the cost, or whether you are being drawn into courses the true character of which you do not realize . . . I beg you not to spurn the counsels of a life-long friend, and I trust that before you take any further steps you will come and have a talk with me . . .[63]

One can imagine the poor Duke's alarm at receiving such a broadside from the newly appointed First Lord, but even so his behaviour was strange. He had Churchill's letter, which was headed 'Secret', retyped and dispatched to Chamberlain with a note remarking that he did not feel there should be any secrets from the Prime Minister of England. He enclosed a copy of the manifesto and asked the Prime Minister innocently, 'I should like to know how it strikes you and what your comments are.'

Chamberlain, whose embarrassment at the affair must have been extreme, did what government officials usually do when faced with such a dilemma — he made no comment at all. Instead he sent Joseph Ball to call on the Duke, and on 28 September Ball reported that he had 'straightened the matter out with the Duke, who was now quite happy about it. He agreed that it was a stupid move *at the present time*.' (Author's italics.) In fact by 26 September the Duke had been sufficiently deterred not to attend the second meeting of the group, although it did take place at his house. Lord Mottistone, who was keeping Chamberlain informed, wrote that this time apart from the usual lords there was 'a sprinkling of MPs'. One of these, an extreme right-winger named Arnold Wilson, read 'a convincing memorandum' to show that Germany could not be worn down by the naval blockade.

This meeting provided Chamberlain with his first intimation of an important diplomatic initiative. Lord Hankey, a member of the War Cabinet, reported that 'the meeting was informed by someone unnamed that the King of the Belgians had a few days ago declared himself privately in favour of an early settlement. It was all rather vague, but I gathered that the King had some scheme in his mind for an appeal in conjunction with the Queen of Holland ...' The unnamed man was in fact Stanley Adams, Chairman of Thos. Cook and Sons, who had just visited King Leopold and had a message from him, which he read. Belgium, the King wrote, was the cockpit of Europe and would suffer horribly if the war was not soon ended. He already had 850,000 men under arms (the King was exaggerating), and they would resist aggression from east or south equally. He begged his friends in Britain to leave no stone unturned in the pursuit of peace. The meeting duly resolved to exert itself in this direction. As we shall see, six weeks later, when the Belgo-Dutch mediation offer did take place, the group was ready to act.

This group of right-wingers, extreme but influential, was more dangerous than the rest for two reasons. Firstly, unlike other 'stop the war' groups, their motivation was sympathy with, or at least a lack of hatred of, Hitler and Nazi Germany. In one paragraph the Duke's manifesto poured scorn on 'the parrot-cry that Nazism, as exemplified by Hitler and his entourage, is an obscenity so hideous that the world cannot resume its ways of liberty and quiet living until it is destroyed'. They liked much of what Hitler stood for, and it is terrifying to speculate about what would have been their attitude if Hitler had ever gained control over the British Isles. Unlike the rest, they cried 'peace' not through any love of peace as such, but because they had much in common with the enemy.

The second special danger was that this group had a better chance than the rest of influencing the Government's policy. They knew members of the Government personally and most of them were Conservatives, members of the party in power. They had a platform in Parliament where as a last resort they could declare their extremist views. Furthermore, though their views were essentially different from Chamberlain's, there were common factors. The group and the Government both disapproved of the Treaty of Versailles. They both believed that *some* territorial concessions at least could justly be claimed from Poland by Germany. They both believed that Germany was militarily unconquerable, and that aerial warfare (in *western* Europe at least) would be the greatest disaster of all. Where they parted company was on the issue of whether or not it was possible to do business with Hitler. Hitler had lied to Chamberlain in Munich. He was untrustworthy and would have to go. This simple, old-fashioned judgement was what saved Chamberlain from his own former appeasement policies and from the wiles of the right-wing extremists, whose promises of peace and 'assurances' about Hitler's future 'moderation' must have tempted him horribly.

These men were supported more honourably, though no less perniciously, by one of the most respected and influential men in Britain, the former Prime Minister David Lloyd George. In his case it was defeatism, not fascism, which led him to do what he did, but the effect of his action was so dangerous that many of his friends never forgave him. It began on 20 September, when some politicians called on Lloyd George at his London home 'Thames House'. Harold Nicolson records:

The old lion sits there in his room at the top of the building with a wonderful view of the river down to St Paul's. He begins by discussing the general situation. He says that he is frankly terrified, and that he does not see how we can possibly win the war. He contends that we should insist immediately on a secret session of Parliament in which we should force the Government to tell us exactly how they estimate the prospects of victory. If our chances are fifty-fifty, then it might be worth while organizing the whole resources of the country for a desperate struggle. But if the chances are definitely against us, then we should certainly make peace at the earliest opportunity, possibly with Roosevelt's assistance . . .

There was a lot of such talk in the drawing-rooms of London during the early days of the war. It was a gloomy time for the country's traditional rulers. The line between them and the Bolsheviks was now 200 miles nearer than it had been at the beginning of the month. Western democracy was in retreat. The ship was not yet sinking, but already those on the fringe were leaving. Extremists of both right and left, who are never really happy in a democracy, who tolerate it only because the alternative is to be without influence at all, saw this as the time to align themselves more openly with fascism and communism, the two ideologies which appeared to be winning. They were joined by the frivolous, the apathetic, the tired and the old, men who still believed in democracy and had defended it stoutly in their day, but who had now lost the stomach for the fight.

Lloyd George's defeatism was strengthened by a strange personal prejudice against Poland and the Polish Government, which he proceeded to demonstrate in a series of three articles in the *Sunday Express*, beginning on 24 September. 'What is Stalin up to?' he asked, and his answer was that Stalin was claiming no more than his due by invading Poland. The Polish Government was class-ridden and imperialistic, he suggested, and it was only because of its 'improvidence' that the country had collapsed. In the circumstances Stalin could not be blamed for liberating his countrymen from the Polish yoke. After all, he was not 'claiming one inch of purely Polish ground'.

The articles were full of over-simplified views and inaccurate facts. That they should have appeared while Poland was in her death throes was the height of tactlessness and cruelty. Count Raczyński, Polish Ambassador in London at the time, found it hard to explain the violence of Lloyd George's attitude. Perhaps, as a Welshman, he had an aversion to such a devout Catholic country. He was a friend of Roman Dmowski, one of Piłsudski's bitter opponents, and so may well have disliked the 1939 Polish Government which followed Piłsudski's ideas. On one occasion in England he snubbed Raczyński in public. The Ambassador made haste to reply to the attacks with two open letters to Lloyd George, which he circulated to a number of leading politicians. He pointed out correctly that Poland's Piłsudski-ite government was no more 'class-ridden' than that of Britain and France. He went on, 'I regret that you should have considered it necessary, in order to convince a generous and fair-minded nation that Poland should be left to her fate, to make her look as black as possible.'[64]

The climax of the former Prime Minister's campaign was a speech in the House of Commons. On 3 October he rose to propose, in language veiled but readily understood by all present, that the Allies make peace with Hitler. He had heard, as had many, that Hitler was about to offer terms for peace. If so, he said, 'I think it is very important that we should not come to too hurried a conclusion. It needs very careful consideration . . . I know how difficult it is to do this sort of thing in the middle of a war. Everybody says that if you begin to talk like that you are weakening the Government. I do not propose to do anything to weaken the Government, but I would ask the House and the Government to pause, not to hurry to come to a conclusion . . .'[65]

With such vague phrases the former Prime Minister, who had ruled Britain through the worst years of the First World War, communicated his fears to the House and proposed, as he had earlier told some MPs he would, a secret session of Parliament. Immediately Chamberlain replied cautiously and politely, promising consideration of Lloyd George's speech but giving nothing away. The worst he said about the speech was that it 'was based on a good many hypotheses'. His real feelings, though, were bitter. It was 'an anxious, almost defeatist speech', he wrote to his sister on 8 October. 'I have little doubt that Lloyd George was encouraged by his correspondence to think that he would get a lot of support for a move that [he hoped] might damage the government in general and the P.M. in particular.'[66]

Others in the debate spoke out more vehemently against Lloyd George and his speech. It was in itself, suggested Duff Cooper, the most weighty argument in favour of a secret session. 'I must say that I deeply regret and deplore that speech,' he said: 'His is a name that is better known throughout Europe and throughout the world perhaps than that of any other member sitting in the House today. His words will be reported and will be misrepresented . . . They will go out to the world with his name on the head of them as a suggestion of surrender.' The dread word had at last been spoken in public. Even the British press, which had been struggling manfully but unconvincingly to exude confidence, felt obliged to comment. On 4 October *The Times* mentioned the speech's 'untimeliness, and the opportunities it offered – however little it was intended by the speaker – for distortion abroad into a symptom of weakening resolve'.

However Lloyd George may have been hurt by such comments, he had little just cause for complaint, for indeed his resolve was weak. He actually had told MPs, although privately, that 'he does not see how we can possibly win the war', and he had made a speech which left little doubt in his hearers' minds that this was his view. He was weak, but at least he was honest, and there was nothing of the Nazi in him. The point was that even in semi-retirement he was close enough to the seat of power to know the facts about Britain's position, that she could muster only a handful of divisions against the one hundred German, that her air force, even combined with that of France, was far weaker in machines and trained personnel than the Luftwaffe. British and French morale was high, but it was built on an illusion. After all, at the end of August, only a few days previously, Polish morale had been high, but this had not prevented her collapse in the face of Hitler's lightning war. Lloyd George had considered Britain's

resources, and felt genuinely that in the light of them her aims —
to destroy Hitlerism, to restore Poland and Czechoslovakia — were
completely unrealistic.

Some, like Churchill, had the greatness and the vision to see that
Britain might slowly but eventually be turned into an efficient war
machine, that in the course of time Britain was likely to attract
allies, while Germany was likely to attract enemies, and that therefore the war must be fought, especially since the only alternative
was to yield to the bully, the blackmailer and the thief. Once upon
a time Lloyd George too had had this greatness, but he was now
seventy-six years old, only six years older than Chamberlain, but
tireder than him, and that meant very tired indeed.

It was a shock to Lloyd George to find that even a statesman as
respected as himself could not take such a line without being
labelled unpatriotic. He tried to get round this with a strange note
which he wrote on 9 October to the Foreign Office. It may be true,
he suggested, 'that Hitler's peace offer has no other purpose than
simply that of a peace offensive to weaken us. That is why I would
have a peace counter-offensive which would baffle him and
strengthen us.'[67] He tried to disguise defeatism as strength, but the
argument was obscure and unconvincing and his views were
written off as discreditable. This was unfair, but, from the point
of view of the national interest, just as well, for there was no
honourable, secure peace to be had. His idea was unworkable and
dangerous.

A fine assortment of 'peacemongers' was flushed out on 7 Nov-
ember, when the Belgian King Leopold and the Dutch Queen
Wilhelmina sent telegrams to the three belligerent heads of state —
Hitler, King George VI and President Albert Lebrun — offering to
mediate peace. Illogically, they did not telegraph the President of
Poland since, as Chamberlain's office noted, 'in her present mood
Germany would have declined to acknowledge it'.[68]

One knows now that the offer was not what it seemed. The
German Secretary of State, Ernst von Weizsäcker, whose loyalty
or disloyalty to Hitler is an enigma to this day, had sent a message
to his Ambassador in Brussels, Bülow-Schwante, at the end of
October asking him to warn the King of the impending attack on
the Low Countries.[69] Thus the Dutch and Belgian offer to act
'before the West European war begins in its full violence' was an

embarrassment to Hitler, as it was meant to be, and may have played a part in his decision that same day to postpone the attack. It would seem that Chamberlain recognized the offer as the ruse it was since, according to Macleod, he was 'much disgusted' by it and dismissed it as a 'manœuvre to prevent Hitler's attacking the Low Countries'.[70]

The possibility of a mediation by King Leopold had been mentioned already on 26 September at the Duke of Westminster's pro-German clique, and it was quickly taken up by some who supported this line. On 8 November, the day after the appeal, Lord Noel-Buxton wrote to Chamberlain asking him to give a 'considered response' to the Belgo-Dutch offer. The next day he signed a joint letter to Halifax with his fellow-peers Brockett, Harmsworth, Darnley, Arnold, Ponsonby, mentioning that they had the support of the Duke of Buccleuch, begging the Foreign Secretary to accept the offer in principle.[71]

Dissatisfied with the Government's lukewarm reception of the offer, the peers put down a motion (15 November) in the House of Lord calling for a secret session of Parliament. Lord Arnold, who had been present at the Duke of Westminster's notorious 12 September meeting, complained that at present 'no really free discussion is possible because we are at war . . . because noble Lords cannot say what they really think, many of them prefer to say nothing at all'. Lord Harmsworth, Chairman of the London *Daily Mail*, claimed, 'We avoid altogether the major problems of policy. And why? Because we do not want to say what we think in an open session . . . we wish to avoid any tendence to shake the confidence of the people . . . we wish very particularly to avoid providing any raw material for an ever watchful foreign propaganda.'

One wonders at the naivity of the noble lords. They were unwilling, they claimed, to shake the people's confidence or to provide ammunition for the enemy's propaganda. Could they honestly believe that such remarks, combined with an appeal for a secret session, would not do precisely that? Could any man who heard or read the debate possibly have doubted that these speakers wanted to ask Hitler for peace? One can imagine the encouragement such remarks gave to those in Berlin whose job it was carefully to eye the British scene.

The group also made the Government's life more difficult by persistent letter-writing to Chamberlain and Halifax, always on the same theme, that the war was unwinnable and Hitler could still be appeased.[72] For instance, a few weeks after the debate Lord Brockett wrote to Chamberlain claiming that public opinion was solidly against continuing the war. The Government's attitude was 'absolutely stiff', he wrote, and it was missing a golden chance of getting most of what it wanted now, by negotiation.[73] The problem was that such letters, however silly, had to be taken seriously. Had Lord Brockett been given reason to believe that his letter was not being seriously studied, had his arguments been met with the flat rejection that they deserved, he could well have taken it into his head to embarrass the Government, and damage the country, by a public outburst in Parliament.

Yet again the activities of the extreme right were mirrored by those of the left. A group of twenty pacifist Labour members of parliament circulated a letter to 138 newspapers. 'It is vital', they wrote, 'that the present [Belgo-Dutch] opportunity for negotiation should not be lost. It is an opportunity which may not occur again for a long time. We should press for a much more considered reply to Hitler's [6 October] speech and a clear declaration that this country is ready to join in a genuine European conference.' They called for 'a new European system in which every country, including our own, would be prepared to sacrifice some measure of national sovereignty in the interest of general security internationally guaranteed'.[74]

These sentiments, which sound admirable in the 1970s, had a naive, silly ring to them in November 1939. George Lansbury, leader of the group which included such well-known socialists as Sidney Silverman, William Sorensen and Agnes Hardie, sent the letter to Chamberlain a few days later complaining that it 'received very little publicity'. The newspapers had largely ignored it. He told Chamberlain he thought Hitler would withdraw from his 6 October position if faced by other European countries at a conference. (Such wishful thinking makes Chamberlain into a Churchill.) Lansbury objected too to President Lebrun's recent reference to a restoration of freedom in Poland, Czechoslovakia and Austria. 'France contemplates the general dismemberment of Germany,' Lansbury accused.

On 24 November Lansbury wrote to the Prime Minister again informing him that he had received 14,000 messages of approval to his letter. Had the press published it in full, he suggested, the replies would have gone into millions. He was probably right. On 8 October Chamberlain had written to his sister, Ida, 'In three days last week I had 2,450 letters and 1,860 of them were "stop the war" in one form or another.'[75] Incredibly, even after Hitler's brutality in Poland, there were still people in western Europe who thought he could be accommodated.

Though what they proposed was in practice the same, the Labour members' motive was different from the right-wingers'. They were pacifist, not pro-German. For years Lansbury had challenged the Government, and sometimes his own party, resisting every effort to strengthen the British armed forces. Inevitably, some of their views had spilled over into the Labour Party leadership. Their leader Clement Attlee said on 28 October 1935, in an election speech, 'We believe that another world war will mean the end of civilization. Modern weapons of war are so dangerous that they cannot be left in the hands of national governments.' In the debate on the introduction of conscription (27 April 1939) Attlee said, 'We are opposed to the introduction of conscription because we believe that, so far from strengthening the country, it will weaken and divide it.'

Stafford Cripps, another prominent Labour member whom Churchill appointed Ambassador to the Soviet Union the following May, maintained these views even after the outbreak of war. On 12 October he asked the Government 'to make a perfectly clear declaration of our own war aims and make an offer to the world to confer on the basis of those proposals. What is the alternative? The alternative is to proceed with a war that will mean the destruction of all the values of civilization.'

Two days later he went to see Halifax. He had it in mind, he told the Foreign Secretary, to ask Roosevelt to intervene and to propose a conference between the belligerents. Peace might be possible, he thought, 'if Herr Hitler would withdraw from countries to which he had no ethnographical claim'. He wanted Halifax to tell him whether his proposal was likely to embarrass the Government.

It is in the face of suggestions such as this that political rulers are most on their guard. In fact, what Cripps was proposing was to allow Hitler to occupy part of Poland provided that he withdrew from the other part. He was ready, which the British Government was not, to let Hitler 'get away with it again', to attain his declared aim by force without having to fight any real war against Britain and France. His seemingly harmless question about whether his idea was likely to embarrass the Government was in reality very dangerous. Had Halifax given him the go-ahead, he would have felt entitled to tell Roosevelt of Britain's generally favourable reaction to his idea. Roosevelt might then have approached Hitler and passed on the message that Britain was ready for peace. This was the last thing that the Allies wanted.

To men such as Cripps the prospect of air bombing was as horrible as that of nuclear warfare is to most people today. Large-scale bombing of big cities, thought Cripps, would cause the death not of thousands but of millions. And it was not only the pacifists who indulged in such over-estimates. In July 1939 it was the view of the British Air Ministry that 'on the outbreak of war air attacks of such intensity might be developed in London that only staffs working in deep underground protection could be expected to carry on work regularly'.[76] How wrong the Air Ministry was would be proved a year later during the London blitz. In spite of the death and destruction, millions were able to work.

Experts had observed the havoc wrought by German bombers during the Spanish Civil War and concluded that the full strength of the German Air Force would be able to lay waste a country and massacre its people. The result would be a wilderness similar to that which one now imagines would follow an atomic attack. Nowadays, to be sure, the idea of world war is totally unthinkable, given that a modern nuclear exchange really *would* kill millions. But if one looks back upon the world of 1939, it is hard indeed to defend the idea 'better Nazism than war'. If ever there was a just war, it was the war against Hitler. Surrender to him in 1939 after the victory in Poland would have strengthened him perhaps irretrievably. It would have meant giving him a free hand to conquer eastern and central Europe. With no war existing between Germany and the Allies, this could probably have been done by threat and submission, with very little fighting. As more and more countries fell, less and less would the peoples of Britain and France have felt inclined to take the monster on and kill him. It is alarming to speculate thus on what would have happened if pacifists like Cripps had had their way.

Fortunately this movement, though part of the Labour Party, did not dominate it. Attlee and the Labour leaders had long fought against Chamberlain's appeasement policy and his early sympathy with German aspirations. But, paradoxically, they shrank back from the logical consequence of their steadfast policy by opposing, right up to the outbreak, any massive strengthening of Britain's defences. Hore-Belisha, Minister of War, had chided them for this in the conscription debate (27 April 1939) with the words, 'Let those whose slogan is "stand up to the dictators" give us the trained men with whom we can stand up.' Only in September 1939 did the Party wake up to this particular reality, refraining from opposition to the massive legislative programme carried by Parliament in the early days of conflict. Hugh Dalton probably summed up the point of view thus: 'The Labour Party has always been, and still is, a peace party. It is fighting today for a real peace, not for a short truce between Nazi aggressions.' Though deeply suspicious of Chamberlain and of all the War Cabinet members except Churchill, the Labour leaders, while refusing to join in a coalition government, did their level best to aid the war effort. But there was a pacifist and left-wing element, perhaps twenty per cent of the parliamentary party, which opposed the war and wanted the Government to ask Hitler for peace.

But those further to the Left – the Independent Labour Party and the Communist Party – opposed the war tooth and nail. Lloyd George's notorious 3 October speech in the House of Commons attracted anger from Labourite and Conservative alike, but only congratulation from George Buchanan of the ILP (who later became a minister in Attlee's government). He praised him 'for having the courage at seventy-six years of age to take a hostile line in this House of Commons'. Buchanan continued: 'I want to go a step further than he has gone. I take an even stronger line about peace than he has done . . . and frankly I say to the Prime Minister that I cannot find this great unanimous desire for the war. Frankly speaking I find the reverse.'

Ten days later the ILP supported the 'peace at any price' candidate Andrew Stewart in a by-election at Clackmannan and East

Stirling. The electoral truce between the main parties provided that any empty seat would go unopposed to the party which previously held it, but the ILP dissented, declaring during the campaign that it 'refuses to support any capitalist government in any war whatever . . . the quarrel between two imperialist states is not a workers' quarrel . . . In view of the Russo-German pact it can no longer be maintained that it is necessary for the British workers to fight against Germany in order to defend Russia.'[77] This party, whose handful of seats in the House of Commons showed that it had significant support in certain parts of the country, was the most militant of all in opposing the war, more so than the Fascists or even the Communists, from whom they differed little except in their dislike of Joseph Stalin. In the event they polled only 1,060 votes against 15,645 for the official Labour candidate, showing how few in number were those prepared to oppose the war actively, even with a cross on a ballot paper.[78] To grumble was one thing, but to oppose, even in the privacy of a voting booth, was another.

The most outrageous attitude of all was displayed by George Bernard Shaw who, in a journalistic article now largely forgotten, declared himself by and large a supporter of Hitler. 'We made all the mischief,' wrote Shaw in the *New Statesman* on 7 October, 'we and the French, when we were drunk with victory at Versailles; and if that mischief had not been there to undo Adolf Hitler would have now been a struggling artist of no political account.' This proposition, though over-simplified, was defensible, but not in the context of the sentences which followed: 'He actually owes his eminence to us; so let us cease railing at our own creation and recognize the ability with which he has undone our wicked work, and the debt the German nation owes him for it. Our business now is to make peace with him and with all the world instead of making more mischief and ruining our people in the process . . .'

Shaw's piece was a vicious mixture of intellectual arrogance and ignorance. Unable to recognize the peril Hitler posed to civilization, he too asked the extreme left-wing question, 'Sacrifice? Yes, but what for?,' continuing with ponderous irony: 'Our aim is first to deliver Europe from the threat and fear of war. And our remedy is to promise it three years more war! Next, to abolish Hitlerism, root and branch. Well, what about beginning by abolishing

Churchillism, a proposition not less nonsensical and more easily within our reach?'

Shaw continued: 'But, we are told, if we do not send Hitler to St Helena he will proceed to annex Switzerland, Holland, Belgium, England, Scotland, Ireland, Australia, New Zealand, Canada, Africa and finally the entire universe and Stalin will help him. I must reply that men who talk like this are frightened out of their wits.' It must have been reassuring to the *New Statesman* readers that Bernard Shaw, at least, was not frightened at the prospect of Hitler's continual aggressions. Indeed, the following issue (14 October) printed letters praising Shaw for his bold stance, and the editor noted that 'we have received a large number of similar letters congratulating us on publishing Mr Shaw's article'.

It may well seem incredible today that such a man as Shaw, a socialist and one of the most brilliant writers of our century, should have committed such an act, for which naivity is the kindest of explanations. Justly concerned by what the working classes of America and western Europe had endured in the previous twenty years, he was unable to distinguish this horror, which though real was curable through economic and social progress, from the horror of Hitlerism which, had it been allowed to conquer, would have left the world barren and uninhabitable to all but the violent and the 'racially pure'. Clearly Shaw had not read *Mein Kampf*, and this is excusable, but he could and doubtless did read the world's newspapers and talk to refugees from Nazi-occupied Europe. What is inexcusable is that he did not draw the conclusion that 'to abolish Hitlerism, root and branch', the aim he and the Duke of Westminster so derided, was essential for the future of civilization.

During the 1930s Shaw was one of the very few eminent English-language writers to be published and performed in Nazi Germany. William Shirer writes that this was 'perhaps because he poked fun at Englishmen and lampooned democracy'. Shirer also points out that Shaw's name was 'conspicuously absent' from the Special List of 2,300 well-known people who were to be arrested immediately after a German occupation of Britain. It is not difficult to understand why.

The timing of Shaw's article – the day after Hitler's 6 October peace proposals – was particularly unfortunate. It was seized upon by the German press and reported, for example, in the first number of the new Nazi-run Warsaw newspaper *Nowy Kurier Warszawski* on 11 October. It also provided basic ammunition for Moscow *Izvestiya*'s 9 October editorial, headed 'Peace or War?'. *Izvestiya* printed chunks of the article on its front page, approving Shaw's thesis and weaving it into its own that 'it is impossible not to accept the fact that they [Hitler's proposals] at least provide a realistic and practical base for talks aimed at hastening the conclusion of peace'.

Like Bernard Shaw and the Duke of Westminster, *Izvestiya* saw no merit in the theory that Hitlerism must now be destroyed 'root and branch'. In one of the most remarkable paragraphs ever to appear in a Soviet newspaper it declared: 'Every person is free to declare his attitude to this or the other ideology. He has the right to defend or refute it. But it is sheer senseless cruelty to destroy human beings because of a dislike for this or the other viewpoint or philosophy . . . No ideology or philosophy can be destroyed by fire and the sword.' One imagines Stalin nodding his head in agreement to these wise words. A wave of pacifism and liberalism seemed to have engulfed *Izvestiya*, the journal which had supported Soviet power through revolution, civil war and massive repression of political opposition. Soviet journalists, guided as ever by their political leaders, were writing about Hitler, if not with approval, at least with kindly indulgence. In this matter they were the epitome of tolerance.

It is doubtful whether this tolerance extended to their comrades of the Communist Party of Great Britain, who were thrown by the outbreak of war into a state of utter confusion. Harry Pollitt, their Secretary-General, never wavered in his detestation of Nazi Germany. His pamphlet 'How to Win the War', published on 14 September, proclaimed: 'The Communist Party supports the war, believing it to be a just war which should be supported by the whole working class . . . It will do everything it can to bring the war to a speedy conclusion.' In such noble sentiments he was supported by his Party's newspaper the *Daily Worker*, which announced on 2 September: 'The mad dogs of Europe — Hitler and his Nazi Government — have set out on their last bloody adventure . . . We are in support of all necessary measures to secure the victory of democracy over fascism.' On that same day the communist member of parliament William Gallacher said, 'I will stick at no sacrifice to ensure the defeat of Nazi aggression.'

These were bold words indeed, for they ignored the great event of the previous week, the signature of the German–Soviet non-aggression pact. 'The situation has changed and we are no longer enemies,' said Molotov on 31 August. Was it not then rash of the British communists to refer to Nazi Germany in quite contrary terms? It took only a day for Gallacher to develop second thoughts. A few minutes after Chamberlain's announcement that war had begun, Gallacher referred to his declaration of the previous day: 'In taking that stand I want to declare here with the utmost confidence, from experience and from knowledge, that I will not come into conflict with the policy of my working-class comrades of the Soviet Union.'

British communists of course knew nothing then of Stalin's secret plan to help Hitler conquer Poland and to share in the spoils. On 16 September, by which time several newspapers were speculating on the basis of articles in *Pravda* and *Izvestiya* that the Red Army was about to invade Poland, the *Daily Worker* printed quotations from them and concluded: 'Our readers will see that the article contains neither the hidden meaning attributed to it, nor does it envisage any Soviet action in relation to the war in Poland.'

One can imagine the *Daily Worker*'s embarrassment when, the very next morning, the Soviet Union acted with military force. 'Soviet Counter-blow against Nazis' was the *Daily Worker*'s huge headline, surely one of the most inaccurate in the history of journalism. The following article explained that the Red Army had acted to forestall Hitler, to prevent him from entering the Ukraine. In the next few days readers were encouraged by tales of the cheering crowds that had greeted the Red Army, of how the Red Army was taking bread to starving peasants and liberating Polish troops. The *Daily Worker* still did not appreciate the facts of life. Its 19 September leader declared, 'It is impossible for the British and French people to even contemplate a surrender to Nazi aggression. The war to halt Fascist aggression must go on with undoubled energy.'[79]

This was too much for the Kremlin, whose whole policy then depended on friendly relations with Nazi Germany and on active cooperation with German forces in Poland. The British representative to the Communist International was sent from Moscow to London with a paper outlining the new policy and immediately the British Party adopted it.[80] An article by Georgi Dimitrov, the Comintern General Secretary, called 'The War and the Working Class of the Capitalist Countries', explained that the struggle between Germany and the Allies was an imperialist war in which no working men ought to take part, and called upon communists in France and Britain to turn the imperialist war into a civil war and a socialist revolution.[81] British communists were instructed to make use of the disruption of society which war was bound to cause to further the aims of the world movement. Harry Pollitt refused to accept this line and was forced to resign from the leadership. For two years the Party did its best to obstruct the war effort, this policy changing only when Hitler invaded the Soviet Union.

Amazingly similar was the attitude of Oswald Mosley and his British Union of Fascists, whose crude xenophobia and anti-semitism still attracted the support of many thousands of Britons, mainly living in the big cities. Although not officially linked with Hitler's Nazi Party, Mosley's blackshirts made use of many of its outward forms and trappings: the raised-hand salute, para-military uniforms, armbands with a flash-of-lightning motif. Like Hitler, Mosley believed in the cult of a 'Leader', a larger-than-life figure projected as a personification of the nation and the saviour of its people. Like Hitler, Mosley had immense personality and the ability to sway a crowd by his oratory. He had a nation-wide organization with branches scattered about the country, providing him with the ability to spread fascist propaganda at public meetings and to recruit members. Another powerful weapon was a weekly newspaper called *Action*. It would be surprising if the British Government, now engaged in war against Hitler's Germany, did not take the existence of such an organization seriously.

Writing in 1968, Mosley justifies by reasoned and skilful argument his decision to oppose the declaration of war in 1939. It risked three consequences, he writes: the disaster of defeat, the triumph of communism and the loss of the British Empire despite victory. True, the first was avoided, and so was the second, but only, he claims, because of the invention of the atomic bomb. Had there been no bomb, the Red Army would have swarmed across western as well as eastern Europe and place the whole continent under Russian domination. He concludes that 'the loss of the Empire and reduction of Britain to the position of an American satellite remain the only clear results of the Second World War'.[82] It should never have been embarked upon, since Britain was the only country which could under no circumstances benefit from it.

It is easy enough to pick holes in Mosley's argument. True, the Empire was lost. Just as well, some would claim. And anyway, it was bound to happen sooner or later, for Britain did not have the economic base to support such a structure. And is Britain an American satellite? An exaggeration, surely. And surely there *were* other clear results of the Second World War? The destruction of Hitler, for instance? Again, Mosley writes, 'The war was fought to prevent Germans joining with Germans.'[83] He ignores the fact that Hitler had already, in March 1939, seized Bohemia and Moravia, areas whose people were in no way German, that by Hitler's own confession the main aim of the invasion of Poland was not to 'reclaim' German lands but to expand Germany's living space at the expense of other countries.

Mosley's arguments, however faulty, are presented in his autobiography with the restraint and apparent reasonableness of which he is sometimes capable. His decision in September 1939, he reminds us, was to instruct his members thus: 'Our country is involved in war. Therefore I ask you to do nothing to injure our country or to help any other power. Our members should do what is required of them, and if they are members of any of the forces or services of the Crown, they should obey their orders.' At the same time he arranged 'an intensive campaign of public meetings in favour of peace'. They were, he writes, 'some of the largest and most enthusiastic public meetings I have ever addressed . . . large crowds not only listened, but cheered our demands for negotiated peace'.[84]

Reading such words of sweet reason, one is liable to forget the viciousness of Mosley's speeches in 1939. Understandably, he is anxious nowadays to play down his role as an anti-semite, as an imitator of Hitler, but his words are on the record and undeniable. On 27 August, for instance, he addressed a large crowd at Hackney in North London, abusing the British Government for creating a situation in which 'if Poland whistles, a million Englishmen have got to die'. The report in *Action* describes with pride the scene, as Mosley's henchmen carried placards with such slogans as 'No War for Warsaw', 'Conscript the Jews', 'The Jews Want War — We Want Peace' and 'We Won't Fight for Poland'. *Action* reports in glowing terms how Mosley 'denounced the war plot to sacrifice millions of British lives in an alien and Jewish quarrel'. The report ends: 'The warmongers have still to reckon with the will to peace of the British people finding expression through the inspired voice of Oswald Mosley! Hail Mosley! Hail Peace!'[85] These slogans were shouted by thousands of Londoners, hands raised in the Nazi salute.

If war came, declared *Action*'s military correspondent, it would be 'the silliest brawl since Jenkins lost his ear'. But it says much for British tolerance that even after the war began Mosley was able to go on making such statements without prosecution or censorship. He seems to have come to some understanding with the British authorities, for on 16 October the Cabinet Ministers were told that Mosley was 'not likely to take action at present which would expose himself to a prosecution'.[86] The British had decided 'to undertake prosecutions very sparingly, unless a case arose in which there was direct incitement to refrain from coopera-tion in the war effort'. As we have seen, Mosley had instructed his supporters to obey orders, so he could not be accused of any such sabotage.

Mosley and *Action* were only very briefly scotched by the out-break. On 3 September itself Mosley was due to address a huge meeting, which he had to cancel because of the universal ban on any large gatherings for fear of air attack. The 9 September edition of *Action* did not appear because of some misunderstanding with the printers over the new system of voluntary censorship, which the fascists were ready enough to observe. On 16 September it reappeared, reduced in size but by no means muted in its invective against almost everyone: Conservatives, Jews, Communists, Labourites, Poles and foreigners in general.

It is a characteristic of extremist movements in Britain that by and large they prefer to remain within the law. The reason for this is that in Britain the mass of the population respects the law and would reject any aspiring demagogue who chose to break it.

When war breaks out, laws are naturally tightened, and Mosley realized that it would have been political madness openly to call for support of Hitler, however much he admired him, so long as Hitler was Britain's enemy. Apart from a small handful, his tens of thousands of supporters would have drawn the line at out-and-out treachery, and probably he would have as well. Nationalism is difficult to export, by definition. For years British and German right-wing nationalists had held meetings and proclaimed their ideological solidarity. But once a conflict starts, a nationalist finds it difficult to put ideology above country, for the two are almost synonymous. This is why conflict with Hitler brought Mosley's men to the point of schizophrenia.

To solve this dilemma Mosley argued in 1937 that 'less than any great nation today her [Germany's] philosophy leads her to think in terms of limitless colonial Empire, which to the Nazi mind suggests loss of vital energy, dissipation of wealth and the fear of detrimental admixture of races. Her national objective lies in the union of the Germanic peoples of Europe ... Thus, so far from the objective of the British Empire clashing with the objective of the new Germany, the two objectives in terms of world stability and peace are complementary.'[87] Whatever Hitler's real objective was in 1937, it soon changed and to answer Mosley's thesis it is enough to quote Hitler's words to his generals on 23 May 1939: 'Further successes can no longer be attained without the shedding of blood ... It is a question of expanding our living-space in the East, of securing our food supplies ... If Fate forces us to a showdown with the West, it will be most valuable to possess a large area in the East. In wartime we shall be even less able to rely on record harvests than in peacetime.'[88] He added that the peoples of eastern Europe would be valuable to Germany as slave labour. This declared plan, which Hitler was soon to put exactly into practice, had little in common with his frequently spoken vow that all he required was a unified Greater Germany, that he had no interest whatever in non-German lands or non-German peoples. By the end of 1939 is was clear that Hitler had lied, but still Mosley preferred to believe Hitler rather than the facts.

'Britain could be made strong enough to defend herself, if necessarily single-handed, against the attack of any nation on earth,' wrote Mosley in *Action* on 16 September. 'Leave the foreigners on the continent of Europe to fight out their own quarrels,' he urged a week later. His plan was to turn Britain into a fortress, to isolate her from the Continent and convert her entire energy towards the development of her Empire. It was identical to the bait which Hitler was then dangling before the eyes of Britain and France, and one must admit that to many it was an attractive and tempting prospect. Still, had Hitler been given a free hand in the East, had he become master of all Europe east of the Rhine, one can hardly imagine that, possessed of such power, he would suddenly have ceased his continual demands. Britain and France would have been easy prey for such a colossus.

So long as the battle still raged in Poland, Mosley's *Action* made it clear that its sympathies lay with Germany. On 11 September the *Daily Mirror* reported with due admiration the Poles' struggle to defend their country from invasion. Every citizen, in or out of uniform, was fighting the German Army, and 'even grandmothers are joining in'. *Action*'s view was that patriotism was all very well for the British or for the Germans, but quite out of place for the Poles. It wrote disapprovingly of Polish 'illegal participation in hostilities'. It was this which the German High Command had already on 13 September made the excuse for its decision to bomb and shell open cities, and one can detect the same sort of thinking in the tone of *Action*'s article on the subject: 'Events of this kind in the less civilized parts of Eastern Europe should not be made the excuse for an outbreak of war frightfulness in the West by either side. If Germany does not blame us for any breach of the rules of war by our Polish allies, no more should we blame them for such measures of retaliation as they have undertaken in the East.'[89]

In fact, as is shown elsewhere in this book, the German Air Force had been bombing everyone and everything in Poland ever since 1 September when the invasion started. The violent resistance of Polish civilians was no doubt a fact, but for *Action* to call it 'illegal' in the light of Germany's unannounced invasion was the height of cynicism. Every moral and legal code recognizes the right of a victim of assault to reply in self-defence.

But although Mosley and his men clearly deplored the alliance with Poland, they did not call upon Englishmen to mutiny against it or against the war that was its consequence. 'Let the people vote,' was as far as they would go, challenging the Government to put the war issue to national referendum. So long as Mosley stuck to such legal and unobjectionable tactics, he would be allowed to run his movement and proclaim his views.

'Stop This War, Let the People Vote,' was the huge slogan spread right across the stage at the Stoll Opera House in London, where Mosley addressed a full house on 15 October. In its usual silly style *Action* told how the audience had given their Leader his customary ovation, and then how 'mingling unanswerable argument with bitter irony, combining appeals to patriotism with demands for social justice, Mosley showed once more his supreme power of leadership, voicing the unspoken yearnings and intense feelings of the people who look to him for a lead in these desperate times'.[90]

But in spite of Mosley's supreme powers, in spite of the people's unspoken yearnings and intense feelings, his campaign won very little success. In spite of the ovations and the huge audiences at his meetings, Mosley's candidates made little headway at three by-elections early in 1940, polling only 1,300 votes in all. Mosley himself admits that 'the overwhelming majority of the people was undoubtedly in favour of the war'.[91]

It was only for this reason that Mosley was allowed to continue. On 16 October the British Cabinet decided that since anti-war propaganda had turned out to be quite harmless and since public opinion generally supported the war, criminal prosecution of the peacemakers would do more harm than good. It was a decision made on pragmatic grounds, not through any excessive respect for Britain's traditional freedom of the individual. In wartime such freedoms have to take second place to national security, even in Britain. The Cabinet confirmed that 'measures would have to be taken if the pacifist elements appeared likely to have any success in spreading a defeatist spirit'. Sure enough, after Hitler's invasion of the Low Countries the following spring it was decided that Mosley could no longer remain at liberty. He and his leading helpers were arrested on 23 May 1940, under Defence Regulations 18B, which temporarily suspended *habeas corpus* and allowed imprisonment without trial.

In France the war seemed closer, the threat more immediate, so the authorities were not inclined to treat with tolerance those who preached defeatism. There were of course the semi-fascists and the defeatists of the right, but these were represented from the top to the bottom of the French administration and even in the Cabinet. To repress these would cause Daladier great political difficulty. Also these right-wingers were by and large lying low, working from within the system. They were not seen to be disrupting the war effort. But then there were the extremists on the other side, the communists, who opposed the war just as strongly and were proclaiming their opposition as loudly as they could. They were an easier and more appropriate target for harsh measures.

The French communists were as confused as anyone about the meaning of the Nazi–Soviet Pact of 22 August. A few days after it they announced in a manifesto, 'It will deprive no nation of its liberty and will hand over no inch of territory belonging to any nation.' They did not know of the Pact's secret protocols with their detailed carve-up of Poland and the Baltic States. They maintained that Nazism was 'the most bestial and the principal warmonger, the most dangerous enemy of democracy' – a line which was contradicted by Molotov on 31 August and within a month dutifully discarded by the French communists themselves. 'Hitler, by recognizing the strength of the country of Socialism, thereby reveals his own weakness,' was the convoluted way they explained the misalliance of the two arch-enemies.

On 28 August the communist newspapers *L'Humanité* and *Ce Soir* were suppressed. Then on 26 September the Party itself was dissolved and it became a criminal offence to propagate the slogans of the Third International. Communists were spreading anti-war propaganda and organizing meetings to disrupt work in Renault and other factories. Justifying this decision after the war, Daladier said in a speech to the French Assembly on 18 July 1946: 'Political tracts distributed by the hundred, by the thousand, throughout a country in a state of war – this is already a serious matter which can have dire consequences. But then there were acts of sabotage. There was the sabotage of aeroplane engines in the Farman factories at Boulogne-Billancourt . . . There were acts of sabotage in powder factories, notably in the factory at Sorgues . . . Yes, ladies and gentlemen, I *did* dissolve the Communist Party.'[92]

Daladier's action may well have been necessary, but of course it was grist to the mill of American and other neutral isolationists, who were maintaining that there was morally no difference between the two warring sides. What right had France now to criticize Hitler's treatment of *his* political opponents? As Molotov said on 31 October: 'One may like or dislike Hitlerism, but every sane person will understand that ideology cannot be destroyed by force. It is therefore not only nonsensical but also criminal to pursue a war "for the destruction of Hitlerism" under the bogus banner of a struggle for "democracy". And what kind of democracy is it anyway with the French Communist Party in jail?'

There were forty-six communist deputies in the French Parliament, and when the Party was banned they were forced to re-label themselves. Officially they left the Communist Party and formed the 'Workers' and Peasants' Group' – a formal change which made no difference to their determination to oppose the French war effort. On 1 October they wrote a famous letter petitioning Edouard Herriot, President of the Chamber of Deputies, to summon Parliament to deliberate the problem of peace. The letter was widely distributed in French factories as a pamphlet under the title 'Immediate Peace', and coming as it did a few days before Hitler's 'peace proposals' of 6 October it was calculated to do great harm.

By 9 October there were thirty-five communist deputies under arrest, their immunity having lapsed as soon as the Parliamentary

The bosses bind France with censorship, having safely locked away the trade unions, the communist party and the newspaper *Humanité* (*Pravda*, 7 November 1939). (Copyright British Museum)

session closed. Several of the leaders managed to escape: Flori-mond Bonté and Arthur Ramette who had signed the letter, Jacques Duclos, the future Party leader, and Maurice Thorez the then leader. Thorez was already conscripted into the Army so his escape was desertion, to escape the consequences of which he decided it was best to spend the entire war in Moscow.

The slavish way in which the Party had adapted its policy to fit in with Moscow's convenience caused disruption in the ranks and brought it into general disrepute. Five of the communist deputies resigned from the Party altogether. Léon Blum and his powerful socialist party described the Pact and the communists' approval of it as 'treason'. He did not support the arrests of communists, partly for tactical reasons, partly because he thought such a move might turn them into martyrs. But his attitude towards them was vitriolic. Their doctrine, he said, was 'the ulti-mate negation of democratic socialism'. He describes how, when a friend read their 1 October letter to him over the telephone, 'I stopped the reader at the end of two sentences . . . Administered in such doses cynicism and hypocrisy become physically in-tolerable and the stomach rejects them like pieces of rotten food'.[93]

In Britain and France it was very much a war of words rather than of bullets. Their job was to defeat Germany, and one would have thought they would have tried to keep their insults for the enemy. That they were not able to do this revealed the extent of their moral unpreparedness. France's disunity was greater than Britain's, understandably, for France was far more vulnerable to attack by the German Army. For her the war was more likely to end in serious defeat, as indeed it did within a very few months. The Allied leaders were forced to devote much of their time to building up internal unity and convincing their people of the seriousness of the task that lay ahead. There can be no doubt that the various 'stop the war' movements damaged the Allied war effort and encouraged Hitler to believe that so long as he stuck to his guns he would gain his ends. Some of these movements were treacherous, others idealistic, but in practice it made little difference. The result was the same.

The Allied leaders felt the need for really efficient propaganda, to quell the dissidents at home, to break enthusiasm for the war in Germany and to damage German credit in the neutral countries. While the Poles endured the bombing of their cities, the slaughter of soldiers and civilians, occupation of their lands and extinction of their state, their British and French allies were only going through the motions of fighting and still concentrating much of their resources on the battle of words. The two warring sides made speeches as they gently sparred, each trying not to destroy the other but to convince him, or failing that to divide or discredit him.

For the Poles it was a truly ignoble spectacle, their allies fiddling while *they* burned. For the Germans it was a welcome alternative to a war on two fronts, then a relaxing breathing-space after the exertions of conquest in the East. For the British and French it was a period in which to sigh with relief and to thank God for delivering them from the horrors of aerial bombardment which would have meant the death of millions, the end of civilization, Armageddon.

In Britain decisions military and political were governed by the partly true but very dangerous belief that 'time is on our side'. Leo Amery writes of Chamberlain, 'Loathing war as he did, he was determined to wage as little of it as possible.' The trouble was that this attitude communicated itself to his subordinates and stunted people's keenness to come to grips with the enemy. On 10 September he wrote to his sister:

> . . . I do not see that I have any particular part to play until it comes to discussing peace terms – and that may be a long way off . . . It may be, but I have a feeling that it won't be so very long. There is such a widespread desire to avoid war, and it is so deeply rooted, that it surely must find expression somehow. Of course the difficulty is with Hitler himself. Until he disappears and his system collapses, there can be no peace. But what I hope for is not a military victory – I very much doubt the feasibility of that – but a collapse on the German home front. For that it is necessary to convince the Germans that they cannot win.[94]

The Prime Minister's touching belief that the German masses could be so convinced was repeated in a letter he sent President Roosevelt on 4 October. In spite of the exhilaration Germany must have felt after her crushing victory over Poland, Chamberlain still stuck to his view that she could be defeated by his blockade, diplomacy, intrigue and propaganda. He hoped to defeat Hitler, a

Die amerikanische Presse

veröffentlicht folgende Einzelheiten:

Göring, des Führers vorbestimmter Nachfolger, verfügt im Ausland über nicht weniger als
RM 30 030 000.-

Göbbels hat in Buenos Aires, Luxemburg und Osaka (Japan) die Kleinigkeit von
RM 35 960 000.-

Ribbentrop ist der Reichste von allen. In Holland und der Schweiz liegen für ihn
RM 38 960 000.-

Heß, des Führers Stellvertreter, versteckte in Sao Paolo und Basel **RM 16 430 000.-**

Ley hat sich bei seinem „A.d.F."-Geschäft gesund gemacht. Er hat **RM 7 564 000.-**

Himmler, der wie ein Lux aufpaßt, daß kein Deutscher mehr als 10 Mark über die Grenze nimmt, verschob selber **RM 10 550 000.-**

Streicher, ist bekanntlich der „Wächter der deutschen Ehre". Er hat im Ausland einen Sparpfennig von **RM 3 000 000.-**

Die Neuyorker Zeitung „Journal-American" bemerkt hierzu:

„Man hört mit Genugtuung, daß so viele Nazi-Bonzen ganz selbstverständlich damit rechnen, daß der Tag kommt an dem sie Deutschland verlassen müssen."

Das sind Eure Führer!

[158]

One of the leaflets the RAF dropped by the million over Germany. This one lists the huge sums of money which the Nazi leaders were supposed to have amassed in foreign banks. (Crown Copyright. Public Record Office. FO 800/317)

man of action and aggression, by closing Germany's western border, blockading her ports, immobilizing her merchant and naval fleet and by wooing the United States and other countries to join against her.

But it was inside Germany itself that the heart of Chamberlain's illusions lay. Military Intelligence had contacts with many Germans, some highly placed in the Army, who wanted to get rid of Hitler. Secret agents, anxious to please as always, exaggerated the generals' readiness to kill or arrest their Führer. Other reports claimed that Hermann Göring had broken with Hitler and was ready to supplant him, that the German economy was on the verge

as find Eure Führer!

Deutsche! Ihr geht in diesen Krieg mit Hungerrationen. Ihr habt seit Jahren den Riemen enger schnüren müssen. Jetzt lest was die amerikanischen Zeitungen bringen, über Eure Führer, die an allem Eurem Leid schuld sind.

Die amerikanische Presse veröffentlichte erstmalig am 20. September, mit allen Einzelheiten, einen Tatsachenbericht, in dem enthüllt wird, daß

Göring	Göbbels	Ribbentrop
Heß	Himmler	Ley	Streicher

durch ihre Strohmänner den ungeheuren Betrag von

RM 142 494 000.-

in Bargeld, Wertpapieren und Lebensversicherungen im Ausland sichergestellt haben.

Die bekannte „Chicago Daily News" schreibt:

„Was auch immer das Schicksal Nazi-Deutschlands infolge dieses Krieges sein mag, Hitlers Paladine werden keine Not leiden. Wenn sie nicht mit heiler Haut davonkommen, wird es wenigstens ihren Familien gut gehen."

Die Neuyorker Zeitung „Journal-American" bestätigt:

„Die Nazi-Vermögen sind bei Banken in Süd-Amerika, Japan, Luxemburg, Holland, Ägypten, Estland, Lettland, Finnland und der Schweiz untergebracht. Außerdem sind große Barbeträge bei Nazi-Agenten und deutschen Schiffahrtsgesellschaften hinterlegt worden."

Das find Eure Führer!

of collapse, that the German people were demoralized and on the point of revolt. Naturally, not all the Government's information was in this vein, and some said exactly the opposite, but so often a statesman is tempted to take the optimistic view, especially when he believes that the only alternative is the Apocalypse.

The British decided to attack Germany not with bombs but with leaflets, appealing to the people to get rid of their evil government. It was the first decision of the war, taken at the first War Cabinet meeting at 5 p.m. on 3 September. According to the minutes of the meeting 'it was believed that these leaflets would have an important effect on German public opinion'.[95] The leaflet campaign was seen as a vital operation, for the Prime Minister's aim was not to defeat Germany in battle but to convince her by reasoned argument of the error of her ways. 'You have been led astray. Repent!'

Der Führer spricht!

„Für uns ist dieser Bolschewismus aber eine Pest... Jede weitere deutsche vertragliche Verbindung mit dem derzeitigen bolschewistischen Rußland würde für uns ganz wertlos sein. Weder wäre es denkbar, daß nationalsozialistische deutsche Soldaten jemals zum Schutz des Bolschewismus eine Hilfspflicht erfüllen, noch wollen wir selbst von einem bolschewistischen Staat eine Hilfe entgegennehmen." (Reichstagsrede vom 30. Jan. 1937.)

„Zu einem einzigen Staate haben wir kein Verhältnis gesucht und wünschen auch zu ihm in kein engeres Verhältnis zu treten: Sowjet Rußland."
(Reichstagsrede vom 20. Feb. 1938.)

„Die Regenten des heutigen Rußlands sind blutbefleckte gemeine Verbrecher."
(Mein Kampf, Seite 750.)

Also sprach Adolf Hitler.

This leaflet quotes some of Hitler's past statements about Poland and Russia, promises which he broke in 1939. (Crown Copyright. Public Record Office. FO 800/317 f 214 and FO 800/317)

was his message to the German people, and like most evangelists he was sure that his words would be listened to. He would not accept the truth, that Germans as a whole were proud of what their Army had just achieved, and full of admiration and gratitude to their Führer for 'reuniting' Danzig and Posen with Germany.

Propaganda was a young art, particularly so in England where a Ministry of Information was set up only on the outbreak of war. Goebbels's more frankly named Ministry of Propaganda had existed for years. True, there had been some contingency planning. In May leaflets had been written and submitted to the Prime Minister for use in the event of war. He and Horace Wilson were a bit doubtful about their content. Would they really impress the

Der Führer spricht!

„Glauben Sie, daß wir unsere Jugend, die unsere ganze Zukunft ist, und an der wir alle hängen, nur erziehen, um sie dann auf dem Schlachtfelde zusammenschießen zu lassen? ... Niemand von uns denkt daran, mit Polen wegen des Korridors einen Krieg zu beginnen."
(Interview mit dem englischen Journalisten Ward Price.
V. B. 20. October 1933.)

„Deutschland hat mit Polen ... einen Nichtangriffsvertrag abgeschlossen, als einen weiteren mehr als wertvollen Beitrag zum europäischen Frieden, den es nicht nur blind halten wird, sondern von dem wir nur den einen Wunsch haben ... einer sich daraus immer mehr ergebenden freundschaftlichen Vertiefung unserer Beziehungen."
(Reichstagsrede vom 21. Mai 1935.)

Also sprach Adolf Hitler.

Germans by telling them that censorship 'has imprisoned your minds in, as it were, a concentration camp'? But since the printing was to cost only £300 it was done and the leaflets were ready.[96] During the night of 3–4 September more than six million of them were dropped over northern and western Germany.

On 27 September *The Times* described the process: 'The pamphlets were loaded into the aircraft in bundles about the size of a heavy brick ... The aeroplanes flew at a great height. At a signal from the pilot the "bricks" were released through the bomb hatches one after the other. The crews had to work at top speed. As the "bricks" fell the pamphlets spread out in a paper shower.' This was the theory at least, but it transpired the affair was not quite so simple. Very often, it was suggested, the papers did not scatter but turned into a soggy lump of pulp as they dropped through the damp clouds, only to land with a dull thud.[97]

It was a situation ripe for crude humour. There was the joke about the R A F pilot who did not return from a leaflet raid, was assumed to have crashed and given up for lost. Then a few days later he flew back to his base unharmed. He was asked where he had been. 'Delivering the leaflets,' he said. But he had misunderstood his orders and spent the time delivering each separate leaflet through German letter-boxes. Noel Coward saw the campaign as an attempt to bore the Germans to death. 'But do we have the time?' he wondered. There was a general feeling that the only result the millions of leaflets were likely to achieve was an easing of the acute German shortage of lavatory paper.

The leaflets, postcard-sized, printed in old Gothic script on coarse yellowish paper, were meant to depress the Germans and to divide them from the Nazis. One of them, for instance, quoted from the *Chicago Daily News* of 20 September thus: 'No matter what may happen to Nazi Germany as a result of the present war, Hitler's right-hand men – if they escape with their lives – will be able to live on the fat of the land.' It claimed they were piling up fortunes for themselves in foreign banks, and listed the actual balances, millions of Reichmarks, of each individual. Hitler's name was conspicuously absent from this list, but another leaflet, headed 'The Führer Speaks!', consisted of telling quotations of his words: '. . . none of us dreams of starting war with Poland over the Corridor' (*Völkischer Beobachter*, 20 October 1933); 'The rulers of present-day Russia are vile, blood-stained criminals' (*Mein Kampf*, German edition, p. 750); 'With one state alone have we sought no relations, nor do we wish to enter upon any closer relations with it – Soviet Russia!' (Reichstag speech, 30 January 1937); 'We have no more territorial claims to make in Europe' (Sportpalast speech, September 1938).[98] Other leaflets presented the Germans with extracts from Chamberlain's speeches – hardly a war-winning exercise.

Soon the Cabinet was getting reports from neutral countries – Denmark, Holland and Belgium – that the leaflet raids were not being successful, that they only showed our reluctance to fight the war properly, and irritated the Germans, who felt patronized by being urged to get rid of their government.[99] But they did not deter the campaign's director, who replied, 'Reference by Göring to British leaflets and extensive measures taken to prevent their being read by the German public have clearly indicated that the Nazi Government regard them as an effective weapon.' In fact what Göring had said, in a speech in a Berlin armaments factory on 9 September, was: 'If British aeroplanes fly through the night and drop their ridiculous propaganda upon us, I do not complain. But if the leaflets are accompanied by one single bomb – then watch out! Reprisals will follow and will be carried out exactly as in Poland.' [100] It hardly showed any great fear on the Nazi leader's part. 'Night after night,' another leaflet proclaimed, 'the British Air Force has demonstrated its power by flights far into German territory. Germans note!' [101] Hardly adequate, one feels today.

On 16 September Lord Halifax told the Cabinet he 'doubted whether any leaflet circulation would counteract the Nazi propaganda in Germany based on the successes of the Nazi arms in Poland'. Chamberlain disagreed. In his view 'this form of propaganda is good, useful and should be continued . . . The fact that the German Government was annoyed showed that the propaganda was bearing fruit.' It was another small example of the Prime Minister's wishful thinking, his unwillingness to believe the worst about the horrible situation his country faced. And there was a certain lack of taste involved in dropping this particular leaflet during the night of 24 September, while simultaneously Allied Warsaw, not for the last time in the war, was being blasted by the enemy into near oblivion.

The new Ministry of Information began receiving advice from all over the country on how the leaflets could be improved. One can see that the scope of the Government's critics was now limited. They could not for instance attack defence preparations, inefficiency of evacuation or even the blackout for fear of sounding like defeatists or trouble-makers. Members of parliament and newspaper editors were easily restrained by Government pressure from criticizing in the normal way. But the propagandists were thought far enough away from the security of the State, and so could be sniped at with impunity. Their work was by its very nature unpopular – censorship, morale-boosting at home – and they monopolized many sources. Many were newly recruited writers or academics, unused to being civil servants, to being unable to reply to their critics. Soon they were the most disliked department of the whole administration.

On 16 September the Minister, Lord Macmillan, came to a Cabinet meeting and told the members that 'the press correspondents in London as a whole, both British and foreign, were in a state of revolt'. The problem was that Samuel Hoare, Lord Privy Seal, had said for the Government on 13 September: 'The press censorship exists for one purpose only – to prevent information being published which would be useful and helpful to the enemy.' But this was just not the way the rules were being enforced. For instance, there was a ban on any discussion of Italian foreign policy, and Polish Ambassador Edward Raczynski's press conference attacking Mussolini's peace plan as a 'manœuvre' had been quashed on the ground that it might provoke the Italians. So was an article by former Premier Lloyd George in 24 September *Sunday Express*, which attacked Poland's 'class-ridden' government and praised the Red Army for liberating their countrymen from the Polish yoke. This article was only released by the censor after Chamberlain's personal intervention.[102]

Harold Nicolson wrote to his wife (14 September) that the Ministry of Information

has been staffed by duds at the top, and all the good people are in the most subordinate positions. The rage and fury of the newspapermen passes all bounds. John Gunther, for instance, told me that he has asked one of the censors for the text of our leaflets which we dropped over Germany. The request was refused. He asked why. The answer was, 'We are not allowed to disclose information which might be of value to the enemy.' When Gunther pointed out that two million of these leaflets had been dropped over Germany, the man blinked and said, 'Yes, something must be wrong there!'[103]

But it was not really a joking matter. Americans were depending for their knowledge of the war on their newspapers' correspondents in Europe, and if those in London were in a 'state of revolt', there was a danger that their irritation might communicate itself to their millions of readers and listeners. Dr Goebbels in Berlin was being much more astute, granting the foreign correspondents such privileges as extra rations, equivalent to those of heavy manual workers. On 28 September William Shirer was allowed to interview the U-boat commander Herbert Schultze.[104] No American in London was being offered such facilities. However sympathetic the journalists felt to the Allied cause, they would not have been human or true to their profession if they did not feel gratitude to the side which gave them the greater scope. In September many were threatening to leave Britain since they could not file their copy. News from Germany was being printed simply because it was the only news available. There can be no doubt that the birth-pangs of British censorship lost the Allies friends all over the world.

But civil servants, like other professional men, close ranks when under attack from outsiders. On 7 November Admiral Usborne, the chief censor, wrote asking all British newspapers not to mention the leaflet-dropping campaign ever again. Criticism of the leaflets' content, Walter Monckton explained, 'is inevitably dangerous. It encourages the enemy and helps him to ridicule an essential part of the war effort.' [105] The newspapers felt that suppression was even more dangerous, but they obeyed.

Before the ban a German refugee wrote to the *New Statesman* (16 September) suggesting that the Ministry's line was unlikely to convince the Germans. It did not help, he claimed, to complain that Hitler had betrayed Chamberlain and lied about not wanting any more territory. Most Germans were cynical about politicians, and anyway wanted Danzig and the Corridor to rejoin the Reich. It *would* impress, though, if they pointed out how Hitler had broken his promises to German workers. He had lowered wages, kept rents static, imposed restrictions on job changing and caused shortages in eggs, butter and meat. He had sold the South Tyrolese down the river to improve his relations with Mussolini, the Baltic Germans to improve his relations with Stalin. He had invaded Poland to add weight to the yoke, not to help the average man. It was a good letter with much food for thought about the art of propaganda, and about what the Allies were fighting for. But after November such things could not be printed.

For centuries British governments had found it possible to minimize censorship and propaganda. But in the autumn of 1939 they had to pay the price for their inexperience. There had been only the meagrest contingency planning. In September 1938 a thirty-eight-page booklet called *Defence Notes and Press Instructions* had been prepared as a general guide for editors. They were forbidden to mention British currency weakness, shortages, movements of Ministers or of the Royal Family. If they did, or printed anything else of possible value to the enemy, they could be prosecuted under Defence Regulations (3). There was also Regulation (39) B, which was aimed at anti-government propaganda, seditious or 'stop-the-war' material, but the idea of anyone being prosecuted under it was thought 'contrary to tradition' and it was never really enforced.

Typically, it was the Foreign Office which pressed for more stringent control. The art of the diplomat is the art of the tight-rope walker. Stability is achieved by the balance of weight against weight. The weights are heavy, so the balance must be very accurate. One little push from an external force and the edifice may collapse. This is how the British Foreign Office has viewed its role in politics. It accepts of course that other government departments have interests which sometimes conflict with that of diplomacy. Vital concerns of defence or finance may force the Foreign Office to shift its position and its relationship to one or another country. But in such cases it will be made aware of what it will be called upon to do and will be given time in which to make the change. Forewarned is forearmed, and it will usually in such cases be able to change step without falling off the wire.

The diplomat sees a free press as a greater danger. In Britain he has traditionally had no control and little influence on what is printed in newspapers, but this has not been the case in many other countries. In some parts of the world a country's press is seen as a reflection of its government's policy. *The Times* of London is still imagined by many, even by educated people, to be the official British Government newspaper. The British diplomat is continually worried lest some tactless or carelessly written article in a British newspaper may offend a foreign country, perhaps undoing in a day some agreement which he has spent years preparing. He will be blamed by foreigners for some insult which he had no part in perpetrating, which if he had known about it he would have tried to prevent. He knows that he can always appeal to the journalist in the name of the national interest, but he knows too that the journalist may resent his interference, suspecting instinctively that the diplomat wishes not so much to protect his country as to cover up some official blunder.

The two professions have a lot in common. Both are concerned with communication and the gathering of information. They form the two main permanent communities in foreign capital cities where, while they see much of one another socially, they are wary of one another professionally and often find themselves in serious conflict. When war breaks out the issues concerning the two professions are naturally more crucial, which increases the likelihood of an angry confrontation.

One such confrontation was soon provoked by an outburst on 13 September in the Rome newspaper *Popolo d'Italia*, which Mussolini owned, bitterly attacking an article by a British member of parliament in the *Glasgow Daily Record*. Apparently it had described Italy as a poverty-stricken country and its army as 'cowardly'. The British Embassy in Rome was outraged and passed the complaint back to the Foreign Office in London, where a strong line was taken by Andrew Noble, a senior official in the press department. 'We are completely at the mercy of "rags" like the *Daily Record* and *Sunday Express*,' he wrote. 'We are now engaged in a life-or-death struggle and cannot afford the luxury of allowing irresponsible newspapers to publish stuff that may undo all that we have done in matters of vital interest.'

The Foreign Office, and particularly the Ambassador in Rome, Percy Loraine, were proud of their diplomatic achievement in Italy. They believed that Italy's failure to enter the war on Germany's side was largely their doing, and for this they reserved for themselves much credit. Andrew Noble was inclined to see diplomacy as the key to keeping Italy out. He really appears to have thought that Mussolini was capable of declaring war on account of some insulting article in the press. Italy is neutral now, he wrote, 'but it won't be if such articles continue'. He came to a predictable conclusion: 'The only remedy is, I am afraid, a complete press censorship.'

It is indicative of the mood of Britain at the time and of Foreign Office attitudes in general that this little matter, an article in a provincial newspaper, was read and considered during days of acute world crisis at the highest possible level – by Orme Sargent, Alexander Cadogan, Halifax and finally by the Cabinet. The attitudes of Cadogan and Sargent are especially alarming. They agreed at once with Noble's diagnosis. 'I fear the Ministry of Information can do nothing without complete censorship powers,' noted Cadogan, and Sargent agreed with him.[106]

A little further investigation revealed how ridiculous was this extreme reaction. The author of the *Daily Record* article was John McGovern, a pacifist of the extreme left wing. His two most famous feats were when he once caused an interruption in the House of Lords during the King's Speech, and when on another occasion he was carried kicking and protesting from the House of Commons by eight attendants. He had never any connection with any British Government. He had been on a cycling tour of Italy with his family, and on his return written the article which appeared on 22 August, before war broke out, and which was quoted in Italy out of context. It took an official of the Ministry of Information to find out these facts and to calm the Foreign Office down.[107] He rallied to the press's defence, pointing out that the *Daily Record* was not a 'rag' but a respectable member of the Kemsley chain. His conclusion, which the Cabinet approved, was that 'none of us at the Ministry are in favour of complete press censorship. It isn't practicable and I don't think it's desirable.'

In this matter at least the Ministry of Information kept its head while other men were losing theirs. Its powers had been carefully calculated to preserve the maximum freedom of speech consistent with the vital interest of a country at war. Legally it could *prevent* the press from giving away information, but only *advise* against anything else. The system seemed liberal, depending as it did on the goodwill of editors, but this did not prevent the 'advice' being given in an arbitrary way. If an editor ignored the 'advice', he ran the risk of being called disloyal in time of war. Some felt they were being subjected to moral blackmail, and would have preferred the Ministry to issue definite rules and orders, to take responsibility for what they were doing instead of shifting it onto others.

The system favoured the irresponsible. For example, on 27 October the chief censor advised all newspapers to publish no details of weather conditions until fifteen days had passed. A few days later the *Sunday Times* printed a long article about floods along the east coast of England. Other newspapers' stories on the floods had been submitted to the Ministry and 'killed'. On 5 November the *Sunday Times* committed a more dangerous lapse, identifying as 'U-14' a sunken German submarine. The editor received 'letters of admonishment' and promised to behave himself in future. If he had dug his toes in, there would have been nothing for the Government to do short of prosecution, which would have been legally and politically very difficult. For months journals and pamphlets continued to be distributed, undermining the war effort and urging the Government to make peace with Hitler, but more than a year was to pass before one of these, the communist *Daily Worker*, was suppressed by government order (21 January 1941). Much resentment was caused by this crude act which could have been avoided if a more definite policy had been adopted at the outset.

The German Government of course had no such problems, its control of its press being absolute. Already Dr Goebbels had years of success to his credit. He had brought his Führer to power and conquest, had won him popularity and later the adoration of millions. It was true that Hitler had enemies in Germany, but his generally radiant image was not to be disfigured by the flea-bites of British and French leaflets. Goebbels could now afford to sow his seed in far countries, and in each one there was at least some fertile ground. To the sophisticated mind his methods seemed crude, but at least he knew his market – the ignorant, the arrogant, the frightened, all those rogues, idealists and honest men who wanted peace at any price.

By mid November Americans were receiving pamphlets through the post from Berlin claiming that Britain had supplied poison gas to Poland. A professor from Basle (Switzerland) named Rudolf Staehelin claimed to have examined German soldiers suffering from mustard-gas poisoning at Jasło near the Slovak border on 8 September. The symptoms were confirmed by a Swedish journalist and by a Mr Deuel of the *Chicago Daily News*. On 12 October the Ministry of Information announced: 'Great Britain has never supplied gas in any form whatsoever to Poland.' But the pamphlets kept coming, 10,000 being received in northern New Jersey alone, written in the style of the following: 'The Poles were the seduced, the British the seducers. Over and above this, the British not only supplied the gas, but made a good business out of it, for, as we have ascertained, John Bull, on top of all this, got his friends to pay for this gas in sound foreign exchanges. Liars,

Further discoveries of British poison gas in Poland!

The following is an official report:

On October 12th, the German Press published in the morning editions of the daily newspapers, details constituting incontrovertible proof that, firstly, poison gas had been used by Polish troops and secondly, that this poison gas had been supplied by Great Britain. The first definite reports concerning these monstrous facts were received as early as September 17th, 1939. Medical experts of international repute and neutral journalists were asked to assist in establishing indisputable and exhaustive proof of the various cases in which poison gas had been used. Only then did we inform world public opinion of the terrible details of this crime against humanity.

What was Great Britain's reply to these detailed German statements, to the expert report of the Swiss professor, Rudolf Staehelin, of Bâle, as well as to the evidence given by such eye-witnesses as the representative of the **Chicago Daily News** and of the **Associated Press,** of the Bâle **National-Zeitung** and of **Stockholms Tidningen?**

On October 12th, the British Ministry of Information published through the Reuter Bureau an assertion that "Great Britain has never supplied gas in any form whatsoever to Poland" (!) This is all that Great Britain had to say to the individually corroborated statements made by Germans or by neutrals regarding the use of poison gas in Poland and its delivery by Great Britain. Evidently the gravity of the accusation and the overwhelming testimony of the facts have this time deprived even the British Ministry of Information of its powers of speech, so that, except for this non-committal dementi, it was unable to produce any facts or evidence which could deny or palliate this accusation.

It is obvious that such a serious breach of International Law as the use and supply of poison gas by Great Britain cannot be done away with by a dementi of this kind.

The use of poison gas is one of the most detestable methods of warfare. It contravenes the International Protocol of June 17th, 1925, prohibiting the use of poison gas in warfare, and the delivery of poison gas by Great Britain, the very country whose leading politicians are constantly preaching humane methods of warfare, is further proof of the hypocritical and unscrupulous forms of warfare of that country.

We have, however, not only to ask in how far Great Britain believes that she can escape this serious question by a laconic reply, but we have today to bring a fresh grave accusation against Great Britain as being implicated in the criminal use of gas in warfare, for, in the meantime, new and definite reports have reached us, according to which poison gas was not only used in Jaslo, the place mentioned in the German Communiqué of October 12th, but also in numerous other places in Poland. In these cases, it could again be proved that the poison gas bombs, or, as the case may be, the poison gas liquid, were likewise taken from the ammunition depot in the neighbourhood of Gotenhafen, which is definitely proved to have contained the deliveries of ammunition brought to Gotenhafen in British ships.

The following fresh facts can today be laid before the world:

1. Near Mlava, a place situated to the south of East Prussia, another huge store of several thousand mustard gas mines has been discovered, which are of proved British origin and correspond in every detail with the mustard gas mines found near Oxhoeft. According to investigations made by the pharmaceutical-toxicological department of the Military Medical Academy in Berlin, all tests made on samples taken at random from the enormous supplies of mustard gas mines stored in Mlava have shown that the poison found here was dichlordiethyl sulphide, i. e. the same kind as was used in the British mustard gas mines already discovered. At the moment, the exact figure of the British mustard gas mines found at Mlava is not available, since their removal must be carried out with the utmost caution. It has, however, already been ascertained that this second large depot of British poison gas is far larger than that at Gotenhafen.

2. To what diabolical uses the Poles put the mustard gas supplied to them by Great Britain is shown by an incident which occurred at Kuczbork, a small town 12½ miles west of Mlava. Here grain was found, the use of

which as cattle-fodder had been prohibited by the burgomaster of Kucsbork. As this store of grain was thought to be suspect, it was put on one side and examined. About ten hours later, blisters appeared all over the bodies of those occupied in clearing it away. Some time afterwards, it was discovered in hospital that not only was there a brown discolouration of almost the whole skin of the persons concerned but also serious burns. A 'closer investigation of the grain showed that Polish troops had infected it with mustard gas, which had doubtless been taken from the large dump at Mlava.

3. In clearing up a Polish battery emplacement near Blozna, in the neighbourhood of Ilza, a large number of canisters, marked with red stripes and weighing between 22 and 33 lbs., were discovered. German infantry soldiers who had examined their contents, were taken to a field hospital suffering from severe burns. Investigations, which were promptly carried out, furnished fresh evidence that these canisters, too, contained mustard gas supplies of exactly the same composition as was contained in the mustard gas mines found near Oxhoeft. From empty mines found in the vicinity, it appeared that the canisters had been put ready to fill these mines, and that a fresh crime had only been prevented here by the speed of the German advance.

4. In a wood to the east of Ostrowiez, the gunners Seidel, Golup and Kotias suffered the most severe injuries due to mustard gas in a similar manner to the infantrymen near Blozna, when they came upon considerable stores of mustard gas in the course of clearing operations. The stores had been partially buried. On this occasion, the note from the Polish military authorities accompanying these consignments of poison gas supplies fell into German hands. From this note it is clear that the poison gas came from the same store near Oxhoeft, the British origin of which was proved on October 12th.

5. A further Polish store of poison gas supplied by Britain has been found in the neighbourhood of Blonis near Warsaw, where German engineers were again seriously injured during clearing operations.

The above are fresh facts showing Britain's share in the poison gas warfare against Germany in Poland.

The question now is, whether the British Ministry of Information still believes that it is possible to refute these outrageous facts by means of a simple lie. The British dementi made on October 12th is on a similar footing with Mr. Churchill's statement with regard to the capture of that German submarine commander who, as is well known, had the honour to send him a telegram after he had safely reached a German port. It is on a par with the reported bombardment of Kiel, the statement regarding which was later withdrawn somewhat shamefacedly by the British Ministry of Information itself. When the mines and the mustard gas supplies were conveyed from Britain to Poland in several ship-loads shortly before the outbreak of the war, it was probably believed in the circles concerned in Britain that Poland would be able to hold out long enough for the Secret Service agents to remove every trace of incriminating evidence against Britain. This assumption, however, proved to be false. Owing to the incredible speed of the German advance, we gained possession of those stores and documents which proved conclusively Britain's guilt.

The detailed statement regarding British poison gas warfare, which appeared in the German Press on October 12th, has aroused a storm of indignation throughout the civilized world.

The appalling condition of the victims of mustard gas poisoning, as described in the German Press, and the irrefutable medical reports, including that given by the Swiss professor, Rudolf Staehelin, have this time confronted the British Ministry of Information with a problem which is insoluble even for them. These facts and proofs are absolutely indisputable. Hence their feeble dementi. But nobody in the world now any longer believes the words of the British Ministry of Information, for, as the daily testimony of the British public confirms, this new British Ministry has already told so many lies that it must produce irrefutable documentary evidence if it is to be believed at all — even in its own country.

In this matter of mustard gas poisoning, evidence is accumulating rapidly. Here, too, the Poles were the seduced, the British the seducers. Over and above this, the British not only supplied the gas, but made a good business out of it, for, as we have ascertained, John Bull, on top of all this, got his friends to pay for this poison gas in sound foreign exchanges. Liars, hypocrites and criminals against humanity — that is what they are, these British war-lords!

A German propaganda leaflet circulated in America. (Crown Copyright. Public Record Office. FO 371/23040 f 287) hypocrites and criminals against humanity — that is what they are, these British war-lords!' [108]

Such ravings probably did little harm to the Allied cause in America, Goebbels's most important target, but they did in other countries. Pamphlets were being translated into all the main languages and sent out by the million. British embassies spent hours collecting samples and sending them home for comment, but there was very little counter-propaganda; it was a fight with only one man doing the punching. Still, even Goebbels's men made mistakes. In Haiti, a French-speaking country, thousands of pamphlets arrived, all in Spanish.

It was Britain that the pamphlets attacked, according to one survey ten times more than France. It was Hitler's belief, and he may have been right, that without the British pressure France would never have fought. On 10 October he told his generals of his plan to attack in the West 'if it becomes clear that England, and under England's leadership also France, are unwilling to end the war'. If he were to attack, it was the French who would have to do most of the defending, having seventy-two divisions along the Line, while the British had only four. It was true, and Hitler may have guessed, that relations between Paris and London were confused, both suspicious the other might leave it in the lurch. It was a situation ripe for 'divide and conquer' tactics.

Prime Minister Daladier in a speech on 21 September had emphasized German outrages against France: 'Germany has tried to make propaganda in France which would dismember the country. She has sought with money to provoke so-called autonomous movements, to separate one province from another. She has printed maps on which France is amputated and sundered. She has disguised Germans as Alsatians, and paraded them at congresses and festivals. She has sought to buy traitors in Brittany and Alsace.' [109] For Daladier it was an eloquent, violent speech and clearly he felt, even in September, that he needed to justify the war. At this stage it was the French Government, not German bombs or bullets, that was causing separation of husband from wife.

Hitler exploited this fact cleverly. On 20 September in the Guild Hall in newly 'liberated' Danzig he made his first speech since 1 September. 'My sympathies are with the ordinary French soldier,' he said. 'What he is fighting for he does not know.' Again, in his 6 October 'peace' speech he said: 'Germany has no further claims on France . . . I have refused even to mention the question of Alsace–Lorraine . . . I have conveyed to France my wish to end for ever our ancient hostility, to bring together our two nations which have such glorious pasts . . .'

Frenchmen too began during September to receive German propaganda through the post, sent at random to addresses in the telephone directory. The letters were gently worded, more in sorrow than in anger, pointing out that Germany was nowhere oppressing Frenchmen, and had wished all along no more than to restore Germans to the fold. Some claimed that the British planned to defeat Germany and to partition her, to restore independent Austria, to achieve 'complete reestablishment of Poland, including the Corridor and Upper Silesia, annexation pure and simple of Danzig by the Poles'.[110] In fact this is exactly what the Allies did six bloody years later.

France too got her rain of words from the skies, most of it over the Maginot Line, but some of it on cities like Bordeaux in western France. 'Frenchmen!' read one typical appeal. 'On the orders of London your press has been forced to conceal from you the contents of this [6 October] speech.' They plugged the theme of France's subservience to Britain, and the injustice of this while France was bearing the main burden of defence. One leaflet was almost beautiful: red-gold in colour and shaped like an autumn leaf, it was almost undetectable as it lay by the million over France in late 1939. On the 'leaf' was written a piece of semi-poetry: 'Autumn. The leaves fall. We also shall fall. Leaves fall because God so desires. But we fall because the English so desire. Next spring no one will remember either the dead leaves or the soldiers who are killed. Life will pass on over our graves.'

One can imagine the effect of such spine-chilling threats on Frenchmen, sad at being so suddenly torn from their families, bored as they dug themselves in along a deathly quiet Front Line. On 10 September Paul Reynaud told British Ambassador Phipps that any German peace offensive 'was sure to gain many more listeners on this side of the Channel'. His was a more general view than that of his fellow-minister Mandel, a stouter spirit, who told Phipps on 7 September that 'anyone here who counted would refuse to listen to Germania's siren voice, and anyone who was tempted to listen would be swept away like a straw by the wind'.[110] Many Frenchmen may have misunderstood as aggression or bellicosity Britain's violent anti-Hitlerism, her announcement of preparation for a three-year war and her rejection of peace overtures. Such posturings, when backed by such a puny army, can seem not only steadfast, but also arrogant and dangerous.

Reynaud told Phipps that 'British troops should be seen at once and photographed marching through French towns and villages'. There might not be very many of them, but at least they should be seen to be there. It might stop the complaints about England's readiness to 'fight to the last Frenchman'. The problem was, though, that the British military leaders opposed any such publicity. 'The greater secrecy the better,' was their motto, and it cut right across the demands of Anglo-French understanding.

On 14 September Gamelin received a letter from Ironside asking him to see that nothing whatever was published about the movements of British troops in the French press.[112] It was the trigger for one of many battles between the generals and the diplomats, the former wanting secrecy, the latter publicity. There was now a complete official censorship over the French press, so Gamelin was able to enforce Ironside's request. The most French journalists could do was to 'lift' stories about the British forces from British newspapers. Thus on 20 September the Paris *Figaro* wrote glowingly from 'somewhere in France' about a day spent 'avec les Tommies', but French newspapers could not use their own men on such jobs. Ambassador Phipps was worried that this situation might undermine the goodwill most Frenchmen felt towards their ally. Kirkpatrick in the Foreign Office agreed. 'In this respect,' he minuted, 'we have something to learn from Germany. The German Ministry of Propaganda has given out a mass of information in regard to military operations and has published a number of photographs.'[113]

After all, the Foreign Office pointed out, the British did have something to be proud of. The movement of the Expeditionary Force had been the swiftest transport ever of an army oversea. The Royal Air Force had been in position in France two hours after the declaration of war, and the naval blockade was likewise enforced immediately, not after a few months as in 1914. It was all very well for the British to be reserved and modest, but these are not qualities which the Frenchman admires most. British understatement was being interpreted as weakness.

The British Air Attaché in Paris was pleading for more inspiring communiqués. In 1939 (although not in 1940) the R A F was not announcing it had destroyed enemy aircraft unless this was absolutely confirmed. True, the French press were doing their best to improve on the stark facts. On 2 October *Paris Midi* quoted an R A F report that fifteen Messerschmidts had shot down five British Battles for the loss of two 'confirmed' of their own. 'As a result of this,' the French paper added, 'the thirteen remaining Messerschmidts were put to flight!' The Allies seemed unable to make propaganda without turning it into something ridiculous.

British officials seemed quite bewildered with their new task. Suspicious of the press even at the best of times, they seemed unable to appreciate that in time of war the traditional conflict between the two professions simply could not be allowed to exist. Few editors begrudged the administration the modest powers they took, a largely voluntary system in which each of them was his own censor. They were prepared to do their bit, to exude confidence and to bolster up national morale, tasks which the press of a free country does not relish or easily fulfil. In return they wanted the right to do their job, to inform the public as far as the national emergency permitted. For this they needed not only freedom, but also cooperation. It was months before the Ministry of Information was able to work out even a reasonable *modus vivendi*. In contrast the German and Soviet ministries had controlled their countries' press and radio for years, so they were not nearly so confused by the emergency. It meant simply that their existing organizations had to move into a higher gear, and continue along the same track, only faster. In Britain and France the idea of communications media being centrally controlled seemed wrong, and it was accepted only as a necessary evil.

In 1939 Germany and Russia were ruled by two very cruel men, both well embarked on a course of mass murder which was eventually to claim millions of victims. When such men govern a country, they govern it entirely, not just its administration, police, post office and foreign policy, but also its industry, press, law courts, education and the movement of its population. Such men hold as a matter of course powers which other governments claim only in time of national emergency. Indeed, they maintain their power by creating the illusion of a permanent emergency, and by exaggerating its threat. Hitler and Stalin were in a war situation already, to which they owed their rise to power, on which they depended for political survival. They spoke its language, Stalin that of class war, Hitler that of race war. So when *real* war came in September 1939, they had a head start over Chamberlain and Daladier, who were men of peace and had little stomach even for a war of words.

One might have thought that Hitler's extreme nationalist and racist views were by definition unexportable. According to his ideology the Nordic race was superior to all others. More than ninety per cent of the world's population was, he claimed, his unalterable inferior. It is a measure of Dr Goebbels's skill that in spite of this Germany was able to win such support all over the world. True, Goebbels was helped by Germany's big battalions, but in his own propaganda battle he showed the initiative and readiness to fight that every winner needs. His convictions were vile, but he had the courage of them, while his enemies apologized to their friends abroad and to themselves for having allowed war to happen.

Hitler won the 1939 war of words. He saturated the world with allegations that Great Britain was weak, brutal, dishonest and the enemy of neutral countries. No one remained uninformed of how tiny was the British Army, her losses at sea, her government of 'ancient men' and the chaos caused by evacuation. He had made a case that the naval blockade was piracy on the high seas, and a brutal attempt to cause mass malnutrition in women and children. The British had supplied poison gas to Poland, torpedoed one of their own passenger ships to try to drag the United States into war, attempted to assassinate the German Führer with a bomb in a Munich beer cellar.

True, the sophisticated laughed at Goebbels's crudities, but they were not the ones he was trying to impress. He flung so much mud that some of it, even if it did not stick, at least smeared a moral issue which should have been clear and obscured the unarguable fact that Hitlerism, however understandable in origin, was an evil which had to be destroyed. And there are always those who are fascinated by violence and admire ruthlessness. These few he successfully enlisted as allies. But his real success was in postponing, for the majority, recognition of his government's viciousness, and of the threat it posed to the whole world.

Socrates made the worse appear the better cause. Goebbels made the worst cause of all seem no worse than any other, not much worse than those of Chamberlain and Daladier. This was the measure of his brilliant short-term success as a propagandist, and of their failure.

6 Truce in the Empire

The countries which declared war on Germany in 1939 to thwart her eastward expansion were the masters of the world's two greatest colonial empires. France, though herself economically weak and politically not very stable, ruled Algeria, Tunisia, Morocco, Lebanon, Syria and most of Central Africa. When France declared war on Germany so did her Empire. Likewise Britain's declaration was assumed to have brought into the war all of the several dozen countries that were legally British colonies. Only with the self-governing Dominions was there any question that the matter might have to be decided outside London, and in each one the speed of decision and depth of commitment were different, emphasizing the various relationships they had with Britain.

The King of England was also King of Canada, Australia, New Zealand, South Africa and (some thought) of Ireland. There were some lawyers who took the view that when the King was at war all territories of which he was Head of State were also at war automatically. This apparently was the opinion of the Australian Government which never in fact declared war on Germany, believing such an act superfluous. There was never any doubt that Australia would fight. On 23 August Robert Menzies, the Prime Minister, assured the world that 'Britain has the fullest cooperation in her magnificent efforts to avoid the injustice and insanity of war. If her great efforts fail, we will stand by her side.' The invasion of Poland served only to raise the patriotic fervour of the Prime Minister's oratory. 'There is unity in the Empire ranks — one

King, one flag, one cause. We stand with Britain,' he said on 2 September. New Zealand Prime Minister Savage felt the same way, for he said in a broadcast on 6 September, 'With gratitude for the past and confidence for the future, we range ourselves without fear beside Britain. Where she goes we go; where she stands we stand.' [1]

In these two countries political argument over the war was confined to matters of degree, to how far they should be ready to make sacrifices to help 'the mother country', as Menzies was then able to call Britain in all seriousness. The Australian Labour Party, for instance, while committed to general support of Britain, was opposed to conscription or to the dispatch of Australian forces overseas. In November they opposed Menzies's plan to send a division of infantry to Europe. But Menzies's government persisted, contributing in addition a naval force of fifteen minesweepers and five armed merchant cruisers, a large number of pilots and other air crew, as well as valuable economic help. New Zealand offered Britain a fully equipped division for service anywhere in the world.

Canada was only slightly less eager, which is surprising when one considers that whereas Australia's and New Zealand's ties with Britain were then so close that they excluded other major countries, Canada had both close ties with and a certain dependence on the United States. There was thus a clear conflict of loyalties. The American people were horrified at the prospect of becoming involved in the war. For Canada to declare war would seem to them like a first step in that direction, for it meant bringing the war to the American continent and to the borders of the United States. In an effort to keep Canada out President Roosevelt had publicly guaranteed Canada's integrity, thus removing the purely defensive need for Canada to join Britain at the outset.

But Canada's leading political forces were unanimous that war should be declared. Mackenzie King, the Liberal Prime Minister, and Dr Manion, the Leader of the Conservative Opposition, approved a declaration on 10 September, a week after that of Britain and France. The delay was important in that it enabled Canada to take delivery of large amounts of war material from the United States before 10 September, when this became illegal under the Neutrality Act, and also demonstrated that Canada was taking her own decision instead of slavishly following Britain's lead, as might well have been said of Australia and New Zealand.

Fortunately for Canada's unity, both Britain and France were in the war, and on the same side, so there was no real reason for the French Canadians to stand aside. Both mother countries were equally involved. The leading French Canadian minister in the government supported the war wholeheartedly. Only in Quebec was there significant opposition from the Union Nationale led by Maurice Duplessis, who decided to put the whole question of Quebec's participation in the war before the provincial electorate on 25 October. It was a serious matter for, in the words of Mackenzie King, 'if the Duplessis Ministry had won, the result would have been hailed throughout Germany as an unmistakable sign of dissension within the Dominion about Canada's entry into the war'. Luckily for the Allied cause, Quebec's separatist movement had not reached the fever pitch that it was to achieve in 1970. Duplessis lost control of the province and six of his nine ministers lost their seats. Canada continued to provide the Allies with assistance: her vast wheat reserves, her nickel, asbestos and woodpulp, and later on her fighting men.[2]

South Africa's decision to fight was even less of a foregone conclusion than Canada's, not surprisingly, for in this part of the Empire lived a large number of men who by and large sympathized with Hitler and his ideology. Then as now the South Africans of European origin were separated from black Africans and others by complicated legislation aimed at preserving political power in the hands of the white minority. It was understandable that they should admire a man like Hitler who also believed fervently that there were basic unalterable differences between the various races of humanity, and that of these the north European race was best in every respect. South Africa had already put this belief into practice, and its economy depended on the availability of cheap labour from black men and women who had small voice in how the country was governed and its wealth divided.

The Afrikaans-speaking whites had of course no reason at all to like the British who, they felt, had attacked and humiliated them in the Boer War at the turn of the century. Some of them were aggressive enough to dream of South African expansion northwards into British territory, a gradual extension of their power as ruling race over the whole of Africa south of the equator. If Britain were defeated in war this dream might become a reality, they thought. By the same token such men could have little objection to Hitler's plans for the conquest of eastern Europe and for the enslavement of the Slavs. After all, he was only doing what they wanted to do, and had already begun. Indeed he should be encouraged, for German domination of Europe could only decrease British and French power in Africa, to the consequent aggrandisement of South Africa. Hitler would rule his European empire and leave South Africa to her African one.

Such arguments, however attractive on the surface to some white South Africans, were as politically naive as they were morally diabolical, for there was little justification for their assumption that a victorious Germany would confine her imperial interests to Europe and leave Africa to others. Hitler's Germany thrived on an atmosphere of crisis and spectacular success. After the great victory it would hardly have settled down to the quiet enjoyment of the gains it had won. Newly born empires do not behave like that. Success tends to go to their heads. They are inclined not to consolidate but to reach out further and further until in the end they overbalance and collapse. And it was obvious that the first piece of overseas territory that Germany would claim after victory would be South-West Africa, which until 1915 had been a German colony and where many thousands of Germans still lived, most of them strongly pro-Nazi. The Treaty of Versailles had placed the territory under South African administration with a mandate from the League of Nations – and everyone knew what Hitler thought of the Treaty of Versailles.

The South African Prime Minister James Herzog had, according to Anthony Eden, 'shown marked sympathy for the German cause',[3] and everyone expected that when war broke out against Germany he would proclaim neutrality – an act which he could do on his own authority, without recalling Parliament. But he had overlooked one thing: that on 6 September the elected South African Senators would reach the end of their ten-year term and that Parliament would have to be summoned to prolong it. The House of Assembly was duly recalled on 2 September, and at once Herzog's Cabinet split on the war issue. His only recourse was now to put the matter to Parliament, which he did on 4 September.

Jan Smuts, then Minister of Justice and a member of Herzog's Cabinet, broke with his boss and proposed an amendment calling for the severance of relations with Germany. South-West Africa was his trump card. In his crucial speech he made the point that if South Africa continued to deal with Germany on friendly terms while both Britain and the other Dominions were at war with her, South Africa would lose all credit among democratic nations. 'When the day of trouble comes,' he went on, 'when we are faced with the demand for the return of South-West Africa at the point of a bayonet, we shall have to say whether we are going to face that issue alone, because our friends would then be against us.' Smuts's amendment was carried by eighty votes to sixty-seven.

It is British constitutional practice that a Prime Minister cannot remain in office unless he has a majority in the elected assembly. This means that if a Prime Minister is voted down and cannot at once obtain a vote of confidence, either he must go or the assembly must go. Herzog decided that the second course was preferable. He went to the Governor-General Patrick Duncan, who represented the King, and asked for a dissolution so that the issue could be decided by the electorate. In a decision of great constitutional importance, quite apart from the matter of peace or war, Duncan refused Herzog's request on the ground that there was no need to call a general election if someone else could be found with a permanent majority in the House of Assembly. Herzog had then no alternative but to resign, and Smuts was invited by Duncan to form a government.

Smuts became Prime Minister on 5 September and declared war on Germany the next day. His only concession to the anti-war men was a speech on 7 September in which he said that South Africa's participation in the war would of necessity be limited by geography, that her first duty was to put her own defences in order and that therefore he could not 'give any encouragement to those citizens who wish to serve overseas'. But he went on, 'The House, which was free to have decided otherwise, takes a stand for the defence of freedom and the destruction of Hitlerism and all that it implies.'

In the days that followed large numbers of South Africans suspected of pro-Nazi sympathies were arrested and interned. Herzog and his followers were furious at being deprived of power by a sort of legal *coup d'état*, and they soon broke completely with Smuts and the Union Party. In an angry speech on 4 November Herzog said that South Africa had been dragged into the war by 'British-thinking jingos'. 'What stronger argument could be found for secession from the Commonwealth?' he asked.[5] He could not imagine a more powerful weapon in the hands of those who wanted to break all ties with Great Britain, although for the time being he did not wish to reckon himself one of them.

All over her Empire, Britain was being called to account for her past mistakes and failures as well as rewarded with cooperation and praise for her successes. Australia and New Zealand were not the only lands to offer unequivocal support. The Sheikh of Bahrain, for instance, presented Britain with £30,000 towards the cost of the war.[5] More important was the Sheikh's kind message: 'Great Britain has protected Bahrain and insured its prosperity by guarding trade and maintaining peace in the Persian Gulf. We are grateful to Great Britain.' In the Gold Coast (Ghana) a formal debate was held on the war: 'The Omanhene of Akwapim first addressed his councillors and chiefs in durbar, stating the case for both Great Britain and Nazi Germany. Debate and consultation followed, at the close of which the chief linguist gave judgement in favour of King George. Three cheers were then raised for King George "for winning the case", and three hoots were given for Hitler whose case was declared to be bad.'[6]

In India the political situation was more sophisticated and delicate, for since 1935 there had been movement towards parliamentary self-government on local level in the eleven provinces, eight of which were in 1939 controlled by the Congress Party, lead by Gandhi and Nehru. In mid September this Party issued a statement in which they asked the British Government 'what their war aims are in regard to democracy and imperialism . . . in particular how these aims are going to apply to India'.

The Congress Party, whose membership was mainly Hindu but which aspired to represent the whole of India, was asking Britain to set a date for total independence, something which at this stage Britain had no intention of doing. The situation was complicated by the counter-pressure to Congress exerted by the

Muslim League, which represented India's biggest minority. (At the 1931 census a total population of 353,000,000 was counted, of which 240,000,000 were Hindus and 78,000,000 Muslims.) The League complained publicly on 15 September that Muslim 'rights and culture are being assailed and annihilated every day under the Congress governments in various provinces'. Muslims would not be able to cooperate fully with Britain until the Viceroy was able to secure them 'justice and fair play'.

The Viceroy replied with a statement on 17 October which both Hindu and Muslim found unsatisfactory, promising only Dominion status, and this only after the war was won. In the meantime it proposed some slight increase in Indian influence through a Consultative Committee on the war and through some Indian representation in the Viceroy's Council, provided that basic agreement could first be reached between Congress and the Muslim League.

Britisches Liebeswerben um Indien:
1857

1939

„Los — an die Kanone — das bist du ja schon gewöhnt!"

Hitler's newspaper recalls cruel British repressions after the 1857 Indian Mutiny. The caption reads, 'Go on, get on the end of that gun, you must be used to it by now!' (Copyright British Museum)

Congress took the view that they themselves were quite capable of deciding the communal question, and that the first step must be majority rule (which meant Congress rule). They decided no longer to cooperate with the British in the administration of India and their ministries in the provinces resigned.

Congress's mid September statement showed that at least they had no illusions about Hitler, for as well as its demands upon the British it declared 'entire disapproval of the ideology and practice of Fascism and Nazism and their glorification of war and violence and the suppression of the human spirit'. But the next few years were to show how difficult it is for people under foreign rule to see any greater evil than the power which actually controls them. When a power which occupies one's own land has an enemy, it is all too tempting to ally oneself with that enemy and help destroy the influence of the occupying power. The Indian nationalists and the Nazis made strange bedfellows, with the latter regarding the former as sub-human, and there were a few Indians who proceeded to help Hitler directly, though this did not apply to Congress Party as a whole.

Of the many cold, harsh facts that Britain was suddenly called upon to face in September 1939, not the least unpleasant was the realization that her hold over her Commonwealth and Empire had weakened. Now that Britain was at war, her close and in some cases master-and-servant relationship with her Dominions and Colonies was suddenly open to question since, to face the brutal truth, the United Kingdom was now a liability to the rest. They would support her for reasons of loyalty and history, but hardly of self-interest, since the conflict was thousands of miles away and no immediate threat to their security. They might sympathize with England and believe in the rightness of her cause, but then so by and large did the United States. One does not involve oneself in war out of sympathy.

Britain's difficulty had automatically raised the question of the extent to which the Commonwealth should help her, and the ensuing debate had opened the door to expressions of resentment as well as of loyalty. All over the world attitudes to Britain and France were being polarized, each country and each shade of political opinion leaping forward to judge them on the basis of recent experience. In such a situation there could be no doubt where Britain would find the deepest hostility and the least inclination to assist – in Ireland.

Britain's treatment of the Irish is the most shameful chapter in her history as an imperial power. Massacred in the seventeenth century by Oliver Cromwell, starved by the million in the potato famine of 1846–7 which Britain did little to relieve, terrorized in the twentieth century by gangs of specially recruited louts they called 'Black and Tans', the Irish have good historical reason to dislike their powerful neighbour. Why Britain should have treated Ireland worse than she treated her other numerous colonies is hard initially to understand. The two nations have exchanged large numbers of their populations and have intermarried. They have become close, not only geographically, but also linguistically and culturally. Perhaps it is this that explains Britain's harshness, for she could not tolerate being rejected by a country which, she felt, was so close to her. The hostility of a friend or relation is harder to bear than the hostility of a stranger. Until the 1920s at least Britain's imperial 'mission' was accepted with little protest in Africa and India. Was it not then the height of irrationality and ungratefulness for the Irish to reject it? Surely those Irish who fought against British rule must be some tiny, vicious minority, unrepresentative of Ireland? They must be criminals, in which case the only way to treat them is by the methods they understand – by force.

By 1939, in spite of having granted independence to all Ireland but the six north-eastern counties, Britain was reaping the whirlwind of her repression. Far from being grateful to Britain for the 'gift' of independence, most Irishmen resented her for holding on to the Six Counties. Britain saw no reason why she should give up her control of the North, which was supported by the Protestant majority who lived there. What is more, she still set much store by Ireland's tenuous link with the British Crown, which had not yet been finally cut. Because of this link, a few optimistic (or pessimistic) Britons might still pretend to believe that the whole of Ireland was British.

Ireland had just endured the tragedy of civil war. This, combined with the uneasy truce with Britain and the unsatisfactory partition, left both countries wounded in their souls. The Irish, forced to choose between collaboration and armed protest, suffered all the heartache that such situations create. Britain had suffered too, for the Irish issue dominated her politics and all but destroyed the Liberals, formerly one of her two great parties of government. It earned her deep odium throughout the world, especially in America whither many Irish had fled to assuage their hunger. It left her with a responsibility for the loyalists of Ulster which was to cause her damage and embarrassment years later.

In 1939 Ireland was the only British Dominion not to follow Britain's lead in declaring war on Germany. Hitler was quick to exploit the potential situation, and on 31 August his Minister in Dublin, Eduard Hempel, had a long talk with the Taoiseach (Prime Minister), Eamon de Valera. Hempel assured De Valera that if war came Germany would observe Irish neutrality. De Valera indicated to him that neutrality would probably be Ireland's choice, but pointed out that 'very special relations' existed between Ireland and Great Britain. The Irish Sea was narrow, he told Hempel, and trade with Britain was vital to Ireland. There could therefore be no question of Ireland being used for espionage, propaganda or any other anti-British purpose by the 'anti-British radical nationalist group'.[7]

For one thing Britain was anxious about Ireland being used to leak information. There were many thousands of Irishmen in Britain, and it had to be assumed that a few of them were fanatically anti-British. Only recently a group of such men had caused a bomb explosion in Coventry and several deaths. Britain thought there would be people like this willing enough to work for Germany, to gather information and write or telephone it home where there was a German Legation. The mail and telephone traffic between the two countries was heavy and Britain would have difficulty in controlling it all. If the Irish language was used, the task would of course be quite impossible, for only the Irish speak Irish and not even very many of them.

De Valera explained this to Hempel and told him frankly that in matters such as censorship, telephone tapping and radio monitoring Ireland would have to collaborate directly with Britain. Hempel was ready enough to accept this small price. Irish neutrality would be regarded by German diplomacy as an important *coup*.

The British Government was unaware of De Valera's intention. At the 1 September Cabinet meeting the Dominions Secretary,

Thomas Inskip, said he assumed that when Britain entered the war De Valera would at the very least break off diplomatic relations with Germany. John Dulanty, the Irish High Commissioner in London, who had been a British civil servant during the First World War, was equally ignorant of his country's policy. He told Inskip 'that he thought that in a week Eire [Ireland] would come in on our side because of attacks on shipping'.[8] According to Churchill, 'He acts as a general smoother, representing everything Irish in its most favourable light.'[9]

It may therefore have been a mild surprise to Britain when on 2 September De Valera spoke in the Irish Parliament (the Dail) and proclaimed neutrality. From the Allied point of view it was not a very encouraging speech. Of all nations, he said, the Irish had known what force used by a strong nation against a weaker one could mean. They had known the meaning of invasion and partition. They were not forgetful of their own history, and so long as any portion of their country was subject to force by a stronger nation, they ought to look to their own country first.

This last sentence was disagreeable enough to British ears, but there were some Irishmen who saw in it an inference that if partition were removed, Ireland would be ready enough to join Britain in war. Whether this is what De Valera meant is hard now to say. Perhaps De Valera did not know himself. A year previously he had told the British Minister for Co-ordination of Defence, Thomas Inskip, that 'if partition could be got rid of it would be comparatively easy for him to make a complete defensive alliance with the United Kingdom'.[10] On the other hand a year later, in 1940, when Churchill offered him a united Ireland in return for Irish support in the war, De Valera refused.[11]

Like all leaders who have ruled Ireland since independence, De Valera had the problem of dealing with the hard core of men who have not forgiven Great Britain for the wrong she did Ireland over the centuries, and who remain Britain's bitter enemies. For instance, at a Gaelic football match in Dublin on 10 September leaflets were handed round proclaiming the old slogan from the First World War that 'England's Difficulty is Ireland's Opportunity' and calling for recruits to the extremist Irish Republican Army.[12] A few months earlier the IRA had sent an 'ultimatum' to Halifax about partition and followed it up with bomb outrages. In June 1939 De

Valera had declared the IRA an illegal organization. In the early days of the war four leaders of the IRA, including two who had signed the ultimatum, were arrested in Dublin and *The Times* rejoiced that De Valera was apparently determined to check such extremists.[13] He was indeed determined to check them, but equally he felt that he could not afford to provoke them by taking any excessively pro-British stand.

De Valera had also to take account of his more respectable political opponents, for instance the Irish Labour Party, which published a manifesto declaring that 'the issue of the war is the supremacy of one bloc of great powers over the other, it is again the clash of conflicting imperialisms'. A few days later the world communist movement would adopt the same line. Referring to De Valera's 2 September speech in the Dail, the manifesto went on, 'We wish to declare that, irrespective of any adjustment that may take place in the matter of the partition of Ireland, we shall resolutely oppose any participation in the war which is causing such misery, torture and suffering to the workers of Europe.' It complained that British newspapers were full of 'war propaganda' and should be banned for the duration.

On 24 September Churchill minuted, 'Three quarters of the people of Southern Ireland are with us, but the implacable, malignant minority can make so much trouble that De Valera dare not do anything to offend them.'[14] But the situation did leave room for *some* conciliatory gestures towards Britain. On 5 September the Cabinet was told that De Valera 'had expressed the desire to help', provided of course that his neutrality was observed. On 22 September he wrote to Chamberlain, adding in his own hand at the bottom of the letter, 'I would like you to know how much I sympathize with you in your present anxieties.' The problem was, though, that the British were fighting for their lives and they wanted more than sympathy. They could not have Ireland as an ally, very well, they would accept this apparently unnatural fact with as good a grace as possible. What they would not accept was German U-boats using Ireland's territorial waters as sanctuary from attack by British destroyers, or as bases where they could refit and refurbish in preparation for attacks on Allied shipping. The ideal place for U-boats to lurk was off the southern coast of Ireland, where they could pick off ships on their way to and from

America. The British sensed that soon this route would become their lifeline, and they were uneasily aware that with Irish help, or even with Irish passivity, Germany might be in a position to cut it.

This led on to the important question of the Irish ports of Berehaven and Lough Swilly. After Irish independence use of these was granted to the Royal Navy, but in April 1938 Chamberlain's government gave them up, a decision which was approved almost unanimously by the House of Commons. Though there was no formal agreement to this effect, it was felt on the British side that use of the ports would be restored in case of dire emergency. In 1938 Winston Churchill was the only well-known British politician to oppose the cession, and this he did passionately, warning the House of the danger to shipping if in any future war the ports were not made available. But at that time his views were thought eccentric and his voice was a lonely one. Ten years later he wrote of the debate: 'There was even a kind of sympathetic wonder that anyone of my standing should attempt to plead so hopeless a case. I never saw the House of Commons more completely misled.'[15]

'What guarantee', he implored his colleagues in Parliament on 5 May, 1938, 'have you that Southern Ireland, or the Irish Republic as they claim to be, will not declare neutrality if we are engaged in war with some powerful nation? The first step certainly which such an enemy would take would be to offer complete immunity of every kind to Southern Ireland if she would remain neutral . . . The ports may be denied us in the hour of need . . .'[16]

So one can imagine Churchill's bitterness when eighteen months later his prophecies were proved so correct. To make matters worse he was now First Lord of the Admiralty and therefore responsible for a naval situation which had been weakened in spite of his protests. The point was that possession of a port in the west of Ireland would have been a great help to destroyers protecting the Atlantic convoys. As things were, the most convenient *British* port for refuelling and refitting the escort ships was Milford Haven, on the west coast of Wales. Berehaven was 200 miles to the west of Milford Haven, which meant that its use would give British ships an extra range of 400 miles steaming in the Atlantic ocean. Also, a damaged ship struggling to get home would have 200 miles less to struggle; and the extra distance would afford greater protection from air attack. Attacking German bombers would have 400 miles further to travel, and they would have to fly twice right across England, running the gauntlet of the British anti-aircraft defences.

On 6 September the Cabinet was told that the Irish were receptive to the idea of stationing a British salvage vessel in an Irish port. It was put to De Valera that this would be in Ireland's as well as Britain's interest, since Irish as well as British trade was in need of protection. The Admiralty felt that if permission could be got for the tugs, this might be the thin end of the wedge, and eventually ships of war would be allowed too. But this raised a difficult problem: if Ireland agreed to harbour British destroyers, how could she as a neutral refuse to harbour German submarines?

This was one of the first problems to which Churchill addressed himself on assuming office. On 6 September he sent a typically terse memorandum to the Director of Naval Intelligence: 'What is the position on the west coast of Ireland? Are there any signs of succouring U-boats in Irish creeks or inlets? It would seem that money should be spent to secure a trustworthy body of Irish agents to keep most vigilant watch. Has this been done? Please report.' Churchill had always been a 'hard-liner' on Ireland, and this note was an early sign that his approach to her was going to be stern, or even hostile.

Then came the bombshell. On 12 September John Dulanty delivered to Anthony Eden on *aide-mémoire* announcing that all submarines, warships and military aircraft of belligerent nations were banned from entering Irish jurisdiction.[18] Only in cases of distress would any exception be made, and then the ship or air-craft would be interned until the end of the war. This was not what Britain wanted at all. An urgent approach to De Valera was now essential.

Britain was caught napping diplomatically as well in that she had no official representative in Dublin. The reason for this astonishing gap is typical of British–Irish relations: a disagree-ment over the envoy's title. Britain wanted him to be called a 'representative', Ireland wanted him to be called a 'minister'. This apparently trifling matter was central to Ireland's strange consti-tutional position, half British and half not. True, she still owed some sort of allegiance to the British King who, for instance,

signed the letters of credence of Irish diplomats, but De Valera
and his supporters had never approved of the link with the Crown
and had practically abandoned it after Edward the Eighth's
abdication. Britain's view was that a 'minister' was a diplomatic
representative in a foreign country, which Ireland was not. Also,
the King was titular head of both states, and could not be asked to
appoint a 'minister' to himself. Ireland, anxious to play down the
functions of the British King, saw no such difficulty.

Whatever mistakes Britain has made over Ireland, it is agreed
on both sides that her appointment of Sir John Maffey as envoy in
Dublin at this crucial time was an excellent choice. He was a tact-
ful, intelligent man who understood the Irish better than most.
His beautifully written accounts of his meetings with De Valera
show equally the breadth of his mind and the difficulty of his task.
Immediately after the receipt of Dulanty's *aide-mémoire* Maffey
was sent to Dublin, and for two and a half hours during the
morning of 14 September he was alone with De Valera. The words
Maffey used left the Irishman in no doubt as to the effect of his
note:

I said that in the last hour before I left Whitehall a grave difficulty
had been created by the presentation of an *aide-mémoire* on the subject
of neutrality presented by the High Commissioner for Eire. It was fully
understood that Eire had adopted a policy of neutrality and the emphasizing of that policy in general terms must be expected. But this rigid
aide-mémoire, dotting the i's and crossing the t's in the way of stringent
rules affecting British ships and aircraft, had been read with profound
feelings of disappointment.

De Valera 'spoke at some length of the difficulties of his position,
his every action studied by men bitterly opposed to any rapproche-
ment with the United Kingdom, critical of any wavering from the
straight path of neutrality'. He also spoke 'of the difficulties in the
way of appointing a "United Kingdom Representative", that is to
say of creating an appointment of a new and special character.
The shout would be raised of "Dublin Castle back again" and it
would be a battle cry for the I R A and the extremists.'

'All this happens,' De Valera continued, 'because you maintain
the principle of partition in this island.' Whereupon, writes Maffey,
'he pointed to a map of Ireland hanging on the wall before him —

Eire jet-black, Northern Ireland a leprous white.' The Irish Premier warmed to his favourite theme: 'Why did not our Prime Minister put his foot down and stop the follies and oppressions of Northern Ireland? Look at what a picture we might have — a united, independent Ireland! Think of the effect in America where the Irish element had ruined and would ruin any possibility of Anglo-American understanding. Why could we not see where the flaw in our armour lay?'

De Valera insisted to Maffey that his desire was to be helpful: 'He had wanted to oblige us by having strict rules about submarines. He understood that that suited us. If he had an order about submarines his critics regarding that measure as entirely anti-German would at once ask what he had done about ships and aircraft.' Maffey countered by emphasizing the danger of laying down a hard-and-fast rule on such a matter without any knowledge of how the problem was going to develop. 'Why tie your hands?' he asked De Valera. 'He could say and do all he liked about neutrality and wait on events.' De Valera probably felt, though, that the rules would not so much tie his hands as chain him to the railings. Without a set code to protect them, the Irish feared that Britain would slowly but surely prise them away from neutrality.

To illustrate his point De Valera told Maffey of an incident a few days earlier where a British military aircraft had come down in Ireland. The Irish had turned a blind eye and the machine had escaped. He had then been obliged to censor all newspaper reports of the event, but 'comment had been widespread', providing ammunition for the enemies of the Allied cause. Then, Maffey writes, 'by a strange coincidence' the telephone rang, and after a few moments' conversation De Valera announced, 'There you are! One of your planes is down in Ventry Bay. What am I to do?' The only way out, he thought, was for the ownership of the machine to be transferred to Ireland. Anyway, he would have to intern the crew. Maffey records, 'We were both much relieved when the telephone rang again an hour later to report that the plane had managed to get away — or rather had been allowed to get away. Clearly problems of this kind lie ahead of us.'

De Valera had some words of comfort for the British envoy. The whole talk was 'very natural and easy', 'more cordial than I expected'. But the kind words were of a general kind, providing no satisfactory answer to Britain's immediate requests. He told of his deep admiration for and sympathy with Chamberlain. 'He has done everything that a man could do to prevent this tragedy . . . Personally he [De Valera] had great sympathy with England to-day.' His most interesting statement was quoted by Maffey verbatim: 'There was a time when I would have done anything in my power to help destroy the British Empire. But now my position has changed. I can see that a united and independent Ireland might well find relationship with it. Moreover there is a change of spirit. I felt that very strongly in the discussions of 1937. And there are strong and growing racial ties.'

That De Valera should express such warm feeling for Britain, the country which had once sentenced him to death, no doubt touched the hearts of the men in Whitehall whose job it was to run the war. Unfortunately, though, Maffey also reported that De Valera 'could not deny the possibility of a German submarine receiving assistance, but he would do his utmost to prevent it'. Maffey reported, 'This does not sound very reassuring. We have no contact with his coastal watch. We may have difficulty in obtaining it as he said a word to me about Eire not wishing to have the burden of our secrets. Cooperation in intelligence cannot work on that formula.' There were those in London who felt that the Irishman was trying to 'sweet-talk' them, to charm them away from specific demands and from the essential issues.

To rub this point home, on the very day of Maffey's talk (14 September) a German U-boat was sunk and prisoners from her told British officers they had been ashore in Ireland. They were found in possession of Irish cigarettes. This fact, later disputed, was discussed animatedly at the Cabinet meeting the next day,[19] and Churchill had the bright idea that it might be used as a lever on De Valera, to persuade him to grant Britain a base. A boom was already built, said Churchill, ready to be placed across the mouth of Berehaven. The Cabinet agreed that Churchill and Eden should pursue the matter since, as First Lord of the Admiralty and Dominions Secretary, it fell into their competence.

Unwillingly De Valera agreed to Maffey's appointment as British 'Representative' in Dublin. He would thus be officially accredited to the Irish Government. On 18 September, the day before he left London, he was instructed by the Cabinet to tell De Valera 'that the present situation might rapidly become a very grave one in which the questions at issue would not be matters of politics but of vital concern to this country'. They were ominous words, and contained a clearly implied threat.

The threat was not being delivered idly. The German Army had been offering little aggression to the Allies, but the German Navy had. The Cabinet knew that in the first week of the war it had sunk eleven British ships, a total of 64,595 tons, and a total of 53,561 during the second week. By First World War standards this was a very heavy loss, and one must assume that it was Churchill who emphasized how grave it would be if such losses were allowed to continue.

Maffey had a second fascinating talk with De Valera on 20 September, a few hours after his return to Dublin. He handed the Irish Premier a letter from Chamberlain, which was read slowly and with great difficulty. De Valera's eyesight was troubling him. Only recently he had received treatment for the complaint in America, the land of his birth. Again the point he emphasized to Maffey was that 'he was known to be pro-British in sentiment on the question of the war'. At present, he said, his government was supported by a large majority, but this support could be undone by any clumsy gesture on his part, and if he had to go the only alternative would be a government of the Left. Already there were members of the extremist Irish Republican Army established in an office in Berlin, stirring up opposition to De Valera's line which, they claimed, was flagrantly pro-Ally. A recent article in the Irish *Standard* had contrasted his neutrality with the real neutrality of Holland. Clearly the Irishman guessed what Maffey was about to say, the requests he was about to make, and he was determined to forestall him.

Maffey noted in his report, 'He is a difficult man to interrupt. But interrupt him you must. He shows no resentment when this happens, and his nimble mind is soon lifted onto the new line you have started.' Maffey judged it right not yet to mention the crucial matter of the ports. 'If such action is vital,' he noted, 'we shall have to take it. But we must think twice and count the gain and the loss.' He seemed to know already what De Valera's answer would be. Instead he proposed joint Irish–British policing of the Irish coastline to prevent U-boats from using it for shelter. De Valera objected to this, but was more receptive to the idea of taking a few Royal Navy officers and men, of Irish origin, to serve on the coastline watch under Irish command.

If any U-boat should be found, De Valera said, 'information of its whereabouts will be wirelessed at once. Not to you especially. Your Admiralty must pick it up. We shall wireless it to the world. I will tell the German Minister of our intention to do this.' He agreed also to consider repatriating British aircraft which, in Maffey's vivid phrase, 'may occasionally land like exhausted birds on Irish shores'.

De Valera pointed out that he had launched a Red Cross campaign. Officially it was to provide medical help to both sides, but in practice only the Allies could benefit. Most important of all were the thousands of Irishmen who were volunteering to fight with the British armed forces. Many of these had fought *against* the British during the independence struggle but, like most Irishmen, had not let the sun go down on their anti-British wrath. 'You would help us', De Valera told Maffey, 'and help yourselves if the men did not come into Ireland in uniform.' Everyone saw the sense of this, and changing-rooms were set up at the departure point for the Irish boat. In Anthony Eden's words, 'Dumps of civilian clothes were provided at Holyhead, where servicemen travelling on leave to Ireland could change into them, resuming uniform on their return. This little device was endorsed by the Cabinet and worked smoothly through the war years.'[20]

The meeting was over. Maffey describes how De Valera 'led me to his black map of Ireland with its white blemish on the north-east corner and said: "There's the real source of all our trouble." He could not let me go without that.' Britain had won only a few minor concessions. The days were past when Britain could bully the Irish, and now the boot was on the other foot. It was Britain whose independence was threatened, and she was having to woo Ireland abjectly, from a position of weakness.

From mid September to mid October there was a lull in the U-boat toll. On 7 September Admiral Raeder discussed with Hitler the French and British inaction on the western front. This, they thought, when combined with the swift and decisive progress the Germans were making in Poland, indicated that the Allies were only going through the motions of making war and would soon be ready for peace. It was decided to exercise restraint at sea as a prelude to Hitler's peace offensive. In the third week of the war the British tonnage sunk had fallen from 53,561 to 12,750 and in the fourth week it fell again to 4,646. (This included losses from mines.) On 1 October the Cabinet was informed that there had not been a single enemy attack on a British merchant ship during the past week. The Irish were being thoroughly cooperative over censorship and communications. They had forbidden the German Minister in Dublin to send messages in code. There were two direct cables from Ireland to the United States, and the Irish were giving the British copies of all messages sent by this route. Dublin by night had been put under partial black-out, to prevent its lights being used to guide German aeroplanes. Ireland ceased to be a constant topic for discussion at Cabinet meetings, and it seemed that a clash with Dublin might not take place after all.

But Churchill's bitterness had in no way subsided. On 24 September he wrote to members of his senior staff in the Admiralty: 'There seems to be a good deal of evidence, or at any rate suspicion, that the U-boats are being succoured from West of Ireland ports by the malignant section with whom De Valera dare not interfere . . . On no account must we appear to acquiesce in, still less be contented with, the odious treatment we are receiving.'[21] If the U-boats became more dangerous, he noted, Britain should 'coerce' Ireland about coast-watching and the use of Berehaven. The idea of a British armed attack on Ireland began to be mooted in Whitehall, especially in Admiralty House.

On 6 October Hitler proposed peace terms, but in a day or two it was clear to him that they would not be accepted. The lull was over and the U-boats once again on the offensive. On 14 October a U-boat made its way into Scapa Flow harbour and sank the battleship *Royal Oak*. An air raid on Scapa Flow on the morning of 17 October brought matters to a head, and Churchill to the boil at the daily Cabinet meeting. He told Cabinet that the Fleet must have alternative harbours. There was fear that Scapa Flow, the main base in the First World War, would be unusable because of its nearness to Germany and vulnerability to air attack. Already the Admiralty was looking for somewhere safer and temporary bases for the Fleet, particularly Loch Ewe down the west coast of

Scotland, were being used and fortified. But clearly Berehaven would be so much better. The time had come, said Churchill, 'to make it clear to the Irish Government that we must have the use of these harbours, and intended in any case to use them'.

Anthony Eden said he did not think De Valera would agree to this. At one with Churchill on most issues over the years, he clearly did not 'support his 'hawkish' line on Ireland. Whereas Churchill wrote in 1939 of 'the odious treatment we are receiving', Eden was to write in 1965: 'As the weeks passed it became increasingly evident that the Government of Eire wanted to do anything it could to be helpful, provided their action did not conflict with their doctrine of neutrality which, I had to admit, the great majority of Irish people wished to see preserved.'[22] Churchill's views by October 1939 were turning into something of an obsession, one that was not shared by his colleagues in the Cabinet.

Eden wondered how the matter should be handled. Perhaps Chamberlain should put the matter to De Valera personally? Still, it was thought unwise to suggest discussions in London. Irishmen are suspicious of discussions in London. They feel they may be subjected to undue pressure there. Cabinet agreed on 17 October that better terms might be got by discussion in Dublin, and Eden was given the unlovely task of advising on the best way of approaching the Irish Government.

Churchill was not one to brook delay. The very next day, 18 October, he offered the Cabinet a paper prepared by his Chief of Naval Staff. In April 1938 the Admiralty had made little protest when the ports were surrendered, but its report eighteen months later emphasized the British shortage of destroyers and concluded that it was 'of vital importance that the port which is naturally situated to control these waters shall be available for the use of the Navy which protects Irish as well as British trade and soil'. Merchant ships supplying Ireland were being escorted across the Atlantic by British warships, and this rankled with the Royal Navy. 'Why should we help them if they won't help us?' the British sailors thought. Eden felt that the danger to Irish trade was the only argument likely to carry weight with De Valera, but his hopes were not high. He had been advised by Maffey: 'It is remarkable how even the "pro-British" group, men who have fought for the crown and are anxious to be called up again, men whose sons are at the front today, loyalists in the old sense of the word, agree generally in supporting the policy of neutrality for Eire. They see no possible alternative.' One must assume that such words impressed Eden, for he wrote to Halifax on 20 October: 'I fear it becomes every day clearer that it is scarcely possible for "Dev" to square neutrality with the grant of the facilities for which the Admiralty ask. And at least eighty per cent of the Irish people favour neutrality. Altogether a pretty problem.'[23] Lord Harvey wrote in his diary (30 October), 'A. E. says De Valera is doing all he can for us',[24] and this was certainly Eden's view.

Churchill had been sent a copy of Eden's note to Halifax, and he answered it the same day: 'Is the neutrality which Mr De Valera has proclaimed a valid condition? . . . What is the international juridical status of Southern Ireland? It is not a Dominion. They themselves repudiate the idea. It is certainly under the Crown. Nothing has been defined. Legally I believe they are "at war but skulking".'[25] Here was the germ of an argument which Churchill was to develop three days later in Cabinet, that Irish neutrality was illegal. Meanwhile Maffey had been recalled from Dublin to discuss the matter. He saw Chamberlain in his room in the House of Commons and returned with instructions to seek an immediate interview with De Valera.

Maffey's account of his ninety-minute talk with De Valera on 21 October throws a fascinating light on the Irish leader and his attitudes. Maffey began by emphasizing that he had come straight from seeing Chamberlain, and that his words were not his own but the Prime Minister's. But it was soon clear to Maffey that he was talking to a man whose mind was made up. De Valera said that if Britain had paved the way to Irish unity, Ireland today 'might' have been able to help. But as things were, the public mood would react violently to any action invalidating Irish integrity. If a demand was made – he fully realized that no demand was actually being made – he would be forced to treat such a demand as a challenge, for if he did what the British were asking, his country would not be able to live and his government would collapse. His sympathies were with the Allies, he would greatly regret a German victory, but if there was today a 'vague majority sentiment' in the Allies' favour, it would be changed overnight by

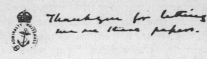

S of 8

Thank you for letting me see these papers.

So far as 'legality' counts, the question itself turns on whether 'Eire is to be regarded as a neutral state'. If this is conceded then the regular laws of neutrality apply. But is the neutrality wh. Mr. Devalera has proclaimed a valid condition, & on all fours with the neutrality of, say, Holland or Switzerland? It is to this point that the attention shd. first be directed. What is the international juridical status of Southern Ireland? It is not a Dominion. They themselves repudiate the idea. It is certainly under the Crown. Nothing has been defined. Legally I believe they are 'at war but Skulking'. Perhaps Sir William will examine this theme.

WSC 20. 8

Churchill's handwritten note launching the theory that Irish neutrality was invalid under international law. (Crown Copyright. Public Record office. FO 800/310) any assault on an Irish interest. There were many people in Ireland, he said, ready to acclaim a British defeat at any price. This attitude might be based on ignorance, but it had its roots in history.

Maffey replied that when the ports had been returned to Ireland 'the path of generosity had been followed as an act of faith and in the belief that in the hour of need the hand of friendship would be extended.' De Valera, reminded perhaps of Britain's treatment of Ireland over the centuries, replied that Britain had no right to derive advantage from what was not hers. At this point the telephone rang, and De Valera spoke to a journalist from Havas, the French news agency, inquiring whether Britain had 'demanded' the ports. De Valera was quick to deny this outrageous suggestion. In his report Maffey ascribes the call to 'quick guessing on the part of the press watching my recent movements'. It did not occur to him that perhaps the call was a contrivance of De Valera's, an attempt to prop up his position still more firmly.

'What British Government would ever surrender the ports of the North after this experience?' was Maffey's last despairing cry. But De Valera was unmoved, refusing either to consider the matter further or to discuss it with Chamberlain. He had thought the matter over very carefully, he had made his decision and he wished to change the subject.

In concluding, De Valera had some sweet words to sugar the bitter pill. He told Maffey 'he found himself in complete agreement with everything that Chamberlain had done . . . England has a moral position today. Hitler might have his early successes, but the moral position would tell.' Moving dangerously close to the naivity and wishful thinking of a Chamberlain, the Irish leader went on to discuss the possibilities of peace. Hitler did not want war, he said, and a reasonable solution embodying a partially restored Poland was to be had. 'How?' Maffey asked. De Valera said he thought some go-between might emerge. It would not be Roosevelt, though, who 'had put himself completely out of court as an arbitrator owing to his inept letter of appeal and remonstrance'. Mussolini, he thought, was the best man to intercede with Hitler and persuade him to come to his senses.

It would no doubt have been politically difficult for De Valera to endanger Ireland's neutrality by leasing Berehaven, but probably not impossible, and one wonders if there may not have been another reason for his refusal. In January 1941 Wendell Willkie, who had just lost the race for the American Presidency, was sent to Europe by the victorious Roosevelt with a letter of introduction to Churchill. On 4 February he flew to Dublin to see De Valera. Being an American, Willkie was in a position to address the Irishman more frankly. 'What about the bases?' he asked. He told Harold Nicolson:

De Valera had produced a map showing how the English still threatened his country by their monstrous occupation of Northern Ireland. Willkie had said that all this did not matter now, but what about the bases? Ireland was definitely proving a disadvantage to the cause of freedom, and American opinion would not be with her. Dev was startled by this and tried to dodge and edge away by accusing the British Government of stupidity. Willkie said, 'But we all know about that. That doesn't count anyway. You want Britain to win?' De Valera assented to this. 'And yet you are making it more difficult for her.' So in the end that fine and obstinate Spaniard was obliged to say that if he leased the bases, Dublin might be bombed. Willkie (having been at Coventry and Birmingham) did not conceal his contempt. 'American opinion,' he repeated, 'will not be with you.' Dev writhed.[26]

Whatever its motive, De Valera's refusal caused consternation in the British Cabinet on 23 October. It showed, said Eden, 'the rigid and unsatisfactory attitude adopted by Mr De Valera'. There were three possible courses of action, he said: to seek further discussion, which would probably be useless; to acquiesce and to try to secure what we could bit by bit, which would not be much; or to seize the harbours by force.

If Britain did this, Eden went on, De Valera would probably not oppose her militarily, but he would indict her before the world and rally his people against her. She would alienate not only the Irish, but also many in the Dominions and the United States. Also, De Valera might then decide to grant facilities to the Germans.

Churchill then spoke and (contrary to the impression given by De Valera's biographers Longford and O'Neill) proceeded to make a strong case for seizure of the harbours by force. The easiest course, he told the Cabinet, would be to accept either the first or the second of Eden's proposals. But this would mean accepting increased destruction of our merchant shipping, and increased strain on the vessels and crews whose job it was to protect them. In his view Ireland's neutrality was illegal. The King was still the Irish head of state, and Germany was the King's enemy. It was improper for Ireland to remain neutral towards Germany, and even more improper for her to maintain diplomatic relations with Germany. As things were the Irish envoy appointed to Berlin had had his letters of credence signed by the King. It was wrong for the King to be represented in an enemy country.

Churchill suggested the Cabinet 'should take stock of the weapons of coercion'. At present Ireland had the best of both worlds: trade preferences, free access to Great Britain, military and naval protection. If she refused to reciprocate, she should be told it was the parting of the ways. It should be brought home to her what she stood to lose by being declared a foreign power. The Law Officers of the Crown should examine the constitutional position. If it transpired that Ireland's neutrality was illegal, Britain should make this fact known to the world. She could then 'insist on the use of the ports'. On the evidence it seems clear that by the word 'insist' Churchill meant 'by force if necessary', and he thought it might be possible to do this without being labelled as aggressor. One could not violate the sovereignty of a non-sovereign power or the neutrality of a power whose neutrality was illegal.

The rest of the Cabinet felt that this was an unrealistic line of argument. Whatever the niceties of Ireland's constitutional position, no legal loophole would justify in the eyes of the world a British invasion of Irish territory. The Dominions would probably oppose it too. Canada and South Africa, for instance, owed allegiance to the Crown, and yet insisted on their own right to declare war. Eden felt that even if it was proved that Ireland's position was legally impossible, the result would not be to make her give up her neutrality, but to drive her out of the Commonwealth. He doubted whether being declared 'a foreign power' would break Ireland's heart.

Chamberlain concluded that Churchill had presented a powerful case, but in his view the case had not yet been established, and it was as yet difficult to claim that use of the ports was a matter of life and death. Until this was so he felt that the risks involved in forcible seizure were too great. He should, however, make his views known to the Dominions, and start shoring up his moral position just in case it should become necessary to take violent action. He told Eden to let it be known among the Dominion leaders that 'the use of the ports in Ireland by the Royal Navy was essential to the security of the Empire, and that the present attitude adopted by Ireland in that matter was intolerable'.[27]

The feverish atmosphere of mid October, with a German attack in the West expected daily, and with good reason, began to quieten down during November. Though the Allies did not know it, the offensive they had been expecting was postponed by Hitler on 7 November, and it soon appeared that western Europe was cooling down for the winter. The tonnage of British, Allied and neutral merchant ships sunk by U-boats dropped during November to about a third of the sinkings during September or October. At the same time Germany began to sow the seas with magnetic mines, a new and terrible weapon which increased November mine losses of such ships fourfold from the previous two months. Suddenly mines were a greater threat to the Royal Navy than U-boats. Churchill and the Admiralty had to shift their emphasis, to solve the magnetic mine rather than the Irish problem. They solved the magnetic mine.

By 23 November, when the report on how to deal with the Irish was ready, the problem was no longer high on the Cabinet's agenda. The urgency was elsewhere. The Cabinet concluded that 'we had obtained control over the U-boat menace in the Western Approaches, and it could not be said that in present circumstances the use of Berehaven constituted a vital interest'. For the moment Ireland was safe in her neutrality.

Thirty years after the event De Valera's decision presents an interesting moral problem. In 1939 Ireland owed Britain nothing, rather the reverse, but no country can totally isolate itself from the world, and neutral or no, whether she liked it or not, Ireland was involved in the war between Germany and the Allies. Of significant European countries only Ireland, Sweden, Switzerland, Spain and Portugal were able to remain neutral, unoccupied and at peace throughout the war, and of these Ireland was probably the one most essential to the Allies' defence. The lull of November 1939 was only temporary. In the twelve months that followed June 1940 the tonnage sunk by U-boats was an average of five times that of November 1939.[28] Eden writes that Britain 'gradually established some useful, if unofficial, cooperation [with Ireland] which was of service to the Admiralty. But no minor contrivance could compensate for the loss of the Irish ports and of Berehaven in particular.' [29] There can be no doubt that denial of the ports helped Hitler's U-boat campaign. It increased the number of British ships sunk and of British lives lost.

So what was De Valera's motive? Certainly there is no reason to imagine that he was in any way pro-Nazi or to doubt his assertion that he hoped for an Allied victory. But in such a conflict action spoke louder than hope, active help was more appropriate than sympathy. It was his case that he was doing everything possible to help, that to do more would be counter-productive. But this conflicts with his statement to Maffey that he might have leased the ports if Britain had given up Northern Ireland, his refusal to cooperate when an end to partition was actually offered by Churchill in 1940, and with his statement to Willkie that his reason for refusal was that he feared Germany would bomb Dublin. One must conclude that his enthusiasm for the Allied cause was genuine but limited, that he was unwilling to put Ireland's interest and his own political future at risk in the battle against Hitler. De Valera must be admired for his patriotism and for his desire to keep his tortured country at peace, but not for standing aside in this particular battle, perhaps the most just and necessary that has ever been fought. De Valera and Ireland preferred to stand aside both in 1939, and again in 1940 when Churchill offered Ireland her unity in exchange for her help. Churchill was a 'hawk' on Ireland, but his 1940 offer was almost certainly a genuine one. De Valera's rejection of it was a tragedy not only for the anti-Hitler struggle, but also for Ireland.

7 Neutral – But on Whose Side?

While the hot, bloody war was being fought in Poland and the phony war on the Rhine, the propaganda war was centred across the Atlantic. Public relations, a skill then in its infancy, were now of the essence. Radio broadcasts, mouth-to-mouth gossip, the press, individually posted pamphlets – all the tools of the new trade were being used in the assault on the western hemisphere. It was not diplomacy, which is a government-to-government channel. The United States *Government* was not the target; its views and policies were known to Hitler, Chamberlain and Daladier and not to be directly changed by propaganda. What could change these policies, though, was American public opinion, the pressure it could exert on the Government through the democratic process. The three main belligerents saw this as one of the keys to the war and proceeded to address themselves to the American people.

President Roosevelt personally could hardly have been more friendly to the Allied cause. On 17 April 1939 a report by the British Committee for Imperial Defence concluded correctly that 'the President can be counted on to do everything in his power to lend support to Great Britain and France'.[1] On 31 January in evidence before the Military Affairs Committee of the Senate, he had announced that the United States would give the democracies, in any conflict with the dictatorships, every possible assistance short of declaring war and sending American troops to Europe. The British Defence Committee, while noting that 'it would be most imprudent to count on armed assistance from that country [the United States]', took the President's words to mean that 'intervention on our side at a later stage is possible and might even, if present trends continue, become probable'. They rightly prophesied that early intervention was likely only if Japan were to ally herself with Germany.

The President had, however, failed to convince Americans during 1939 that there was any threat to their own interests from far-away Germany and Italy. There were strong pressure groups which disapproved of his showing undisguised sympathy for one side of the conflict. Perhaps they did not hate Hitlerism and fascism as much as the President did. At any rate, they thought that the war was not America's quarrel, and they feared that the President's scarcely disguised partisan attitude might sooner or later drag them into it. It was an understandable attitude, even in Britain. On 27 September Halifax wrote to his Ambassador, Lord Lothian: 'I have never been tempted to be surprised by the isolationist movement, which is a first reaction to the insane behaviour of Europe. It is, I always think, instructive to reflect that it was only on 6 February last that we, on the fringe of this mad continent, formally assured France unconditionally of our assistance to her if she became the object of aggression from any quarter. We cannot expect the Government or people of the United States to evolve quicker than we did.' [2]

The reaction of the American press to Hitler's invasion was universally hostile. The *New York Sun* wrote: 'Hitlerism has brought about this war; its fitting end must see Hitler irreparably crushed.' The *New York Herald Tribune* concurred: 'It is doubtful if ever the head of a great nation has taken upon himself so frankly the full and sole responsibility for starting a war . . . Negotiation? Mediation? Arbitration? Hitler would have none of these. What he wanted was Poland. So he attacked. He has written the history of his infamy in his own words.' The *New York Times* was equally uncompromising: 'The world will echo the words of Mr Chamberlain that the responsibility for the outbreak of hostilities between Germany and Poland lies squarely on the shoulders of one man – the German Chancellor.' [3]

But if the initial reaction was one of horror and anger against Hitler, the second reaction was one of alarm, followed immediately by a desire to shrink away from what had just happened. This was apparent when at 10.30 a.m. on 1 September, eleven hours after the Germans had invaded and eight hours after he had been woken up and told the news, Roosevelt held a press conference in the White House: 'A reporter observed that the question uppermost in everyone's mind just now was, "Can we keep out of it?" The President cast his eyes downward for a moment as he pondered the request for comment. Then he replied, "Only this – that I not only sincerely hope so, but I believe we can, and that every effort will be made by the Administration to do so." ' [4]

Whether the President was sincere in this statement is much disputed. Probably he was. But in either case he had no alternative but to make it in the face of those powerful men who opposed his pro-Ally stance. Already the issue had been drawn into domestic politics by opponents of the New Deal, an alliance of Republicans and conservative Southern Democrats. The newspaper chain of Randolph Hearst was particularly hostile. His *World Telegram*, for instance, while blaming Hitler for the outbreak of hostilities, continued: 'But we, who are so fortunate as to live on this side of the Atlantic – it is not for us at this time to assess the responsibility for the tragedy that has overtaken Europe. Rather should all our energies and all our resolutions turn to efforts to prevent our own involvement.' [5]

Unfortunately, the war confronted Roosevelt with an immediate problem which he could not avoid. He had to declare America's neutrality, that went without saying, but he had also to enforce a series of practical measures which Congress in a fit of isolationism had embodied into law in 1937. This Neutrality Act, without interfering with the free expression of opinion or sympathy, made it the duty of the Government 'not to permit the making of its territory or territorial waters subservient to purposes of war'. Therefore on 5 September the President, as was his obligation, published a list of 'acts forbidden to be done'. One of these stipulated that no American could serve with a belligerent army, but the most serious of all consisted of a total arms embargo. Under the Act no arms could be purchased from America by Germany, Britain or France, even if paid for.

Norman Davis, a friend of Roosevelt's who was then Chairman of the American Red Cross, told Lord Lothian 'that the

President felt very badly about having to issue his neutrality proclamation when every fibre of his being sympathizes with Britain and France. But he and his advisers were clear that they could not afford to give to the isolationists any ground for saying that he was not obeying the law'.[6] Churchill told Ambassador Kennedy how 'terribly discouraging' was the announcement of the President's measure at such a time.[7] But even before the outbreak Roosevelt had decided that if war came he would seek repeal of the Act. Early in September Daladier told Ambassador Bullitt: 'If we are to win this war, we shall have to win it on supplies of every kind from the United States. We can hold for a time without supplies, but England and ourselves cannot possibly build up sufficient production of munitions and planes to make a successful offensive possible.' Bullitt agreed. Every Frenchman who knew the facts, he said, believed that unless supplies were forthcoming 'German victory would be certain'.

Chamberlain too agreed. Whatever the result of the debate of repeal, he told Kennedy, it would be one of vital importance for the Allies. If it were passed it would give them 'the greatest psychological lift they could have at this time', while if it failed 'it would be sheer disaster for England and France'.[8] It seemed to leave little room for half measures. Roosevelt announced his intention of recalling Congress on 21 September to request repeal of the Act.

During the evening of 3 September Roosevelt delivered one of his famous 'fireside chats' to the American people on the radio. It was a speech with two aims, to reassure and to arouse. He had to quash those of his critics who were busy telling Americans that their President was leading them on a headlong slide into war. 'I hate war,' he said. 'I say that again and again.' From the point of view of American public opinion he could not say it often enough. 'Let no man or woman thoughtlessly or falsely talk of America sending its armies to European fields,' he said too, no doubt picturing in his mind the millions of American mothers listening to his words, fearful that their sons were about to be taken from them and thrown into battle.

But calming words were not enough. The President knew that sooner or later he would have to wake his people up to the realities of the world situation and the danger it posed to everyone, not only to Europeans. He would have to do this gradually, for were he to attempt to shock Americans out of their complacency too violently their first reaction would be to turn against him personally, to blame him for inflicting upon them the bitter truth. He had to tread softly so that their awakening would not be too rude. At this moment the most he could afford was a gentle warning: 'It is easy for you and me to shrug our shoulders and to say that conflicts taking place thousands of miles from the whole American hemisphere do not seriously affect the Americans, and that all the United States has to do is to ignore them and go about its own business. Passionately though we may desire detachment, we are forced to realize that every word that goes through the air, every ship that sails the sea, every battle that is fought, does affect the American future.' [9]

From the British and French point of view the President's most encouraging words were these: 'This nation will remain a neutral nation, but I cannot ask that every American remain neutral in thought as well. Even a neutral has the right to take account of facts. Even a neutral cannot be asked to close his mind or his conscience.' Already the President was entering the realm of the controversial, for he was deliberately repudiating the advice President Wilson had given Americans before they entered the First World War, to remain neutral in thought as well as in deed.

The President's bold statement received much support. His friend Felix Frankfurter, Associate Justice of the Supreme Court, telegraphed him: 'Many thanks and especially for not requiring us to be neutral in thought.' [10] The *New York Times* wrote: 'No scruples of strict neutrality can conscript the underlying sympathies of the American people.' [11] But others were alarmed by the President's words. The contrast between them and Wilson's words was apparent, and one did not have to be very old to remember how, in spite of Wilson, the United States had slowly but surely been drawn into war in 1917. How would America be able to keep out of it this time with a President so obviously committed in sympathy to the Allied cause?

This is why such a newspaper as the *New York Herald Tribune*, while also sympathetic to the Allies, wrote of 'the colossal costs which military intervention must entail' and called for a rejection of 'any course which fatalistically assumes any repetition of the incidents which tended to lead us into military intervention last time, and must inevitably produce military intervention again'.[12] Another danger signal to Roosevelt was a Gallup poll which showed that Americans, while approving by a large majority the recall of Congress, split fifty-fifty on whether the law should be changed to favour the Allies.[13]

In September the first wartime Roper poll showed how divided America was.[14] Those who favoured supporting Germany were few in number, 0·2 per cent of the sample. It was not these that the President would have to contend with. His problem was the hard core of isolationists, a good thirty per cent of the population, who wanted nothing to do with any warring country, not even trade with them on a cash-and-carry basis. This figure was to remain constant for most of the two years that preceded American entry. It included of course members of most of the extreme political groups, the communists and the fascists, united as they so often are when parliamentary democracy is under threat. It followed too that few Americans of German or Italian origin would support any active intervention on the side of their mother countries' enemies. Likewise there were many Irish Americans ready to cheer for anyone who was fighting against England.

Those who advocated immediate American entry into the war on the Allied side were a mere 2·5 per cent. A further 14·7 per cent favoured American entry if ever Britain and France looked to be in real danger of losing. Meanwhile they were ready to supply the Allies with war materials and food, but not Germany. A little less interventionist were the 8·9 per cent who favoured supplying the Allies, but rejected any idea whatever of helping them militarily. These groups, actively pro-Ally but to varying degrees, had a combined strength of 26·1 per cent.

The biggest group favoured a middle-of-the-road line between isolationism and interventionism. They were the 37·5 per cent who wanted to 'take no sides and stay out of the war entirely, but offer to sell to anyone on a cash-and-carry basis'. By taking this line they were being loyal to the Roosevelt Administration, and as long as he had this large group's support the President could reasonably hope for a majority in Congress for his modest proposals. He could count on the help of the actively pro-Ally groups and thus enjoy a combined support of some two thirds of the population for the laws he wanted Congress to pass.

But the isolationists were by no means prepared to let the matter go without a fight. Their argument that the President was far too sympathetic to the Allies, that his behaviour was quite un-neutral, and that what he really planned was eventual American entry into the war, was both plausible and dangerous. If they could project it, they might hope to convert millions of Americans and dozens of Congressmen during the weeks of debate that preceded the vote. Most of all they hoped the President would make a mistake, revealing himself as the warmonger he was.

Lothian reported to Halifax: 'They have been taught that they were tricked into the last war partly by Wall Street finance and partly by British and French propaganda.' He concluded, 'It is obviously going to take a long time to re-educate 130 million people into a truer perspective.' His problem was though the Americans were clearly going to be ultra-sensitive to any attempt to 're-educate' them into the war. Fortunately most of the British realized the danger that propaganda might well be counter-productive. 'Such re-education can only be done by the Americans themselves,' Lothian concluded as early as 5 September.[15]

Robert Bruce Lockhart, the famous Scottish author and veteran secret agent, had toured America on a lecture tour early in 1939. At the end of it he wrote, 'The effect of my lectures, like that of most British lecturers, was insignificant if not indeed harmful, and the only benefit of my tour was self-education.'[16] There were many in Congress ready to shout it across America that, in the words of Robert Sherwood, 'All "furriners", particularly Englishmen and Frenchmen, are slick deceivers who are out to pull the wool over the eyes of poor, innocent, gullible Uncle Sam the while they deftly extract the gold from his teeth.'[17] Lockhart summed up thus the view of many of his audience: 'We Americans went into the last war to save democracy. We pulled you out of a hole and we received very grudging thanks. At Versailles and after Versailles you trampled on democratic ideals. Now, largely through your own fault, you are in trouble again and you want our help. Well, we've learnt our lesson.'

While emotional feelings such as these were urging America to curl up like a hedgehog in the face of danger, cold facts and reasoned analysis were forcing Roosevelt and his men at least to take note of the war and to make contingency plans. One of his biographers wrote in 1947 of the President's conviction, after the Nazi-Soviet Pact was signed, that sooner or later the United States would be obliged to enter the war.[18] Historians writing later have found little support for this view. So much is plain, that Roosevelt wanted the Allies to win and was in no doubt of the vital dangers America would face were they to lose. His administration would do what they could to prevent this catastrophe, but if it came to the crunch with the Allies on the brink of defeat it was by no means decided that America would come to the rescue. Indeed we have Assistant Secretary of State Berle's personal view that, were this to happen, America would do better to go into even deeper isolation. 'That combination must eventually break up,' he wrote of the new Nazi-Soviet alliance. 'Even if it is victorious, we should be in a position to hold a powerful and almost impregnable line for a few years. And those years ought to see this tremendous combination tear itself to pieces internally after which Europe will tend to re-emerge. But they will be ghastly years.'[19]

Only with sympathy and kind words was the President able to be free and generous. 'My dear Chamberlain, I need not tell you that you have been very much in my thoughts during these difficult days,' he wrote on 11 September. 'I hope you will at all times feel free to write me personally and outside of diplomatic procedure . . . I hope and believe that we shall repeal the embargo within the next month and this is definitely part of the administration policy.'[20] But already there was an acute problem of transatlantic communication. Americans, like the citizens of belligerent countries, were having their right to travel abroad severely restricted. Passports were being given only in cases of emergency. Letters were taking up to a month to cross the ocean. All this increased Americans' feeling of isolation from Europe. Even Roosevelt's letter took three weeks to reach the Prime Minister.

Chamberlain replied the next day (4 October): 'My own belief is that we shall win not by a complete and spectacular military victory, which is unlikely under modern conditions, but by convincing the Germans that they cannot win. Once they have arrived at that conclusion, I do not believe that they can stand our relentless pressure, for they have not started this war with the enthusiasm or the confidence of 1914. I believe that they are already

10, Downing Street,
Whitehall.

Your letter of the 11th of last month has just reached me and I am very grateful to you for your sympathetic and encouraging words.

These are indeed difficult days and there are many more before us but I retain full confidence that we shall come out successfully in the end

My own belief is that we shall win not by a complete and spectacular military victory, which is unlikely under modern conditions, but by convincing the Germans that they cannot win. Once they have arrived at that conclusion I do not believe they can stand our relentless pressure, for they have not started this war with the enthusiasm or the confidence of 1914

*I believe there are already
half way to this conviction & I
cannot doubt that the attitude of
the U.S.A., due to your personal efforts,
has had a notable influence
in this direction. If the embargo
is repealed this month. I am
convinced that the effect on
German morale will be devastating.*

*I hope so much that
one day I may have the great
pleasure of meeting you personally
and discussing with you
the happy results of the
actions of our two countries
in this testing time for
democracy,*

Chamberlain's first handwritten draft of his letter to Roosevelt. This
letter encapsulates the basic error behind the Prime Minister's thinking,
the theory that the Allies could probably defeat Germany without an
all-out military confrontation. (Crown Copyright. Public Record Office.
Prem 1/366)

half-way to this conviction . . .' If the Neutrality Act was repealed, he added, 'the effect on German morale will be devastating'.[21]

Roosevelt can hardly have found this letter inspiring. The 'relentless pressure' to which Chamberlain referred was presumably the blockade, for in no other way were the Allies interfering with the normal life of Germany. But everyone knew that the effect of the blockade was a doubtful quantity, and indeed it turned out to be quite small. Again, Chamberlain's bald assertion that the German people were already half-convinced they would not win was based upon nothing but personal intuition and the usual wishful thinking. The theory that German morale was crumbling was not consistent with the advice that Chamberlain himself was receiving, nor with the first-hand information Roosevelt had from his representatives in Germany.

Lothian wrote to Halifax describing the line he was taking with Roosevelt. The British Naval blockade, he said, 'will in the long run be effective partly because Germany starts short of money, supplies, and partly because it is not going to be at all easy for her to secure large supplies – except oil from Rumania – from Russia'.[22] Halifax wrote back to him on 27 September approving this line: 'Economic pressure may eventually induce a collapse in Germany. So far the blockade is being successfully applied. The submarine menace appears to be well in hand . . . On the economic side, we feel pretty sure that the position of Germany must deteriorate whilst our armaments position should relatively improve . . . Generally, therefore, we think that time is on our side.'

This rosy view was by no means universally shared, either in America or in Europe. Adolf Berle, Assistant Secretary of State, was a particularly pessimistic American. He wrote on 3 September: 'In this war we cannot, so far as I can see, count on a military victory of Britain, France and Poland. Should they be on the eve of defeat, the square question would be presented to us whether to enter the war using them as our outlying defence posts; or whether to let them go, treble our navy, and meet the ultimate issue between us and a Russo-German Europe bent on dominating the world, somewhere in the Middle Atlantic. My mind is rather running on the latter.' To Jay Pierrepoint Moffat, chief of the State Department's Division of European Affairs, the issues involved seemed 'so terrible, the outlook so cloudy, the probability of Bolshevism so great, and the chances of a better peace next time . . . so re-mote that if one stopped to think one would give way to gloom'.[23]

On the British side Hore-Belisha told Ambassador Kennedy that 'if our Neutrality Act were not modified, the Soviet Union, Italy and Turkey would decide that Britain could not win the war and would hasten to side with Germany. He also said that if Britain did not obtain the right to buy war goods in America, the situation was hopeless for her, and even if she did obtain it he wondered how long she would be able to pay for her requirements.' Apparently this view was shared by the French. On 20 September the American Ambassador in Paris cabled Washington that he had spoken to Daladier, Léger, Gamelin and others, and his impression was that 'all Frenchmen who knew the facts agreed Germany would surely win if the embargo were continued'.[24]

However confused Roosevelt may have been by such contrary information, he can have been in no doubt of the supreme impor-tance both for America and for Europe of his plan to amend the Act. His preliminary soundings indicated that he would obtain a majority. On 7 September Ed Halsey, a Senate clerk, estimated that about sixty senators would vote for repeal and twenty-five against, with the rest doubtful.[25] Roosevelt knew, though, that if by any clumsy gesture he gave Americans the impression that this was to be the first step towards active involvement, opinion would swing against him immediately.

He decided to disguise what he was about to do. He would present the measure before Congress not as an act deliberately designed to assist the Allies, but as something else. On 13 Sep-tember he did what everyone expected and summoned a special session of Congress. Frankfurter suggested to him one line of argument: 'A so-called neutrality law which in practical operation favours the forces of aggression must be fundamentally wrong in conception.'[26] Roosevelt approved it and plugged it in his message to Congress on 21 September. He and his British and French friends knew that this was a crucial speech in which he would have to tread warily and not say everything that he felt. His political opponents would be listening intently for any word indicative of a movement towards active involvement in war. If they could de-tect just one such word, they would magnify it before the American people and rally senators and congressmen to the isolationist side.

The argument Roosevelt rested his case on was 'that by repeal of the embargo the United States will more probably remain at peace than if the law remains as it stands today'. It was his candid judgement, he said, that he would succeed in keeping his country out of the war, but his task was being complicated by the Neutrality Act, which he had himself signed but which he now considered 'most vitally dangerous to American neutrality, American security and American peace'.[27] He spoke of the inconsistency of the present position in which wheat, copper, raw materials and incomplete war machines *could* be exported to belligerents, *and* in American ships. Was this isolationism? A more respectable policy surely would be to ban all trade with Britain, France and Germany. The present Act was merely discriminatory against the power which controlled the seas, that is to say, against Britain.

His Secretary of State, Cordell Hull, writes, 'Nowhere in his message did the President mention the thought that had been in the minds of all of us, that lifting the arms embargo would assist Britain and France.' Indeed at times he seemed to speak in terms that were almost isolationist. 'Destiny has made the United States and the sister nations of this hemisphere joint heirs of European culture. Fate now seems to compel us to assume the task of helping to maintain in the western world a citadel in which that civilization can be kept alive.' His only aim, he tried to convince his audience, was to keep American ships away from war zones and to avoid any sort of participation.

Given that, as Hull later admitted, Roosevelt's real aim was to assist the Allies, his argument appears subtle to the point of spuriousness and clever to the point of deceit. It was well summarized, though with equal cynicism, by a leader in *The Times*:

> It is no business of America to attempt to influence the course of the present struggle . . . It so happens that they [Americans] can be prevented from supplying munitions and other contraband goods to one side. But that disability is established not by American action but by the British fleet. For American law to impose a further disability and forbid trade with the belligerents who can buy would evidently be an attempt not to protect the interests of American merchants but to redress the balance between the combatants – that is, an intervention in the war.[28]

But this argument ignored the question whether it was proper for America as a neutral to supply arms to belligerents in the first place. Roosevelt pointed out that it was international practice and 'ordinary American trade policy' so to do, but he would have found it hard if pressed to answer the question why he was infusing such speed and effort into a piece of legislation that would in practice give great assistance to one side and none to the other. Although in theory the new Act would enable Germany as well as the Allies to buy arms, everyone knew that she would not, for she had no means of transporting them home.

So on one level it was politics at its most dishonest. The President was proposing a law for the simple reason that it would help the Allies, but he was concealing the fact of this motivation from American people. His decision to push the new Act through was pure partisanship, a breach of neutrality in the moral sense of the word, and no verbal contortions could conceal this from any man of intelligence. With his statement that the new Act would help to keep America at peace the President was sticking rather closer to the truth. The administration was, Hull writes, 'sincere in our belief that the new legislation would afford us a better chance of keeping out of the war than the old legislation, because if Britain and France won the war we should remain at peace, whereas if Germany won there was every chance that we should soon have to fight'.[29] But here again this was not the rationalization that was told to the American people. To them the Act was presented as one of just neutrality, the reversal of an unfair advantage which favoured one of the belligerents — Germany. And this it in fact was not.

Even to many who were not isolationists it was an undignified sight, the President going to great lengths to conceal his favouritism for the Allied cause, both from the Americans who saw such an attitude as dangerous to peace and from the Germans who saw it as a clear breach of neutrality and international law. Hans Dieckhoff, German Ambassador to the United States, who had been in Berlin since the anti-Jewish outbursts in Germany of November 1938 when both ambassadors were recalled for 'consultations', wrote clearly enough on 7 September: 'The President doubtless intends to repeal the arms embargo as soon as possible in order to be able to assist England and France with arms deliveries as well . . . Anyone who knows the President and his attitude cannot doubt that he is working towards this goal with all his energy.'[30]

Petitions began flooding into Washington asking Senators and Congressmen to vote against repeal, particularly from the Middle West where most of the Americans of German origin lived, but they were rightly interpreted as the shoutings of the noisy minority. The German Chargé d'Affaires, Hans Thomsen, had few illusions about the result of the vote. That battle was already lost, he reported, and Berlin would be well advised not to fight it too strenuously. If she did, she would add humiliation to defeat. 'The sympathies of the overwhelming majority of the American people are with our enemies, and America is convinced of Germany's guilt,'[31] he reported with commendable frankness. '. . . They want Britain and France to win the war and us to lose it.'[32] At the same time he wrote bitterly in criticism of Roosevelt's double attitude: 'America is putting herself into a preposterous position from the standpoint of international law. On the one hand she participates in the war against us by most actively supporting our enemies with war material. On the other hand she demands that we respect all rights to which neutrals are entitled.'[33]

The President's tactics were doubtless necessary in the context of his internal political position, given that he was working for the anti-Nazi cause, the best of all possible causes. But they did subject him to the risk of being labelled a trickster and a dishonest man. 'I wish I trusted him more,' noted Charles Lindbergh, an arch-isolationist who was then busy lobbying senators to resist the 'mad plunge' which the President was leading. 'I do not intend to stand by and see this country pushed into war,' he noted on September 7. 'Much as I dislike taking part in politics and public life, I intend to do so if necessary to stop the trend which is now going on in this country.'[34]

At the back of the isolationists' minds was the lurking personal dislike of Roosevelt which conservative Americans always felt, the suspicion that what Roosevelt was really after was dictatorial powers, and that he realized he was more likely to get these with his country at war than at peace. On 24 August Senator Nye spoke strongly against leaving the administration of American neutrality in the sole hands of the President. To do this would be to permit a slow but inexorable slide into war. 'We need the neutrality law. We need restraints upon a President', he said.[35] On 14 September Senator Borah, the high priest of the isolationists, said in a radio broadcast that European wars were merely 'wars brought on through the manipulation and unconscionable schemes of remorseless rulers'.[36] To sell arms to such rulers would be to take sides in an evil war, which was unthinkable.

'The dreaded Borah', as an American official historian calls him, led the fight with stirring speeches in the Senate. The call for the new Act, he said, came not from the American people but from 'the war hounds of Europe', while the war itself was 'nothing more than another chapter in the bloody volume of European power politics'.[37] Senator Hiram Johnson foresaw that under the new Act 'we will be pushed around and shoved along by those wily men who play the game of power politics in which some of our people, some of those who are snobbish, imagine they can play better than the diplomats of Europe'.[38]

Amid such outpourings of thinly disguised xenophobia the best Roosevelt could do was to sit still and not rock the boat. He was forced, for example, to defer a visit to his home at Hyde Park from the Governor-General of Canada, Lord Tweedsmuir (the novelist John Buchan). He wrote to him: 'The first [reason] is that you could not "slip down inconspicuously" to Hyde Park because under existing circumstances it would be bound to be front-page news both in your papers and mine. The second reason is that, as you have probably sensed, I am almost literally walking on eggs and, having delivered my message to the Congress and having good prospects of the bill going through, I am at the moment saying nothing, seeing nothing and hearing nothing.'[39]

American newspapers were at the same time full of the deliberations of the House Committee on un-American Activities. In August 1939, under the control of Congressman Martin Dies, it published a report which called down a plague upon all foreigners and, by implication, upon the President for getting himself involved with them. 'War propaganda is at full blast in the United States today', it said, reducing the causes of the European conflict to simplistic terms. '. . . Certain nations have empires and want to keep them . . . other nations do not have empires (not imposing ones at least) and want to acquire them.'[40] Britain, Germany, France, Italy, Russia — all the potentially belligerent countries were guilty of conducting propaganda, and all had agents working openly in the United States, registered with the Secretary of State as required under the law of 8 June 1939.

In 1939 as in the 1950s, the communists were seen as the most 'un-American' of them all, and they were Martin Dies's primary target. Earl Browder, their General Secretary, was interrogated at length. At one point he caused consternation among the committee by claiming that a group of Republicans had tried to bribe him to appoint Roosevelt the communist candidate in the 1936 Presidential election, in order to discredit him among his Democrat supporters. Ben Gitlow, one of Browder's predecessors, declared that the American Party received direct financial aid from the Comintern, and confessed to have appropriated much of the one million dollars raised in America for the relief of famine in Russia in 1922.

Fuel to the flames was added by a currently famous defector, Walter Krivitsky, who was said to have been head of Soviet Military Intelligence in Western Europe. (In 1941 he was assassinated in America by the NKVD.) He told the committee that of course Stalin was the real head of the American Communist Party. During October Congressman Dies several times alleged that American Government officials were helping the communists by sponsoring Red Front organizations, and he implied that Roosevelt had done this, although unwittingly, by showing hospitality a few weeks previously to the American Youth Congress. American communists, said Dies, were serving 'Moscow's special interest', which was that Germany and the Allies should destroy one another.

Also indicted before the Committee was the German–American Bund, men of German origin and Hitlerite sympathy, led by a local 'Führer' called Fritz Kuhn. Based in Chicago, they claimed two million members and spent the month of September agitating for a constitutional amendment which would ban the use of American soldiers on foreign soil and oblige the President to call a national referendum before he was allowed to declare war. Dies reported that pro-Nazis had appeared before his Committee with 'fantastic tales of Jewish plots'. He concluded that 'these tales have won acceptance among many Americans who now openly declare their partisanship towards the Rome–Berlin axis on this basis alone. Witnesses have appeared before this Committee with the frank avowal that they hail Hitler as the world's saviour from International Jewry.'[41]

But Dies' condemnations were not confined to the agencies of the dictatorships. He had hard words for the way the British and French were conducting 'a well-organized attempt to influence public opinion, either to enlist us actively or financially in war'. His was a feeling common among Americans at that time, that the cunning Europeans were once again trying to seduce them. Acutely conscious of the extent to which their civilization is derived from Britain and France, Americans have developed a strange attitude to those two countries, a mixture of admiration and resentment, and the outbreak of war served only to intensify both these emotions. As Douglas Fairbanks Jr wrote to Lord Stamp in October: 'We as a nation suffer a multitude of inhibitions — an inferiority complex being not the least of them.'[42] He deplored British 'lack of foresight in wooing American sympathy over the last twenty years' and suggested ways by which this might be put right. A particularly pro-British American, he wished he could be in Europe helping the Allied cause, but feared the effect that any such gesture would have on American opinion. The House un-American Activities Committee had just concluded that 'many well-meaning Americans have already become the unwitting dupes' of foreign agents. The gibe was meant partly for Roosevelt, partly for the overt communists and pro-Nazis, partly for such men as Douglas Fairbanks.

The British and French were in a cruel dilemma. They were accused of trying to seduce America, and it was true, they *were* trying to seduce her. On this level the German propaganda task was much easier, for they expected less. They knew that by and large America was sympathetic to the Allies and that it was little use their trying to attract American help. The most they could achieve was to deny such help to their enemies, and this they could do by appealing to Americans to be fair, to be genuinely neutral. The Germans could appear as supporters of the chief American aim, which was to keep out of the war. Their propaganda could claim with some justification that Britain and France were trying to involve America in the war, while all Germany wanted was to keep America neutral and at peace.

Britain and France were therefore forced to disguise their

seduction and to restrain their advances. For instance, when war began Lord Beaverbrook had the bright idea of setting up a radio station on a British island in the West Indies to broadcast to America his country's point of view. It was just the sort of clumsy scheme that would be grist to the mill of the isolationists, and he was rightly dissuaded from his plan. The Foreign Office ordered its Washington Embassy to soft-pedal all propaganda, and publicly announced as much in a statement which was reasonable to the point of naivity: 'We feel that it is for you and you alone to form your own judgement about ourselves and about the war. That of course is your inalienable right. This is what we mean by saying that the British Government conducts no propaganda in this country.'[43]

No wonder, then, that the Foreign Office was disturbed at the prospect of a visit to America by Duff Cooper, a hard-line anti-Nazi and vociferous critic in Parliament of Chamberlain and Halifax. In late August, just after the Nazi–Soviet Pact was signed, an article of his appeared in the French newspaper *Ordre*: 'Once again the governments of the democracies have let themselves be surprised. Once again they find themselves presented with a *fait accompli*, against which they had been warned, but in the possibility of which they refused to believe.'[44] This line, which was that of Churchill and his group, and which may now be claimed to have been justified by history, infuriated the British Ambassador in Paris Eric Phipps. In a wild note to London Phipps called it 'most mischievous', and actually asked London for authority to ask the French authorities to suppress any further articles by Duff Cooper. It was an astonishingly hostile attitude for an ambassador to take to a man who had so recently been a Cabinet Minister. (Cooper was a Privy Counsellor and had only the previous year resigned as First Lord of the Admiralty. In 1940 Churchill brought him back into the Government and in 1944 appointed him Ambassador in Paris.)

Warned of Cooper's transatlantic voyage, Halifax wrote to Lothian on 13 October to ask for reports on all Cooper's speeches. Lothian was asked to warn Cooper, wisely, against any suggestion of American entry into the war and, perhaps not so wisely, against 'entering into any old and, I hope, effete controversies over Munich'.[45] Cooper was to be personally informed 'of the various dangers that he should avoid in his public speeches, and in particular no doubt of the great importance of saying nothing'. The tone of Halifax's message, condescending to the point of arrogance, is a good indication of how deep was the division within Britain's governing Conservative Party, deep enough to be a continual danger to the Government's relations with Allies and friendly neutrals in time of war.

It was true that any Briton or Frenchman who actively sought American sympathy was at best wasting his time, at worst spoiling his own case. The sympathy of the American Government and of most Americans was with the Allies already. It did not need to be sought, and the more it was sought, the more it confronted Americans with their main preoccupation which was more important than any matter of sympathy – how to keep out of the war. As Douglas Fairbanks wrote, 'in the nation's anxiety to avert participation it seeks refuge in condemnation of the standards of British morality'.[46] Congressman Martin Dies had no sympathy for British and French appeals to America on the basis of democratic solidarity against the German, Russian and Italian dictatorships. The British and French were apt to portray themselves as angelic and the others as satanic, said his report. Such arguments were an 'instrument of deception' which 'has been used to an alarming degree in this country'.[47]

Dies quoted from a book called *Propaganda in the Next War*, edited by the famous Captain Liddell-Hart: 'In the last resort alliances spring from the hope of material advantage, not the possession of a common ideological belief.' Sinisterly the British writer had continued, 'In our propaganda we must make the facts fit our case as far as possible.' Perhaps overlooking the ideological similarities between the Nazi and Soviet systems, Dies found confirmation in the recently signed Pact for his argument that countries with opposing ideologies would always be ready to ally themselves militarily, if this was in their national interest. Conversely, ideological sympathy was no proper basis for military assistance.

Anyway, Dies's report continued, Britain and France had no monopoly of righteousness. 'Surely no one will deny,' he admitted, 'that the governmental forms of England and France are far more in accord with those of the United States than are those of Germany and Italy?' But – and here was the Allies' main propaganda difficulty — 'it is also true that London and Paris control the two largest empires in the world today'.

There were many Americans who saw the war simply as a quarrel between imperial powers. True, Hitler had invaded Austria, Czechoslovakia and Poland, and was busy establishing his colonial rule in these lands, but was not this exactly what the British and French had done in the past? 'This is a war between Rome and Carthage,' said Walton Butterworth of the American Embassy in London to John Balfour. 'Which is which?' Balfour was tempted to ask. And he could with some ease have picked holes in the analogy. The British and French empire-builders had occupied, often without resistance, non-European countries which were at that particular time politically and economically under-developed. Furthermore, they had done this in previous centuries when the only international law was that of the jungle and of 'might equals right'. By the 1930s the right of a country to self-rule was on its way to acceptance, even by the main imperial powers. Mussolini's aggression into Abyssinia had reversed this trend, and Hitler's into eastern Europe confirmed the reversal. The first attempts at world cooperation, symbolized by the creation of the League of Nations, had been sabotaged by the rampages of the two dictators, which were beginning to be a threat to the imperial powers themselves — Britain, France, Holland and Belgium. These countries, whose power stretched like the tentacles of an octopus around the circumference of the globe, were soft and vulnerable at the brain-centre. What use was it that they ruled half the world, when their capital cities could in a matter of hours be blown to pieces by the German Air Force? So long as Hitler remained, every foreign policy had to be subordinated to the need to defend oneself against him. Orderly economic and political progress was impossible so long as this man who refused to obey the rules was allowed to run riot.

But on a very superficial level it was possible to tar with the same brush all the imperial powers: Britain and France as well as Italy and Germany. These were of course the years when Americans took great moral pride in the fact that they did not possess colonies. They had once been a colony, they knew what it was like, and they supported those peoples who strove to throw off the shackles — for example the Cubans and the Irish. They tended then to see themselves as pure and innocent of any sins of oppression.

Professor T. N. Whitehead of Harvard University wrote the Foreign Office an interesting letter about the basis for such anti-British attitudes: 'India, for example, is commonly presented as a fairly homogeneous country of intelligent Asiatics prevented from enjoying the blessings of democratic self-government by the iron control of English regiments, kept there to fill the pockets of English merchants.'[48] Men of the perception of Roosevelt knew that this was to over-simplify, but he was aware of how many Americans took a simpler view of the evils of imperialism. On 14 December he raised the issue with Lothian at lunch:

He [Roosevelt] thought that we ought never to cease hammering at the point that one of our war aims was the right of self-government for all people, because that always struck a responsive note here. He suggested to me that it might be very useful if you could in one of your forthcoming speeches point out that while in the seventeenth and eighteenth centuries Great Britain, together with France, Holland, Spain, Portugal and other nations, went in for Empire buildings, that we had long ago learnt the lesson that the only foundation for a stable international system was national autonomy. He said that the most convincing approach to the American public was to admit the errors in the past while pointing to a change of heart in the present, that Germany was trying to force the world back to methods which had been discarded by the United States in the Monroe system and by Great Britain in the modern British Commonwealth which had not yet reached self-government, all its peoples were on the way there and that the process of development of self-government would continue.[49]

This was one of the few points which revealed a clear divergence of opinion between the President and the British Prime Minister. Halifax handed Lothian's important letter to Chamberlain, who scribbled in the margin: 'Be careful about India, Burma, Ceylon etc. who think they ought to have autonomy at once. Why must we admit errors in order "to approach the American public"? I doubt if that would conciliate them. Anyway I should not be prepared to admit that what would be errors if done now were necessarily wrong at the time when they were done. One cannot defend everything in the past, nor can anyone else. But need we suggest that we have been worse than the others?'[50]

Robert Vansittart, Halifax's Chief Diplomatic Adviser, noted, 'I strongly agree with the Prime Minister's marginal comments.' The idea of admitting errors, he thought, was 'simple lunacy when one is once at war (and even when one is not, so far as the United States are concerned)'. It would provide 'jam for German propaganda and for all the American isolationists to boot'. 'This folly leads easily to the next stage,' he went on, recalling a speech which the actress Sybil Thorndike had just delivered to an audience of women. She had suggested that Britain confess her past imperialist sins to Hitler, and then, in Vansittart's words, 'that we could then easily kiss and be friends – on the basis of common turpitude presumably'.

Certainly, Americans had only to look at the Empire to find ample basis for their allegations of British hypocrisy. This led many to develop their attitudes into more damning accusations of trickery and dishonesty. For instance, many felt, not only had they been tricked into the First World War, but they had also been tricked into lending Britain huge sums of money to fight it – *money which twenty years later had still not been repaid*. And now here was Britain again, through the agency of the American President whom she appeared to have duped, requiring Congress to allow her to fight another war with American weapons. True, for the moment Britain was actually offering to *pay* for these weapons, but it would not be long, they thought, and rightly, before Roosevelt would be proposing to hand them over free of charge.

'In fact,' wrote Professor Whitehead from Harvard with great astuteness, 'we are beggars on horseback. We do not pay our war debts, but we claim a leading part in world affairs as if by right. We assume a position of superiority which the American half acknowledges and half resents.'[51] His letters were so well put that within a few months he was invited to return to England and join the American desk at the Foreign Office.

Examples of this resentment were soon to be found in extreme form, culminating in the cruel suggestion that the United States should ask Britain to hand over some of her West Indian possessions in lieu of war debts. Senator Lundeen of Minnesota even suggested sending the American Army to seize them by force, adding that this would be quite easy since the British 'were pretty busy on the Western Front'.[52] Charles Lindbergh also thought this would be a good idea, his argument being that so long as European powers retained any possessions in the Western Hemisphere, the United States was bound eventually to become involved in European wars. Lindbergh was also furious when Canada declared war on Germany, proclaiming in a radio broadcast on 13 October: 'Have they [the Canadians] the right to draw this hemisphere into a European war simply because they prefer the Crown of England to American independence?'

Such strong views were naturally most prevalent among Americans of German, Italian or Irish origin. 'Many Irish were opposed to anything that would help the British,' notes Elliott Roosevelt in his edition of his father's letters,[53] and it is probably true that the Irish in America were more anti-British than the Irish in Ireland, who could view the war at closer range and perhaps understand what would happen to them if Britain lost. Between them the Irish, Italians, Austrians and Germans were able to turn the Roman Catholic Church in America into a force for isolationism. A few of its representatives, for instance the famous radio personality priest Father Coughlin, were strident anti-British propagandists. The other side did have its say. On 2 October Bishop Sheil called upon Catholics to support repeal of the embargo, but in view of the way in which Catholic Poland had just been devastated it is surprising how lone was his voice.

For instance on 8 September the International Catholic Truth Society organized meetings in many large American cities under the slogan 'What can *you* do to keep the United States out of the war?' This society also proposed the introduction of a bill before Congress requiring a national referendum before America could declare war. (A similar suggestion was also being canvassed by the German–American Bund.) On 26 September Bergen, German Ambassador to the Holy See, was able to send to Berlin a file of reports and cuttings demonstrating 'the large extent to which sentiment against involvement in the war already exists among American Catholics and is promoted by influential individuals in these circles'.[54] The Catholics were presumably unaware of Hitler's plan, already under way, to render harmless the Polish nation by arresting and killing its natural leaders, among whom of course were Catholic priests.

But it was not ignorance so much as complacency that Roosevelt really had to fight against. A Gallup poll in September showed that eighty-two per cent of Americans thought the Allies were going to win the war, though on what basis it is hard to comprehend. Even by the end of that month, after the conquest of Poland and the active participation in it of Soviet Russia, very few Americans could see the war as any threat to *them*. The President took it all much more seriously. He said to Lothian 'that one of his difficulties was to make the American people understand the tremendous risks that they themselves were running at present. His military advisers were by no means certain that we would win the war, and if we lost it the United States would be faced with intolerable difficulties.'[55] The President was particularly worried that Britain, forced to make peace with Germany on unfavourable terms, might have to transfer to Germany some of her sea bases, including perhaps some in the West Indies, and part of her Navy. The United States would then find it impossible to defend the Monroe Doctrine. Germany would be able to force into her economic system the countries of South and Central America, thus replacing the United States as the dominant power in that continent.

But such thoughts placed the President in somewhat of a quandary. It was in his interest and, he believed, in America's interest to shock his people out of their complacency and to make them face up to the dangers that threatened. But to do this he would have to address them in terms which envisaged an Allied defeat. Could he take such a risk? Would it not boost German morale to the sky if the most pro-Ally of all the neutrals began to indulge in defeatest talk? After all it was precisely this, a collapse of German morale, that Chamberlain was relying on for his quick victory. The Prime Minister was deluding himself, and maybe the President realized this, but it would not be easy for him to make speeches which boosted Germany and thereby undermined the British plan.

Privately, of course, Lothian lost no opportunity to point out to the President the risks involved in American aloofness. He would ruminate about the need for Britain 'to yield up the sceptre to America'. But such talk merely irritated the President, who knew the disastrous effect such words would have on the American electorate, whom in no more than a year he was going to have to ask to reappoint him for an unprecedented third term. Americans were in no mood to have any European 'sceptre' foisted upon them, and it was unrealistic of Britain to try to push him into a position where he would not even be able to survive as President.

He allowed himself the occasional outburst, for instance in a letter to a British writer friend called Robert Byron. He wrote that he was getting thoroughly tired of this British attitude of *morituri te salutamus* (we who are about to die salute thee). If the British wanted cooperation they should make America believe that they could lick the other guy on their own. The President concluded that 'what the British need is a good stiff grog'.[56]

But as well as braver talk, and perhaps braver action, the President required from Britain a realistic appraisal of the consequences of defeat. To this end, at the request of Ambassador Kennedy, the Foreign Office embarked upon the extraordinary task of preparing a paper on what would happen to America if Britain and France were defeated. Then as now, the idea of a Hitler victory is a spine-chilling thought, so it is interesting to note on what particular horrors the various Britons who compiled the document decided to place their emphasis: 'The defeat of these two powers, and especially of Great Britain, would shatter the fabric of international finance and trade . . . The United Kingdom would inevitably disappear as an important market, and, seeing that she is the best customer of the United States, the direct loss to the latter's export trade would in itself be little short of disastrous.'[57]

The reason why the Foreign Office thought it necessary to make this point so prominently seems strange in retrospect. The illusion created and fostered by so many prominent men in Western Europe and America, that Hitler was a necessary bulwark against communism, or 'Bolshevism' as it was then commonly termed, had only recently died in Britain and France, while in America it was still very much alive. For two or three years, to be sure, Hitler had been behaving very badly. His repression of German Jews, his racist legislation and destruction of Jewish property on *Kristallnacht* in 1938, can have left few in doubt even in 1939 that he was hell-bent on a murderous rampage. His successive aggressions had by now given the lie to his claim that all he required was 'reunification' of the German peoples of Europe. At long last

Chamberlain had appreciated that Hitler was the greater danger, as well as morally the worse, for Stalin's internal repression was of a different character. True, it was murderous class hatred and internal security gone mad, but it was not racism and incipient genocide. By 1939 Stalin had already slaughtered tens of thousands, but it was done haphazardly, insanely, and it was within the Soviet Union's defensive barricade. It was an *implosion* of terror, whereas Hitler was clearly on the point of exploding his hordes against the bulk of the human race. To anyone who had observed the man's actions and read his words, so much was apparent, but many Americans still had not. They were still more likely to be impressed by threats to their finances than by wild talk about the evil of Hitler.

Expanding upon this theme, the Foreign Office authors fore-saw 'the smaller European countries reduced to vassal states . . . chaos in India, colonial war in South Africa'. But let no one assume that only European interests would suffer. A German victory would leave the Far East 'exposed without the bulwark of British and French sea power to the designs of a predatory Japan'. It would be 'a potent threat to the internal orientation and stability of the Latin American republics'.

Only towards the end of its text did the British report feel able to turn to loftier issues: 'Whatever their shortcomings, France is the hearth of intellectual sanity and England the home of intellectual freedom and representative government.' The whole world would suffer if, as might reasonably be assumed, 'having once consolidated their hold over them, the rulers of Nazi Germany would demand that Great Britain and France should remodel their forms of government to approximate more closely to the system at present obtaining in Germany?'

So what? Would that be such a terrible tragedy? Anyway, what has it to do with us? Such questions would not have been the *typical* American reaction, but they would have been asked by many still unaware of what Hitler really stood for. For their benefit the report appended some apt quotations from *Mein Kampf*:

Man has become great through perpetual struggle. In perpetual peace his greatness must decline[58] . . . Foreign policy is only a means to an end and the sole end to be pursued is the welfare of our own people. This is the sole preoccupation that must occupy our minds in dealing with a question. Party politics, religious considerations, humanitarian ideals — all such and all other preoccupations must absolutely give way to this[59] ... A state which, in an epoch of racial adulteration, devotes itself to the duty of preserving the best elements of its racial stock must one day become ruler of the earth.[60]

All this led the writers to the conclusion that 'if Western Europe and America cannot find some means of combining to defeat the common enemy, they may both find themselves dangerously threatened by internal convulsions, arising from loss of markets, a growing spirit of lawlessness, unemployment, famine and pestilence'.

It was strong stuff, written in the sort of language that one does not usually find in Foreign Office memoranda, all the more lurid for the fact that it was designed not to be declaimed at some public assembly but to be read soberly and digested diligently in government offices in London and Washington. Knowing that their document was primarily for American consumption, it was of course in the writers' interest to paint the situation as colourfully as possible, but looking back with the knowledge of what Hitler was about to do one can hardly accuse them of exaggeration. At the time they may well have thought they were exaggerating in a good cause, but they were not. They might for instance have included details of the Nazis' treatment of Jews and political opponents in Germany, but this was not thought appropriate. The point emphasized was that an Allied defeat would be for America an *economic* catastrophe.

For the fight against American complacency the document was formidable ammunition, but unfortunately it also had its built-in dangers. If it were to become widely known that the British Foreign Office was envisaging defeat and writing memoranda on its possible consequences, the result might be disastrous. In America it might cause contempt for the British war effort, and if through America it became known in Germany, which was more than likely, it would boost German morale. For this reason, although it was at Ambassador Kennedy's request that the document was compiled, the British decided that it would be too dangerous to show him the finished text.

There was another reason, one acutely embarrassing to both

countries. The fact was that the Ambassador's behaviour was causing alarm in Whitehall, and was soon the subject of page after page of critical official comment. Joseph Kennedy had accumulated a multi-million-dollar fortune in banking and investment before his friend the President appointed him to the London Embassy, his first governmental post. On 14 April 1939 Harold Caccia, then one of Halifax's Private Secretaries, wrote: 'Although a newcomer to diplomacy, Mr Kennedy has proved during the short period since his appointment here as Ambassador that he possesses every quality necessary for the success of his mission.'[61] His entertaining was lavish. His children were young and beautiful.

But the outbreak of war seemed to induce a sort of panic into the Ambassador. At an interview with Chamberlain he declared frankly that he thought Britain was going to lose. He did not even think that the President would succeed in repealing the Neutrality Act. It was of course quite in order for the Ambassador to express this private view to the Prime Minister, however much it may have depressed him. But soon Kennedy began airing his defeatist views in conversation to anyone who cared to listen. It was not long before the British authorities began to hear of his loose talk, and their reaction was an angry one.

On 20 September a young British diplomatist called Berkeley Gage recorded a talk he had had with 'a friend of mine in the Coldstream Guards'. Apparently 'after an informal dinner with the US Ambassador (with whom he is on close terms through one or all of his daughters) Mr Kennedy had after a somewhat competitive exchange of toasts expressed the opinion that we should be badly thrashed in the present war'. The officer was probably Lord Hartington, who married the Ambassador's daughter Kathleen in 1944 and was killed shortly afterwards. It was his opinion that Mr Kennedy took relish in expressing this opinion because of 'the delight inherent in most Americans in seeing the lion's tail twisted'.

The Ambassador adduced several reasons for his pessimism. (For pessimism it was. The evidence shows that he took no delight whatever in the idea of an Allied defeat. The Guards officer had misinterpreted the tone of his host's remarks.) He feared that Japan and Turkey might soon join Germany. He declared that 'the Germans knew where our aircraft factories were and we were ignorant of the position of theirs', to which Alexander Cadogan was moved to reply: 'Why Mr Kennedy should think that we don't know where German aircraft factories are located I can't imagine. I suppose Colonel Lindbergh told him.'

John Kennedy, the future President, was at the dinner party which took place a day or two before the family returned to America (21 September). He was then twenty-two years old and working on a thesis which in spite of much adverse criticism was later published under the title *Why England Slept*. Most unusually, he and his elder brother Joseph had been appointed by their father as attachés in his embassy. That evening John confirmed his father's gloomy forecasts. Even if the Neutrality Act was repealed, he said, it would not help Britain much since she did not have enough gold or dollars for large armaments purchases. (It is a fact that for half a year after repeal Britain bought American arms only at the rate of two million dollars a month.[62]) Gage noted: 'We are of course aware that Mr Kennedy attaches importance to the views of one of his sons who recently returned from Germany very impressed by what he saw and whose views on the subject Mr Kennedy telegraphed to the State Department.'

The Foreign Office was very angry with the American Ambassador. Graham Hutton wrote, semi-prophetically, 'Kennedy's real ambition is the White House, and he has a great chance of achieving it. He is not a career man in the American diplomatic service. He wants to get back into the domestic arena. And he has annoyed most of his own staff in the London Embassy by his rather peculiar and personal (and even familial) conduct of diplomacy and reporting to Washington.' John Balfour mentioned Kennedy's concern 'to make sure that he is not tainted with the pro-British brush' and of his Irish predisposition 'to twist the lion's tail, the more so when the animal appears to be in one hell of a jam'.

The file of complaint on Kennedy made its way up the pyramid of seniority, as is the Foreign Office custom, until it came to an Assistant Under-Secretary called David Scott. Scott disagreed with his subordinates. 'Mr Kennedy is entitled to his opinion and to express it when and where he likes,' he noted, only to be quickly reversed by his boss Alexander Cadogan whose view became the definitive one: 'He occupies a privileged position by virtue of his being accredited here, and he enjoys access to people in the highest authority. Surely the least one can ask in return is that he should exercise some discretion.' This note was shown to Halifax and to Chamberlain who concurred.

During those last days of September there is a noticeable lack of objectivity and 'cool' in the British papers – understandably, for it was then that the challenge to Whitehall's pre-eminence or even existence became revealed as a real and terrifying one. The Kennedy case is a good example of this deterioration. The files are full of second- and third-hand gossip about him, like the report which claimed 'there were funny stories about him and his dealings in the City'. The word had been passed by a Swede called Baron Palmstierna and 'the inference, though this was not explicitly stated, was that Mr Kennedy's stock exchange activities, whatever they may be, are capable of being interpreted as affording evidence of anti-British proclivities'.

The logic behind this note is hard to detect. Kennedy was not anti-British; he simply thought that Britain was going to lose the war, and if that was the case it was a bad enough situation for the world without the Kennedy family losing money into the bargain. Evidence that this was Kennedy's real view was given to the Foreign Office by an American journalist, William Hillman, who said: 'Mr Kennedy was a professing Catholic who loathed Hitler and Hitlerism almost, though perhaps not quite, as much as he loathed Bolshevism, but he was also a self-made man who had known poverty and did not want to know it again.'

What Kennedy feared, according to Hillman, was that the war would go badly for Britain and France until, with the Allies on the brink of defeat, the United States would be forced to come to their aid. The result would be the collapse of the western financial and social order, followed by a Bolshevik take-over. He said to Hillman, 'Bill, I'd sell a hundred Polands down the river any day rather than risk the life of a British soldier or the loss of a British pound.' It was a crude way of putting it, but all the Ambassador was really saying was that since the Allies were probably going to lose the war, they should never have begun it, that to break a treaty was a lesser evil for a government to commit than to lead its people to defeat in war.

But wherever his sympathies lay, the fact remained that the

Ambassador was casting gloom over London society, proclaiming his woeful prophecies even to neutral journalists, for example, it was reported, to a Swiss called Kessler. It was intolerable, and David Scott was ordered to write to Lothian in the following terms: 'It has come to our notice through various unofficial sources that Mr Kennedy has been adopting a most defeatist attitude in his talks with a number of private individuals. The general line which he takes in these conversations, as reported to us, is that Great Britain is certain to be defeated in the war, particularly on account of her financial weakness.' For the moment Lothian was not required to take any action, but he was warned to be ready 'in case it should later become necessary to ask you to drop a hint in the proper quarter'. It was a very diplomatic threat, but a real one nevertheless. The British were considering the possibility that they might have to ask Roosevelt for Kennedy's removal.

It followed that Kennedy was putting as much if not more gloom into his reports to Roosevelt. Particularly dangerous was the impression he was giving Roosevelt that Britain herself had no stomach for the war and was only looking for some way of getting out of it. On 11 September he wrote to Washington about the coming peace offensive: 'It seems to me that this situation may crystallize to a point where the President can be the saviour of the world.' But Roosevelt did not see himself cut out for such a role. He wired back to Kennedy immediately: 'The people of the United States would not support any move for peace initiated by this Government that would consolidate or make possible a survival of a régime of force and aggression.' [63]

On 30 September Kennedy wrote the President an even more unhappy letter, implying that the mood of London was one of total gloom and defeatism. He had spoken to John Simon, who was in despair about the joint declaration which Germany and the Soviet Union had issued two days previously. Even if Hitler could be removed, moaned Kennedy, there would be chaos in Germany and, worst of all, the country might well go communist. Whatever happened the war would be ruinous for Britain and France. 'Why go on?' Kennedy asked Simon. The restoration of pre-war Poland was obviously impossible, so what was Britain fighting for? To this question Simon had only one answer, that if he and his colleagues 'were to advocate any type of peace, they would be yelled down by their own people, who are determined to go on'.[64]

All this brought Kennedy to his conclusion: 'I have yet to talk to any military or naval expert of any nationality this week who thinks that, with the present and prospective set-up of England and France on one side and Germany and Russia and their potential allies on the other, England has a Chinaman's chance . . . England and France can't quit, whether they would like to or not, and I am convinced because I live here that England will go down fighting.'[65]

When one considers the importance Britain then attached to her relations with the United States, it becomes difficult to understand how Kennedy was able to maintain his loud opinions as well as his position as Ambassador. The issue was not so much his reports to Washington. British officials did not see these, of course, though they rightly assumed they would be very defeatist. It was not the reports that infuriated London. There were even those who thought they might do some good. Berkeley Gage noted, 'Putting the wind up President Roosevelt might also conceivably have advantages as we know that he, at least, has no illusions about the threat to America should we be beaten.'[66] Britain's legitimate complaint lay not here but in the Ambassador's wagging tongue.

The Foreign Office apparently did not proceed with its threat to report the Ambassador to the President, but one can imagine the effect that his presence was having on London's relations with Washington. As a channel of communication he can hardly have been very effective, for after the experience of the first few weeks of war the British began to withhold information from Kennedy, especially information of a depressing character, for fear that it would be blurted out at some dinner party. The following year the President took the unusual step of sending a special representative, William Donovan, ostensibly to coordinate intelligence. In fact one of his main tasks was to check up on Kennedy.

Hints were of course dropped. Kennedy was given to understand that he should curb his tongue, but he was incorrigible. With his great wealth, and safe in the knowledge of the services he had rendered the President in the past, he felt that he could get away with behaving as he felt fit. He made speeches on controversial subjects. During a visit home in December he told an American audience that the British Government 'does not have the slightest belief that the United States will get into the European war. They understand our position perfectly.'[67] On 11 December he told a meeting of parishioners from a church in Boston where he had once been an altar boy, 'There's no place in the fight for us. It's going to be bad enough as it is.'[68] British morale was excellent, he told another group, adding cruelly, 'It seems to perk up every time a British ship gets sunk.' Informed of these remarks, Alexander Cadogan minuted, 'I don't think these utterances are so bad in the circumstances. I should not have been surprised by worse.'[69] Cadogan's lack of anger on this occasion can be seen as a measure of the strength of the general Foreign Office feeling against Kennedy.

After Germany's lightning conquests of Holland, Belgium, Norway and France in the early summer of 1940, it was to be expected that Kennedy's gloom would increase, and sure enough it did, for on 1 July Chamberlain wrote in his diary, 'Saw Joe Kennedy who says everyone in USA thinks we shall be beaten before the end of the month.'[70] By then Chamberlain had been replaced as Prime Minister by Winston Churchill, and an immediate problem arose about the letters which the new Premier was sending the President at frequent intervals. It would have been normal to hand these letters to the London Embassy for dispatch across the Atlantic in the American diplomatic bag. But by then the Kennedy affair had reached such a stage that both governments thought that the American Embassy in London would be an 'undesirable channel'. The Foreign Office was again concerned about Kennedy's 'openly expressed defeatism', and Sumner Welles, the American Under-Secretary of State, actually suggested to Lothian that it might be better to send the letters to Washington by British courier 'for reasons of security'.[71] Nevertheless, in spite of the grave allegation implicit in these remarks that Kennedy might be expected to misuse or reveal private correspondence between Churchill and Roosevelt, no move was made to replace him as Ambassador until the following year when he returned to America.

It would be a mistake to get the Kennedy affair out of proportion and to suggest, as some have, that he was pro-Nazi. He was not pro-Nazi, but he was probably less anti-Nazi than he was anti-communist, and he was recognized as such by the Germans. On 22 October Thomsen reported to the German Foreign Office that he had heard that Kennedy was using his influence against repeal of the arms embargo on the ground that this would intensify the war. Robert Vansittart noted on 26 October, 'Mr Kennedy is so afraid for the old and wealthy order of this world that he is now, I feel pretty sure, an appeaser.' [72] But he was probably only anti-British in his resentment against the part she had played in getting the world, his world, into its present mess. His personal opinion, hardly unreasonable in the circumstances, that Britain was going to lose the war only increased his resentment against her.

He did not like the way that Britain had embarked upon her dangerous adventure, involving not only herself but also America in dire peril, and safe in the knowledge that if she were on the brink of defeat America would be forced to bail her out. Britain was gambling not only with her own money, but also with that of her rich American cousins. There was nothing disreputable about such an opinion. 'We were living on a knife edge and everyone knew it. Kennedy was only putting into words what everyone who knew the facts secretly felt,' says John Balfour in 1971. Kennedy is to be blamed not so much for his opinions as for his gross indiscretions, which amounted to an abuse of the important and sensitive post he held. His fears were such that he could not control his tongue, and the result was to place a strain on Anglo-American relations at a most difficult time. On one level his story is a strong argument in favour of career diplomats, for his indiscipline was only made possible by his inexperience of diplomacy and his financial independence. On another level Kennedy was the epitome of that feeling in the West that made Hitler possible, that blind terror of Bolshevik Russia that justified making an ally of the Nazi devil. It took such men a long time to realize which of the two was the greater danger.

There were other prominent Americans who shared Kennedy's terror of Bolshevism but not his understanding of the danger and evil of Hitlerism. During September and October several of them travelled to Italy and Germany, and after conversations with the dictators were deceived into aiding the German cause. For example, James Mooney, Vice-President of General Motors, had an interview with Göring on 19 October and was led by him to believe that peace was quite possible to achieve. It was the old story of Göring the leader of the liberal, reasonable wing of the Nazi Party, whose efforts to restore independence to the conquered lands were being thwarted by the so-called 'wild men', led by Goebbels and Ribbentrop. Göring apparently told him that Germany was quite ready to agree to create a Polish state of 14 million people, to 'guarantee the political and cultural integrity of the Czechs' and perhaps to set up a Jewish state in the south-eastern corner of Poland.[75] The trouble was, said Göring, that many Germans felt that by his speech on 12 October Chamberlain had slammed the door on any negotiations, and so it was difficult for him to pursue the matter further.

Mooney reported his talk to William Bullitt, the American Ambassador in Paris. All that was required from the Allies, said Mooney, was a word of encouragement to Göring and his men. Göring's hand would then be strengthened. He would be able to override the 'wild men' and steer Germany towards peace. Hitler would either be persuaded or removed.

The British had dealt with such vague proposals before, in particular through the agency of the Swedish businessman Birger Dahlerus. As Halifax wrote to Lothian on 21 November: 'We are almost daily the recipients of peace feelers from various quarters in Germany. It is very difficult to assess these at their real value. A number of them seem to be traceable to Göring . . .' Halifax concluded, though, that 'it would be impossible either for us or the French to enter into discussion of any proposals with the present government of Germany'.[74] He and his subordinates were by then thoroughly suspicious of these vague overtures, which seemed to be aimed not so much at securing peace as at finding out how deep was general British and French enthusiasm for the war, and how much they might be ready to concede as the price of ending it.

So it was with a certain lack of tolerance that the British addressed themselves to James Mooney. Alexander Cadogan described him as 'apparently connected with the automobile industry' — hardly a fair description of a man who was Vice-President of General Motors. A telegram from Lothian warned London to beware of him for 'he was formerly quite an important and responsible man, but is believed by his friends to have quite gone off his head'.[75] On 23 October Bullitt reported his conversation with

Mooney to Washington, adding that he assumed the State Department did not wish in any way to support Göring's proposals. This was confirmed from Washington the same day.[76]

Three other wandering Americans had been causing consternation as they passed through London on their way to Central Europe. Chief among them was a certain W. R. Davis whose job it was to purchase oil for Germany from Mexico, and who was in direct contact with Göring through the German Embassy in Mexico City. When war broke out Göring invited him to visit Berlin, which is why in mid September he found himself in London with two American companions, Rickett and Ben Smith.

Rickett, Smith and Davis were soon alarming London with stories which seemed to show that Roosevelt was working for peace in direct contact with Berlin behind the back of London and Paris. Rickett said they had been sent on a personal mission by the President because he thought that Kennedy and Bullitt were too pro-Ally, and that the American Clipper had been held up for him in Lisbon on the President's instructions. He was ready enough to give his personal view about the war, which was that it was just an imperialist squabble with nothing much to choose between either side, and that no decent democratic country ought to touch it with a barge-pole.

Of course frantic telegrams were dispatched to Lothian in Washington, and on 25 September came the reassuring reply: 'The State Department says that these men are catspaws of the Nazi Government who are trying to use them to put over a tale that Göring is working against Hitler behind his back and that peace overtures should be started through Göring, presumably with the encouragement of President Roosevelt. The State Department say that the idea of the Hitler–Göring split is moonshine and that the whole plot is a frame-up. None of the men mentioned has the slightest chance of getting to the White House doorstep.'[77] Frank Roberts noted from this that Britain should bear in mind that the United States would not welcome any attempt to play Göring off against Hitler. (This was after all the line that Göring was feeding London direct through Dahlerus, and London was at that stage quite interested in it.)

Where Lothian got his information from one cannot say, but anyway it was false. Davis *had* in fact seen the President and received from him, if not a mandate, at least some words of encouragement for his mission to Berlin. An American official historian writes that Roosevelt 'was certainly intrigued by the possibilities suggested by his visitor [Davis], including reports that Göring might be planning to take over the German Government, or that the Army might engineer a *coup d'état* to oust Hitler. In any case the President gave Davis to understand that he would consider the possibility of mediation, though only if the interested governments officially requested it'.[78]

Contrary to what Lothian was told by the State Department, the President had spoken to Davis, had expressed interest in Göring's alleged plan to remove Hitler and had given cautious approval to the idea of American mediation. Official denials of all this must presumably have been due to American embarrassment at the indiscretions of the three 'envoys' and the consequent British suspicion that Roosevelt was scheming behind London's back. Of course there was no reason whatever why Washington should not have its own contacts with Berlin, but it does seem that the three men were not very well chosen for such a sensitive mission.

Davis was given VIP treatment in Germany, with a lightning tour of the Siegfried Line and occupied Poland. On his return he again spoke to the President and wrote two reports to which the President paid close attention. The gist of these was that peace was to be had for the asking. The President had only to offer his good offices and Göring would combine with the German General Staff to make peace on the basis of the moderate 'sixteen-point programme', the reasonable solution to the Polish dispute which Germany had pretended to offer in the last days of August.[79] But Roosevelt was not to be moved by such vague though tempting proposals. He would only act if officially asked by the German Government, he said, and even then he doubted if the British would accept any solution so long as the existing military *status quo* lasted. All in all, Roosevelt was less willing to act than he had been when he saw Davis in mid September. Not only was such mediation likely to prove embarrassing to Britain and France, but it would also embroil the United States deep in the European quarrel. This was the last thing any American wanted. Davis and his friends followed the other amateur diplomats of the period away from the councils of his nation and back into ordinary life.

But their brief flurry into fame caused British officials to write numerous worried memoranda full of concern and doubts as to what the President might be up to. By coincidence Robert Vansittart, head of the Foreign Office until 1938, had a family connection with James Mooney in that his brother worked for General Motors, so that in a sense Mooney was his boss. Vansittart noted that he could not agree with the universal damnation of Mooney, or that Mooney should be put in the same category as the other three who were 'very shady characters with considerable dossiers in their disfavour'.[80] Mooney was probably not as bad as all that, he thought. But the general view in London was that all such interlopers were thoroughly dangerous and a menace to world security. With the world in such a disastrous state, with the whole of civilization resting on a knife-edge, there could be no excuse for such private individuals, responsible to no one, rushing about Europe, accepting the Nazis' hospitality and returning home with misleading promises that raised false hopes of an early end to the war. Some of them were Nazi sympathizers. Their motive was apparent to all. Others like those just mentioned were merely foolish and incautious, rushing in where angels fear to tread and then proclaiming their valueless and dangerous opinions. And this, with the vote on the Neutrality Act only a month away, could do great harm to the Allied cause.

As October progressed and the day of the vote drew nearer there were pro-Nazis in America clutching at straws to prevent the passage of the President's Act. On 18 October the *New York Times* and other newspapers published an alarming statement which a certain Gustav Anderson, a travel agent from Evanston, Illinois, had sworn before Congressmen Case, Brooks and Pierce. Anderson had been a passenger on the British ship *Athenia* which had exploded and sunk west of Scotland at 9 p.m. on 3 September – the first important event of the war. At once it was assumed that a German torpedo had done the deed which cost the lives of 112 people, twenty-eight of them American, and the first reactions were of horror at an unspeakable Nazi crime and of terror at the prospect of unrestricted submarine warfare.

But the next day the German Secretary of State, Ernst Weizsacker, called in the American Chargé d'Affaires, Alexander Kirk, to tell him that no German ship was involved, that there was no

U-boat anywhere near where the *Athenia* had been hit.[81] He remembered how the United States had been brought into the First World War, by the sinking of the *Lusitania*, so that evening he went to see Grand-Admiral Raeder to urge him not to provoke America in this way. Raeder assured him that no German U-boat could possibly have been responsible.[82]

Raeder and Weizsäcker were sincere in their protestations, for in his 31 August directive Hitler *had* ordered restraint in warlike operations against Britain and France, even if the two countries were to declare war.[83] 'Even when German U-boats lay in a favourable position near the French battleship *Dunkerque* he [Hitler] refused to authorize an attack,' claims Albert Speer.[84] On 5 September Hitler's newspaper *Völkischer Beobachter* assured the world: 'There was no German warship anywhere near the Hebrides. In any case, Hitler would never dream of violating the rules of war. The whole story is a typical Northcliffe lie.' Maybe, the article continued, the ship sank because of an accidental explosion, or maybe — and here was the germ of an idea for Goebbels's propaganda — 'maybe Churchill had the bomb planted in the ship himself'.

But in their heart of hearts the German leaders could not be sure that one of their submarines was not responsible. While at sea the U-boats could not report their activities by radio. Such broadcasts if intercepted might give away valuable information, as well as the U-boat's position. On 7 September Raeder noted in his diary, 'No attempt to be made to solve the *Athenia* affair until the submarines return home.'[85] So his denial of responsibility, while sincere as far as it went, was made in the knowledge that it might turn out to be incorrect. On 16 September he moved a step further away from sincerity by inviting the American naval attaché to come and see him, and informing him that he now had reports from all his submarines which showed that none of them could possibly have been responsible.[86] In fact, not all his U-boat commanders had reported, and one who had not was Oberleutnant Lemp of the U-30.

Raeder's commander of submarines, Karl Doenitz, must have had a guilty conscience about the U-30, for when she returned to port at Wilhelmshaven he was waiting on the quay. In evidence at the Nuremberg Trials he told how Oberleutnant Lemp confessed to having torpedoed the *Athenia*, having mistaken her for an armed merchant cruiser on patrol. Doenitz had Lemp flown at once to Berlin for questioning, but it was decided not to court-martial him since he had acted in good faith. Doenitz himself ordered all mention of the *Athenia* cut out of the U-30's log, and the crew sworn to secrecy. He even deleted all comment on the affair from his own diary.[87]

Of course such mistakes do happen in wartime, and lives do get lost as a result, so although a U-boat was in fact guilty of the sinking, it cannot really be called a Nazi 'crime', certainly not when compared to what was to happen later. But typically, not content with covering up their responsibility for the deed, the Nazi leaders decided to turn it to their own advantage by means of a big lie. They would change the idea first suggested in their news-paper on 5 September that the British had blown up their own ship from a ludicrous hypothesis into a fact, or at least into a plausible version that might well convince a few Americans and confuse a few more. The Americans are hostile enough to us in any case, they may have thought, so we have little to lose.

The Nazi lie was given verisimilitude by the events (or rather the inaction) which followed the sinking. As the days passed and no other passenger ships were attacked it emerged that the *Athenia* affair was an isolated incident. German submarines were torpedo-ing Allied merchant ships and ships of war, but not indiscrimin-ately or in such a way as to cause great loss of life. German aeroplanes were not bombing open towns (except in 'remote' Poland), and any American could see that the bestialities of ordi-nary war were just not happening. Americans began to have second thoughts about the *Athenia*. Who stood to gain by the outrage? Surely not Germany. Their war would not be won by the slaughter of a few innocent lives. But what about Britain and France? The frantic way in which they were trying to involve America in the war was plain for all to see. Could they not just possibly have manufactured a second *Lusitania*? On the one hand it seemed incredible to believe Britain and France guilty of such a ruthless, inhuman act, but on the other hand . . . One must re-member that war is a ruthless game. *Inter arma silent leges*, and their is an English proverb to the same effect: 'All's fair in love and war.'

That such thoughts were rife is shown by the result of an opinion poll taken at the end of September, which showed that only sixty per cent of Americans believed that the Germans had sunk the *Athenia*. The men in Goebbels's ministry may have read this and concluded that here was something to work on. Then came Gustav Anderson's astonishing affidavit sworn before three Congressmen to the effect that the *Athenia* had been carrying guns, that her decks were strengthened for use as a raider, and that the crew were constantly nervous and seemed to know there was going to be an explosion. His testimony was gleefully taken up by the German press.

In his propaganda, Anderson could be seen to be falling between two stools. The German Embassy was propagating two possible versions of the incident. The first, the more restrained, claimed that the *Athenia* was not really a passenger ship but was armed as a ship of war. As such she was fair game for a U-boat attack. The second version was the brazen lie that Britain had destroyed her own ship. The fact that the first theory contradicted the second was pointed out by the more subtle of Anderson's audience, but it cannot be denied that on the face of it his words were convincing, and very dangerous to the British cause, coming as they did nine days before the Senate vote on repeal of the Neutrality Act.

On 22 October, four days after Anderson's testimony appeared in the press, Goebbels broadcast the definitive German version, one personally authorized by Hitler on the theory that in propaganda as in battle attack is the best form of defence. 'Churchill sank the *Athenia*,' proclaimed Hitler's *Völkischer Beobachter*, and within a few days thousands of pamphlets were arriving through the letter-boxes of prominent Americans. These began: 'The British steamer *Athenia* was sunk by order of the First Lord of the Admiralty, Mr Winston Churchill. The idea originated in his own mind and he caused this most shocking crime ever devised by human brain to be carried out systematically. Can the British people in the name of their country continue to back this criminal?' [88]

The German press and radio made great use of Anderson's testimony. True, Anderson was soon discredited. Other survivors from the *Athenia* were quick to give their version of the affair, which quite contradicted what Anderson had sworn. Also it emerged that he was a man of extreme right-wing views. A report in the British files claims that 'he shouted his views all round the Savoy Hotel'.[89] But in a war of propaganda the crude lie can often be a useful blunt instrument. It may not deceive the clever and sophisticated, but what about the rest, the vast majority? Churchill admits that 'this falsehood received some credence in unfriendly quarters',[90] but this is to underestimate the effect of the German propaganda. Goebbels fooled millions, in and outside Germany, with bigger lies than this one.

If his job had been to approach America as a friend and to enlist her help, his task would have been harder. Friendship and trust cannot be built up by spreading the sort of dirt that was his speciality. But his was a more modest task, merely to soften the hostility of a potential enemy, and for this it was enough to confuse the moral issue, which for most Americans was clear-cut and in favour of the Allies. In their natural desire to avoid active involvement in the war, Americans were particularly at this moment receptive to seeds of doubt about the justice of Britain's and France's cause. In a few days' time their representatives were to vote on a vital piece of legislation which, if passed, would favour the Allies and be interpreted in Germany rightly as a hostile act. It took the black cunning of a Nazi to turn the unwitting crime of a U-boat commander into an act of deliberate mass murder by their arch-enemy Churchill, and to present a case that many people half believed.

A few days later the isolationists grasped at a final straw. King George VI sent a Bible to the Episcopalian Church at Hyde Park, where Roosevelt lived, and while consecrating it the Rector read the usual words from the Anglican Book of Common Prayer: 'Strengthen him [the King] that he may overcome all his enemies.'[91] The vigilant American press noted this most un-neutral prayer and made it into a lead story, which was later quoted in the House of Representatives as an example of the President's favouritism. Roosevelt had of course had nothing whatever to do with the consecration and was able to laugh the matter off as a storm in a teacup.

On 26 October Roosevelt was able to return momentarily to the offensive, having been told by Senator Byrnes that 'everything is all right' and that the vote would be the next day.[92] He said in a radio address: 'In and out of Congress we have heard orators and commentators and others beating their breasts and proclaiming against sending the boys of American mothers to fight on the battlefield of Europe. That I do not hesitate to label as one of the worst fakes in current history. It is a deliberate setting-up of an imaginary bogey-man.' [93] He went on to repeat for the umpteenth time that America had no intention whatever of sending her sons to Europe or of getting involved in the war in general.

The President had succeeded in his task. His tactic of keeping out of the controversy and playing down the division in American politics was about to pay dividends. The isolationists had tried to whip the country into anti-war hysteria, but they ended by over-playing their hand and boring the nation into apathy, which helped the administration. The last days of the great debate in Congress passed in a blaze of disinterest, with floor and public gallery all but empty. [94] On 27 October the Senate passed the new Act by sixty-three votes to thirty, a bigger margin even than the two-to-one which Hull had predicted. On 2 November the House of Representatives also passed it.

On 4 November Roosevelt signed the new Neutrality Bill and it became law. The next day he broadcast to the nation the gist of

Moscow's view of Roosevelt's plan to repeal the arms embargo. The arms salesmen are ready for the race to Europe. 'On your marks,' says the man with the starting pistol. (Copyright British Museum)

French and British customers queuing for 'Uncle Sam's Autumn Sale' of tanks, guns and aeroplanes (*Pravda*, 26 October and 7 November 1939). (Copyright British Museum)

its contents: 'American ships cannot now proceed to any port in France, Great Britain or Germany. That is by statute. By proclamation they cannot proceed to any ports in Ireland nor to any ports in Norway south of Bergen; nor to any ports in Sweden, Denmark, the Netherlands or Belgium; nor to Baltic ports.' [95] But American ships could go to neutral ports in the Mediterranean, to all ports in the Pacific, belligerent or not, and to most in Canada. Weapons of war could now be bought and exported by any country, but only in the ships of belligerents, and only for payment in cash.

Chargé d'Affaires Thomsen telegraphed the bad news to Berlin more in sorrow than in anger: 'The House of Representatives, which only a few months ago resolved to maintain the arms embargo, voted today by an unexpected majority of sixty-one to raise it. This change of sentiment is due both to the strong pressure brought to bear by the Administration on representatives subject to party discipline and to events abroad in recent days.' [96]

He was referring particularly to Molotov's speech of 31 October which seemed to indicate that there would soon be another move of Bolshevik expansion, this time into Finland. 'Our demands are minimal,' Molotov had said. 'What we want is only a small area of a few dozen kilometres north-west of Leningrad, in return for which we are willing to give them an area twice that size. We are also asking for a naval base at the western end of the Gulf of Finland. We have now a naval base at Baltiski in Estonia on the south side of the Gulf. We want a similar base on the north side.'[97]

It was in fact only a month since the Soviet Union had acquired the Baltiski base under duress from Estonia. Americans, however isolationist, were beginning to see these successive German and Soviet demands and aggressions as part of a pattern, and if there was one thing they did fear, it was the gradual bolshevization of the world. Molotov's speech, with its polite request which was indeed followed by armed invasion a month later, may well have swayed a few Congressmen to Roosevelt's point of view that it was in America's vital interest that the Allies win the war.

As Lothian wrote to Halifax on 3 November, the day after the crucial vote, 'Public opinion by an overwhelming majority wants the Allies to defeat Hitler — and more recently to keep Russia at bay — partly for ideological reasons, partly because the success of the Allies will remove the Hitlerian menace to American security, especially in South America, while their defeat would leave the United States face to face with a totalitarian Europe.' For six weeks the arms embargo had been debated and the result had been to produce a certain equilibrium in public opinion: 'The United States has decided to place its industrial resources behind the Allies on the "cash and carry" basis, and at the same time has also decided with practical unanimity that it is utterly against being drawn into the war in Europe . . . Both the President and the Isolationists have had a partial victory and the present Neutrality Act represents very fairly the compromise between the two.'[98]

It is doubtful whether many of the isolationists agreed with this view. They saw the new Act as a definite defeat, as indeed it was, and one should not underestimate the extent of Roosevelt's victory, his achievement in providing the Allies with material support, and more importantly moral support, during these early days of the war. True, the new Act did not help the Allies very much immediately, for neither Britain nor France had the money necessary to buy what they needed, but the President's prompt action did help in arousing American public opinion to the great dangers they faced, and it was an essential first step towards 'lend-lease', the system whereby Britain was provided with armaments on credit, although before that could be considered the Allies' position would have to worsen considerably.

The great American debate had rendered the Allies another important service. In the United States of all countries public opinion can be expressed loudly and in all its different political shades. Their mass media, the radio and the press, were already the most developed in the world, and in addition there were speeches of the Senators and Congressmen. After the debate was over Britain and France could no longer cherish any illusion about the success or failure of their foreign policy in recent years or about the kind of help they could now expect from America. In an outburst of frankness America declared her attitude to European 'democracy' and 'dictatorship', an attitude which was almost totally anti-Nazi, even more anti-Bolshevik, but far from committed to the idea that Britain and France were the fountains of world freedom. And even if there was widespread sympathy for the latter, it by no means followed in American minds that such sympathy should be converted into active assistance.

Equally the debate brought home to the Allies an axiom of diplomacy which in the emotion of the moment some of them were apt to forget, that responsible leaders of states make decisions not on the basis of sentiment or even of morality, but on the basis of their countries' national interest. In 1939 it was clear to most Americans that the German Government was immoral and cruel, perhaps the most vicious government that had existed anywhere for centuries. Its treatment of countries like Poland, with which America had friendly historical ties, was seen and agreed by all to be abominable, as was its treatment of Jews, always a force to be reckoned with in American politics. But however convinced of the satanic quality of Hitlerism — and in America as elsewhere there were still men to be found who would defend the Nazis or at least protest that they were not as evil as the world painted them — no influential American would think of launching his country on a crusade, whether to defend the good or to destroy the Devil.

War could be waged only in self-defence, even Roosevelt believed that, and it was hard to find many Americans more pro-Ally than him. The problem was that, while Roosevelt realized that a Nazi-controlled Europe was a distinct possibility, that if it happened it would be a disaster for America, most of his fellow-countrymen did not. Morality did indeed have an indirect bearing on the case. Roosevelt found it intolerable to think of a Europe dominated by Hitler partly because of the evil of Hitler's ideology, his rejection of free expression, of a free parliament and the rule of law, of elementary human rights. A super-power governed along such lines would be hard to deal with. She would be a bad neighbour, and every year science was narrowing the Atlantic and would be bringing Europe closer. It is unpleasant to have to live close to someone whose ideals and behaviour one finds distasteful.

But more important than this were Hitler's and Stalin's recent adventures in aggression and expansion. In the first two months of war the dictatorships made spectacular territorial advances by swallowing up Poland and the Baltic States, and astute Americans rightly assumed that within a few days Russia would be moving against Finland. The claw of the bear was moving not only towards western Europe, but also towards America. There was another alarming prospect — that the Soviet Union, having allied herself with one enemy, Germany, might decide to court a second strange bedfellow, Japan.

The imagination boggled at what might happen then. Germany, probably with Italian support and perhaps with Spanish, would move against France. Russia would sweep across Finland, Sweden and Norway, joining forces with the Nazis in Denmark. Japan, with Russian help, would make short work of China and proceed to mop up the Pacific, island by island, while the British, French and Dutch which ruled the area were preoccupied with survival at home and unable to resist. In Africa rule by the French, Belgians, British and Portuguese would soon collapse for the same reason. America might become faced by a vast dictator-ruled Euro-Afro-Asian land mass, hostile to every ideal on which the United States was based. The American possessions in the Pacific would become indefensible and would have to be ceded. Her armed forces would have to seal themselves up in Fortress America.

Then South America, whose countries were ruled more by dictators than by parliamentary democracy, would be open to infiltration and subversion by the new super-power. The 'new order' would spread over the south before creeping up through Central America towards Mexico and the borders of the United States. How long the United States and Canada would be able to survive as an island of democracy, hostile to the rest of the world, no one could say, but they would certainly be doomed. The world would become a political void, a cultural desert. The Dark Ages would begin again.

The above thesis is of course over-simplification, but it is not fantasy, as anyone will confirm who lived through the events of 1939 and was *au courant* with their political reality. Civilization really was in peril. Britain and France realized this, but then it was easier for them because the threat to them was immediate. It took a particularly far-sighted and worldly American to appreciate that the threat to his country was just as inexorable, even though it might be delayed a year or two.

On 28 October Lothian made a moving speech in New York to the Pilgrims of the United States. 'I quite realized that you had to make it at an exceptionally awkward moment,' wrote Halifax to him in congratulation, 'and I much admired the skill with which you managed to speak frankly without incurring the charge of making propaganda.' [99] Lothian concentrated on the broader issues of the war, emphasizing that it would decide not so much rivalries between imperialisms, but more the sort of government and ideals that would rule the world in the future. 'The real issue in this war,' he said, 'is whether there is going to be power behind the kind of world in which France and Great Britain believe or far more relentless power behind the world in which National Socialism or Communism believes.' Lothian did not wind up his argument by telling his audience that France and Britain believed in the same world as America did. The atmosphere of the time was such that it would have seemed presumptuous. It would have been dangerous, too, for those were the very days when Congressmen and Senators were casting their votes.

Lothian then quoted some lines from Victor Hugo. Amid the gloom of 1939 they seemed absurdly optimistic, but as the years pass they have seemed more and more likely to come true: 'A day will come when those two immense groups, the United States of America and the United States of Europe, shall be seen placed in the presence of each other, extending the hand of fellowship across the ocean, exchanging their produce, their commerce, their industry, their arts, their genius, clearing the earth, peopling the deserts, meliorating creation under the eyes of the Creator.' [100]

8 Russia the Great Enigma

Meanwhile what about the Russians? One would hardly imagine their remaining inactive or indifferent to the war which had erupted on their doorstep, but this was certainly the impression given to readers of the Soviet press during the first days of September. The picture given, in the words of Alexander Werth, was 'that this was a small local war, of no particular consequence to the Soviet Union, where life, thanks to the wisdom of Comrade Stalin, was going on normally and peacefully'.[1] Of the six pages of the 2 September edition of *Pravda* only page five mentioned war or foreign affairs. The momentous events appeared only in one short article based on a TASS communiqué, headed 'Military Operations between Germany and Poland'. A similar amount of space was given to the war between Japan and China.

The Soviet Government had good reason to be reticent. On 23 August it had completed one of the swiftest and most sudden about-turns in the history of diplomacy, signing a non-aggression pact with Nazi Germany and so rendering useless the military discussions with Great Britain and France still in progress. It was an act of extreme cynicism and, in Churchill's words, of 'cold self-interest'. Stalin had convinced himself that Britain and France would not make suitable allies in the face of the European war which seemed to him inevitable. He decided that in the short term his country's interest lay in making a deal with his arch-enemy Hitler, who seemed to be on the point of attacking Poland, Russia's neighbour. If this happened and Poland were overrun, as seemed probable, Stalin preferred the idea of sharing in the spoils than of allowing the German Army to advance right up to his western border.

Stalin therefore took the precaution of agreeing with Hitler a 'Secret Additional Protocol' to the published non-aggression treaty:

In the event of a territorial and political transformation of the territories belonging to the Polish State, the spheres of interest of both Germany and the USSR shall be bounded approximately by the line of the rivers Narev, Vistula and San. The question whether the interest of both Parties make the maintenance of an independent Polish State seem desirable and how the frontiers of this State should be drawn can be definitely determined only in the course of further political developments. In any case both Governments will resolve this question by means of a friendly understanding.[2]

In other words, what was agreed between Russia and Germany on 23 August was a share-out of the territory of Poland after her defeat, with a small, politically insignificant Polish state probably allowed to remain. What was not agreed was exactly when and how the Soviet Union would employ its army to secure these territories. Hitler was resolved upon action within a very few days. The Soviet Union was not prepared for any such important military move. She had already been worsted once by the Poles, in the war of 1920, and had had to give up large tracts of territory. She would hesitate before committing herself to a hard-fought war against Poland, but a mopping-up operation or a military takeover of an already conquered country was another matter.

The Soviet Union was therefore careful in the days which followed 23 August to give no indication that it was about to move into Poland. In an interview published in *Izvestiya* on 27 August Klement Voroshilov quashed firmly a suggestion that his Red Army might take part in the coming conflict, indicating that there was no reason why the Soviet Union should not supply Poland with weapons and military equipment. In his 31 August speech to the Supreme Soviet, meeting to ratify the treaty with Germany, Molotov warned against 'those amateurs who read into the Pact more than is written in it', who 'set on foot all sorts of conjectures and insinuations'.[3]

William Seeds, British Ambassador in Moscow, telegraphed the Foreign Office on 4 September: 'My own opinion, shared by

Polish, Turkish and American ambassadors, is that Soviet Government will not be lured into military assistance to Germany but will maintain attitude of isolation for the time being at any rate. Undue importance should not, we think, be attached to the alleged Soviet Military Mission in Berlin, which may well not amount to more than a new set of service attachés . . . Moreover actual war news has so far been presented by Soviet press in an objective and impartial manner.'[4] Interestingly, the German Ambassador was equally pleased with the tone of the Soviet press. It was 'as though transformed', he reported.[5] There were no attacks on Germany, indeed, accounts of the war and foreign affairs were based often on German news reports. Anti-German literature was being removed from the bookshops. One cannot help feeling that such matters, if observed, would have spoilt the British Ambassador's misplaced optimism.

The evidence shows that Russia had in fact agreed in principal to move into Poland when the time was ripe, but she had not committed herself to any date. Her army was mobilized only on 31 August, with a second call-up on 4 September, and her commanders believed it would be many weeks before it was ready to go into action. But action there would certainly be.

Meanwhile she was ready to help the German invasion in little ways. Early in the morning of 1 September a senior signals officer of the German Air Force got in touch with Ambassador Schulenburg in Moscow. He wanted the Soviet telecommunications ministry to give navigational aid to the invading German airplanes from its broadcasting station at Minsk, just a few miles from the then border with Poland. The Russians were asked to 'send out a continuous dash with intermittent call-sign "Richard Wilhelm I.O" in the intervals between its programmes, and introduce the name "Minsk" as often as possible'.[6] The Soviet Government agreed to repeat the word 'Minsk' and to extend broadcasting by two hours on that day. It would not introduce the call-sign since this might attract attention. How much this helped the German bombers is difficult to discover, but at least it proved that the Russians were willing to behave like allies.

It was now in the German interest to draw Russia into the conflict more actively. On 3 September Ribbentrop wired Schulenburg. Germany expected to have beaten the Polish Army within a few weeks, he said, and would then keep its allotted share of Poland under military occupation, in which case it might find itself compelled to take action against Polish forces in the areas allotted to Russia. 'Please discuss this at once with Molotov', Ribbentrop went on, 'and see if the Soviet Union does not consider it desirable for Russian forces to move at the proper time against Polish forces in the Russian sphere of interest and, for their part, to occupy this territory. In our estimation this would be not only a relief for us, but also be in the sense of the Moscow agreements, and in the Soviet interest as well.' [7]

Molotov saw Schulenburg at midday on 5 September and gave him a reply to Ribbentrop's request. He agreed that 'at a suitable time' Russia would have to take action, but felt that this time had not yet come. He was worried that 'through excessive haste we might injure our cause and promote unity among our opponents'.[8] Apart from their lack of readiness, it appeared there was another reason for Soviet hesitation: they were concerned about how it should look. The Soviet Union was still a beginner in diplomacy. One cannot imagine that 'world opinion' counted for much when Stalin was making decisions. But for Soviet internal consumption it was important to camouflage any aggressive move.

At this stage it was in the Soviet interest not only to refrain from attacking Poland herself, but also to delay the German conquest. Had Germany overrun Poland immediately and without much of a fight, perhaps even before Britain and France could come into the war on her side, Germany would sweep across the Polish plains before there were any troops of the Red Army ready to confront them along the agreed line of demarcation. This was probably why Ambassador Sharonov suggested to Beck on 2 September that Russia might be able to supply Poland with military equipment. Although it seems unlikely that the Russians would have run the risk of offending their new German ally by such manoeuvres, they did doubtless hope that the Polish Army would prove strong enough at least to give them a breathing space.

It is often forgotten that the Soviet Union was already fighting a little war of its own. Japanese mounted raiding parties had been operating in Mongolian territory and had several times come into contact with Soviet patrols. On 20 August a fair-sized battle had taken place in the Mongolian desert at Halkin Gol, and although soon after this the Japanese requested a cease-fire, the problem was a thorn in the Russians' flesh.

To add to the Russians' embarrassment the Germans proceeded to overrun Poland more quickly than anyone, except perhaps Hitler, had expected and on the evening of 8 September they announced their entry into Warsaw. Molotov followed his famous message of congratulation to Germany with another the same day (9 September) promising Soviet armed intervention 'within the next few days'.[9] The fall of Warsaw would at least remove one difficulty. Intervention could now be justified to the Soviet masses as an act aimed at protecting the several million Ukrainians and Byelorussians who lived in Poland, and made necessary by the collapse of Poland's capital city and administration. It meant too that if the Red Army was not quick the Germans would be in possession of the whole of Poland, while the Russians were still pulling themselves together. That same day therefore another large batch of reservists, some as old as forty-five years, was called up into the army, and it was announced that this was 'in connection with the German–Polish war which is assuming a more wide and threatening character'.[10] Schulenburg reported to Berlin that certain foods had disappeared from the shops, that petrol was hard to find and that schoolrooms were being converted for use as hospitals.[11]

This frenzied activity subsided somewhat the next day (10 September) when it transpired that the announcement of Warsaw's imminent fall was premature. That afternoon Molotov told Schulenburg how surprised his Government had been by the rapid German successes. 'The Red Army had counted on several weeks, which had now shrunk to a few days,' he said.[12] Although three million Red Army men were now mobilized, two or three weeks' preparation was required before they could act. Schulenburg gathered that Molotov had the previous day promised more than his army could live up to. He emphasized again the importance of swift action by the Red Army. Molotov explained that when this happened his Government would want to explain the move as one of aid to the Ukrainians and Byelorussians 'threatened' by Germany. He must have realized that this theory would not be to the Germans' liking, but apparently he still thought it important to find some plausible justification for what he was about to do.

On 11 September the Soviet press at last broke its silence. A *Pravda* editorial headed 'A Review of Military Activity' gave quite a balanced account of the war's progress. The rapid German advance was attributed to lack of fortification on Poland's borders, to German superiority in technical equipment and in the air, and to lack of effective help from Britain and France. 'As for Poland's military prospects', it concluded, 'one can say that in spite of considerable military forces that remain, having retreated across the Vistula, the Polish High Command will hardly be able to offer serious resistance, as they are deprived of almost the whole of their military and economic base.'

Another ominous sign was the 11 September decision of Ambassador Sharonov to leave Krzemieniec where he had just arrived with the other diplomats.[13] He told Beck's deputy Jan Szembek that he wished to telephone Moscow and, there being no connection from Poland, he would have to cross into the Soviet Union. He would return in a day or two. He collected his family and most of his staff, leaving just a couple of Russians in charge of things in Poland, and drove off on the morning of 12 September just before the German bombers blew the village apart. 'It would be interesting to know the connection between these events,' noted Clare Hollingworth.[14] There is no evidence to support her suspicion that there was collusion over the bombing, but obviously the Russians wanted to extricate as many of their people as possible before attacking.

It was 14 September before the world finally woke up to what the Red Army was about to do. A front-page article appeared in *Pravda*, headed 'The Internal Reasons for Poland's Defeat' and explaining that there were reasons for Poland's quick collapse other than those suggested on 11 September. There were 'the internal weaknesses and contradictions of the Polish state'. Only sixty per cent of its population was actually Polish, it claimed. There were eight million Ukrainians, three million Byelorussians, as well as Jews, Germans and other minorities. One would have thought, *Pravda* went on, that the Polish Government would have made things easy for these groups, giving them their own schools, cultural centres and a certain autonomy. But no: 'The Polish rulers did everything to worsen relations with the national minorities and to bring them to a state of extreme tension.'

In eastern Poland, the lands won from Russia in the 1920 war, *Pravda* claimed that the minorities 'are subjected to the most coarse and shameless exploitation on the part of the Polish land-owners'. It was 'a colony without rights, handed over to Polish overlords for them to loot'. These non-Poles had no chance of getting jobs in the administration, where Polish was the only language used, as well as in courts of law. The rulers believed in stirring up inter-minority hatred and strife, in division and conquest. No wonder that the Polish Army, consisting in part of these hostile groups, had no stomach for the fight.

Although Polish cultural domination of minority groups was an undeniable fact, there was of course much exaggeration in this report. In particular, whatever one says about pre-war Poland, no one can deny that its army fought bravely in September 1939, and this was manifestly apparent even on 14 September. Such an article could have but one explanation and one consequence, and to ram the point home *Izvestiya* carried three more alarmist reports, also on 14 September. 'Rebellion in Eastern Galicia', it proclaimed. '. . . The local Ukrainian minority is protesting against a number of Polish orders. In the area between Kołomyja and Śniatyń several Polish farm houses have been burnt down by Ukrainian peasants.' The Byelorussians too were showing their 'extreme dissatisfaction'. They were refusing to join the Polish Army and – a significant point – 'demanding the setting up of an independent republic'. There were reports too that Polish aircraft had violated Soviet air space. Schulenburg wired Berlin that 'the purpose of the articles is to provide the political justification mentioned by Molotov for Soviet intervention'.[15]

Molotov was still worried though about the stubborn Polish defence of Warsaw. He told Schulenburg that same day that he did not want the Red Army to act until Warsaw had fallen. 'When would this be?' he asked. But Warsaw was the one place where German plans had gone seriously awry. Lying only eighty miles south of the border with East Prussia, it was vulnerable to attack and the original Polish plan had not envisaged defending it seriously. It made more sense to retreat across the Vistula. But as things turned out, Warsaw had become an island of defiance, a stubborn blot on the board which the German Army had all but swept clean. In a day or two they would have Warsaw as well, they believed. Hitler had already arranged to deliver a major oration in the enemy capital on 19 September. But the German generals could not of course guarantee that it would be theirs by then, either to Hitler or to Molotov.

Still, Molotov was able to say that his army had got itself ready earlier than expected, and that action could now take place quite soon. The evidence is that Stalin had now taken a decision to intervene within a few days, if possible during the brief interval between the fall of Warsaw and the final Polish surrender. In this way he would have the soundest of pretexts. The next day (15 September) Shirer noted in his diary: 'I heard today on very good authority that Russia may attack Poland.'[16] That night he telegraphed his suspicions to his head office in America, and the German censor did not object.

On the evening of 15 September senior Red Army commanders were told of the impending action,[17] having read that morning in *Izvestiya* an inspiring article about their 'sacred duty'. It reported that Polish soldiers were following a scorched-earth policy, burning villages in Byelorussia as they retreated, that women and children were fleeing across the border into neutral Lithuania. That day Ribbentrop sent Molotov another message aimed at rousing him to action.[18] The Polish Army was almost crushed, he told him, and Warsaw would fall 'in the next few days'. Reading rather more into what Molotov had just said than was justifiable, he assumed that the Red Army 'intends to begin its operations now'. The German Government was glad of this, since it relieved them of the need to pursue the remnants of the Polish Army right up to the Soviet border. This hint was well taken. Stalin had no desire to see the German Army anywhere near Soviet territory.

Ribbentrop went on to say that he was worried about the possibility of a political vacuum in eastern Poland. If Russia did not intervene, new states might spring up. There had, of course, been newspaper reports the previous day of Byelorussians demanding an independent republic, and there were similar rumblings in the Ukraine. He proposed a joint Soviet–German communiqué deploring the 'intolerable economic and political conditions' existing in 'the former Polish state' and declaring their joint intention 'to restore peace and order in these their natural spheres of influence'. He did not approve Molotov's idea of using a German threat to the Ukrainians and Byelorussians as a pretext for Soviet intervention. In the first place, it would be contrary to German intention as set out in the pact, which was confined to interest in western Poland. Secondly, it would not be in the spirit of the pact and would 'make the two states appear as enemies before the whole world'. He now requested the Soviet Government to 'set a day and an hour on which their Army would begin their advance' and to send him 'an immediate reply by telegraph'.

A few hours after receiving this message Molotov gave his answer,[19] receiving Schulenburg at 6 p.m. on 16 September. The Red Army's intervention was now imminent, he said. Stalin was at present in consultation with his military leaders to decide the exact time of the attack, which would be communicated to Schulenburg that very evening. Molotov agreed to modify the Soviet explanation of its action, and to remove any reference to a German 'threat'. Its justification would now run as follows: 'The Polish State had disintegrated and no longer existed; therefore all agreements concluded with Poland were void; third powers might try to profit from the chaos which had arisen; the Soviet Union considered itself obligated to intervene to protect its Ukrainian and White Russian brothers and make it possible for these unfortunate people to work in peace.'[20] Molotov admitted that these arguments might contain 'a note which was jarring to German sensibilities'. But he and his colleagues were in a difficult position, he claimed. The Soviet Union 'had to justify abroad, in some way or other, its present intervention'. So he asked the Germans 'not to stumble over this piece of straw'. The tone of all these exchanges indicated that Germany was trying to recruit the Soviet Union onto its side as actively as possible, but that the Soviet Union was unwilling to commit itself irrevocably.

Sure enough that night, as 2 a.m. on 17 September, Schulenburg was received by Stalin personally and told that the Red Army would cross into Poland at 6 a.m. that day. Soviet airplanes would begin to bomb the areas east of Lwów, he said, so he would like the German Air Force not to operate there or east of Brześć, another town the Poles still held. A joint German-Soviet commission would meet at Białystok, north-east of Warsaw, to coordinate the action, and a joint communiqué would be considered in a few days' time.

An hour later Polish Ambassador Wacław Grzybowski was summoned by deputy Foreign Minister Potyomkin to be told the bad news, which consisted of a note embodying the arguments listed above. 'The Polish–German war has revealed the internal bankruptcy of the Polish State,' it began, and went on to elaborate on the idea that Poland no longer existed: Warsaw was no longer its capital; its government had collapsed and showed no sign of life; its people had been left leaderless and its land without administration, all of which was a potential danger to the Soviet Union and meant that it could no longer remain neutral. It would do its best 'to free the Polish people from the miserable war into which they had been drawn by their incompetent leaders, and to give them the chance to begin a new life in peace'.[21]

The blow can hardly have been a total surprise to Ambassador Grzybowski. His London colleague Count Raczyński writes that it was 'like the sensation one feels in the theatre when a crime which has long been impending is finally perpetrated'.[22] But for the Poles it was none the less horrible for that. Potyomkin too had tears in his eyes, Grzybowski noted, as he heard the Ambassador's vehement protests against the note's contents, but of course his words counted for little. Out of touch with his government and his army in tatters, he was an ambassador in name only. But he kept his dignity. He left the Foreign Ministry, having declined to accept Potyomkin's note.

In spite of the violence that was being done, the Soviet Government still found it necessary to go through a bizarre diplomatic charade. They were strangely embarrassed by Grzybowski's refusal to accept their note. British Ambassador Seeds records: 'When he [Grzybowski] returned to his embassy he found that the note had been quickly dispatched and was waiting for him. He immediately sent it back by hand to the Narkomindel [the Soviet Foreign Ministry] but the doorkeeper there had received the necessary instructions and the Polish messenger had to bring the envelope back to the embassy. Mr Grzybowski, undefeated, immediately consigned the document to the Narkomindel through the Soviet post, and its subsequent fate is to me unknown.'[23] The legal basis for what the Soviet Government was about to do was tenuous indeed, but its forms had to be properly observed.

As with the German attack sixteen days earlier, the first news the British had of what was happening was given by a journalist who telephoned Ambassador Seeds. What were Poland's allies to do? The British Chiefs of Staff had reported the previous day that, if Russia attacked Poland, Britain was obliged to declare war on Russia.[24] They were wrong, since the guarantee to Poland covered only aggression by Germany. Seeds telegraphed London: 'I do not myself see what advantage war with the Soviet Union would be to us, though it would please me personally to declare it on Mr Molotov.'[25] One can understand how the Ambassador felt, even though he must have known that his country was nowhere near strong enough to indulge such whims. On the other hand it was his view that 'the Soviet invasion of Poland is not without advantages to us in the long run . . . German–Soviet close contact in the occupied countries under war conditions etc. should lead to a desirable friction.' In the light of Britain's desperate situation, the Ambassador was clutching at straws, but in this case he had alighted upon an important point.

The efficiency of the Red Army was hardly tested during the advance. At 6 a.m. by Moscow time, which means at 4 a.m. by Polish time, their vehicles crossed the frontier along its whole length, from Latvia in the north to Rumania in the south, a distance of nearly 1,000 miles. To meet this invasion there were only twenty-five battalions of the Polish Frontier Corps.[26] An eye-witness has described the scene to the author. It was dawn, and morning mist covered the flat countryside as the sparse Polish patrols stood manning their unwieldy eastern border. Suddenly they saw shapes looming towards them through the mist – a few tanks but mostly horse-drawn carts full of Red Army soldiers. 'Don't shoot!' they shouted at the Poles, 'we've come to help you against the Germans.' White flags fluttered from many of the vehicles. This thoroughly confused the defenders, and in many cases the invaders were simply allowed to pass. A Soviet colonel writes that the Red Army advanced about sixty miles during the first day, suffering only insignificant losses. They were greeted by the population without much hostility, but with a sense of puzzlement.

In a few places there was a little fighting, near Wilno and near Białystok, but by and large the Poles and Russians avoided contact. According to de Wiart 'on some roads the retiring Polish troops were already marching side by side with the Soviet forces in apparent friendliness'.[27] The American military attaché actually spoke to some Red Army men who told him that their job was to help the Poles against the Germans.[28] This is confirmed by General Jaklicz, who was told of a scene where Red Army soldiers had stopped for a rest, and Polish soldiers were sitting among them talking.[29] Even by midday the situation was little clearer. Marshal Rydz-Śmigły gave orders for the 'Bolsheviks', as the Poles called them, only to be opposed if they offered violence.

The Polish Prime Minister Sławój-Składkowski seems to have been particularly ill-informed. 'Joyful news this morning,' begins his diary entry for 17 September. 'In a series of night attacks General Sosnkowski has smashed several German tank units fighting east of Lwów . . . At last something good in this war.' He was to learn of the Soviet attack only at 10 a.m. 'We were completely dumbfounded,' he continued.[30] Maybe he was. Trapped newsless for days in this scrap of Polish territory he was unaware of the propaganda build-up to the Soviet move. 'Just when it looked as if we were going to be able to resist the Germans,' he complained, and Chief of Staff Stachiewicz spoke in similar terms to Colin Gubbins. Poland was now surrounded by a total of 200 hostile divisions, the Prime Minister noted, and 'in such conditions it is hard to organize any effective, lasting resistance'.

Desperation was driving the usually ebullient Poles into uncharacteristic understatement. Gone were the grandiose plans for a massive counter-attack and a march on Berlin, gone was the plan to hold the 'Rumanian bridgehead' and wait for Gamelin's offensive, the best the Polish leaders could hope to do now was to escape and to take up the fight again from an allied country. 'When the war began I fully understood that it was bound to be lost on the Polish front,' wrote Marshal Rydz-Śmigły, but this was in December 1939, after the event.[31] Before September he and his colleagues had felt much more confident. But whatever the outcome the Marshal realized that his army's performance was *politically* very important: 'The greater Poland's sacrifice, the more she will have the right to demand from her allies after victory.' Every day Poland was able to endure was crucial to her future, and now that defeat was inevitable, every soldier who could be extricated was worth his weight in gold.

Jaklicz and Beck were told what had happened a little earlier, about 6 a.m., i.e. two hours after the attack, but even so Beck knew nothing of his Moscow ambassador's interview with Potyomkin five hours earlier. At 7.30 a.m. he found Kennard and gave him the news. Kennard wired London: 'He cannot explain the sudden invasion or whether it is with German connivance, but fears the worst.' [32] Beck protested about the attack to Kennard and to as many foreign diplomats as he could find, but most of them were already in Rumania. Kennard, Norton and Hankey still maintained a 'British Embassy' in the dentist's house in Kuty half a mile from the border. 'Better the Russians than the Germans,' their hostess remarked when she heard the news, but she was Jewish which made a difference. For most Poles there was little to choose between the two invaders. It was the same old story, Poland's traditional enemies once more converging and about to swallow her up.

The Englishmen were surrounded by rich Poles begging them for British visas, without which they would not be allowed to cross into Rumania. Poland's neighbours were embarrassed at the prospect of the exodus which in a few hours was to turn from a trickle into a flood. No country likes the idea of being suddenly descended upon by hundreds of thousands of foreigners, all with worthless money and worthless documents. At best they would become a drain on Rumania's resources. At worst they would provoke Germany to attack her.

Poland had a mutual defence agreement with Rumania against Soviet aggression, so legally Poland could have asked Rumania to declare war. 'I did not invoke this *casus foederis*,' Beck writes, 'being persuaded that there was no chance of Rumania respecting it.' [33] This was certainly wise. Treaties are all very well, but when the bullets start to fly and countries are being wiped off the map, they run the risk of being reduced to mere scraps of paper. By 'generously' releasing Rumania from the main treaty Beck hoped to gain more favourable consideration for his request for permission to cross Rumania with his governmental colleagues *en route* for France, where the Polish Government and Army would be reconstituted and continue to exist under international law. Already on 16 September Ambassador Biddle had wired Washington from Cernauti that this was about to happen, adding the hope that foreign missions would remain accredited to this government on foreign soil. There was a precedent for this action in that of the Belgian Government during the First World War.

Meeting the Marshal and the Prime Minister at Kołomyja, the Polish headquarters, Beck expounded his view that 'the Polish State should remain not a passive but an active element in international events'. France had agreed to give the government permanent accommodation (*droit de résidence*), and Rumania was expected to provide transit (*droit de passage*). There was no reason why she should not do this, since according to the Hague Conventions of 1887 and 1907 transit rights for a government would not be a breach of neutrality. Beck returned to Kuty and found the Rumanian Ambassador Gheorghe Grigorcea who had come across the frontier bridge. He formally offered him transit facilities in the name of King Carol, then walked back across the bridge into Rumania.

The problem was that on 12 September Ribbentrop had forbidden the Rumanians to do any such thing.[34] Various German 'demands' were put before the Rumanian Government: not to grant asylum to the Polish Government or High Command but to intern them 'under strict confinement'; to disarm and intern all Polish soldiers who crossed into Rumania; to forbid the transit of war material. The German Minister was instructed to obtain a 'binding declaration' to this effect, and with the power of the German armed forces behind him his approach, however undiplomatic, could hardly be ignored.

But for the prominent Poles, huddled down in the south-east, Rumania was the only way out. The short border with Hungary was still reachable, but Hungary had close ties with Germany. 'If we cross the Hungarian frontier we shall at once be interned,' the Prime Minister noted, 'but the Rumanians are our allies and have clearly defined obligations towards us.'[35] This fact had not escaped the Soviet leaders who had ordered the delivery of a particularly fast 'left hook' from the southernmost point of the front. General Anders, under whom Polish troops were to fight so bravely in the Italian campaign, was captured by Red Army troops near the border and told by a Soviet major that his job was to stop Polish soldiers from escaping across it. 'The Russians, it was clear, were doing their utmost not to allow the Polish Army to be reconstituted abroad,' Anders concluded.[36] That same afternoon Soviet cavalry and motorized units had forced the River Dniestr, where they had paused for a rest. This river was not much of an obstacle during the dry season, being fordable in several places. It was clearly only a matter of a few hours before the Polish-Rumanian frontier was cut.

Inconveniently for the British, the Red Army had invaded on a Sunday, and Prime Minister Chamberlain did not see fit to return to London at once from his country week-end at Chequers. Hardly any ministers were present at the War Cabinet meeting called to discuss the sudden development, which was chaired by John Simon. Ironside's deputy Ronald Adam expressed the not-very-daring opinion that 'this Russian invasion would tend to hasten the military collapse of Poland'. But it would not, he said, if the Russians concentrated their attack on the northern part of the front. Why he should suppose that the Red Army would attack the north is not clear. By now there were hardly any Polish soldiers north of Brześć; the bulk had retreated southwards. Furthermore, by now there was no front, only a few strongly-held points and a mass of Polish stragglers. Clearly the British politicians and military men knew next to nothing of the state of the fighting. (The military mission's wireless had broken down early in the war.) They resolved to telephone Chamberlain their extraordinary conclusion 'that the Russian advance would almost certainly be very slow'.[37] In fact the Red Army was well embarked on one of the swiftest and least opposed advances of modern warfare.

The British General Staff had, however, been put right on one important point. In their 16 September report they had assumed that if Russia attacked, Britain would have to declare war on her. The Foreign Office had quickly explained that the treaty with Poland covered only aggression by Germany, which was just as well, since otherwise it is alarming to think what this ill-informed 'skeleton' War Cabinet of 17 September would have decided was necessary to meet the emergency.[38] One important point they did spot was that if the Red Army occupied the Rumanian border — which they were to do within twenty-four hours — the German Army would be cut off from any move into Rumania, which many Allied experts thought might be its next step. It could now attack Rumania only by sending troops through Hungary, and that country had already shown itself unwilling to allow such outrages, refusing its territory as a base for attacks on Poland.[39]

In the Soviet Union itself the reaction to its army's move was one of predictable joy. 'The heroic regiments of the valiant Red Army are honourably fulfilling their duty,' *Pravda* announced. 'The whole Soviet people welcomes the wise policy of the Soviet Government.'[40] Well, if it did not, it was not going to admit it. At 11.30 a.m. Molotov spoke on the radio telling the people his version of recent events, and asking them not to hoard food or essential supplies. There was enough for everyone, he said, and no intention of imposing rationing. His speech appeared in full the next day in Hitler's daily *Völkischer Beobachter*. Factories and offices were passing resolutions commending the government for its bravery and wisdom. Party activists were explaining the complexities of the situation to those less versed in politics, describing the unhappy lot of the Ukrainians and Byelorussians in Poland, 'afraid of even dreaming in their own language, singing their national songs in a whisper'. 'And now our boys are going in,' *Pravda* quoted one such as saying, 'the hatch of a tank will open and our Soviet lads will leap out, laughing and singing songs.'[41]

It followed that, in the words of the Soviet official history, 'the workers of Western Byelorussia and Western Ukraine welcomed the Red Army ecstatically', while the peasants 'came out with bread and salt', the traditional mark of welcome and respect.[42] After all, the history states incorrectly, the Soviet move took place 'after the flight of the Polish Government into Rumania and the collapse of the Polish State'.[43] The Red Army was only 'fulfilling its international duty, affording the only assistance possible in the given circumstances to its neighbouring people. It was a campaign aimed at forestalling the capture of the Western Ukraine and Western Byelorussia by the German fascist forces.'[44] The history does not explain, nor has any Soviet printed work, that the German–Soviet partition of Poland was agreed, and the Red Army's advance into Poland was envisaged, in a document signed by Molotov and Ribbentrop on 23 August 1939.

It takes Molotov to task on one point only, his speech to the Supreme Soviet six weeks later (31 October) in which he said: 'A short blow at Poland from the German Army, followed by one from the Red Army, was enough to annihilate this monster child of the Treaty of Versailles.'[45]

This cruel remark showed the hostility felt by many in the then Soviet leadership, and probably by Stalin himself, to the very existence of a Polish state. True, Stalin changed his tune two years later, but at the end of the war he was again toying with the idea of absorbing Poland into some north-east European superstate dependent on the Soviet Union. The most Stalin was prepared to allow was a Poland 'friendly to the Soviet Union', which in practice meant 'under my control'. He had spent time there as a young man and recognized the deep historical rivalry between the two countries, each one taking it in turns to build empires on the other's territory. For more than 100 years, until independence was restored in 1918, a large part of Poland was ruled by Russia, and although Lenin's new Soviet state admitted Poland's right to reconstitute itself, this was seen by the Poles merely as a sign of weakness which they were quick to exploit by invading the Ukraine and Byelorussia in 1920, by defeating the Red Army in a short war and by imposing on Soviet Russia a disadvantageous peace which left large tracts of formerly Soviet territory on the Polish side of the new border. Then again in the mid 1930s Stalin, paranoid in his belief that spies, imperialists and Trotskyists were plotting to destroy him, pinned much of the blame on the Poles who lived on his borders and were supposedly harbouring legions of enemies of the Soviet Union. By 1938, when Stalin dissolved the Polish Communist Party and killed those of its leadership upon whom he could lay hands, the very word 'Polish' was a term of abuse in Moscow.

Briefly, this was the background to Molotov's outburst which, in the words of the official history, 'was in contradiction to historical truth and to the aims of the Soviet soldiers' campaign of liberation'.[46] No explanation is given, though, of how this chauvinistic remark came to be made, or of why it was not contradicted. One can only conclude that in 1939 not only Molotov but also Stalin was distrustful of Poles as such, and opposed to the very concept of their state. Every man has his prejudices and in 1939 Stalin's were anti-Polish. In that country he thought he saw the ultimate in everything he hated — traditional anti-Russianism, fervent anti-communism, Trotskyism and a delight in middle-class values.

Poland was now reaping the whirlwind for her sudden rise from the ashes of partition and extinction to the superficial grandeur of a country with imperial pretensions but without the armed forces to back them up. Apart from this she had the appallingly bad luck to find herself squeezed between two powerful countries, hostile both traditionally and presently, and ruled by two of the cruellest men who have ever lived. She tried to bluff her way out of it by claims to illusory strength and by a stubborn refusal to compromise. She failed, and at 4 p.m. on 17 September her government, meeting in Kuty for the last time on Polish soil, was forced to face this fact.

Beck told the ministers of the success of his talk with the Rumanian Ambassador. The government was to be allowed to proceed either to the port of Constanza or to a Rumanian land frontier. It was requested only that they make their way as quickly as possible across the country to minimize any embarrassment. The Prime Minister gathered that 'as for Marshal Rydz-Śmigły, the High Command and the members of the armed forces – there would probably be some formal difficulty, but they would all be able to proceed to France'.[47] This was just as well, for during the meeting the Mayor of Śniatyń, twenty miles north-east of Kuty, telephoned to say that the Red Army was already at the gates of his town and had closed the border crossing point. The frontier was marked by the River Cheremosh, and Kuty had the only bridge still in Polish hands. They decided to cross that evening and drew up a proclamation explaining why.[48]

Ambassador Kennard having crossed at 1 p.m., the only foreigners remaining on the Polish side were the members of the allied military missions. Starved of news like everyone else, they tried to tune their radio set to London to hear the BBC, only to find that what was being broadcast was a Sunday afternoon tennis match. This ended and was followed by a music programme, which began with the immortal song 'We're Gonna Hang out Our Washing on the Siegfried Line'. After this it was no surprise to Gubbins when he found himself being insulted by a Polish staff captain. 'Aren't you British at war?' the Pole asked him. It was a difficult question to answer.

By now a queue of cars several miles long led up to the border, though at this stage it was mainly private citizens who were crossing. Prime Minister Sławój-Składkowski found that his role had been reduced almost to that of a traffic control officer. 'The Rumanian customs post at Vyjnitsa was working with no undue haste, no faster than during the good times of peace,' he wrote. He was worried that the Russians might arrive before the queue had crossed, or that the Germans might hear of its existence and start to bomb it, or that disorder might break out and the road become blocked. At 8.15 p.m. he telephoned Beck, who had driven a few miles up the road to the village of Kosów with Rydz-Śmigły to await the arrival of his General Staff from Kołomyja, and told him that Soviet cavalry was now only fifteen miles away. The only armed forces available to oppose the Red Army's advance, according to Beck, consisted of the Presidential Guard, a total of fifty or sixty men. This is confirmed by the Prime Minister and by the historian Pobóg-Malinowski, but contradicted by communist historians who allege that whole regiments were diverted and sacrificed to facilitate the government's flight.

So about 10.15 p.m. the President set out from Kosów in melancholy procession towards the frontier bridge, which he crossed within the hour. The Marshal followed shortly afterwards, having apparently decided at the last minute to leave Poland and continue the struggle abroad. He was met by the Rumanian military attaché in Warsaw, who was able to persuade the frontier police and customs men to speed up the flow of traffic. The Marshal decided to wait at the frontier for the arrival of his senior officers, while the government leaders were escorted to Cernauti (Czernwitz), the nearest Rumanian town of any size, and accommodated in the palace of the local bishop.

All through the night the exodus continued, though by now it consisted mainly of Polish soldiers. For them it was the moment of surrender, for they were obliged to hand over their arms as soon as they crossed into neutral territory. It would be hard to exaggerate the horrible effect of such a moment on men who for seventeen days had fought bravely but without success, constantly on the move and usually in retreat, and now were cornered in a narrow neck of Polish territory, whose Ukrainian inhabitants were potentially hostile, with two great armies bearing down upon them. 'It is sad to behold our magnificent Polish rifles being handed over to the semi-civilian Rumanian soldiers, who do not even know how to hold them properly,' the Prime Minister noted, the bitterness of the moment bringing out the Pole's traditional disdain for all Europeans who live east of his own borders.

Some soldiers left their arms on the Polish side of the bridge, but it was not much of a choice. The Russians would soon be there, and most preferred to reward an ally rather than an invader. Colin Gubbins, who crossed over with his military mission around 1 a.m. that night, remembers a different picture — the soldiers throwing their rifles over the bridge and into the river rather than surrender them to any foreigner. The little border brook became a graveyard of rifles, machine guns and revolvers by the hundred, then by the thousand, as the exhausted Poles were deprived in mid stream not only of their country but also of their means of defending it. 'It was one of the most tragic sights I have ever seen,' says Gubbins.

The Red Army did its best to woo the Polish Army onto the Soviet side, and it may well have had some success with those soldiers who were Ukrainian or Byelorussian. But the Russians thought it worth their while to bombard the Polish soldiers too with calls to mutiny. Poles were told in an appeal from the commander of the Byelorussian front, M. Kovalov, that 'your blood-suckers, the landowners and capitalists, have flung you into the fiery pit of a second imperialist war'. They were assured that 'the people of Soviet Byelorussia, helped by the great Russian nation, has constructed a joyful, prosperous and happy life'. They were advised, 'turn your arms against the landowners and capitalists. Do not shoot at your class brethren.'

A few days later the commander of the Ukrainian front, S. Timoshenko, told Polish soldiers in another leaflet that their army was defeated and that men were coming across onto the Red Army's side in tens of thousands. 'Do not trust your officers,' it said. 'Officers and generals are your enemies. They want your death. Soldiers! Kill your officers and generals. Do not obey the orders of your officers. Drive them from your land . . . Believe us, your only friend is the Red Army of the Soviet Union.'[49]

It seems that not very many Poles accepted Timoshenko's advice, for about 200,000 of them were captured by the Red Army by force. Also about 85,000 of them managed to escape into neutral territory, some into Hungary, Lithuania or Latvia but most into Rumania.⁵⁰ Wired enclosures had been hastily prepared to take the non-VIP refugees, for international law required Rumania to intern belligerent soldiers, though not civilian administrators. But no undue officiousness was displayed by the reluctant gaolers. Most of the Poles were able eventually to make their way to France and join their reconstituted army. De Wiart, Gubbins and the military mission were likewise belligerents and liable to internment, so as they crossed the River Cheremosh their car was directed into the enclosure. They drove once round the perimeter and out through another entrance, making their way home overland by train.

Once people were in Rumania, at least they could commmunicate with the outside world. The journalists could send back their reports, the ambassadors their telegrams. By the morning of 18 September the world knew that the battle for Poland was over, that except in a few strong points Polish resistance was crushed, and that the immediate cause of this sudden collapse was Russia's intervention. The reaction in Britain was angry. 'A stab in the back' was the heading on a vitriolic leader in *The Times* which presumed that 'Germany was to do the murder and Russia was to share the estate'. It declared that 'to the Soviet belongs the base and despicable shame of accessory before and after the crime and the contempt which even the thief has for a receiver who shares none of his original risks'. As for the strategic position, it was *The Times*'s view that 'Stalin has wiped out the unqualified boon of 500 miles of neutral territory'. What exactly the writer meant is hard to deduce, since the lands the Red Army was invading were not neutral but belligerent on the Allied side. But one can assume that they would not have remained so for long, whether Russia moved in or not.

Chamberlain's reaction was also an angry one, and his mood at the 18 September Cabinet meeting cannot have been improved by Churchill's announcement that the aircraft carrier *Courageous* had been sunk by a U-boat the previous evening. By admission he had 'extreme distrust' of the Soviet Union, and this strong feeling made it possible for him to trust Hitler at Munich in 1938 and not to think of an alliance with Russia until it was too late. That morning he proposed that his Government proclaim their 'horror and indignation' upon learning of the Russian attack. The Polish

Ambassador had asked him to protest formally, he said, but he did not think this would be necessary since the government's announcement 'would be regarded as embodying our condemnation of the action of the Soviet Government'. The Cabinet agreed that Halifax should prepare the statement for release that afternoon.

But in the next few hours this plan was to be replaced by one of greater caution and restraint. No one knew the precise meaning of the Russian action. It could be a move to forestall the German Army or even to oppose it. At the other extreme it could be the preliminary to a more open Russian–German alliance, even to a Soviet declaration of war on Britain and France. The previous day the 'Sunday' Cabinet had discussed rumours that Soviet Ambassador Maisky was closing his embassy and preparing to leave the country. This was gloomy and disquieting news. Then Ambassador Seeds wired London from Moscow: 'I have no means of knowing whether the Soviet Government intends us to go to war. It seems likely, however, that with their fundamental caution they will not wish to commit themselves too irrevocably with Germany.'[51] The British leaders quickly rethought the position and concluded that whatever Russia's intention, whether she was potentially ally or enemy, it would be unwise to provoke her with hard words.

The French agreed, and in a note to Halifax dated 18 September they expressed themselves against 'pushing Russia into belligerence by a categoric declaration' or 'tightening her ties with Germany'. That same day the Chiefs of Staff reported to the Cabinet that if Russia declared war on Britain 'our strategic position though serious would not be desperate'.[52] These were not encouraging words, and Chamberlain soon saw that he would have to moderate the language he had first envisaged using.

Clearly he could not let such a great event pass in silence. He was Poland's ally, and Poland had been invaded. On 18 September Ambassador Raczyński handed Halifax a note asking the British to protest against the Soviet aggression, and adducing the relevant treaties which, in his view, the Soviet Union had violated: the Soviet–Polish Non-aggression Pact of 25 July 1932, the convention signed by Ambassador Raczyński and Foreign Commissar Litvinov at Harrington House in London on 3 July 1933 and the Protocol signed in Moscow on 5 May 1934.[53] It was the Soviet

Government's view, contained in the note handed to Polish Ambassador Grzybowski early in the morning of 17 September, that the Polish Government and state had ceased to exist and that therefore these agreements were invalid. The Polish view was that whatever difficulties their government, state and army faced during the early morning of 17 September, they certainly still existed. The British and French accepted the Polish view, but saw little good coming out of any diplomatic approach to Stalin. 'All highly relevant,' was Frank Roberts's reaction to Raczyński's note and the attached documents, 'but as we don't want to quarrel with the Russians until we are forced to, the less we "feature" these documents the better'.[54]

Seeds too had come to the conclusion that Russia's final aim was doubtful, but that in either case to provoke her would be to play the German game. Was the aim to assist the Germans or to forestall them? Opinions were divided about this, Seeds reported, but his own opinion, incorrect as usual, was that 'Soviet mobilization and the precipitate invasion of Poland came as a surprise to the Germans'. Several British envoys confirmed this wrong view. Preston reported from the Baltic States that 'the advance of the Russian Army caused the greatest dismay in Berlin'. His sources of information had deteriorated since his accurate report three weeks earlier that the Germans and Russians had arranged a partition. Palairet wired from Athens that the Russian move 'came as a surprise to the German Government' and Lothian from Washington that it 'took place sooner than was expected or desired' by them. This was the opinion of the American experts, he said. 'Still,' wired Seeds, in qualification of his basic opinion which was erroneous, 'that does not mean that in principle (if such a word can be used of this band of blackguards) the eventual partition of Poland was not foreseen by M. Stalin and Herr von Ribbentrop.'[55] Seeds was a colourful telegraphist but an unreliable informant.

All in all it was a horrible situation for the Allies, and no wonder some of their officials gave way to extremes of optimism and pessimism. It took a real expert in self-discipline to keep a level head amid such a succession of calamities. It was only human nature for them to try to convince themselves the Russians meant them no harm, to under-emphasize past and future Russo-German collaboration in aggression. On 18 September Hore-Belisha told the War Cabinet his view that 'the Empire was faced with a situation of grave peril, and he thought the country should be stirred to make far greater efforts and submit to far greater sacrifices than were at present contemplated'. Those who write Cabinet minutes are known for the way they blunt the edge of what their Ministers have just said. They are adept at taking the sting out of an argument, so much so that they seem sometimes to be aiming at an ideal of perfect blandness. The Minister of War's appeal blares forth like a siren amid the approving murmurs of the other ministers. One must assume that it was quite an outburst.

Chamberlain decided to quell this 'horror and indignation', and by the time the matter was debated in Parliament on 20 September he had managed to moderate his language. The Soviet attack 'could not be justified by the arguments put forward', he said tamely, adding that 'the full implication of these events was not yet apparent'. But nothing would alter the British intention to fulfil their obligations to Poland 'and to prosecute the war with all energy until these obligations had been achieved'. They were brave words, although their meaning is hard to pinpoint. What was Britain's obligation? To restore Poland's independence perhaps. But which Poland? The Poland of three weeks ago? It was apparent to any realistic Englishman that this aim was hardly attainable, involving as it would the defeat of both Germany and the Soviet Union. A country only able to put five well-equipped divisions into the field should not indulge in such talk. It was mere frivolity.

The 20 September debate produced several more interesting lines of thought. Robert Boothby, a young MP and a member of Churchill's group, the 'glamour boys' as Chamberlain's supporters called them, took a less hesitant attitude to the Russian move and made it clear that by and large he supported it. Had the Red Army done nothing, he pointed out, the Germans would by now have reached points far further to the East. He said, 'I am thankful that Russian troops are now along the Polish–Rumanian frontier. I would rather have Russian troops there than German troops.' The matter was not one of morality, he added, although 'there is nothing this country likes better than to take a high moral attitude'. The key to the problem was that 'we want all the support we can get; and I hope and believe that one day we shall get the support of Soviet Russia'.[56] They were wise, prophetic words.

In two days the British press had cooled down remarkably also. The 18 September outburst in *The Times* was nowhere repeated. Clearly it had been dashed off in a fit of initial surprise and anger, before word was sent from Downing Street that tongues should be guarded and hasty judgements restrained. Some newspapers were going to the other extreme. The *News Chronicle*, for instance, wrote that morning that the inhabitants of eastern Poland 'are hailing the Red Army as deliverers' and that Russian troops were 'telling the people that they have come as friends and comrades'. This was the *Pravda* line and a crazy over-simplification. The communist MP William Gallacher of course quoted it delightedly to the House of Commons. Where he was right, though, was in emphasizing that the Red Army had 'drawn a line across Poland beyond which the German troops dare not, must not, pass'.

No one knew the whole truth. Russia's intention was, in Churchill's famous words, 'a riddle wrapped in a mystery inside an enigma' and it would have taken more than a group of parliamentarians to master it. The workings of Stalin's mind were probably not known fully even to Ivan Maisky, his popular ambassador in London, who was listening to the proceedings in the diplomatic gallery. Lord Strabolgi bumped into him after the debate, asked him to tea and reported the conversation faithfully to the Foreign Office.[57] The Ambassador made two important statements: that his country did not want Germany to win the war, and that it did not want the Germans on the shores of the Black Sea. He indicated, as was briefly the policy of both Hitler and Stalin, that Poland would not be extinguished completely but would be left 'a homogeneous, compact people of 18 million as a buffer state'. He added somewhat illogically that this country 'would be between two very great powers which would be a safe-guard'. A safeguard against what, one may well ask. Against Polish imperialism, perhaps, but hardly against the theft of Polish independence, which was what had triggered Britain and France into war. What really bothered Maisky was the possibility that Britain might now be ready to make peace with Germany and accept Poland's loss as a *fait accompli*. Strabolgi assured him that 'the whole Nazi system would have to go'.

It was on the basis of such scraps of information that relations with Moscow were arranged. Maisky was popular personally but no great help diplomatically. 'Quite useless talking to him. He knows nothing and is told nothing by his government,' wrote Cadogan in his diary (27 September). Ambassador Seeds and his staff had but the slenderest of contacts with Soviet officials, thousands of whom had in the past few years been arrested and killed on false charges of sabotage and espionage. It was precisely this contact with foreigners that was the kiss of death to any Soviet bureaucrat, however eminent. No British or French diplomat in Moscow had reliable friends in the administration, only business acquaintances, so there could be no question of any informal approach to find out what lay at the back of Soviet policy. When French Chargé d'Affaires Payart asked Potyomkin formally for an 'explanation' of what his government had done, he was told simply to mind his own business.

On 13 October Eden lunched with Maisky, and again their talk was encouraging as far as it went. The Ambassador explained that 'Russia was compelled to pursue a policy of isolation. In order that that policy may be effective, it was necessary for Russia to ensure that certain vital strategic points should be under her own control.'[58] He promised too that Russia genuinely desired neutrality. Eden concluded that Maisky truly wanted to improve relations with Britain, but wondered how far this wish was shared by Stalin. Like all the Allied leaders Eden was completely confused. Whose side was Russia on?

In what little was left of Poland the two invading armies seemed to be getting on well enough. The city of Brześć was one point the Poles still held on to after their Government left on 17 September, but within a couple of days the Germans had occupied most of it. One fort still held out until the arrival of the Red Army and only surrendered after being bombarded by combined German and Russian artillery.[59] Having won this great objective, the German commander Heinz Guderian was told to his horror that he would have to evacuate the city by 22 September. 'It seems unlikely that any soldier was present when the agreement about the demarcation line and the cease-fire was drawn up,' he writes.[60] He was hardly given enough time to collect his equipment together for withdrawal, and all the material he had captured in battle from the

Poles he had to leave behind. Luckily he got on well with the Red Army commander Krivoshin, with whom he was able to discuss such problems in French, and they arranged a military ceremony during which the city was handed over. He writes, 'A farewell parade and salutes to the two flags in the presence of Krivoshin marked the end of our stay in Brest-Litovsk.'[61] The world was becoming used to the strange sight of the Red Flag and the Swastika flying side by side.

On 22 September forces of the Red Army occupied Białystok and set about mopping up Polish soldiers who had taken refuge in the forest of Augustów nearby. That same day the Poles surrendered their garrison of Lwów (Lvov). The Red Army had drawn near to the city within a day or two of their invasion. The Soviet commander F. I. Golikov, writing in 1969, relates characteristically: 'Finding that our forces were clearly superior, the Germans began to withdraw quickly westward during the night of 20–21 September. They were afraid of being surrounded.'[62] Golikov thus gives the false impression that his orders were to forestall the Germans, whereas in fact he was to assist them, and that the Germans regarded the Red Army as an enemy.

According to Golikov the Polish commander General Langner said to him, 'We would rather surrender Lwów and its garrison to the 'Red Army than to the Germans, because we are Slavs.' Golikov claims that he released all soldiers and officers whose homes were in the area and that 'their joy knew no bounds'. (What he probably means is that he released the Ukrainians but kept the Poles, thousands of whom were due for deportation.) One not released was the former Polish military attaché in Berlin, Antoni Szymański, who in three weeks had made his way from Germany to Eastern Poland by a roundabout route, only to fall into the hands of the Red Army on arrival. 'The Asiatic hordes poured into Lwów,' he remembers.[63] On 23 September *Izvestiya* reported that Red Army units held 120,000 Polish prisoners, and there is no doubt that a large part of these were immediately sent deep into the Soviet Union, where they suffered nearly two years of horrifying imprisonment. 'For many of us it was a convoy of death,' Szymański writes accurately, for thousands were to perish in the forced-labour camps and thousands were shot by the Soviet Security Police (the NKVD) in Katyń Woods. This fact goes some way to explaining the attitude of Poles like Szymański, a bitterness amounting almost to racism.

Another account of the capture of Lwów is given by Nikita Khrushchev in his 'memoirs':

> If the Germans had had their way, they would have entered the city first and sacked the city. But since our troops, under the command of Golikov, had gotten there ahead of them, the Germans were careful not to show any hostility toward us. They stuck to the letter of the treaty and told Yakovlev in effect, 'Please! Be our guests! After you!' Hitler was playing for high stakes, and he did not want to start a fight with us over small change. He wanted us to think he was a man of his word. So the German troops were pulled back to the border which had been set by the treaty.[64]

Khruschchev was well qualified to know the facts since he was First Secretary of the Ukraine and himself moving towards Lwów in the wake of Timoshenko's army.

On 18 September a joint Soviet–German communiqué declared that the two armies' activities 'threatened neither German nor Soviet interests and were in no way contrary to the non-aggression pact'. The truth was that the armies were working closely together – a fact which post-war Soviet historians and generals do their best to play down, often at the expense of the truth. The British and French were right to fear that more active cooperation would develop. There were many who assumed briefly that Germany had succeeded in recruiting Russia as an active ally against Britain and France as well as against Poland. If this were the case the Allies' position would be perilous indeed. Still, there were also the optimists, and Churchill was one of them. He could not, as his ally Boothby had done, proclaim his approval of the Russian action in the House of Commons, but he did on 25 September write a paper for the War Cabinet in which he said, 'I was determined to put the best construction on their [the Russians'] odious conduct.' He did not, he writes, 'give way to the indignation which I felt and which surged about me in our Cabinet at their callous, brutal policy'.[65] Chamberlain and his men, meeting on 18 September, had heaped abuse on the Soviet Union for her action of the previous day. But it was Churchill's view that 'in mortal war anger must be subordinated to defeating the main immediate enemy' and he was pleased that 'the left paw of the Bear has already closed the pathway from Poland to Rumania'.

Churchill had no means of knowing Stalin's motives or of guessing how deep went his agreement with Hitler. But he was wise to draw attention to another important point: 'It is impossible for Germany to denude the Eastern Front. A large German army must be left to watch it. I see that General Gamelin puts it at at least twenty divisions. It may well be twenty-five or more. An eastern front is therefore potentially in existence.' With typical boldness he proceeded to put this view on public record in a B B C broadcast on 1 October:

> Russia has pursued a policy of cold self-interest. We could have wished that the Russian armies should be standing on their present line as the friends and allies of Poland instead of as invaders. But that the Russian armies should stand on this line was clearly necessary for the safety of Russia against the Nazi menace. At any rate the line is there and an eastern front has been created which Nazi Germany does not dare assail . . . I cannot forecast to you the action of Russia. It is a riddle wrapped in a mystery inside an enigma. But perhaps there is a key. That key is Russian national interest. It cannot be in accordance with the interest or the safety of Russia that Germany should plant herself upon the shores of the Black Sea, or that it should overrun the Balkan States and subjugate the Slavonic peoples of south-eastern Europe.[66]

In this as in other important matters Churchill's minority view prevailed over that of the weaker majority in the War Cabinet. In a few days Chamberlain changed his mind about Russia's action and wrote to his sister, 'I take the same view as Winston, to whose excellent broadcast we have just been listening. I believe Russia will always act as she thinks her own interests demand, and I cannot believe she would think her interests served by a German victory followed by a German domination of Europe.'[67]

He was right, of course, and it is to the Prime Minister's credit that he was ready to undergo this swift conversion, to change his attitude to the Soviet Union which had previously been one of unmitigated mistrust and hostility. It was certainly pleasanter to believe that Russia might eventually be wooed onto the Allied side, and doubtless this thought encouraged him to reconsider. The only pity is that he did not do this several months previously. Had he been able to overcome his distrust, he might have been able to convince Stalin that he meant business, that he really was going to put a stop to Hitler. This was what Churchill and his friends had urged all along. It *might* have prevented the Nazi–Soviet pact.

Even so there were appeasers in Parliament who refused to follow their leader's line, and understandably, since to anyone unversed in his political thinking he must have seemed very inconsistent. The Italian newspaper *Messagero* was quick to play up such doubts. 'What is the explanation of the silence of Franco-British circles vis-à-vis Soviet Russia?' it asked. '. . . Not one voice is raised to call Russia to account for her sudden intervention. The restoration of Poland and even Bohemia is demanded, but nobody makes any specific mention of the Polish provinces now occupied by Muscovite troops.'[68] A member of parliament asked Chamberlain publicly about Churchill's views, whether he was speaking on behalf of the Government, and was told by him that although they were Churchill's 'own personal interpretation' there was nothing in them 'at variance with the view of His Majesty's Government'.[69]

Churchill's guesses as to Russian intentions were amazingly accurate. He was not impressed by the pro-Hitler posturing which Stalin and Molotov had suddenly cultivated. He was not carried away by the immorality and selfishness of what Russia was doing for, however one interpreted her ultimate plans, her present actions were there for all to see, and they did not look pretty. Whatever the Soviet Union felt about Hitlerism, and however much she feared it in the long term, no one could deny that for the moment she was deriving much benefit from the perverted alliance with her ideological arch-enemy. There is nothing so good as a hated third party to bring two adversaries together. Poland was providing both Russia and Germany with emotional common ground as well as with booty, and this was enough to make the extraordinary Nazi–Soviet friendship far more than a façade.

There were still many details to arrange over how this booty should be divided, and in the circumstances, with the German Army still flinging itself victoriously eastwards, Stalin understandably felt some concern. On 17 September he told German Ambassador Schulenburg of his worry that Germany might not withdraw to the agreed line. Schulenburg did his best to reassure him that of course the German Government would keep its word, to which Stalin replied that he did not mistrust Germany, far from it, but 'his concern was based on the well-known fact that all military men are loath to give up occupied territories'.[70] We know now how Guderian felt about having to withdraw from Brześć (Brest), so clearly Stalin had a point. Two days later the same point was raised with Schulenburg by Molotov, who 'with evident agitation' asked about a German map, on which a demarcation line was drawn leaving Lwów on the German side.[71] The Ambassador had to telegraph Berlin twice for authority to reassure the Soviet leaders, which he did on 20 September, when he was able to report that 'our intention to withdraw . . . is no longer doubted'.[72] To make sure that this agreement was on record, on 23 September and for the five following days *Pravda* and *Izvestiya* published a map marking the dividing line, which left Bialystok, Lublin, Lwów and east-of-the-Vistula Warsaw on the Soviet side. Frontiers meant little in those heady September days while the small countries of Europe feared for their very existence.

German propaganda, serving Hitler's aim to conclude peace on his terms with Britain and France, was now encouraging rumours that a 'rump' Polish state would be created as a buffer state between her and Russia. The western press was full of the idea,[73] and it is likely that Hitler actually favoured the idea in principle, provided of course that this new 'Poland' was entirely subservient to him and under his protection, as was Slovakia. On 1 October he told Count Ciano that he regarded the prospect of administering Poland simply as a burden.[74] He said 'he had found Poland in so run-down and rotten a condition that he wanted to have as little to do with it as possible'. This certainly represented part of his feeling on the subject, but it was complicated by his resolve that the Poles were to be Germany's slaves. At best this 'Poland' would have been a short-term measure, a sop to the Allies to allow them to make a peace and still save face. It would not have changed his long-term plan to colonize the vast plains of eastern Europe, to build his Greater Germany.

It was Stalin who decided that it would be simpler to kill Poland outright. On 20 September Molotov gave Schulenburg to understand that 'the original inclination entertained by the Soviet Government and Stalin personally to permit the existence of a residual Poland had given way to the inclination to partition Poland along the Pissa–Narew–Vistula–San Line'.[75] He suggested that talks on this take place as soon as possible in Moscow. Schulenburg agreed, but when Molotov suggested they both announce publicly their agreement to the Line he objected that 'the final determination of the political boundary had not yet been made and was reserved for further negotiations'.[76] But to press the objection in the light of what had gone before would have been to arouse Stalin's suspicion, which for the present Hitler wanted at all cost to avoid. He withdrew and allowed details of the dividing line to be published in *Völkischer Beobachter* on 23 September, ordering Foreign Minister Ribbentrop to fly to Moscow on 27 September for the talks.

On the evening of 25 September Stalin had an important talk with Schulenburg and told him that his 'inclination' to abolish Poland had hardened. 'Anything that in the future might create friction between Germany and the Soviet Union must be avoided,' said Stalin, which meant that 'he considered it wrong to leave an independent residual Poland'.[77] He had yet another important new proposal, a direct territorial swap, a variation of the 23 August share-out. Germany should waive her claim to Lithuania and receive in exchange Russia's only allotted chunk of purely Polish territory, the lands between Warsaw and Brześć, between the rivers Vistula and Bug, roughly up to the Curzon Line. Russia would still be left with about five million Poles, mainly in Lwów, Białystok, Wilno and other cities, but the countryside she took would now be almost entirely Byelorussian or Ukrainian.

While he refrained from challenging Stalin's opinion, Hitler was not yet convinced that a 'rump' Poland was out of the question. Its future, Secretary of State Weizsäcker noted on 26 September, 'depends on whether the western powers should now say they are willing to come around'.[78] Another imponderable was whether a Polish Government could be found ready and able to conclude peace with Germany on Hitler's terms. This question was put to Hans-Adolf von Moltke, who for eight years had been German Ambassador in Warsaw.

Von Moltke's attitude to the country where he had lived for so long can be judged from a report on 'the special structure of the Polish population' which he had submitted on 1 August. 'The great masses of Polish peasant population are obtuse and ignorant . . . The Polish workmen, who live in very poor social conditions, are mostly marxists, which is in itself sufficient to make them hostile to National-Socialist Germany. [*This was of course twenty-three days before the Nazi—Soviet pact was signed.*] . . . A lower middle class of a distinctively Polish character hardly exists in Poland, its place being taken by a strong Jewish element without national feeling . . .' These quotations are from a German propaganda book sold in the United States in 1940.[79] Amazingly, Goebbels's men seem to have imagined that such abuse would justify Germany's aggression in neutral circles.

On 25 September von Moltke reported more realistically that 'it is not likely that politicians of standing would make themselves available for the formation of a government'.[80] The only hope, he thought, would be to create a Poland whose western frontier was that of Germany in 1914 and whose eastern frontier ran from Grodno to Przemysl, i.e. from north to south about 120 miles east of Warsaw. This would have the advantage of eliminating completely a German—Soviet frontier, and it was possible that some Poles would be 'more or less satisfied' with such a state. But, he added, 'it would be necessary to impose firm restraint on the new state in order to keep its foreign policy permanently amenable towards us'. Stalin's proposed variation of the dividing line would place most of this territory at Germany's disposal, but its 'independence' would only be a device to get Britain and France out of the war.

But the immediate problem was to secure the best possible bargain with the Russians. 'Secure Augustów and the forest for Germany if possible,' Ribbentrop wired Schulenburg on 21 September,[81] but two days later he felt that Germany's aim might be better served if he flew to Moscow himself. 'In view of the general situation my sojourn in Moscow will have to be limited to one or two days at the most,' he wrote,[82] and on 26 September he decided to leave for Moscow the very next morning. Clearly a man of energy and resilience, he spent the night in talking about the forthcoming negotiations, stealing only an hour or two's sleep before arriving at Berlin's Tempelhof Airport at 9 a.m. They took off and, in the words of Under-Secretary of State Andor Hencke, 'hardly were we in the air before office routine resumed, just as in the Wilhelmstrasse or the special train. The Foreign Minister worked as usual.'[83] The typewriters kept tapping, and Ribbentrop talked to Soviet Ambassador Alexander Shkvartsev, who came along for the ride. At 11 a.m. they landed in Königsberg in East Prussia for a quick meal and were handed news of the capitulation of Warsaw. Hencke mentions that all of them, German and Russian alike, saw this as a good omen for the coming negotiations.

At 3.50 p.m. German time, 5.50 p.m. Moscow time, they landed at Khodynka Airport which was flag-strewn in the extravagant Soviet way. Hencke was 'singularly impressed' and reflected that until a month ago the swastika flag had probably never flown from a Soviet building. The next few hours were 'busy' and 'filled with conversations as well as telephone calls' in preparation for the first talks which began at 10 p.m. It was an intimate little gathering that was to decide the future of eastern Europe – just Stalin, Ribbentrop, Molotov, Schulenburg and the interpreters. The junior men sat in an adjoining room in case they were needed. 'Conversation with the [Russian] aides did not flow readily,' Hencke mentions, so they spent the time drinking Narsan mineral water, smoking strong Russian cigarettes and reading newspapers. At 1 a.m. the Germans adjourned to their Ambassador's residence, where Ribbentrop stayed up until 4 a.m. dictating his report for Hitler, which was at once encoded and telephoned to Berlin.

Hencke had been able to tell from his boss's face that the talks had gone well. They were 'friendly throughout in tone', Ribbentrop recorded in his first paragraph. He had to decide, firstly, whether to accept Stalin's proposed variation of the 23 August split-up, secondly, to try to improve the deal from Germany's point of view. There were arguments for both proposals which Ribbentrop was careful to enumerate. Stalin's preference was clear. He was against splitting the territory with purely Polish population. 'History has proved that the Polish people continually struggle for unification,' he pointed out astutely, which presumably raised the question in the German's mind of against whom the Poles were now to struggle? Having just beaten the Polish Army so decisively Hitler may not have been too worried by the prospect of having to keep them under control, but clearly Stalin was. Ribbentrop wondered whether it was in Germany's interest to relieve Russia of the Polish problem. But by and large he agreed with Stalin that to divide this area might lead to friction between Germany and Russia. It would be better for one of them to assume the whole burden.

Germany would be loath to give up Lithuania, since there were many thousands of Germans in the Baltic States who, if Germany withdrew her influence entirely, would have to be abandoned or resettled. But retreat in Lithuania and advance in Poland would leave Germany with a tidier, more homogeneous, more defendable sphere of interest in which, Ribbentrop observed ominously, 'the Polish national problem might be dealt with as Germany thought fit'. This could mean that Germany was thinking of granting the area some autonomy, or it could mean something more terrible.

Stalin too had much to gain from the variation he had proposed. To be sure, his strategic aim was to push his country's frontier westward as a cushion against any future German attack. But there were disadvantages in pushing it too far. By advancing to the Vistula he would add 250 miles to his lines of communication, and this across country which, though not all Polish-inhabited, was certainly not Soviet and was therefore potentially hostile. Also its railway system was on the European gauge, which is narrower than the Russian. Supplies would be more difficult to transport. And although the frontier would have a natural defence in the four rivers, it could easily be outflanked from East Prussia or Lithuania, which would jut 100 miles east of the line, and then the Red Army might suffer heavy losses in trying to get behind its original fortifications. Colonel Firebrace, the aptly named British military attaché in Moscow, concluded that the Russian advance would not help her defensive potential at all, except perhaps in freeing Moscow and Leningrad from the threat of air bombardment.[84] But then the job of military attaché in Moscow is not an easy one. Frequently he is led astray.

Having dicatated his memorandum and asked Hitler to inform him by telephone which of the two deals he should press for, Ribbentrop retired to bed to refresh himself for the next round of talks which began at 3 p.m. on 28 September. Hitler decided to agree to Stalin's variation, and a note to this effect was signed by Ribbentrop and Molotov.[85] All that afternoon was devoted to a discussion of details of the carve-up. Two rooms near Molotov's office were set aside for the negotiators, one full of cartographers, the other full of stenographers. Hencke writes: 'The boundary, at first sketched in great sweeps, was made more and more precise by use of maps until finally it was settled. During this time many changes and consultations were of course necessary. The draughtsmen had no easy task keeping their entries current. The greatest care had to be taken here, for later, in actually marking the boundary on the ground, the slightest error – or even too heavy a line – might be important.'[86]

At last a map with a line down the middle of it was ready, and was presented for the signatures of Ribbentrop and Stalin. Stalin signed, remarking with his inimitable humour, 'Is my signature clear enough for you?' At 7 p.m. they all repaired to the grand palace of the Kremlin for one of those bizarre banquets that Khrushchev, Churchill, Djilas and Stalin's daughter Svetlana have described so vividly. Krushchev says, 'I don't think there has ever been a leader in a position of comparable responsibility who wasted more time than Stalin did just sitting around the dinner table eating and drinking.'[87] It was the usual crowd – Beria, Voroshilov, Molotov – and the table was laden with the usual amount of vodka and caviar. Molotov kept toasting his chief, and Stalin felt called upon to make another of his jokes: 'If Molotov really wants to drink, no one objects, but he shouldn't use me as an excuse.'[88]

After dinner Ribbentrop allowed himself a short break from work to visit a production of *Swan Lake*, while Stalin negotiated with a Latvian delegation one of his famous 'Mutual Assistance Treaties'. But after one act the indefatigable German was back at work. He spoke with Hitler on the telephone and at midnight negotiations resumed. At 5 a.m. all was ready for formal signature by Ribbentrop and Molotov, not only the main boundary agreement but also a series of others. One of these allowed for the repatriation to the Reich of Germans living in the Baltic States, which would now be taken over by Russia.[89] Another planned 'to promote by all means the trade relations and the exchange of goods between Germany and the USSR'.[90] The Soviet Union was to supply Germany with raw materials, some of which she needed desperately in order to be able to prosecute her war against Britain and France, while Germany was to supply manufactured goods. In particular Russia agreed to supply Germany with the total annual oil production of south-east Poland, receiving in return German coal and steel piping. This oil was vital to Germany, since the British blockade effectively prevented her from importing any from overseas. Russia also agreed to give Germany transit facilities to Rumania along the one-track railway through Lwów and Kołomyja. It was through this railway line, one recalls, that the Allies had originally planned to supply Poland with military equipment. Now it was to be used with Soviet assistance to enable Germany to trade with Rumania, which was also rich in oil.

There was another agreement of a more ominous nature: 'Both parties will tolerate in their territories no Polish agitation which affects the territories of the other party. They will suppress in their territories all beginnings of such agitation and inform each other concerning suitable measures for this purpose.'[91] In practice this meant that the Gestapo held regular meetings with the NKVD, its Soviet equivalent, to coordinate their efforts against any Poles so foolish as to try to reinstate their country's independence.

Of course none of this was made public. The actual treaty stated merely that Germany and the Soviet Union viewed it 'as exclusively their task, after the disintegration of the former Polish state, to re-establish peace and order in these territories and to assure to the peoples living there a peaceful life in keeping with their national character'.[92] They also released to the press an appeal for an end to the war between Germany and the Allies. Such a result 'would serve the true interest of all peoples', the statement said. What about the Czechs and the Poles, some were tempted to reply. But it was the statement's final paragraph which the Allies found most menacing: 'Should however the efforts of the two governments remain fruitless, this would demonstrate the fact that England and France are responsible for the continuation of the war. In such a case the governments of Germany and of the USSR shall engage in mutual consultations with regard to necessary measures.'

Ribbentrop and Molotov signed the documents. According to Hencke, 'Stalin observed this ceremony with obvious satisfaction.' Indeed he had good reason to rejoice. At the price of a small military operation, which according to Molotov cost the Red Army no more than 737 killed and 1,862 wounded,[93] the Soviet Union had pushed its western frontier 150 miles further from Moscow and, which was from the strategic point of view more important, had won from Germany a free hand in the Baltic States. Khrushchev quotes Stalin as saying: 'Of course it's all a game to see who can fool whom. I know what Hitler's up to. He thinks he's outsmarted me, but actually it's I who have tricked him.'[94] He told Khrushchev, Beria and Voroshilov that 'because of this treaty the war would pass us by for a while longer. We would be able to stay neutral and save our strength.' Khrushchev admits, though, that 'for their part, the Germans too were using the treaty as a manœuvre to win time. Their idea was to divide and conquer...'[95]

One cannot but admire Ribbentrop for his physical endurance. The early morning of 29 September found him without having had any sleep for three whole nights. One might have thought that having signed his agreement with Molotov, having redrawn the map of Europe, acquiring for Germany vast areas of territory as well as essential raw materials, he might have felt able to retire for a well-earned rest. But no, the German colony of Moscow was waiting to receive him at the Embassy, honoured to be the first to congratulate him on the agreement which 'had created for them too a new basis for their work in the Soviet Union'. The whole of that morning was taken up with receptions, and it was only at midday that Ribbentrop and his entourage left for Moscow Airport and he was able to relax during the flight back to Berlin. 'With us,' writes Hencke, 'we took an experience of historical importance, a wealth of interesting impressions.' They landed at Tempelhof Airport at 6 p.m., having been away no more than fifty-seven hours.

The military defeat and partition of Poland was accomplished by the German and Soviet armies which, as the previous pages have shown, were throughout the campaign in constant and close communication. Even today, and in spite of conclusive documentary evidence, the Soviet authorities have not admitted this simple fact. The official Soviet history of the war, published in 1960, still maintains that the German Army 'intended to advance further east'. They still say that the Nazis 'were most disappointed that the Soviet action would prevent their plan to advance to the Soviet frontier', and that 'convinced of the Soviet Government's determination to repulse the fascist aggressors they considered it wiser in the given circumstances to agree to the suggested peaceful solution to the conflict'.[96] In fact there was no Soviet determination to repulse the fascist aggressors. The moves of the two sides were well coordinated, and both lived up to their promises.

As to who was the rightful owner of the areas of western Poland the Red Army had seized, it is one of those unanswerable questions. Before the First World War they were divided between Tsarist Russia and Austro-Hungary. Then for brief periods, while the new Bolshevik nation was in a state of flux, part of the Ukraine was independent and self-governing. Khrushchev says quite plainly that 'from a purely territorial point of view, you'll see that we gained practically nothing except what we were legally entitled to — that is, the Byelorussian and Ukrainian lands which were seized by Piłsudski in 1920.'[97] This is not a claim which can be totally dismissed, for the areas in question were indeed won by Poland in battle. The population was mixed: Byelorussian, Ukrainian, Jewish, Russian and Polish. In fact the only conclusion one can draw is that ethnologically and historically their ownership is unclear.

Soviet propaganda of course claimed that the Red Army was greeted everywhere as a liberator, even by the Poles. The pre-war régime, declared *Izvestiya* on 9 October, 'was based on lawlessness

Moscow's view of the Polish government-in-exile in Angers, France. Ambassadors present their credentials at the 'Presidential Palace' (*Pravda*, 21 October 1939). (Copyright British Museum)

and the subjection of all people who inhabit Poland, not excluding the Polish people', and was supported by no one but the Polish ruling classes. The post-war official history claims falsely that any Poles who wished were allowed to emigrate to the West: 'Some came into the main part of the USSR, where Polish patriotic organizations were being set up, or left for France.' [98] In fact the Soviet authorities did allow some Poles to cross into the German-occupied area, but did not permit them to go to France. According to the history, the working classes 'began with great enthusiasm to build a new life . . . Soon there began to appear the first collective farms and the first machine tractor stations.' [99] The only opponents of the new system were 'a small proportion of the Polish armed forces, colonial settlers and gendarmes'. The evidence shows though that of the several million Poles in the Russian-occupied areas only the handful of communists actually supported the entry of the Red Army. The Polish population as a whole opposed it strongly.

In some ways indeed the Poles endured the Soviet occupation less hopefully even than the German. Although Hitler treated them far more brutally than Stalin, they were as slow as the rest of the world to realize exactly what the Nazis had in store for them and in all too many cases clung pathetically to the belief that they would be better off under the Germans, an orderly, disciplined race, than under the 'barbaric' Russians. Here they were mistaken, but in another respect they were quite correct. They were convinced that the Nazi occupation would not last, that Hitler was hell-bent on a suicidal as well as a murderous journey, that the further and faster he went the sooner he would reach the end of the road where there was nothing but a sheer plunge into the depths.

What really depressed people about the Soviet occupation was that there was no real prospect of its disappearance. Britain and France were at war with Germany but not with Russia. They had promised to drive the Germans out of Poland – and in spite of overwhelming evidence to the contrary the Poles believed they would – but not to drive out the Russians. Accustomed to think of themselves historically as the outpost of Catholic civilization, east of which there is nothing but a cultural and religious desert, they felt like those rugged men who try to farm on the edge of the

Sahara, who frantically build walls to keep the sand at bay, knowing that once they are swamped it will be for ever, that they will never reclaim their soil. Rightly or wrongly there were many Poles who, as they watched the Red Army's hundreds of tanks and thousands of horse-drawn carts clatter through Lwów, Wilno, Białystok, and the countryside Poland had won in battle in 1920, felt themselves being infested irrevocably by the forces of barbarism.

This is why, even when they realized the full horror of what Nazi occupation meant and was going to mean, the Poles would not accept or even reconcile themselves to the idea of liberation by the Red Army. For they thought of it not so much as the army of international communism, although that was bad enough, but rather as the army of a historical enemy and an alien civilization. They continued to work for a liberation that would come from the West with the British and French. Once bitten twice shy, one would have thought. Did they really hope that the British and French, who had done so little to prevent Poland's defeat, would be able to rescue them? Would the Western Allies really be prepared, even assuming that they were able to conquer Germany, to advance their armies hundreds of miles further East at the risk of a confrontation with the Red Army, to restore the Poland of 1939? True, they had restored Poland in 1918, but this had been in the West's political and strategic interest, to make sure that there was a buffer state between Bolshevik Russia and the cradle of Bolshevism, Germany. Also, in 1918 Russia was in a state of semi-collapse and in no better position than Germany to resist the terms imposed by the French, Americans and British at Versailles. In 1939 it was surely logical for Poles to consider that maybe the Nazi–Soviet Pact would some day collapse. There were plenty in England who foresaw this, Churchill for instance. But Poles refused even to admit this possibility. Their attitude to Russia was such that they would regard liberation from the East not as liberation but as corruption. As Rydz-Śmigły said to the French Ambassador just before the outbreak, 'With the Germans we may possibly lose our freedom, but with the Russians we would lose our soul.'[100]

It must be admitted that Polish–Soviet friendship was hardly encouraged by the behaviour of the Soviet forces who occupied the eastern part of the country. The Russian conquerors did not of course consider themselves superior racially to the Poles. They did not feel they had the right or the duty to turn them into helots. But they had persuaded themselves that the Poles as a whole were a danger to their internal security, and soon let loose among them those cruel men who usually follow in the wake of Soviet armies when they invade foreign countries, their secret police, the NKVD.

On 28 September Ribbentrop and Molotov had finally agreed in Moscow for the Soviet Union to take just over half the area of the pre-war Polish state, about 200,000 square kilometres. But for the most part this was flat farming country with little industry, so its population was little more than half that of the German share. What is more, of the 13 million who inhabited the eastern areas, only about 5 million were Poles, the rest being Ukrainians, Byelo-russians, Lithuanians and Jews, almost all unassimilated. The Soviet authorities therefore felt they could treat the Poles not as the rightful owners of these lands, but as a minority, and what is more as a minority which for years had oppressed the Ukrainians and Byelorussians to whom the country really belonged.

It was not that the Poles treated the non-Poles whom they ruled viciously, but they showed them little understanding. After more than a century of national eclipse and foreign rule, Poland had gained independence only by a fluke, through the military collapse of two of the partitioning powers, Germany and Austro-Hungary, and the military weakness of the third, the young Bolshevik state whose leader Lenin had been ready enough to give up the Polish areas which had caused his Tsarist predecessors so much trouble. The men who governed this resurrected Poland partly owed their power to the western Allies who decided in 1918 that, strategically placed between defeated Germany and newly socialist Russia, she would help the stability of the area and prevent the export of the new ideology. This was the birth which Hitler described on 6 October as an abortion. No wonder the Poles felt touchy and complex-ridden about their national existence.

The 1920 Soviet–Polish war, the result of a Polish attempt to seize the Ukraine with the aid of the Ukrainian nationalist leader Simon Petlura, ended in Polish victory only after Red Army troops had occupied eastern Poland, set up a communist government there, and been within an ace of capturing Warsaw. The Polish rout of the Red Army troops who were besieging their capital, the so-called 'Miracle on the Vistula', is now seen as one of the most decisive battles in the world's history. Had the Red Army taken Warsaw, it might have carried its march westward into Germany with who knows what consequences. As it was, Poland was left in possession of large areas of western Ukraine and western Byelorussia, and many millions of non-Poles.

It can be seen that Poland had none of the security and stability which leads a country to take a tolerant, enlightened attitude towards its national minorities. The areas taken from Russia in 1920 proved more trouble than they were worth. The Poles tried to assimilate their inhabitants. Polish was made the only official language in government and in the schools. Rich Poles owned vast estates in the east where Ukrainians worked as peasants. It was not a happy state of affairs, and there can be no doubt that Polish rule was unpopular in many parts of the eastern territories. Many Ukrainians and Byelorussians welcomed the Red Army in September 1939, a few out of enthusiasm for communism and world revolution, but mostly out of a general desire for change which, who knows, might well be a change for the better.

Another thing Stalin had against the Poles was that they had been causing disruption in the communist movement. During the purges of the late 1930s almost all the leading Polish communists had been summoned to Moscow, arrested and liquidated. The Polish Communist Party with its large Jewish element[101] was accused of 'cosmopolitanism' and 'Trotskyism' and in the summer of 1938 had been dissolved by the Comintern under Stalin's order for supposedly allowing Polish intelligence agents to infiltrate.

The NKVD, following in the wake of the Red Army with instructions to eliminate all hostile elements, took its task literally and fulfilled it more than conscientiously. In such a situation they decided it was not possible to investigate every suspicious individual. To do this would have taken years. Instead they established organizations and categories of the guilty. Anyone who had served the Polish state in an official capacity, however menial, could be accused of being a 'socially unreliable element', tried before a three-man court and deported to forced labour in Siberia. Politicians, postmen, army officers, policemen, dustmen, bankers and of course communists — all these became natural targets. This fact is half admitted nowadays even by communist historians, for instance by the Pole Marian Malinowski who writes: 'The Soviet authorities were taking repressive measures against the forces of Polish reaction in these areas. As a result of distortions of justice, and sometimes simply of misunderstandings, these repressions also fell sometimes on Polish anti-fascists and communists.' [102]

The first cross the Poles had to bear was a wave of disorder, perpetrated not by the Red Army but by the non-Polish inhabitants of the occupied areas. Bands of Ukrainians seized upon the collapse of Polish power as a fine opportunity to get their own back for the years during which they had been forced into an inferior position. This action began in mid September, while the Polish army was still in existence, and there were one or two instances where the Poles took reprisal against such bandits. As in the case of 3 September, 'Bloody Sunday', at Bydgoszcz, the Polish army can hardly be blamed very much for reacting violently when sniped at in the rear in such a situation. But the incidents certainly provided ammunition for the Soviet press and justification for future repressions, as had 'Bloody Sunday' for the Germans. On 14 September *Izvestiya* announced rebellion in the Ukraine and mutiny in the Polish army. On 15 September it reported that the Polish army was setting fire to Byelorussian villages. This was stage-setting for the 17 September invasion. After this, when Polish administration had disintegrated and was being replaced by Soviet power, attacks against the former rulers became widespread and very brutal. Many Ukrainians and Byelorussians were anxious to ingratiate themselves with their new communist rulers, to take revenge against their now helpless Polish former rulers, and if possible to gain a little plunder in the process. For a few weeks there was anarchy, murder, looting and rape. The Soviet press was delighted to report that inhabitants of the occupied areas were collaborating with the Red Army in their round-up of notorious Polish 'enemies of the people' – generals and gendarmes, officials of the Ministry of the Interior, even a certain Prince Radziwiłł. [103] But of course it went much further than that. Harmless minor officials were also being arrested by the thousand and sometimes simply killed. As Malinowski admits with commendable frankness but with gross understatement: 'At first there were certain irregularities in the behaviour of the Soviet authorities.'

This phase lasted only a short time, and once Soviet power was consolidated it scotched such disorganized killing. The Polish émigré historian Pobóg-Malinowski, not known for his love of the Soviet Union, writes that 'the Soviet soldier in the occupied towns behaved generally correctly'.[104] They did not hold mass executions in towns and village squares as the Nazis were doing on the other side of the demarcation line. It is true they stole the Poles' watches, unable to overcome a passion for this fascinating machine which was a commonplace in Poland but a rarity in the remote parts of Russia most of them came from. It is true they fixed the rouble at parity with the Polish *złoty*, in spite of a fourfold difference in purchasing power, and that this soon led to empty shops and food shortages. It is true that the invaders were led to believe that Polish landlords were brutal sadists, that Polish officers were enemies of the Soviet Union, that Polish policemen and officials were their contemptible lackeys, that Polish communists were potential traitors to the movement. Such distorted propaganda obviously had its effect on the soldiers and encouraged them to commit acts of cruelty.

Within a few weeks Soviet power was established and imposing drastic changes upon the newly occupied territories. The Polish language ceased to be official and in practice was replaced by Russian. Publication of Polish books and newspapers was subjected to the strict Soviet censorship, with the result that with the exception of a few communist publications like the Lwów *Czerwony Sztandar* (Red Banner) they vanished completely. Schools were divided up by nationality, and while the Polish schoolchildren were still taught in their own language, they were of course deprived of all instruction in religion. An area where the Catholic Church had previously held a powerful position was within a few weeks completely secularized. The crucifixes and images of the Virgin Mary which hung in abundance throughout public buildings and institutions were removed. Churches were turned into social clubs. History books were replaced with others which provided a different version of controversial events. Schoolteachers and priests were the first to be suspected of disloyalty, because of the influence they exerted on young people the first to be damned as 'socially unreliable elements'. They were arrested in large numbers.[105]

The agricultural estates, many of which were owned by Polish landlords, were confiscated by the state and divided among the peasants who worked them. But whatever delight there was in such new-found property was short-lived, for very soon the peasants were pressurized into joining collective farms and again dispossessed. Large industrial enterprises were of course nationalized immediately, and while a few small businesses were allowed to continue, a system of taxes and regulations soon made their existence impossible. The unilaterally imposed exchange rate enabled newcomers from other parts of the Soviet Union to plunder the area of goods, much of which was at once transported eastwards.

Worst of all were the mass arrests. The Soviet official history implies that members of the Polish army were released shortly after capture. In fact most of the Polish officers and many of the Polish soldiers were at once deported or placed under restriction. It was a lottery. Poles with the same background, with the same record of guilt or innocence from the Soviet point of view, were treated to the senseless capriciousness of the NKVD. A Pole might be allowed to go completely free, or placed under restriction of residence, or sent to work in a remote locality. But many thousands were arrested, treated to some mockery of a trial and imprisoned in labour camps. Tens of thousands of these never returned.[106] Then more than now obsessed by the idea of threats to her own security, the Soviet Union behaved viciously, like a trapped animal, towards all those whose profession or way of life indicated a rejection of socialist values. Among these there were no doubt some who would have fought the invader, some who were relentless enemies of the Soviet system. The NKVD was determined to catch those it thought dangerous, and not particular about how many innocent men suffered in the process.

No one knows how many suffered in the mass arrests of the year that followed September 1939. Probably it was between one and two million. The official Polish émigré history of the war puts it at between 1,050,000 and 1,200,000.[107] Another well-researched book called *Soviet Justice* quotes a figure of 1,692,000, broken down as follows: 990,000 arrested in mass deportations, 250,000 arrested individually, 230,000 prisoners of war from the September Campaign and the rest conscripts into the Red Army.[108] The conditions of their imprisonment were horrible – extreme cold, starvation rations, life-breaking work – a combination indescribable except by such a writer as Alexander Solzhenitsyn. In a few cases, such as in the Katyń Forest in 1940, the NKVD massacred Poles by the thousand. Such crimes have not yet been forgiven or forgotten by the mass of the Polish population.

To compare the Soviet and Nazi treatment of occupied Poland is an impossible and pointless exercise. The most one can say is that the approach was different. The Nazis saw Poles and Jews as racial inferiors and treated them as such with logical, orderly method. The NKVD, suspicious of Poles for various reasons semi-valid by their own peculiar standards, acted not out of racial aggression but in a sort of self-defence. The Soviet terror was more disorganized and haphazard, but perhaps because of their kinship with the Poles as fellow-Slavs more effective in killing subversion and rebellion. Grót-Rowecki, the heroic leader of the anti-Nazi Home Army until he was arrested in 1943, reported to his Government in London, 'The Bolsheviks are not so quick to shoot people as the Germans.' But, he went on, they were far better at penetrating all aspects of Polish life, and their various arrests and conscriptions 'decimated the ranks of those who could have become material for our organization'.[109]

In two years the Soviet authorities succeeded in arresting about one fifth of the Poles they governed. In five or six years the Nazis managed to *kill* about the same proportion of their Poles. The NKVD succeeded in stamping out armed resistance to their rule. The Gestapo and the SS did not. The Poles of course ended the war with feelings of bitter hatred against both countries which oppressed them. But while their hatred against Germany was probably stronger than the hatred against Russia, and while it was recognized that in the end it was the Red Army who delivered them from the Nazis, their contempt for the Russians was in no way diminished. They remained inclined to dismiss their fellow-Slavs as 'primitives' or 'Asiatics', to judge them not by the genius of Tolstoy or Dostoyevsky but by the behaviour of the Russian peasant, or perhaps of the Soviet policeman.

No wonder Nikita Khrushchev, First Secretary of the Ukrainian Communist Party, and since March a full member of the Politburo, felt obliged to approach seriously the task of spreading the Soviet ideology in the newly conquered lands. In a speech at Lwów on 4 October 'Mr Khrusheff', as *The Times* quaintly spelt him, announced that the area would be completely and relentlessly bolshevized. In the colourful language that was to delight and infuriate the world from 1953 to 1964 he said 'he knew that in Lwów there had been so many political parties that they could hardly remember their names. He declared war with all possible means against all opponents of the Communist Party . . . He did not believe that everyone in Lwów greeted the Red Army as a liberator. The workers did, but there were those upon whom the decaying capitalist order supported itself.' In his 1971 'memoirs' Khrushchev admits that under his rule 'the Polish population felt oppressed',[110] but in 1939 he felt no need for such modesty or frankness. Work had already begun, he said, distributing the land-lords' estates and replacing factory directors with ordinary workers. He was confident that in the forthcoming elections a majority would vote for the Soviet system. In any case, he added, 'if anyone tries to stop us, we will knock him into a cocked hat'.[111]

This was the Soviet way of calling a general election, the date being fixed for 22 October. As usual in such affairs, there were no opposition candidates, and the voters could merely accept or reject the names on the ballot paper, 2,410 previously prepared candidates, many of whom were already Soviet citizens. The area was large and transport facilities meagre, but still 94 per cent of the electorate was declared to have voted, and of these all but 4 per cent in favour of the official list. With amazing speed the votes were collected and counted in time for the results to be published in *Pravda* on 25 October.

Two days later this Ukrainian Assembly in Lwów petitioned the Supreme Soviet in Moscow 'to annex into the Soviet Union the areas of former Poland occupied by Soviet troops'. The way this decision was taken is described in *Izvestiya* on 28 October: 'Landlords' Poland, which existed through the exploitation of millions of Ukrainians and Byelorussians and of Polish working men, has collapsed,' the delegates were told. Hearing the news of the proposed annexation, they were 'seized with immense enthusi-asm. Everybody rises to their feet. Long applause. From the depths of every heart come shouts: "Long live Soviet power!", "Long live our fellow-countryman Comrade Stalin!' 'The question is put: "Who is in favour of accepting the proposal to establish Soviet power in the western Ukraine?" Over the heads rises a forest of hands. "Who is against?" No one votes against. "Who abstains?" No one abstains. The motion is carried unanimously!'

'Death to the White Eagle!' was the slogan at a similar meeting in Białystok, the new capital of Western Byelorussia, a no less lurid account of which appeared in *Izvestiya* on 29 October. ' "Stalin, Stalin, Stalin!" they shout, again and again,' wrote the correspondent. Finally the Chairman called to his fellow-delegates, somewhat superfluously:

'Comrades, what power shall we choose?' For a second the hall falls silent in amazement. On such a matter can there possibly be any doubt? Should such a question be asked? Can there be any other answer but one? And so the delegates, rising as one man, answer the Chairman's question as it could only be answered by a people exhausted and injured, which has endured slavery and exploitation, which has gone through misery and torment, finally to catch sight of the clear beam of joy and freedom. 'Soviet power!' the cry echoes through the hall. 'Long live Soviet power everywhere in the world!'

Wilno, like Lwów, was a Polish city in a non-Polish area seized by the Polish army in 1920, in this case from Lithuania. In mid September the Red Army occupied it and administered it for a month before handing it over to the small Lithuanian Republic on 27 October, according to the terms of the treaty of 10 October. 'All clocks in the city have been moved two hours forward,' wrote an *Izvestiya* correspondent on 9 October, 'and from now on Wilno lives by Moscow time. Also introduced have been Soviet standards of work and life . . .' It was a candid enough admission that, whatever Article Seven of the treaty might say about 'sovereign rights' and 'non-intervention in internal affairs', the country was to be controlled by the Soviet Union through their legation in Kaunas and their Chargé d'Affaires Pozhniakov, with the help if necessary of Red Army units based in the country under the terms of Article Four.

This treaty, and those with the other Baltic states Latvia and Estonia, were another example of Stalin's sensitivity to world opinion and to his own propaganda. Unlike Hitler, he was not prepared to seize territory by pure right of conquest, by the rule that might equals right. He felt he had to go through the motions of granting self-determination. In the particular case of Eastern

Poland, or Western Ukraine and Western Byelorussia as the communists called it, Stalin perhaps had some vestige of a case, even though his invasion was brutal and in flagrant breach of international law. Certainly this was the view of the British Foreign Office. His popular elections, though ludicrous, did take place, and even if he would probably have lost a free vote, it is hard to say who would have won. Certainly few Ukrainians or Byelorussians would have voted for Foreign Minister Beck, for Prime Minister Sławój-Składkowski and the successors of Piłsudski.

But the peoples of the Baltic states were not Slavs, and here a popular acclamation of Soviet power by the customary 90 per cent majority would have looked even more ridiculous than it did in Poland. This is why Stalin thought it necessary to conclude the 'mutual security pacts' as an interim measure, to cushion the blow he knew his reputation would suffer if he simply seized the Baltic states outright. Of course there was no one who could have stopped him seizing them. By the terms of his agreements with Hitler they were his, and he must have known that no other world power would lift a finger to save three countries so small and remote. When he did decide to end the show and absorb them into the Soviet Union a few months later (June 1940), there was hardly a whisper of protest. But for the moment, as Schulenberg reported from Moscow to Berlin, 'the Soviet action must somehow be justified to those on the outside'.

The irony was that the British and French Governments, once converted to Churchill's view that 'in mortal war anger must be subordinated to defeating the main immediate enemy', felt bound to acquiesce in Stalin's bloodless conquests. Not surprisingly there were those among the Allies who objected to such a cynical approach, to judging Russia and Germany by a double standard. The violently anti-Soviet M.P. Henry Channon, for instance, wrote in his diary on 10 October: 'Russia helps herself to a new country every day and no one minds. It is only German crimes which raise indignation in the minds of the English.' Morally Channon was on firm ground here, but less admirable was the way Englishmen like him condemned the Soviet leaders not so much for their cruelty and ruthlessness as for their rude, uncouth behaviour, for their rejection of the 'generally accepted' rules of drawing-room conduct. For instance, Channon was almost insulted when his boss R. A. Butler asked for the use of his house so as to lunch unobserved with the Soviet Ambassador Maisky. He wrote in his diary on 28 November: 'I never thought that the Russian Ambassador would ever cross my threshold. I checked up on the snuff-boxes on my return but did not notice anything missing.' This remark illustrates well the pettiness and spitefulness of the Chamberlain-adoring, Hitler-appeasing group which Channon represented, their total incomprehension of the workings of the mind of someone like Maisky, a man respected by many who opposed vigorously the policies of the Soviet Government.

In solid contrast to the middle-class attitudes of Channon, the cool *Realpolitik* of Churchill is like a breath of fresh air. His view and the policy he persuaded his colleagues to adopt had little to do with justice or morality, but his prophecies and proposals were uncannily correct. More than any other it was the Red Army which defeated Hitler, and this achievement was only possible because in 1941 it had this extra territory in the West, this extra room for manoeuvre and withdrawal. Had the German Army been allowed to occupy the whole of Poland in 1939, it would have been able to launch its attack on Russia (22 June 1941) from a line 200 miles nearer Moscow and Leningrad. It might well have seized these key cities and defeated the Soviet Union in its first assault.

Speaking in 1939, Churchill did not of course know that Stalin had prearranged his move with Hitler. If he had his private thoughts about the callousness of Soviet policy would doubtless have been even stronger. But it would hardly have changed his view of the practical benefits the Soviet advance afforded Britain and France. It is this practical argument that modern Soviet historians use to justify the whole of Stalin's policy on this issue. Apart from small details like Molotov's cruel remark about Poland on 31 October, the policy of those days has never been criticized officially in Russia. It is still maintained that Stalin acted not only in the Soviet national interest, but also in the long-term interest of the crusade against Hitler, that he helped the Ukrainians and Byelorussians by delivering them from the Polish yoke, and the Poles by saving them from the Germans. It was a noble decision, aimed at the good of humanity as a whole.

This is of course an over-simplification, indeed a gross distortion, but the real motive behind Stalin's decision will not be known until that fascinating day when Soviet official archives are thrown open to historical study. It is undeniable that one reason for the Red Army's advance was to protect the western border against Hitler. Khrushchev writes, 'It was like a gambit in chess. If we hadn't made that move, the war would have started earlier, much to our disadvantage. As it was we were given a respite.'[112] Stalin convinced himself incorrectly that Britain and France did not intend to fight Hitler. He felt obliged to look after his own country first. On this basis it is hard to counter Soviet claims that the decision was taken in what Stalin believed was his country's national interest.

But there is a point where defence ends and turns into aggression. To defend his western cities Stalin felt obliged and entitled to push his frontier further west. To defend the eastern end of the Baltic and the approaches to Leningrad he felt he had the right to absorb the Baltic states. For the same reason he decided to provoke a war against Finland. While admitting that every country has the right to defend itself and to promote its legitimate interests, one must conclude that Stalin put a very wide interpretation on the concept of defence. It seems indeed that here was the germ of the idea which he was able to fulfil successfully after the war was over, to surround his country with a ring of buffer states. It is at about this point that self-defence ends and becomes imperialism.

This is the argument of those who take a less tolerant attitude to the Soviet advance. Ambassador Raczyński, for instance, told the author in 1970: 'Stalin could see that Hitler was about to invade Poland and knew this would mean war between Germany and the western Allies. This suited him very well. He wanted to be the *tertius gaudens.*' And indeed, while defence against Hitler was one reason, maybe the main reason, for the Soviet move, it is hard to imagine that Stalin was averse to the side-effect of an enlargement of the Soviet Union. Why should Stalin be unwilling to increase his empire? Such modesty would surely be to deny his own character as well as the Marxist-Leninist crusade he led. After all at Teheran and Yalta, when the war was approaching its end, he insisted on retaining not only the conquests of 1939 but also areas of Rumania and Czechoslovakia through which the Red Army was about to pass, and Churchill and Roosevelt were orced to agree. He was a skilful negotiator with his ideological enemies, and judging purely from the standpoint of Soviet national interest it is hard to fault the decision he took to 'sign up' with Hitler in 1939. It was not this decision that was so terrible, but the way Stalin proceeded to supply Hitler with everything he needed, to repress with the utmost cruelty the Poles he had absorbed and to make few contingency plans for a German invasion of Russia which, Soviet historians now tell us, was always, even in 1939, thought likely. It is by these standards that Stalin's policy emerges as thoroughly bankrupt, both practically and morally, for it left Russia with debts of honour which have yet to be repaid.

9 The Peace Offensive

September 1939 was a month of world political hysteria, with countries deprived of their freedom, borders redrawn and alliances busily reshaped. We have seen how at the end of August the British and French Governments were still reasonably confident of their ability to deter Hitler from war, in blissful ignorance of his 22 August order to invade Poland. Then on 25 August the combined weight of Mussolini's defection and the Polish–British Treaty were enough to make Hitler hesitate and be seen to hesitate. This increased British and French confidence that Hitler would never go through with his mad scheme, that he was bluffing. They had made *some* preparations for war and they were ready to send such forces as they had into action, but psychologically they were counting on this not being necessary. Maybe there were exceptions. Maybe there were some less optimistic who realized the strength of Germany's armed forces and thought that maybe Hitler was *not* bluffing. But the evidence shows that most British and French leaders were confident that they had the situation in hand. The morning of 1 September brought them a very rude awakening.

The days that followed brought shock upon shock, two of which were enough to send them reeling: the lightning German conquest of Poland and the Soviet intervention in German support. France and Britain controlled the two greatest empires in the world, but in three weeks they were turned from rulers into beggars, forced to pay court to every little neutral country, to woo from what was now almost a kneeling position. One can imagine the trauma this sudden change of events caused in the minds of the several hundred administrators who controlled Allied policy. In their memoranda one detects a note almost of panic, and at the same time a contradictory feeling that it is all too bad to be true and must therefore be untrue. European civilization had been centuries in the building. Was it now to be destroyed in a few days by the bombs of a barbarian ideology?

The thought was enough to drive people's imagination to extremes. Some preferred to turn a blind eye to the terrifying facts. The clouds would pass, the sun would shine and Hitler would disappear, presumably by magic. Others felt that Armageddon was a few days away. They all breathed this heady mixture of wishful thinking and panic, and it was strong enough to affect adversely the superbly trained brains of the administrators. The cream of French and British universities was used to making reasoned decisions on the basis of facts, analysis and discussion. But events were suddenly moving so fast that this process could no longer always be carried out, and decisions were having to be made on the basis of personal opinion and emotion. This diversified and confused national policy. For years British and French leaders had tried to curb Hitler by appeasing him. That policy had failed. Then it had been to restrain him by vague threats and to encourage him with vague promises. Now that policy had failed too. Circumstances were not the best in which to work out a new national purpose, to arrange new relationships with foreign countries. All this had to be done at high speed.

During the last days of September there was a vacuum in British and French thinking which Hitler was bound to exploit by proposing peace on his terms after the conquest of Poland. On 11 September Moley Sargent noted: 'There is every indication that the Germans are afraid of a long war and would like to conclude peace on their own terms as soon as possible.' The second supposition was correct, but hardly the first. On 1 October Ivone Kirkpatrick observed in a memorandum initialled by Cadogan and Halifax: 'It is clear that the German Government is about to embark on a peace offensive with the moral of if not active support of Russia.'[1] The Allied aim, he went on, must be to avoid concluding a peace which would enable Hitler to prepare an attack on Britain and France, secondly, to counter Hitler's attempt to throw onto the Allies responsibility for continuing the war.

There was also a third aim of British policy, one which has hitherto received little historical attention. Some British leaders also wished, if possible, to make peace with Germany and end the war. This hardly surprising. The war was going to be a disaster for the human race. Obviously it was desirable to end it. The question was, on whose terms? Clearly there would have to be compromise on both sides. In that case, what would Britain be ready to concede? Would she be ready to take part in another Munich and approve the cession to Germany of certain areas of Poland? There were those who thought that if this were the price of peace, it should be paid.

Kirkpatrick's memorandum continued: 'It is, however, for consideration whether we should not reply that we favour a conference that will achieve a just and lasting settlement.' But the real difficulty, he said, was that Poland and Bohemia had been deprived of their independence, and that because of Hitler's aggressions European governments who wished to improve the standard of living of their peoples were being forced to maintain huge, expensive armed forces and to mobilize at frequent intervals. Kirkpatrick's view was that 'if Germany will give guarantees that these claims will be considered and met, we are prepared to agree to a conference. But in view of the discrepancy between German promises and performance we must insist on solid guarantees, such as the evacuation by Germany before the conference of those areas *which are inhabited by Poles and Czechs.*' (Author's italics.) In other words they would no longer insist on total German evacuation from Poland before opening negotiations.

Here already there was a significant retreat in British policy. As Halifax wrote to Lord Lothian on 27 September: 'Hitherto we have insisted that we could consider no settlement except on the basis of the evacuation of Poland, but with the Soviet in occupation of more than half of that country we obviously cannot emphasize the point about evacuation unless we are prepared to eject the Soviet by force of arms.' [2] Halifax was making a valid point, but he was ignoring another one. The Allies were at war with Germany, but not at war with the Soviet Union. In a peace conference they would be negotiating with Germany, not with Russia, and in the circumstances it was Germany that would have to provide the guarantees to make the conference possible. Was it now British policy not to require Germany to withdraw entirely from the Polish territory they held, but only to withdraw partly?

Halifax admits in his letter that this was one aspect of British policy that would have to be discarded. What then remained? It was hard for the outsider to detect. Ostensibly Britain had gone to war in defence of her Polish ally. But when another country, the Soviet Union, invaded Poland, there was no declaration of war against her. The truth was of course that Britain and France were concerned not so much with Poland as with their own national interests. Halifax admitted that for public consumption the liberation of the Poles and Czechs must remain high on the list of Allied war aims. But, he went on, 'essentially it is a fight against a whole conception of policy, almost against a state of mind. We are fighting for intangibles and imponderables.'

It was not woolly thinking. Halifax did know what he meant, even though not many other people did, and even though he felt it necessary to explain himself to Lothian, one of his ambassadors: 'Our main objective remains the same. Put colloquially, it is that Hitler must not be allowed to get away with it again. If that were to happen he would be confirmed in power, and life in Europe would continue to be as unendurable as it has been these last two or three years. In one way or another his latest adventure must be shown a failure and a disaster for Germany, so that the German people will resolve not to allow themselves to be led into such errors again.'

But if Britain was now prepared to concede Germany territory in Central Europe, in another sphere her attitude had hardened. Hitler's invasion of Bohemia in March was a personal betrayal of what he had told Chamberlain at Munich, that he had no further territorial demands to make in Europe. His invasion of Poland had compounded the betrayal and infuriated Chamberlain *personally* so much that it was soon an axiom of British policy that, whatever terms for peace might be negotiated, they were useless if guaranteed only by the word of Hitler. Removal of Hitler became a non-negotiable demand from which the Allies never budged.

Chamberlain wrote to his sister Ida: 'To my mind it is essential to get rid of Hitler. He must either die, or go to St Helena, or become a real public works architect, preferably in a "home".' [3] But the Prime Minister's insistence on this did not necessarily rule out all plans for peace. There were several ways in which Hitler might disappear. He might voluntarily retire. (There were actually people in authority who believed this was a possibility.)[4] He might be edged out of office by 'moderates' in the Nazi Party, led by Hermann Göring. He might be deposed in a military *coup d'état*. Halifax wrote on 27 September, 'It would be best if the German people could realize the error before it is too late, and contrive themselves to throw off the yoke.'[5] To his logical English mind it seemed unimaginable that a well-educated nation should support such an unbalanced rabble-rouser. But he was wrong. They did support him. As Chamberlain wrote uncomprehendingly in December, 'All accounts agree in reporting that the people there are still devoted to Hitler.'[6] The evidence of Hitler's popularity was so strong that logically the British leaders had to accept it. Even so, emotionally they continued to believe the German people would come round to their point of view. It was an example of the triumph of heart over head.

Previous chapters have shown that after 1 September the main channel of communication between London and Berlin was not a diplomat but a private citizen, a Swede named Birger Dahlerus. His attempt to avert the 3 September declaration of war is outlined in published documents as well as in his book *The Last Attempt*. Giving evidence in 1946 before the Nuremburg Tribunal on behalf of his friend Hermann Göring, Dahlerus felt obliged to explain his dubious role: 'At the time I thought I could contribute something to preventing a new war. I could definitely prove that nothing was left undone by the British Government to prevent war. But had I known what I know today, I would have realized that my efforts could not possibly succeed.'[7]

The Tribunal accepted this statement: 'Dahlerus of course had no knowledge at that time of the decision which Hitler had secretly announced on 22 August, nor of the German military directives for the attack on Poland, which were already in existence.' Norman Birkett, an eminent British lawyer and one of the judges at Nuremburg, even agreed to write an introduction to Dahlerus's book in which he describes him as 'an honest man' and as 'one actuated by the highest motives'.[8] The impression was given that Dahlerus, while perhaps a little naïve and over-generous in his affection for Göring, had done his level best as an impartial mediator to avert the catastrophe, and that the British Government had done well to make use of his services.

It is only after the opening of the British official papers for 1939 that certain inconsistencies emerge in Dahlerus's words and behaviour. In particular it is hard to understand how he could honestly have called his book *The Last Attempt*, ending as it does on 4 September, for at the end of that month he made another far more strenuous attempt to bring Britain and Germany together. Its details are interesting in that they show not only the extent of Britain's resolution to carry on with the war if necessary, but also the conditions under which she might have been ready to make peace.

Göring kept in touch with Dahlerus during the early days of September and spoke to him in Stockholm by telephone. On 18 September Dahlerus visited the British Minister there, Sir E. Monson, to report Göring's attitude. Göring had spun Dahlerus a tissue of lies: 'The Germans and Russians had now reached the line agreed upon between the governments and did not intend to advance any further . . . Germany would insist on the retention of the whole of the Corridor, Danzig and Upper Silesia. And Russia would probably have to be given Vilna as a reward for her services. In return Germany would agree to disarmament and to give suitable guarantees . . .' [9]

The British were sceptical of Göring's assurances. Too often in the recent past the Nazis had deceived them, and we know now that this was yet another attempt to do exactly that. In the words of Norman Birkett, 'The efforts of Göring were not those of the single-minded seeker after peace, but were rather in conformity with the usual Nazi practice of seeking to isolate an opponent to make the task of destruction easier and more certain.'[10] But at the time the British felt there was a chance that Göring was 'on the level' and that this chance could not be ignored.

Dahlerus's message from Stockholm was the first move of a campaign to 'sell' Göring to the British as an acceptable and respectable alternative to Hitler. On 10 September Göring sent Dahlerus letters from two R A F prisoners of war shot down during leaflet raids over Germany. He gave his word that the men were being looked after. Dahlerus passed the letters on to London as an impressive proof of Göring's good faith and general humanity. He told Monson that Göring 'in contrast to the rest of the German Government was absolutely trustworthy and would stake his reputation on the observation by the German Government of terms, and any truce negotiated by himself personally. In this he would receive the support of the German people who were tired of war . . . Herr Hitler's popularity was declining, as the German people had never believed he would allow them to be involved in world war . . . Göring was the only man possessing everyone's full confidence . . .' [11]

One wonders who was Dahlerus's source of information for such sweeping statements, presumably Göring himself. But however guarded the welcome his words received in London, it seems clear that they were not rejected outright. Firstly, they were what the decision-makers wanted to hear and believe. Many of them knew Göring personally. A few had even hunted with him. They liked his bluff manner, his sense of humour, his relish of the good things of life.

Hermann Rauschning was a German émigré who had until 1935 been President of the Danzig Senate and a friend of the Nazi leaders. On 14 November he made a wise statement to Campbell Stuart: 'It is easy to see why the British like Göring. He is almost the only leading Nazi with *Kinderstube* [manners]. To put it crudely, he does not pick his teeth during diplomatic talks like Herr Hitler. But one must not forget that Göring was in the thick of everything Nazism has committed. He has inspired the Reichtag fire, as admitted in conversation to Dr Rauschning. He was responsible for the shooting of conservatives and right-wing Nazis on the thirtieth of June [1934]. He represents the spirit of the present régime just as much as Hitler.' [12]

It may well be that Göring felt inclined to end the war that September. There may well have been a difference of opinion between Göring the 'moderate' and 'wild men' like Goebbels and Ribbentrop. But how wide was that difference? Rauschning felt that British intelligence was exaggerating it, and he was right. There is no evidence to show that Göring was prepared to jeopardize his position with Hitler to bring the war to an end. True, he may have used Dahlerus to dangle the bait of Hitler's removal before the British, to draw them out and test their reactions to the idea of making peace with a Germany still Nazi but ruled by more 'moderate' men. But he would hardly have done such a thing without keeping Hitler informed. Loyalty to the Führer united all Nazis and most Germans. For the Nazi leaders themselves to challenge this unity was unthinkable and there is no evidence that Göring was ready to do this.

Göring was a more comprehensible figure than the others. His bad qualities – his flamboyance, vanity, greed and arrogance – showed him as more of a human being than men like Hitler, the aesthete and fanatic. He had none of that Hitlerian intensity which mesmerized so many Germans, but which the English found almost physically repugnant. To them the earthiness of Göring was a welcome relief. The French on the other hand had no liking for such a type. Chaim Weizmann was told in Paris that the British were making a mistake by trying to divide Hitler from the German people: 'They say that to all intents and purposes the Nazis *are* Germany. They are the directing influence and the only people who count. Hitler can rely on millions of younger men, and it is only among those over forty that criticism of the régime exists.' [13] A Germany ruled by Göring, they said, 'would be as terrible a menace as Hitler Germany, indeed worse'.

It would be unfair to Halifax to suggest that he received Göring's approaches with any great enthusiasm. He wired to Monson in Stockholm: 'I would not wish him [Dahlerus] to come on a vain errand and I must therefore say at once that I can conceive of no peace offer which the German Government are likely in present circumstances to make that could even be considered by His Majesty's Government or the French Government . . .' [14] But this reaction was not quite as negative as it sounded, for Halifax went on to suggest that Dahlerus find out from Göring the nature of his peace proposal, whereupon Britain 'would be able to examine it and state definitely their attitude'. As for British war aims, the only indication Monson was empowered to give was a repetition of Chamberlain's 20 September statement in the House of Commons that Britain's aim was 'to redeem Europe from the perpetually recurring fear of German aggression and to enable the peoples of Europe to preserve their independence and their liberties'.

En route for Berlin, Dahlerus stopped over at Oslo to speak to his friend George Ogilvie Forbes, the former Counsellor at the British Embassy in Berlin, now attached to the Legation in Norway. Forbes passed on Halifax's discouraging message, to which Dahlerus replied that initially his only plan was 'to test the water' in Berlin, to find out if there were any ideas for peace that he thought Britain and France would even consider. If there were not, he said, he would not pursue the matter any further for the present and would return to Sweden.[15] But if there were he would come at once to London.

He thought it might be possible to 'keep Hitler out of it' by confining the discussions to Göring, who would meet in some neutral country a British negotiator who spoke German and knew 'soldiers' language'. If Göring was able to confront Hitler with the *fait accompli* of an agreement, his position would be strengthened and Hitler would find it hard to reject the terms. Dahlerus said that Göring had been telephoning him 'every other day' to ask if the British were showing some signs of willingness to talk peace. It was a strange idea that he was suggesting, that Göring was prepared to go over Hitler's head to discuss peace – an act little short of treason. A day or two earlier he had told Monson that Hitler's popularity was declining, but to Forbes he said exactly the opposite, that 'he considered Hitler's position in Germany to be stronger today than it was a fortnight ago, owing to the speedy occupation of Poland'.[16] In that case one wonders how Dahlerus can seriously have believed that Göring would defy his Führer.

And indeed it transpired that there was no question whatever of 'keeping Hitler out of it'. Two days later Dahlerus had his talk in Berlin and was received by Göring and Hitler together. The account of their talk made by Hitler's interpreter Dr Schmidt reveals no difference of opinion whatever between Hitler and Göring. The gist of the German message lay in Hitler's parting words: 'The British can have peace if they want it, but they will have to hurry.' He and Göring spoke in a thoroughly aggressive way towards Britain and was full of hate towards Poland. There was no sign of conciliation.[17]

At Nuremburg Dahlerus claimed he had 'discussed with Hitler on what conditions he would be prepared to make good the harm he had done to Poland, and make peace'.[18] But Dr Schmidt's account makes no mention of such bold speaking. According to him, Dahlerus's opening remark was 'that the British were such great egoists that they were now deliberating, in view of the difficulties of the present situation, how they could extricate themselves from the whole affair'. He said that Forbes had told him that 'Poland was considered lost' and that for the British 'it was now a matter of at least saving their own skins'.

Such talk was of course grist to the mill of Hitler who replied by deploring the way Britain had consistently interpreted as weakness his considerateness and forebearance'. Their declaration of a three-year war was another example of their provocations. Hitler 'would soon wage the war toward the West also in such a way as to stun the British. He had destroyed Poland in three weeks. The British should stop and think what could happen to them in three months . . . An abysmal hatred for Britain was gradually spreading among the German people.'

Dahlerus repeated that 'British egoism' was the best hope for peace, but quoted Forbes to emphasize the need for a formula by which Britain could save face. She could not afford to be seen to be abandoning her Polish ally completely. But even such a weak, compromising approach, unrepresentative of the British Government's attitude, was unacceptable to Hitler. 'Germany had won a victory in Poland that was without precedent in history,' he pointed out. 'In fourteen days he had completely destroyed a country of 36 million inhabitants which had an army of forty-five divisions [this was incorrect], in part well-equipped, and whose soldiers had fought bravely. In these circumstances the Führer had no intention of allowing anyone to interfere in the Polish question . . . a condition of peace discussions would be to allow him a completely free hand with regard to Poland.' Göring added that the Polish question was in any case now settled not only by Germany, but also by Russia.

Hitler told Dahlerus he was prepared to give 'assurances' to the countries of western Europe, including Belgium and Holland. 'The West Wall was the unalterable western border of Germany,' he said. (This would have sounded strange to anyone who had read *Mein Kampf*, where there are references to 'a final reckoning' and 'a last decisive struggle' against France.)[19] He now claimed that 'Germany did not wish any conquests in the West or in the

Balkans. In the Balkans she had only commercial interests.' But he planned to 'reincorporate' the former German and Austrian parts of Poland, to 'reshuffle' and 'resettle' the rest. If he could do this, an 'asylum' could also be created for the Jews. The whole operation would remedy 'the tremendous backwardness and demoralization of Poland'. He spoke of his 'awful impressions of Poland during his trips to the front'. It was madness that 'now for this wretched country millions of Englishmen and Germans were to lay down their lives'. And 'it was insolence for such a debased country as Poland to dare to turn against a country like Germany'.

Six and a half years later Dahlerus recalled his reaction to this outburst in reply to questions from Göring's lawyer, Dr Stahmer: 'I then realized that his aim had been to split Poland and Great Britain, and thus, with the consent of Great Britain, to have the opportunity of occupying Poland without running the risk of being involved in a war with Great Britain and France.' At last Dahlerus had reached the all-too-obvious conclusion. To imagine that he had not reached it earlier is to give him the benefit of a great deal of doubt. One can be generous to him and accept that he was deceived into believing Göring's protestations about peace, about his plan to negotiate behind Hitler's back, but if that was the case Dahlerus was undeceived as soon as he arrived in Berlin. At the 26 September interview it was made plain to him that Hitler's and Göring's aim was identical. It was either to make peace on their terms, conceding next to nothing and confirming their claim to be allowed a free hand in Eastern Europe, or to continue the war of aggression against other European countries. The interview can have left Dahlerus in no doubt.

In that case, had Dahlerus been an honourable mediator and as 'honest man', he must surely have stopped trying to persuade the British to make peace and to place their trust in Göring. Hitler's words, and the tone in which they were phrased, can have left him in no doubt that the Allies could only make peace by abandoning Poland entirely to the tender mercies of Hitler and Stalin. Had he felt — a cruel but arguable point of view — that the Poles must be sacrificed to the cause of world peace, that Britain and France should be ready to break their treaty obligation to Poland rather than plunge the world into years of unforeseeable horror, he could at least have told the British fairly and squarely that this was the position and that this was what negotiation with Hitler would entail.

Instead Dahlerus decided to carry on the deception. He had told Forbes that unless Berlin produced proposals that had a chance of being accepted by the Allies he would return to Sweden. Hitler's plan for peace involved no more than an Allied recognition of his conquests and his own unenforceable 'guarantee' of the *status quo*. Dahlerus resolved to come to London and to present Hitler's proposals not as what they were but as concessions to be grasped as the key to peace. He thus became a knowing accomplice in Hitler's plan to extend his rule over large areas of eastern Europe, to impose on the Slav inhabitants a form of slavery, and eventually to dominate the whole continent.

The day after his interview Dahlerus left Berlin for The Hague where Neville Bland, the British Ambassador, had urgent and specific instructions. Dahlerus, referred to in Foreign Office telegrams sometimes as 'Mr D——' and sometimes as 'person', was to be issued at once with a visa, and his departure to England expedited. It was at this point that a worrying thought crossed Halifax's mind. What would the French think about it all? Officially they knew next to nothing about Dahlerus, and they might perhaps be understandably annoyed if they discovered that their allies were negotiating closely with Hitler behind their backs.

Henry Channon noted in his diary for 28 September: 'Very secret. "The Walrus" is in London . . . No one knows of this. What nefarious message does he bring?' Again on 29 September: 'The now fabulously mysterious "Walrus", i.e., Mr Lazarus, was interviewed secretly yesterday . . . This morning he walked about the Foreign Office openly . . . Also Cadogan had a talk with him and a report of their conversation was given to Lord Halifax, who read it I believe at the War Cabinet. It is the usual personal plea for peace, and again hints at making Göring head of the German State.' For Channon to have known so much and to have taken the risk of recording what he knew in writing shows that the affair was not being treated with deep secrecy. Channon was a Member of Parliament, a Private Secretary to a junior minister but not a member of the Government. The Foreign Office's 'need to know' principle would seem to have been broken in this very important case. It was not long before the French got wind of what was going on.

Identical German proposals were being simultaneously communicated to Britain by an entirely different route. In Ankara the British Ambassador, Hughe Knatchbull-Hugessen, was in touch with the German Ambassador, Franz von Papen, through the Dutch Minister, Philips Christiaan Visser, and on 22 September he reported to Moley Sargent: 'Papen stated that he is in direct correspondence with Hitler behind the backs of Ribbentrop etc. In order to prove this von Papen showed Visser letters from Hitler, though Visser says he did not read them but only looked at them. Papen stated that Hitler had charged him with the express duty of pressing for a conclusion of hostilities and of some arranged peace at the earliest possible moment.' Von Papen himself was apparently strongly in favour of peace. Although he thought Germany might well win the war, he realized 'that there will be nothing much left of anybody at the end of it all'.[20]

Several tempting thoughts and ideas were dangled before the British Ambassador. German troops in Poland were ready to withdraw 'very far indeed'. The Czechoslovak problem too might be solved since 'the Germans would be quite glad to get rid of it'. Most enticing of all was Von Papen's suggestion that it might be possible to get rid of Hitler: 'According to Visser, Papen's first idea was to make Hitler a kind of figurehead President and to constitute a new government, Probably with Göring, which would be prepared to talk sense. Papen as far as I could make out went on to say that Hitler was in an extremely agitated and nervous condition and that it might be possible to take the line with him that he had done all he could for his country and that he had better take a good long rest.' Visser's idea was that Göring and von Papen were leading members of a 'peace party' in Germany that was ready to deal with the Allies certainly behind the backs of Ribbentrop and Goebbels, and possibly behind the back of Hitler.

Von Papen's ideas were of course moonshine, and while the Foreign Office received them sceptically it felt it could not ignore them, especially as they tallied so closely with the suggestions of Dahlerus. 'Papen is an arch-intriguer,' noted Ivone Kirkpatrick. 'I don't believe that he can get rid of Hitler. But personally I should pause before rejecting out of hand a solution on the lines of: disappearance of Hitler, reconstitution of Poland and Bohemia (not necessarily with the same frontiers), disarmament.'

The record shows that many British policy-makers thought this way, that the prime objective was to get rid of Hitler and the secondary objective to restore the countries Hitler had conquered. They would have supported making peace with a Germany which, though no longer ruled by Hitler, was still broadly Nazi, and would have supported this new German Government's claim to incorporate certain areas of occupied Poland and Czechoslovakia as a price for the evacuation of the rest. Kirkpatrick's reference to Bohemia shows that he probably would not have insisted on the re-establishment of Czechoslovakia as such but only on the sovereignty of the Czech lands. The Sudetenland would remain German and Slovakia would remain independent and fascist. Had Germany been ready to consider such ideas, there might well have been the basis for negotiation. But peace on such a basis would have been a far greater surrender than Munich.

Churchill and his group would not have approved such terms, but there were other members of the Cabinet who for years had approved the policy of appeasement and who were still unwilling to face the prospect of a fight to the finish. Samuel Hoare, for instance, apparently took quite seriously the idea that Hitler might be induced to retire. On 7 October he wrote to Lord Lothian in Washington about Hitler's speech of the previous day: 'I had imagined that he would take one of two courses. Either he would make a very attractive peace offer, possibly going to the point of offering to retire himself in the interests of peace . . . or he might have made a truculent speech ending with some kind of ultimatum.'[21] It was indeed an astonishing thing to write. The mind boggles at how a man like Hoare, with his detailed knowledge of Hitler's behaviour over the past years, could imagine such a possibility. The idea of Hitler voluntarily giving up power, especially at such a time, in the midst of the elation of victory, was quite absurd. Hitler had plans for Germany (and not only for Germany) which were only just beginning. They involved a gamble, Hitler admitted as much, and by the end of September it was clear that his first throw was a shattering success. It was not the moment for anyone to try to persuade him to retire to a life of ease in some quiet, luxurious palace.

On 1 October Visser communicated to Britain through Knatchbull-Hugessen a set of peace proposals which he said the Dutch

Government had received from Berlin and which had been suggested by von Papen. They were quite unbelievably generous.
Germany would evacuate the whole of its share of Poland with
the exception of Danzig. Hitler would abdicate. Czechoslovakia
would regain its independence. Von Papen would restore the
monarchy under a Hohenzollern prince, or perhaps a Bavarian
prince (von Papen was a Catholic). Visser said 'the above proposals had Herr Hitler's consent'. The British Ambassador asked
London what he was to say to these ideas, and an immediate and
'most secret' telegram was sent instructing him to say nothing.
This was as well, for the next day Visser had changed his tune.
He was now sure 'that Herr Hitler will disappear and agrees to
the importance of getting rid of all the Nazi leaders except Field
Marshal Göring, whom he puts in a different category and regards
as a necessary bridge between one régime and another'.[22]

Considering the inconsistency and the sheer improbability of
von Papen's claims, they were treated with remarkably deep
attention in London. They were too good to be true, but London
was apparently inclined to grasp even at such vague straws as
these. Any hope was better than none. Von Papen had apparently
told Visser that Hitler would be removed, either with or without
Hitler's consent. But in his memories von Papen gives a different
picture of his intentions. He writes that his plan was merely to
restore Poland and Czechoslovakia, not to remove Hitler at all.
On the contrary he writes: 'I hoped I would be able to persuade
him [Hitler] that a Polish buffer state would only be an advantage,
and that an allied Czechoslovakia would be sufficient guarantee
for Germany's security.'[23] This assumes that von Papen knew
nothing of Hitler's plan to colonize the East, or at least that he
thought he could talk him out of it. In either case his schemes
emerge as at best very silly, at worst as yet another attempt to
confuse the Allies and to tempt them into revealing the price they
were prepared to pay for peace. London was wise enough not to
fall into this trap at least.

Although von Papen's peace proposals did not materialize,
there is evidence that they struck a chord in the heart of many
British officials, including that of the Prime Minister, and induced
them to believe that there was a strong political movement in
Germany ready to undermine Hitler. Chamberlain wrote to his

sister on 10 September of how the declaration of war had been delayed by 'the secret communications that were going on with Göring and Hitler through a neutral intermediary [Dahlerus]'.[24] On 11 November he wrote again of the necessity to remove Hitler: 'His entourage must also go, with the possible exception of Göring who might have some ornamental position in a transitional government.'[25] There is a striking similarity between this phrase and the suggestion made by Visser and von Papen in Ankara.

Finally, Chamberlain mentions his hunch that the war would be over by the spring: 'It won't be by defeat in the field but by German realization that they can't win and that it isn't worth their while to go on getting thinner and poorer when they might have instant relief and perhaps not have to give up anything they really care about. My belief is that a great many Germans are near that position now and that their number, in the absence of any striking military successes, will go on growing with increasing rapidity.' In the words of Iain Macleod, one of Chamberlain's biographers, 'What was not sound, but also never publicly stated, was his private view that Nazism might conceivably be destroyed and Hitler overthrown without a frontal clash between Germany and the Allies.'[26]

Dahlerus's and von Papen's efforts did create a certain optimism in London as the time approached for Hitler to make his offer. Frank Roberts noted, 'These telegrams all support the suggestion that some acceptable peace offer might come from the Papen–Göring team, if they can persuade or compel Hitler.'[27] The main hope was pinned on Dahlerus who on 27 September, the day after his talk with Hitler and Göring, left Berlin for The Hague. The British Ambassador Neville Bland had instructions to issue him at once with a visa, and he arrived in London to an atmosphere of great expectation. On 29 September he met Chamberlain and Halifax, but his main business discussions were with Alexander Cadogan, the non-political Head of the Foreign Office, a man like all civil servants outside the limelight but with immense influence over Britain's policy. No details of this talk have appeared in Dahlerus's book or in published British documents.

Hitler's terms for peace, as outlined by Dahlerus to Cadogan, bore little resemblance to what Hitler had actually told him three days earlier. Dahlerus censored all the bombast, arrogance and threats which Hitler had uttered, and presented the 'proposals' in an exaggeratedly reasonable light. The gist of his message was a repetition of Göring's offer to fly to a neutral country to meet someone who spoke German and 'with whom he could speak as soldier to soldier', someone like General Ironside.[28] The basis of their discussion would be, according to Cadogan's notes dated 4 October,

> an 'independent' Poland in economic vassalage to Germany and subject to military restrictions to prevent her being a threat to Germany. Germany would occupy the old Reich frontier in Poland. Germany would say nothing about Poland on the other side of the demarcation line – she was not interested in that. Frontier rectification in Slovakia – particularly in that region where Poland encroached last March. Disarmament. A colonial settlement, either by restoration of former German colonies or by 'compensation'. No war aims against France or England. No territorial claims in Europe and particularly not in the Balkans. This to be subject to 'suitable guarantees'. Ready to guarantee French and British empires. Settlement of Jewish question by using Poland 'as a sink in which to empty the Jews'.[29]

These ideas, even after being watered down and dressed up by Dahlerus, sound horrific enough in Cadogan's version. They provided no long-term security for Britain, France and the rest of democratic Europe against Hitler's recurring aggressions. In the short term they meant abandoning the Poles and the Jews. In the circumstances Cadogan's answer was a strange one: 'All of this, or some of it, *may be very nice*,' he wrote [author's italics], 'but we cannot trust the word or the assurance or the signature of the present rulers of Germany.' It would be wrong to say that he reacted positively to Dahlerus's message or that he gave him any reason for encouragement. But equally he did not make it clear to Dahlerus that such a settlement, particularly the abandonment of Poland, was out of the question.

'He really hadn't much to say. He's like a wasp at a picnic, one can't beat him off,' wrote Cadogan about Dahlerus in his diary.[30] But where Cadogan failed was in allowing Dahlerus to leave this important interview believing that a settlement was still attainable, that the terms themselves provided the basis for negotiation, that the real stumbling block was the British mistrust of Hitler. It was on this problem that Dahlerus concentrated his mind during the night of 29 September, and when he saw Cadogan again the next morning he was ready with a brainwave.

He told Cadogan that he did not think Hitler could be removed, but that 'if it was impossible to accept the word of the German Government, would it be possible to accept the word of the German people expressed by a plebiscite?' The Germans would be asked to vote on whether they favoured independence for the Poles and Czechs. Dahlerus expected that they would accept this idea. Then, Dahlerus asked Cadogan, 'would it not be more difficult for a Nazi régime, even supposing that it survived the plebiscite, later to follow a policy that was in direct conflict with what the whole German people had been allowed to proclaim?'

Cadogan said he felt this was all too hypothetical, as indeed it was. Presumably the Nazi leaders were to agree to hold such a plebiscite as one of the terms of a cease-fire. But this would leave many open questions. Would they honour their pledge and even hold the plebiscite? The British had no reason to trust that they would. Would it be an honest vote? Elections organized by dictatorial régimes are seldom in any way meaningful. Which way would the vote go? A majority of Germans might vote against relinquishing their recent conquests. Even if the vote was held and went the right way, would that really force Hitler to obey it? Would he not be able to find some excuse? And even if he obeyed it, in what way would he obey it? He could never afford to evacuate the Polish and Czech areas completely. He would have to keep some military or security forces there to ensure that the two countries did not immediately rearm, join, mobilize and fight against him. It is hard to believe that Cadogan was impressed by Dahlerus's plan which was probably aimed at giving the British the face-saving formula which, he believed, was all they really required.

Again Cadogan, while not accepting this idea, did not reject it. He told Dahlerus that 'if he were able to let us know what they [the German Government] were prepared to do in this direction I was sure His Majesty's Government would be ready to consider that and decide whether such procedure would afford any prospect of reaching an agreement'. It was a dangerous thing to say, for it left Dahlerus with the impression that his idea might well be accepted. At 2 p.m. that same day (30 September) Dahlerus again left London for Berlin. He was to play a part in forming the peace terms which Hitler was known to be preparing.

It was clear that Hitler's peace offensive would make diplomatic difficulty for the Allies. Neutral countries were alarmed by the first month of the war. In spite of the muted press reports, the suppression of the full horror being inflicted on the Poles, most neutrals appreciated that a new and particularly horrible war had just started, that it might well spread and engulf them too if allowed to continue. Governments were trying frantically to remain neutral in their attitudes to the two warring sides, to blur the moral issue and the undoubted fact that Hitler's attack on Poland was an act of aggression.

Hitler's diplomacy had to this extent succeeded. The postures of the two sides were now reversed. A month earlier it was the Germans were were angry and aggressive, the British and French who were conciliatory. Now the Germans had achieved their immediate aim and could afford to seek peace, thereby appearing to be generous. The Allies were the angry and the outraged. They were the ones now who made the warlike noises, while Hitler offered the hand of peace. It was inevitable that when the Allies rejected this hand, which they had to do, they would lose the sympathy of some and be blamed for prolonging the war.

Ivone Kirkpatrick noted on 1 October that one of Britain's aims must be to 'counter the German effort to prove that the Allies will be responsible for continuing the war', and it emerges that Britain was particularly worried about the effect of the 'peace offensive' on Italy and Spain. 'As you know, I have always been more afraid of a peace offer than of an air raid,' Chamberlain wrote to his sister Ida on 8 October.[31] On 1 October Ciano was in Berlin, and he had a $2\frac{1}{2}$-hour interview with Hitler. Kirkpatrick thought that the visit would mean Italian involvement in the German offer, and that Hitler's aim was 'if possible to secure from Italy an assurance that she will come into the war on Germany's side should the peace effort fail'.[32] Britain was very worried at the prospect of Mussolini again offering himself as intermediary. Cadogan noted, 'If Signor Mussolini were cast for the role, and we turned down the peace proposals, that *might* push him into the German camp.'

Moley Sargent also assumed that Italy would support the

German offer since, faced with the dilemma of supporting Germany and risking disruption or of abandoning her ally, she was bound to do everything to end the war. He noted on 13 September:

The Germans are most unlikely after their military successes to be ready to propose any solution which would be acceptable to Poland, and we might therefore be in a better position with the Italians if we were to limit ourselves to the condition that the proposals must have regard to the independence and the vital interest of Poland, and not insist on the evacuation of Poland before beginning to negotiate. The Italians supported by the Germans would naturally argue that it would be quite impossible to evacuate Poland before negotiations, since in that event the Poles would be certain to reject even the most favourable terms, and the victories won by German arms would therefore be rendered fruitless. On the other hand if we do not insist on the prior evacuation of Poland, we shall be abandoning the condition on which we insisted before the outbreak of war and which the press under our inspiration has been repeating since, and this would certainly be regarded in many quarters as clear evidence of weakness. If the Polish Government insist on the prior evacuation of Polish territory, we should of course have to support them, but we might leave them to raise this issue first.[33]

So important to Britain were the new cordial relations with Italy that there was actually talk of breaking treaty obligations so as to preserve them. 'We are through Loraine in very close touch with Ciano,' wrote Halifax to Lothian. The Foreign Office felt it had accomplished a superb coup by keeping Italy out of the war and it was prepared to go to some lengths to consolidate this gain – a feeling which was not shared in France, where strong forces actually favoured provoking Italy and launching a preventative war against her.[34]

Italy was indeed steering a perilous course, trying to keep on good terms with both sides in the conflict. Offended by Hitler's decision to sign an agreement with Bolshevik Russia without even consulting him, Italy had assured Britain and France that she would not fight against them when war broke out, then made a genuine effort to prevent the outbreak of war. Publicly Hitler had to pretend that Italy's refusal to fight meant nothing to him, but privately he was angry with her for what was in fact a breach of the Pact of Steel. On 3 September he had sent Mussolini a note polite enough in tone but implying that he resented the betrayal.

'Even though we now march down different paths, Destiny will yet bind us one to the other,' Hitler wrote.[35] Mussolini replied that 'he had to disagree most emphatically' with the first part of this sentence. 'On the contrary, agreement was complete as to the road and the goal, and he had done everything, especially in the military field, that the Führer now wished him to do.'[36] In the days that followed Mussolini and Ciano were at pains, while congratulating Hitler on his military victories, to urge upon him the need for a 'generous settlement'. 'With a new [Polish] government it would be possible to conclude peace if an honourable offer were extended,' said Mussolini on 9 September to the German Ambassador in Rome, Hans George von Mackensen.[37] On 15 September Ambassador Attolico told Weizsäcker in Berlin of the Duce's desire for 'a really magnanimous offer of peace'.[38] On 19 September, two days after Russia had invaded Poland, Ciano told von Mackensen that 'he was particularly gratified to learn that Russia's action was entirely within the programme agreed upon'.[39] The remark drew attention to Italy's dislike of the pact with the Soviet Union, and to her resentment against Germany for concluding it without prior consultation.

At his 1 October meeting with Hitler, Ciano pressed the Führer for details of the Polish rump state to be set up as a condition of peace. How large would it be? What population would it have?[40] Hitler was evasive, as well he might be, for only six days earlier Stalin had told him of his objection in principle to any residual Poland. At such a stage clearly Russia was the more important ally. Hitler said he wanted to have as little to do with Poland as possible. He would be glad to be rid of it. But nothing could be finally decided until hostilities were ended, order restored and the area 'pacified'. We know now what Hitler had in mind, but Ciano presumably did not. Ciano was also embarrassed to be told that Britain only signed her final 25 August treaty with Poland because she knew in advance that Italy would not fight.[41] Ciano assured Hitler falsely that England had had no prior information. Schmidt's account of the talk indicates that it contained several such tense moments. Observers were quick to note that the joint communiqué after the talks said nothing about identity of views, simply that Ciano was returning to Rome to inform the Duce of them.

In the circumstances Ciano and Mussolini had less than their usual influence with Hitler, which was never very great. Still Ciano tried to persuade Hitler to be generous, to make concessions that would make peace possible, but he detected that after his great victory Hitler was in no mood for peace. He seems to have analysed Hitler's frame of mind correctly, for he wrote in his diary: 'Today to offer his people a solid peace after a great victory is perhaps an aim which still tempts Hitler. But if in order to reach it he had to sacrifice, even to the smallest degree, what seems to him the legitimate fruits of his victory, he would then a thousand times prefer battle.' His father-in-law Mussolini, he added, 'is somewhat bitter about Hitler's sudden rise to fame'.[42]

General Franco in Spain was similarly urging upon both sides the need to make concessions and end the war. Generally his sympathies lay with Hitler, who had helped him to gain power, but like Mussolini he was anxious at the prospect of world war, vaguely sympathetic to the misfortunes of Catholic Poland, and shocked by the pact with Stalin. On 19 September von Mackensen reported from Rome: 'The *Caudillo* [Franco] had apparently recovered from his initial dismay over German–Russian co-operation, which at first had caused him grave concern because of its impact on the Spanish people, whose memory of the war against the Reds was still too fresh, and whose Church circles moreover always saw in Moscow the Antichrist with whom there could be no compromise.'[43]

On 2 October Franco said at a press conference that Poland could have been saved even after the outbreak of war: 'Every day of victory places the winning side in a position to demand more. Thus, once the Polish front had broken, complete rout was absolutely certain. A wise and prudent policy would have been to save for Poland all that could have been saved. But there was only one way of doing that, by arranging an honourable surrender. By refusing to do this, thousands of lives were uselessly sacrificed.'[44] The next day the Spanish Ambassador in Berlin told Weizsäcker that Spain considered the moment ripe for making peace and was ready to act as mediator. Like Ciano, he emphasized that 'without provision for a rump Poland nothing can be done, because France and especially England must be given the chance to save face'.[45]

Although they pressed him to concede more than he was ready

to in Poland, Spain and Italy assisted him in his peace offensive by the greater pressure they exerted on Britain and France. Allied officials did not expect that Spain would come into the war on Hitler's side for the moment. Some thought that Italy might, but the country that most concerned them was the Soviet Union. Ribbentrop had just returned to Berlin from a second very successful trip to Moscow, where he and Molotov issued a joint declaration calling for the end of the war. Unless peace was now signed, it said, 'England and France will bear responsibility for the continuation of the war, in which case the German and Soviet Governments will consult together on the measures that should be taken'.[46] At first sight it looked suspiciously like an indication that the Soviet Union was about to enter the war on the German side. The British Chiefs of Staff felt the need to plan for this eventuality in which case, they reported, the British position 'though serious would not be desperate'.

No such small encouragement could disguise the peril Britain and France faced militarily, diplomatically and even internally. Panic was in the air, and during late September its flames were fanned by a tiny event, a chance remark made by Hitler in his speech at Danzig on 19 September. 'Do not deceive yourselves,' he said. 'The moment may come when we shall use a weapon which is not yet known and with which we would not ourselves be attacked. Let us hope that we shall not be forced to use this means.' Even now it is not certain what he meant, what this 'secret weapon' was, but his words caused an immediate and horrified reaction in London. 'The implication is,' Halifax noted the next day, 'that if the war continues and economic pressure on Germany is not lifted, Hitler is determined to resort to frightfulness.'[47]

What could this weapon be? The idea of such a thing in the hands of such a man was enough to turn the blood cold. Halifax confessed that the Foreign office had no precise information. Once or twice in conversation Hitler had hinted that he possessed 'some new destructive chemical'. Another report was of 'the construction of two batteries of 24-inch howitzers, which are alleged to be capable of penetrating the Maginot Line to a depth of 75 feet'.

Within a few days reports were reaching London of what was

in store for the Allies once Germany decided to commence the war in earnest. Percy Loraine had heard that, as well as massive air and submarine attacks, there would be 'sabotage by groups of desperadoes landed by parachute in various remote corners of Great Britain and France'. A report from Holland alleged that German agents planned to send germs through the post from neutral countries – lavatory paper, bandages, brushes and bristles which would cause deadly disease in anyone who opened the envelope. Another story told of 'a large and very long tube placed vertically with the mouth just above the earth, connected to motors producing millions of kilowatts'. The electric force would apparently 'dislocate hostile planes and force them to land'. A German general had claimed to possess a 'power ray' which would annihilate the Allied armies. Its only disadvantage was that it worked off the sun and so could not be employed until next summer.[48]

Theories only slightly less fantastic were mentioned in a report of the British Joint Intelligence Sub-Committee, commissioned by the Chiefs of Staff on 5 October. Among 'weapons with which Germany is reported to have been experimenting' the report listed gliding torpedoes, the rays of the sun, inflammable-gas shells, a 'death-ray' and, in the same category of probability, 'the use of atomic energy as a high explosive'. The Sub-Committee had heard 'that a cavity has been made in one of the Hartz mountains and is to be used as a super-cannon which by electrical propulsion would discharge a shell of 100 tons to a distance of 400 miles'. It would need only twelve such shells to destroy London completely.[49]

The report concluded that the weapon Hitler most probably meant was German air power, and most probably it was, if his words meant anything at all. It suggested though that maybe the Luftwaffe would drop bombs containing 'a new or secret explosive', or perhaps chemicals or even germs. Anthrax and psittacosis were diseases that might be caused in this way, though the chief fear was of contamination of milk or water supplies by enemy agents. But this danger had been foreseen and stocks of vaccine and serum were ready. As for chemicals, there were definite rumours of 'a new poisonous gas against which it would be difficult or impossible for us to provide protection'. On 30 September the

British Cabinet authorized dispatch of gas bombs to France, to be used if Germany did so first, and on 11 October the War Office requested facilities to increase production of mustard gas from 310 tons a week to 1,200 tons.[50]

One must not forget that Goebbels was alleging that Britain had supplied poison gas to Poland, and that the Poles had used it during the campaign. Neutral doctors and journalists were persuaded or deluded into supporting this false accusation, and on 12 October the British found it necessary to deny it officially.[51] The lie was aimed at discrediting Britain throughout the world, nothing else, but at the time there were many in London who thought it meant that Germany was about to use gas against them and to claim that she was only retaliating in kind against British and Polish barbarity. Some thought that Germany should be deterred from this by a public announcement that if Germany used gas Britain would too, but others thought that any such announcement would make the Germans think that Britain was about to use gas anyway. Germany might launch a preemptive strike. Such vicious circles of reasoning tormented the decision-makers of London.

The Sub-Committee's report reveals the limited extent of British knowledge of the German chemical industry and other matters vital to British security. But on 12 October Chaim Weizmann had a talk in Zurich with Professor Willstatter, a leading German chemist who had emigrated a few months earlier, and was able to give Britain information of great value. Willstatter said he thought there was no 'secret weapon', certainly not a chemical one, since 'chemical invention in Germany had practically ceased'. For the moment Germany had no gases more destructive than those used in the First World War – mustard gas and arsenic. But these she had in huge quantities, and a large bomb of, say, 500 kilograms would lay waste miles of country und effect the whole population. Gas masks would not be much use against such an attack, certainly not the primitive machines issued to the population at large, and unless the Allies were able to retaliate in kind there was a real danger of Hitler using this horrible weapon.[52]

It was hard for the decision-makers of Britain and France to do their job well while facing the prospect of such disasters. In British eyes the possibility of Russia joining Germany outright was real and terrifying. In Paris American Ambassador Bullitt reported strong fears that Russia was about to support Germany in an attack on France, at least with the Red Army Air Force.[53] The Foreign Office put its heads together to consider how to prevent this. The problem was that Russia had just invaded Poland, Britain's ally. For this same offence Britain and France had declared war on Germany. Why had they not on Russia? On 19 October the British Government explained the limit of its guarantee, that it covered Germany and not Russia,[54] but there were many who saw this as a hypocritical approach. Why should Russia get away with it?

Then there was the question of Poland's territory. On 19 October a British Minister (R. A. Butler) was asked in Parliament, 'What area does he intend to recognize as the boundary of Poland?' Butler's answer was evasive, and no wonder, for Halifax had just written, 'Obviously we cannot emphasize the point about evacuation unless we are prepared to eject the Soviet by force of arms.'[55] One appreciates that were Russia to get the idea that Britain and France planned to throw her out of the lands she had just entered, she would be tempted to help Germany more actively against them.

The British Ambassador in Moscow, William Seeds, therefore, as was his duty, considered whether it might not be necessary to sacrifice part of his Polish ally's interest so as to appease the Soviet Union, whose hostility Britain at this point feared and would scarcely have been able to endure. He pointed out to London that the 'portion of Poland allotted to the Soviet is undoubtedly inhabited to a great extent by a Russian or nearly Russian population, while Hitler's share is entirely non-German. I therefore wonder if it would not be possible to drive a wedge between the two aggressors, and perhaps keep this country [Russia] out of war, by suggesting in some way that our war aims are not incompatible with settlement on ethnographic and cultural lines . . .'[56]

Ivone Kirkpatrick thought there was much force in Seed's argument. The reconstitution of Poland had become 'much more difficult, if not wholly impossible', and for Britain to proclaim her belief in the old boundaries 'would render inevitable a conflict with Russia'. He submitted a map showing that the Soviet–German demarcation line was almost the same as the Curzon Line, from which he deduced that Britain could 'stand for an ethnographical and cultural Poland without treading on Russian toes'. Britain would be wise to take this line, at least until Russia declared herself an enemy.

The woolliness of this argument would not have escaped the keen minds of Whitehall at a less frantic time. No one pointed out, for instance, that Hitler's share of Poland was *not* 'entirely non-German' but contained a large German minority, or that there were several million undoubted Poles in the Soviet-occupied areas. A scholarly note by Daniel Lascelles did point out that if the Soviet Union by reason of its Russian component had the moral right to absorb 'near relations' like the Ukrainians and Byelorussians, then it had also the right by reason of its Turkic component to claim Turkic-inhabited areas of Iran, Afghanistan and China, to weld them into a greater Turkestan. Likewise since there were more Finns in the Soviet Union than in the whole of Finland and Estonia, these countries also could be claimed. Lascelles's conclusion put the matter in a nutshell: 'It is hypocrisy, *though perhaps a necessary hypocrisy*, to suggest that it [the Soviet Union] has any right to expand on ethnological grounds.'[57] Furthermore, Seeds had not mentioned the Soviet expansion into the Baltic States, countries which had no ethnological ties with Russia at all.

In politics, and especially in wartime, morality is the child of necessity. The Allies could not afford to go to war against Russia, they simply had not the strength, so it would have been madness for them to provoke Russia unnecessarily by challenging the demarcation line which the Soviet press was now calling 'the sacred frontier of the Motherland'. It was true that Poland had suffered an injustice at Soviet hands as well as German, but it was one which the Allies for the moment had to ignore. They could not defend even a just cause beyond the limit of their physical strength. The Poles were forced to appreciate that the Allies were their only hope of eventual re-emergence as an independent country. Only by winning the war could they help Poland, and only by a careful and restrained diplomacy could they win the war.

The Allies decided not to challenge the Soviet invasion. What is extraordinary about their behaviour is not this decision itself — that was unavoidable — but the frantic way senior officials cast about for *moral justification* of their necessary concessions to injustice, of their unavoidable betrayals. They would not admit that 'all's fair in war' or that 'the end justifies the means'; such formulae were too crude for them. Their memoranda show them as strangely anxious to convince one another that their moral purity was inviolate, and to this end they adduced arguments whose emptiness would have been apparent to men with half their education. Even when faced with a Hitler or a Stalin, they insisted, the game must be played according to the rules. And so, as Lascelles gently pointed out, they fell victim to hypocrisy.

The Poles were forced to fall in with this line, however much they hated the Russians for stabbing them in the back. In November the new Prime Minister of Poland, Władysław Sikorski, visited London and, although for the moment he had no country, he was received with the ceremony due to a head of government. During his talks he expressed some interesting, prophetic views about Poland's territory: 'If it proves impossible to recover from Russia what has been lost, he aims at finding compensation elsewhere which would at the same time increase Poland's security. In this connection his mind is turning towards East Prussia as the means for finding such compensation.'[58]

The reaction to this idea in London was not encouraging. There were still hopes in London that the German people or the German military were going to throw Hitler out. Clearly they would not if they were going to be deprived of territory by Britain and France. Almost every day messages were reaching London by devious routes from anti-Nazi German generals enquiring about British and French war aims and hinting at a change of government. High hopes were placed in their endeavours. Ever optimistic, Chamberlain and his men over-estimated the power and the resolution of these men, and were unwilling to discourage them with any hint of encroachment on Germany's territory. Ivone Kirkpatrick wrote (25 November): 'I am sorry to see that General Sikorski is toying with the East Prussian ambition which always struck me as rather silly when endorsed by the wilder Polish imperialists before the war.' Within a few years Sikorski's idea was to emerge as less silly. It became the basis for the territorial rearrangement of Central Europe.

Sikorski had another fantastic idea, only this time it really was no more than a dream. At this moment Polish minds were turning towards the idea of some sort of federation with Czechoslovakia, Hitler's other non-German victim. A Foreign Office note reported: 'Sikorski discussed this in general terms with Beneš [the Czechoslovak President], though they did not take matters very far. Both sides made it a condition that their countries should maintain their complete independence, but Sikorski at present seems to favour some kind of visible and symbolic bond between them in the shape of a monarchy.'

This was an amusing enough idea in itself. 'The Poles are incurably romantic,' noted William Strang. But better was to come. During his visit Sikorski toured Scotland and met the Duke of Kent, the King of England's brother. Sikorski was favourably impressed and suggested the Duke as a possible choice for King of the new federation.[59] Was he serious? No one can tell now, for three years later the Duke was killed in an aeroplane crash, and a year after that so was General Sikorski. It seems though that the Duke heard of the idea, even in this tentative form, for years later the Duchess mentioned it to her son, the present Duke.

The knowledge that Hitler was to announce his proposals for peace in the Reichstag on 6 October served only to increase the agony of expectation in London and Paris. For days the German press had pointed out the uselessness of continuing the war. Its line was as simple as ever: Germany wanted nothing from Great Britain and France, nowhere did she threaten British or French interests, all she required was a free hand in Central and Eastern Europe. So why fight? To many Germans the British and French behaviour was incomprehensible, explainable only by some attitude of vindictiveness towards Germany, and to her acquisition of what was rightly hers. Germans wanted peace, but since the great victory in Poland their confidence was boosted and their reluctance to make war diminished.

On 3 October Dahlerus telephoned the British Legation in Stockholm: 'New proposals have been put forward. Shall I come to London?' Again London was cautious, unwilling to give Dahlerus and his German friends the impression that they were ready to end the war. Only he could decide whether his journey was worth while, he was told, but 'if he comes, arrangements will certainly be made to see him at any time convenient'. Again

London was hedging her bets, torn between the need to present a bold front and the natural desire to end the war.

The next day (4 October) Dahlerus told London, this time through Neville Bland in The Hague, that he would not come yet 'as proposals are not yet sufficiently advanced'. Two days later there was a complication. Bland was told: 'I think it is unnecessary to trouble Mr Dahlerus to come over here again. He can surely transmit through you any information he has to give us. *Moreover his movements are causing suspicion in certain quarters.*'[60] (Author's italics.) A danger had crept into the British flirtation with Göring. Dahlerus's activities as go-between had not been communicated formally to Paris. But stories of his comings and goings had begun to reach French ears. Unless something was done quickly there would be mistrust between the Allies. The French could with justice protest vehemently about being kept in the dark. They might even accuse their ally of negotiating with the enemy behind their backs.

On 5 October Halifax noted: 'M. Corbin called to see me this afternoon and, as I had reason to know that M. Daladier had some indirect information as to the visit of the Swedish individual who had been in touch with Field-Marshal Göring, I thought it was desirable to speak to him on this matter myself.'[61] The conversation seems to have been an embarrassing one. Corbin's reaction was one of subtle rebuke. He told Halifax that 'the French had had a similar intimation of a Swede who was prepared to go to Paris. They had however refused him a visa, feeling the great danger on the morale of the army if it should become known that any talks of the nature suggested were in progress.'

Both sides realized how foolish it would be of them to quarrel as they faced the common danger of Hitlerism. The French could have made much of the fact that such information had been withheld from them, but they did not. And still they did not know the whole truth, the full extent of Dahlerus's role as go-between. Halifax explained that the negotiations implied no lack of enthusiasm for the war, far from it, and that their only aim was to drive a wedge between Hitler and Göring. But there was much that he was concealing. The French were not told that senior British officials were discussing possible peace terms among themselves in inter-office memoranda. Only on 16 October, by which time

Dahlerus had been given up as a bad job were any documents about him given to Corbin for transmission to Daladier, and then it was only the last few telegrams, which had been totally discouraging on the British side.

Meanwhile the peace-mongers were being encouraged by the reports of neutral diplomats in Berlin to believe that Hitler's terms would be moderate and generous. Some reports even repeated the ridiculous theory that Hitler was now ready to retire in the interest of peace. 'All Europe awaits the word of peace from London. Woe to them who refuse it. They will one day be stoned by their own people,' proclaimed Hitler's *Völkischer Beobachter*.[62] On 1 October the British Cabinet was told that a whole week had gone by without an attack on Allied merchant shipping and two days later Chamberlain hailed this fact in Parliament as a great victory for the Royal Navy.[63] It was a foolish thing to say. The U-boats had not been swept from the sea; they were withholding their torpedoes on Hitler's orders as part of his peace offensive, to put moral pressure on the Allies. Now if they refused they would be branded as warmongers, if they made peace they would be discredited as cowards. Sargent noted (2 October): 'Once we agree to discuss with Hitler or his emissaries we abandon straight away the strongest argument in our armoury, for we will thereby implicitly have recognized that a permanent peace with Hitler is possible.' There was no way out of this dilemma.

The Italians were here Hitler's full allies. They wanted peace for their own reasons, so they could support the 'offensive' wholeheartedly. The feeling in Rome, as reported to London, was that it was madness to continue the war since, win or lose, the only real winners would be Bolshevik Russia.[64] 'This is the feeling behind all the peace moves in Europe and this country,' noted Frank Roberts, but there was not much enthusiasm for the Italian theory which appeared to lead to the conclusion that almost any peace with Hitler was preferable to continuing the war and furthering communism. As for the Italian Government, after Ciano's 1 October meeting with Hitler it can have been in no doubt that the only peace available was peace on Hitler's terms, which required the abandonment to him of Central and Eastern Europe. On this point Hitler would make no concession, and in trying to persuade the Allies that he would the Italians were simply playing his game.

Oratory can do much to cover up the most abominable of crimes. A superb example of this was Hitler's 6 October speech, which even today can momentarily convice the reader of Hitler's honest desire for peace and universal goodwill.[65] William Shirer was there in the Reichstag, and he writes that it 'sounded — if you overlooked his latest victim — like a decent and reasonable peace'. Of his two enemies he spoke more in sorrow than in anger: 'My chief endeavour has been to rid our relations with France of all trace of ill-will, to make them tolerable for both nations . . . Germany has no further claims against France . . . I have devoted no less effort to the achievement of understanding between Germany and England, indeed of friendship between our countries. Nowhere have I ever acted contrary to British interest.'

So long as war continued Hitler was resolved to wage it humanely: 'In the war with Poland I endeavoured to restrict aerial warfare to objectives of so-called military importance.' He hoped sincerely that the Red Cross and the Geneva Convention would restrain wicked men from the worst horrors, even though 'Mr Churchill and his friends may well interpret these opinions as weakness or cowardice'. What was needed was a conference 'to tackle the solution before millions of men are uselessly sent to their deaths'. This could be done only 'if all the nations inhabiting this continent decide to work together'.

What then of the Poles and the Jews, those peoples whom Hitler was resolved to destroy — a process which had already begun? Here Hitler could offer no more than vague hints that something might be arranged for them at the conference. They would discuss 'an attempt to reach a solution and settlement of the Jewish problem' and 'the formation of a Polish state'. Urgent measures were needed 'to alleviate the terrible distress prevailing there [in Poland]'.

But lest anyone conclude that he really was ready to make serious concessions as the price of peace, Hitler pointed out quite bluntly that the Polish problem could 'perhaps be discussed but never solved at a conference table'. What he wanted was a completely free hand: 'The states of Europe should be grateful that Russia and Germany are prepared to turn this hotbed into a zone of peaceful development and that these two countries will assume the responsibility and bear the burdens inevitably involved. The

Reich undertakes this task in no imperialistic spirit, for it will take some 50 to 100 years to fulfil it.' In the long run all Europe would benefit from Germany's selfless effort in agreeing to govern the 'barbarous' Polish lands. Hitler concluded, 'At this moment I can only thank God for so wonderfully blessing us in our struggle for our rights. I beg him that he may lead us and all other nations to the right way, so that both Germany and all Europe may once more obtain the blessing of peace.'

Chamberlain wrote to his sister (8 October): 'I was I confess anxious when I read Hitler's clever speech and especially when the first American reaction was reported, viz. that he had made a very attractive set of proposals and that his tone had been surprisingly friendly to Great Britain.'[66] But it can only have been the very naïve who were taken in by Hitler's sweet words. William Shirer wrote in his diary (6 October): 'I doubt very much if England and France will listen to these "proposals" for five minutes.'[67] Some of his colleagues disagreed, not because they in any way believed Hitler's protestations but because they thought it might be smart of the Allies to make peace and leave Germany and Russia to come to inevitable blows along their new frontier.

Chamberlain writes, 'I refused to think about the speech that night but next morning I was clear in my own mind that it offered no real advance in mind or spirit towards a real peace and that it must be rejected.'[68] The official British historian writes that 'the War Cabinet did not even consider the possibility of accepting it',[69] but this is to oversimplify just a little, for although the British never considered acceptance, they certainly made heavy weather over the rejection. At the 7 October Cabinet Meeting Halifax said 'there could be no two opinions as to the unsatisfactory nature of the speech itself, nevertheless time was required for consideration as to the form of the reply'. The Dominions and the United States would also have to be consulted. Again it was not the proposals themselves that were the stumbling block. In Chamberlain's words, 'the difficulty is that you cannot believe anything Hitler says'.[70] The War Cabinet was clear enough that its primary aim was to get rid of Hitler, but it feared that to proclaim this would be counter-productive, that it would simply unite Germany around him. 'What was required,' the Cabinet decided, 'was a statement ending on a note of enquiry rather than on a direct rejection. Hitler should be left with the choice between answering our questions and starting war in earnest in the West.'[71]

This was all very well, but again it gave the impression that the Allies were hesitating. The British Government's public reaction to the speech was critical, describing the proposals as vague and pointing out that no reparation was offered to the countries Hitler had wronged. But it went on to promise that the proposals would be 'carefully examined'. And so the position remained for six whole days, while the Government consulted and worked out the precise terms of the rejection, leaving the door open to all kinds of speculation about British weakness.

Dr Goebbels had millions of copies of the speech, or at least the more friendly parts of it, prepared in leaflet form in English and French ready to be dropped by air to show Hitler's enemies how reasonable he was being. In Britain the exercise proved un-necessary, for the speech was printed in full in *The Times*, but in France it was censored. French soldiers at the front were showered with leaflets. 'Frenchmen! On the orders of London your press has been forced to conceal from you the true contents of this speech,' they began.[72] Georges Bonnet, a Cabinet Minister, claims that not even he was able to get hold of a copy of the speech until much later.[73] He and de Monzie complain that Daladier rejected the proposals without consulting the Council of Ministers. 'He continues the war because he is unable to stop it. The ideological machine will not be halted by mere logic,' writes de Monzie,[74] but of course these were the two chief defeatists and most of the French leaders were of sterner stuff. The censored press, men-tioning only the fact of the offer without any of the detail, was naturally hostile to it. On 8 October *Le Temps* wrote 'Hitler is beating the air . . . While affirming his desire to end war, he demands that we should bow before the *fait accompli* of the destruction of Poland . . . We are amazed at such impertinence.'

In America the feeling was the same. The *New York Times* called the proposals 'barrack-room statesmanship' and even the anti-British *New York Enquirer* called Hitler 'without doubt one of the most unconscionable liars in the records of history'. But whatever his sympathies, Roosevelt was under pressure to help Hitler in his peace offensive. The American press was hinting that he should. On 7 October he wrote to Marvin McIntyre: 'If you believe this morning's papers you will expect me to be in Berlin talking peace with Hit next Monday morning. Fortunately you agree with me about what one reads in the papers.'[75] Clearly any offer by Roosevelt to intervene would be harder for the Allies to reject, and the attempt to enlist him was part of the general German plan to brand Britain and France as warmongers.

On 8 October senior State Department officers held a long meeting to consider their attitude to the proposals. While some thought the time was ripe for America to step in, the majority appreciated that whatever peace might be concluded Hitler was not going to give up Austria, Czechoslovakia or Poland, that Britain and France would probably be forced to continue the war and that it was unfair to put them in a position of having to reject an American suggestion.[76] The next day the German Government announced publicly that they would accept an American offer to mediate and attend a peace conference in Washington, an idea which was supported by Belgium under threat of German invasion and by Finland under strong Soviet pressure. In Italy the *Giornale d'Italia* (8 October) wrote that Hitler's speech 'provides a clear framework for stability in Europe and the foundations of peace'.[77]

The Soviet press supported Hitler's plan in language almost identical to that of Hitler and Mussolini. Moscow's *Izvestiya* agreed with *Giornale d'Italia* that it 'provides a realistic and practical base for talks aimed at hastening the conclusion of peace'. Poland was castigated as a country 'based on lawlessness and subjection of all peoples who inhabit Poland, not excluding the Polish people'. Like Hitler, *Izvestiya* took pride in Soviet and German selflessness in 'taking upon themselves the task of restoring order and peace in the territory of former Poland'. The country's amazingly swift collapse had proved, claimed *Izvestiya*, that it was incapable of sustaining life. The implication was that Poland had disappeared by spontaneous implosion, not by the violent assault of her two neighbours, and that for the Allies to try to restore her was a useless and dangerous undertaking, 'a senseless shedding of blood'.

From all over the world pressure was building up against the war and in favour of anything that would stop the fighting. The world seemed mesmerized into grasping the short-term benefits of negotiation and ignoring the prospect of a Hitler-dominated Europe which would have been the inevitable result of British and French acquiescence. As the tension increased relations between the Allies were bound also to suffer. On 5 October Corbin had his awkward interview with Halifax about Dahlerus, and on 8 October Corbin was again at the Foreign Office, this time with criticism of the British handling of Hitler's speech.

Cadogan reports that Corbin told him: 'There was some uneasiness in Paris as to the procedure that we were adopting in regard to Herr Hitler's speech. He referred to the press reports to the effect that His Majesty's Government were giving careful consideration to Herr Hitler's proposals and that a statement by the Prime Minister might be expected on Wednesday. He feared that this was making too much of Herr Hitler's speech, which in fact contained no proposals and was not really deserving of attention.' What worried Corbin and the French Government was the long delay, six whole days, before Chamberlain was due to answer. During this time 'Hitler's proposals would be discussed in the press and would gradually grow in importance'. Cadogan felt that on the contrary the passage of time would show merely how impractical the proposals were, to which Corbin said he still believed it would be better to pass over in silence such a nebulous and unsatisfactory offer.[78]

A third bone of contention was the different British and French attitudes to Göring, to the possibility of his succeeding Hitler. As we have seen, this idea was fed to the British leaders with some success by Dahlerus. Had it been possible the British might have accepted it as a basis for ending the war. But the French would not have. Corbin said, 'He doubted very much whether the German régime under [Göring] would differ very much from what it was at present', to which Cadogan replied, 'I could not help believing that the disappearance of Herr Hitler would produce an immediate and possibly favourable change in the situation.'

Fourthly there was the problem of war aims, and it was here that British and French policy was in danger of diverging seriously and to the detriment of the war effort. What were the British fighting for? The British were by now clear on that point. It was to make Europe a secure place to live in, to free it from Hitler's recurring aggressions and the consequent need to maintain huge armies. So what would the Allies do when they won? They would replace Hitler and his government, that went without saying, but what of Germany herself? Would she be divided, truncated and forced into paying vast reparations as she had been in 1918? Or would she merely be restored to parliamentary democracy and left in peace?

Believing that there was a chance the German Army would overthrow Hitler and end the war, Chamberlain was at pains on several occasions to demonstrate his goodwill towards the German people, to make it clear that his only quarrel was with the Nazi régime and its treacherous leader. 'In this war we are not fighting against you, the German people, for whom we have no bitter feeling, but against a tyrannous and foresworn régime which has betrayed not only its own people but the whole of western civilization and all that you and we hold dear,' said Chamberlain in his 4 September broadcast to Germany.[79] In his speech on 12 October he amplified this theme. 'It is no part of our policy to exclude from her rightful place in Europe a Germany which will live in amity and confidence with other nations . . . It was not therefore with any vindictive purpose that we embarked on war but simply in defence of freedom . . . We seek no material advantage for ourselves. We desire nothing from the German people that would offend their self-respect. We are not aiming only at victory but rather looking beyond it to the laying of a foundation of a better international system.'[80]

These conciliatory noises found no echo in Paris, where little reliance was placed on the emergence of an alternative to Hitler. The French, the non-defeatist French at least, saw little to be gained in wooing the German people whom they assumed to be united by and large in Hitler's support. In an interesting letter to Lord Lothian dated 21 November Halifax discussed the whole issue of war aims which, he said, 'might at this moment lead us into disastrous controversy with the French'. The two allies were exchanging notes, trying to resolve their points of view, but Halifax feared that 'sooner or later we shall have to face up to the fundamental difference of opinion'.[81]

Halifax summed up the French point of view thus: 'The mass of French people have been saying "*Il faut en finir*" ["We must dispose of the whole business"] without, I rather suspect, any clear idea of how to achieve that object. They have only a vague idea that war has come upon them again owing to our having taken the teeth out of the Versailles settlement, and having ever since shown a sentimental spinelessness in dealing with Germany. If they have any definite idea, it appears to be the dismemberment of Germany. I hope they will keep that to themselves, as any such proclaimed object would be more calculated, I should say, to weld the Germans into a solid bloc. My highest hope would be that Germany should disrupt from within, and we should do everything we can to encourage that process, but my conviction is that it cannot possibly be imposed from without.' Halifax only hoped that Britain would be able 'to wean the French from their worst fallacies'. Quite understandably he concludes: 'I find that this letter contains a certain amount of explosive material and it might be better therefore that you burn it after perusal.'

There were thus several rows brewing between Britain and France at the time when they should have been preparing a simultaneous and united answer to Hitler's speech. It was significant that Daladier did not wait for Chamberlain's 12 October announcement but himself rejected the German proposals on 10 October in a radio broadcast: 'We have taken up arms against aggression and we shall only lay them down when we have the guarantee of a security which will not be put in question every six months.' He had not consulted his Cabinet on the speech. 'Did he perhaps fear that he would not find it unanimous?' a French historian wonders.[82] We know that Bonnet and de Monzie would have had something to say against total rejection. The former told the author as much in 1971 and on 9 October 1939 the latter wrote to the Socialist deputy Peschadour, 'Whatever happens there is every reason for us to proceed by mediation.'[83] Mussolini thought he detected signs of hesitation even in Daladier's speech and was only convinced of Allied determination to proceed after Chamberlain's speech two days later. Attolico, Mussolini's ambassador in Berlin, told Weizsäcker on 9 October he thought the speech 'would probably not be purely negative'.[84]

Hitler's attitude during these days of uncertainty is hard to fathom exactly. On 10 October he repeated his readiness for peace and his reluctance to fight the Western Powers at a Winter Help Rally in Berlin's Sportpalast, but that very morning he had outlined to his generals plans to invade France through Belgium, Holland and Luxemburg. The question whether or not he wanted to end the war was one which even he was finding it hard to answer. The British and French entry into the war on 3 September had been an initial shock to him. He had hoped to be able to crush Poland without involving them and momentarily he was proved wrong. But during the past month the Allies' failure to fight the war seriously and Germany's brilliant military success had restored his self-confidence, rehabilitated his judgement and increased his prestige. He had tasted the sweet fruit of victory, and the delight of it was tempting him to abandon his original intention of a quick war and a quick peace in favour of more elaborate indulgence. He wanted peace, but only just, his inclination was moving more and more towards war with every day that passed. He had felt forced to make his 6 October offer. To have made no offer at all would have antagonized all the neutrals, friendly and unfriendly, and disappointed the German people who, while they varied from one extreme to the other in their enthusiasm for the war, were generally speaking more ready for peace than Hitler was.

On 11 October Berlin Radio broadcast falsely that the British Government had fallen and that there would be an immediate armistice. William Shirer describes the wave of happiness that covered Berlin that morning as the news spread: 'Old women in the vegetable markets tossed their cabbages into the air, wrecked their stands in sheer joy and made for the nearest pub to toast the peace with *Schnapps*.'[85] But their delight was short-lived as the news was corrected, and when the next day Chamberlain finally delivered his speech they can no longer have been in doubt that the war was going to continue.

There were of course the sentences conciliatory to Germany which have been quoted, but in the absence of any word of tenderness or tolerance towards Hitler and his government it was obvious that there was little that could be done to end the war. For once it was a good speech, full of the resolution and oratory essential to a war leader, and for once the Prime Minister was congratulated by an almost unanimous House of Commons. He spoke movingly of the 'wanton act of aggression which has cost so many Polish and German lives'. Convinced at last that 'Polish towns and villages were bombed and shelled into ruins and civ''ians were slaughtered wholesale',[86] he had nothing but scorn for Hitler's assurances and guarantees. Hitler had broken promise after promise. He had told the world at Munich in September 1938 that he had no further territorial claims, then seized Prague the following March. He had vowed repeatedly that his aim was merely to reunite Germans into his Reich, and now here he was proposing to govern millions of Poles and Czechs for an indefinite period.

It was this background which had brought the Prime Minister to the policy which he now summarized: 'The repeated disregard of his [Hitler's] word and these sudden reversals of policy bring me to the fundamental difficulty in dealing with the wider proposals in the German Chancellor's speech. The plain truth is that after our past experience it is no longer possible to rely upon the unsupported word of the present German Government.'

What the Allies required was acts not words, Chamberlain concluded: 'Either the German Government must give convincing proof of the sincerity of their desire for peace by definite acts and by the provision of effective guarantees of their intention to fulfil their undertakings, or we must persevere in our duty to the end. It is for Germany to make her choice.'

Chamberlain had, he believed, followed the decision of his Cabinet and delivered 'a statement ending on a note of enquiry rather than on a direct rejection', but this was not the way it appeared to Hitler and his government. The German Press Department issued a circular a few hours after the speech:

Chamberlain's speech is an outrageous affront to Germany. With incredibly scurrilous insults against the German Reich and its policy Chamberlain rejected in his speech the hand of friendship held out to him by the Führer . . . Chamberlain and Britain's warmongers under the cloak of hypocritical phrases are bent on exterminating the German nation. Chamberlain's speech reveals the true nature of the British war aim, which is war to annihilation against the German people and the German Reich. The English Prime Minister's speech is founded on lies and culminates in a lie. While he accuses German policy of breaking its word he forgets that the world knows that England's world empire is built on nothing but force and broken word. England wanted the war . . .[87]

That was that, one would have thought. After such an exchange of abuse surely the war was now going to begin in earnest, and surely there could be no more talk of peace. Even if Hitler had wanted peace he would not have got it, not at least without offering to retire as Chancellor. But by now his inclination was just the opposite. He wanted not to reduce his power but to extend it. He now had his excuse to cease uttering the peace-loving noises which came so unnaturally to him and to stand proudly before his people as the man who had led them to victory.

The Nazis' 12 October outburst was meant mainly for home consumption. It did not mean they were immediately going to cease their efforts to get Britain and France out of the war, or to dig and probe in attempts to find out the extent of Allied resolution to fight, and perhaps to cause division in the enemy camp. In Ankara von Papen was still doing his best to confuse the issue. He told Knatchbull-Hugessen through Visser that the 6 October speech had originally been postponed and was only delivered in its present form because his own 'moderate' group was overruled at the last minute by Ribbentrop and the hard-liners. Von Papen said that he was nevertheless encouraged by the fact that the passage in the speech about peace proposals was delivered in a measured, unsensational tone, while the rest of the speech was the usual tub-thumping. He wondered whether perhaps Hitler had been carried away by the applause of his audience and spoken more aggressively than he really meant. By now such feeble excuses cut little ice in London. Roger Makins of the Foreign Office noted on 8 October: 'Von Papen has been a very unreliable source in this matter and it is hard to see what has been at the back of his activities.'

The amazing Dahlerus was quite unabashed by the non-appearance of the new proposals he had promised. In spite of the unhelpful tone of Hitler's speech he was still able to convince himself that his duty was to induce Britain to make peace. Even more strangely, he still seemed to believe there was a chance he would succeed. On 11 October he had wired Bland a slightly amplified version of the vague concessions Hitler had offered in his speech. He promised 'a new Polish state within German orbit. Extent of territory to be considered, but that in Soviet occupation not subject for discussion.' He added that the Germans had accepted the 'brainwave' he had mentioned to Cadogan on 30 September: 'Any agreement reached at conference would be endorsed by national plebiscite in Germany.' But there was no hint of a concession on Czechoslovakia, and most important of all was his final sentence: 'If His Majesty's Government is not prepared to negotiate with present régime in Germany, proposals fall to the ground.'[88]

This in itself was enough to demonstrate to the British that peace was for the moment unobtainable. 'Past experience has shown that no reliance can be placed upon the promises of the present German Government,' Chamberlain was to say the next day, and we know that he had already made up his mind that the war must be continued until Hitler and his entourage were removed. In the circumstances it is extraordinary that Dahlerus thought it worth while to continue sending his telegrams. Why did he do it? One can only conclude that his amateur diplomacy was incompetent to the point of dishonesty. So thrilled was he by the role of international peacemaker that coincidence had thrust upon him that he was determined to maintain his impossible position by every possible means, even after it was obvious that his role was ended, that the only thing left for him to do was to retire from the stage. For weeks he had been a pernicious influence, painting for each side a rosy picture of the possibilities of agreement. This was why both sides continued to talk to him and use his 'good offices'. The Nazis had a use for him since the lies they fed him caused great confusion in England. Had he told the British the truth they would have realized he could do them no good. To keep himself in the company of the powerful he was forced to suppress vital information, causing misunderstanding certainly in London and possibly also in Berlin. Because of him both sides came to believe that the other was ready to make serious concessions, the Germans to relinquish their conquests, the British to acquiesce in their retaining them. The result was to strengthen the faint-hearted in Britain and France who could not face the prospect of real war.

Some blame too must be laid at the door of Alexander Cadogan for neglecting to make quite clear to Dahlerus at their 29 and 30 September meetings the British determination to stand firm, if not for Poland and Czechoslovakia, at least against Hitler. He allowed Dahlerus to return to Berlin with some justification for believing that two small German concessions, a puppet Polish state and a vague promise of a plebiscite, would buy peace. No doubt Dahlerus exaggerated Cadogan's readiness to negotiate, but on a matter so important it was Cadogan's duty to din into Dahlerus's head the vital non-negotiable points, to leave him with no illusion about the British will to continue the war. On the evidence of his own memorandum Cadogan failed to do this, and the result was to encourage Hitler's belief in British decadence and irresolution.

Through Dahlerus and Bland there came also a message from Göring that no reply would be made to Chamberlain's 12 October speech which was a 'declaration of war'. But two days later up bobbed Dahlerus again with strange hints that the atmosphere in Berlin was now 'distinctly more hopeful' and that there were new proposals worth discussing at a conference. But by now London's patience was wearing thin. 'Mr Dahlerus is being rather tiresome,' noted Ivone Kirkpatrick.[89] Dahlerus was now hitting the Foreign Office with petulant and untimely complaints that Britain was not showing him due respect. He resented being treated as a mere messenger boy between Berlin and The Hague, he told Bland, and he wanted assurances that as soon as these 'new proposals' were ready he would be able to bring them to London himself.

This time at last it was made clear to Dahlerus that his diplomacy was unwelcome and so would be his presence in London. The reply Halifax signed on 17 October pointed out to Bland that 'it is impossible to keep Dahlerus's movements secret, and his visits will almost inevitably cause misunderstanding in various quarters'. After his embarrassing interview with Corbin twelve days earlier one can appreciate Halifax's position. Here was yet another way in which Dahlerus was serving the Nazi cause, by causing suspicion and driving a wedge between Britain and France.

The next day Dahlerus made yet another approach through Bland enquiring what action and guarantees were likely to satisfy the British other than a change of government in Germany. One would have thought this was a question the Allies had answered many times already, but however much of a nuisance he was now considered London still thought it necessary to give him a reply on the highest level. On 19 October both Chamberlain and Halifax signed a statement that their government 'could consider no proposals that did not effectively right the wrongs done to other nationalities, and which did not by provision of practical guarantees both for this reparation and for future protection of Europe against aggression securely re-establish confidence that actions of present German Government have destroyed'. Once again the emphasis of this statement indicates that German withdrawal from the East was demanded not so much for the subjected countries' sake as to provide a sign of German good faith and future good behaviour.

Dahlerus was to re-emerge briefly once or twice more, for instance during the Belgian–Dutch mediation offer of early November. 'I recommend that no definite stand be taken for several days on the appeal,' he wired Göring with cool authority. 'I shall in the meantime seek to ascertain from England whether the British are interested at all and if so what their conditions are.' He handed this message to Wied, the German Minister in Stockholm, for transmission through the German Foreign Ministry. It was an act that made complete nonsense of his claim to be dividing the 'moderate' Göring from 'wild man' Ribbentrop, for of course the telegram was shown to the latter who was Foreign Minister. 'The German Government is no longer interested in his [Dahlerus] sounding out England, because the official attitude of the British Government has already indicated unequivocal rejection of the German position,' was Ribbentrop's reply to Stockholm.[90]

And that was the end of Dahlerus the amateur diplomat. It had at last penetrated Hitler's mind that the British and French were not going to give him peace on his terms. He was now busy planning his offensive in the West, in the face of violent opposition from his generals who had just forced him to postpone, though only for a few days, an attack originally scheduled for 12 November. He was no longer in any sort of a mood to play games with Dahlerus. Dahlerus did visit London again in December and spent an hour with Cadogan to no avail,[91] but thereafter he withdrew to well-deserved obscurity in Sweden.

An interesting series of notes beginning on 23 October shows how little the British Government knew of Dahlerus's background at the time when they were placing so much trust in him. Frank Roberts had discovered that 'Mr Dahlerus's wife was a German and that she owned farm property in Germany the value of which Mr Spencer estimated at about £250,000. Before he was married Mr Dahlerus was not a particularly wealthy man, although now he had a great deal of money in addition to his wife's property.' It followed, Roberts pointed out with restraint, that 'however honest Mr Dahlerus's intentions might be, he may also have been influenced to some extent by his wife's personal stake in Germany'. Roger Makins scribbled 'Interesting' in the margin of this alarming report which was shown forthwith to Halifax and Chamberlain.[92]

The amazing thing is that this information, which would if known have put the whole of Dahlerus's mediation in a different and more doubtful light, reached the ears of the Prime Minister and the Foreign Office only after his role had come to an end. Roberts's informant was a prominent British businessman who knew Dahlerus well, but it appears on the evidence that he was never asked by any official about the background of the man who was to play such an intense if brief part in world affairs. Nor was it known, as Dahlerus revealed in 1945 in his book, that it was Göring's personal intercession which had removed German official objections in 1934 to the marriage of Birger and Elisabeth Dahlerus, or that Dahlerus had taken under his protection Thomas Kantzow, the son of Göring's first wife who was Swedish and who died in 1931.[93] For months the British Government had allowed itself to be delayed and confused by an intermediary who they thought was neutral, but who in fact had close personal ties with Göring and a financial interest in Germany.

One could of course argue that because nothing came of Dahlerus's mediation, the British Government's ignorance of his background, their mistaken belief in his neutrality, turned out to be of small importance, and that in the final analysis little damage was done. But this would be to over-simplify the effect his diplomacy had on the British leaders, particularly on the Prime Minister. Firstly, the two-day delay in Britain's declaration of war was partly Dahlerus's doing. Chamberlain admitted as much in a letter to his sister on 10 September.[94] Secondly, Dahlerus also succeeded in convincing Chamberlain of the reality of the Hitler–Göring split, even of the extraordinary theory that Göring was ready to plot with the British to secure Hitler's removal from power. This theory is confounded by overwhelming evidence which shows that, while Göring may just then have been personally less inclined to fight a serious war than some of his political rivals, his function during the 'negotiations' through Dahlerus was to find out exactly what Britain was ready to pay as the price of peace. He was not working behind Hitler's back.

Dahlerus's reports served only to bolster that school of thought in Britain led by Chamberlain which believed in the possibility of 'a collapse on the German home front'. The historian A. J. P. Taylor points out astutely that Italy's unexpected neutrality, while hailed as a great diplomatic success, deprived the Allies of their planned easy victim for the first months of the war. The French Army was not prepared to assault the Siegfried Line but it might have been able to invade Italy from France and Italian Libya from Tunisia or Algeria. The British Army was not much, but probably enough to attack Italian Abyssinia from Kenya and Libya from Egypt. These easy victories were to be called 'knocking down the props'. Taylor believes this policy was calculated 'to provide the sensations of war and of victory on the cheap. Finally at some remote time there would be a victorious attack on Germany herself − an attack again almost without effort, since Germany was supposed to be already on the point of economic collapse.'[95] Such were the fallacies that led to Chamberlain's belief that Germany would soon reach the conclusion that she

Moscow's view of the British naval blockade. The British Lion, sitting on a pile of 'contraband lists' and 'confiscated goods', stands guard to prevent ships approaching the 'small neutral countries' (*Pravda*, 12 November 1939). (Copyright British Museum)

could not win the war, after which she would make terms. Dahlerus helped to foster these fallacies.

In the summer of 1939 Liddell Hart wrote, 'If war came now these nations [Germany and Italy] would be starting from the same point of undernourishment that Germany reached after two or three years of the last war.'[96] It was widely believed in England that an effective blockade of Germany's ports would cause swift economic deterioration leading eventually to a situation where it was impossible for her to continue the war. On 10 September the three Chiefs of Staff – Ironside, Newall and Pound – issued a report on bombing policy with the following extraordinary statements: 'We have behind us a free and united nation and Empire with vast resources of all kinds. The Germans on the other hand are already to some extent an exhausted and dispirited nation who are by no means united behind the Nazi régime.'[97]

Here was fertile ground for Dahlerus to sow the seeds of irresolution, complacency and delay. 'There is such a widespread desire to avoid war, and it is so deeply rooted; that it surely must find expression somehow,' wrote Chamberlain touchingly but pathetically.[98] His faith in human nature was deep, embracing almost

Churchill: „Verlassen Sie sich ruhig auf mein Neutralitätsversprechen, meine Herren!"

The Nazis and the blockade. Churchill is saying, 'You may rely on my promise of neutrality, gentlemen' (*Völkischer Beobachter*, 1 October 1939). (Copyright British Museum)

everyone in Germany, not Hitler himself, perhaps, but certainly Göring who he thought should be allowed 'an ornamental position in a transitional government'. There can be little doubt that Dahlerus's pernicious diplomacy fixed these dangerous ideas more firmly in the Prime Minister's mind and contributed to his government's series of decisions not to prosecute the war with much energy or violence. 'What we ought to do is just to throw back the peace offers and continue the blockade . . . I do not believe that holocausts are required,' Chamberlain noted in October.[99] What *was* required was a little less gloom and torpor, a little more inspiration. But given the quality of the man this was just not possible.

In the light of these facts it is hard to see why Norman Birkett felt called upon to call Dahlerus 'an honest man' and 'one actuated by the highest motives'. The record shows that he consistently withheld information from the British side and that he did his best to extract from British officials declarations of policy which would have given Berlin valuable information. He was not neutral. On the contrary he had vested interests in Germany. His machinations and secret visits to London undermined Britain's reputation with the French and encouraged everywhere the forces of appeasement. Whether he was consciously trying to help the Nazis is doubtful, but what is certain is that he was ready to distort the truth to preserve his grand position as the bridge between the two warring sides and as the personal friend of powerful men.

His baleful influence shone like a searchlight into the offices of Whitehall, even that of the Prime Minister, pinpointing those most willing to do business with the Nazis and tempting men of influence to reveal how lukewarm was their resolution to fight. A one-season *prima donna*, he nevertheless dug deep into the British Government machine, far more deeply than a man of his limited competence and integrity should have been allowed to. It is shocking to think that so much trust was placed in him at such a time, without even checking a few elementary facts about his family and background. It is alarming to see from the record how trustingly the British leaders clutched at him, a man of straw indeed who could not have saved a fly from drowning, let alone a world from war.

Yet as far as ground fighting was concerned the war was virtually

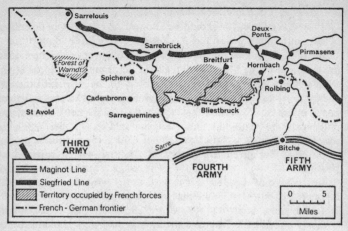

The Maginot and Siegfried Lines, 1939.

at a standstill. On 16 October the German Army advanced into the area between the Rhine and the Moselle, driving those few French troops Gamelin had left in Germany back to the Maginot Line. On the eastern front a German–Soviet boundary commission was busy making out the new frontier in detail. Germany now had quiet on her eastern and western borders. True, there was frantic digging-in. Fortifications were being built on either side of each line by men of the French, German and Red armies to block the tanks which had proved themselves so well in September. And so, quietly, the winter was spent.

'It is obvious from the broadcasts of Ed and Tom from London that the Allies are exaggerating their action on the western front,' wrote Shirer in his *Berlin Diary*.[100] On 10 October he travelled by train to Switzerland and skirted the French frontier for 100 miles. The train crew told him that not one shot had been fired in this sector since the war began. He wrote, 'We could see the French bunkers and at many places great mats behind which the French were building fortifications. Identical picture on the German side. The troops seemed to be observing an armistice. They went about their business in full sight and range of each other. For that matter one blast from a French "75" could have liquidated our train. The Germans were hauling up guns and supplies on the railroad line, but the French did not disturb them. Queer kind of war.'

Both sides patrolled the no-man's-land between the two lines, and it was here a few casualties took place on the rare occasions when patrols encountered artillery fire, mines or each other. A feature of the German Army's minelaying technique was to attach detonators to brightly coloured 'souvenir' objects. Unsuspecting French soldiers would pick these things up and be blown to oblivion. A British journalist reported from the French lines that 'one unit had the bright idea of driving a flock of sheep before them, with the result that they suffered no further loss, though the unfortunate animals doomed ultimately to the butcher's knife in any event suffered some casualties'.[101]

The British soldiers in France were bored by lack of action and embarrassed by the puny contribution they were making to the combined Anglo-French force. 'They have plenty of warm straw, the barns are solidly built, free from draughts, and the general living conditions are excellent,' The Times told its readers reassuringly, but anyone better informed knew that militarily their situation was bad. They were short of supplies, with scant air cover and in many places, along most of the Belgian frontier for instance, without any prepared defences. They had hardly any armoured vehicles and were short of ammunition, the bulk of which was being used by the RAF. George Turner, then of the Ministry of Supply, is definite in his view: 'They could not have fought the war seriously in 1939.'

The soldiers were indulging in the self-confident good humour which in England is so often a substitute for real strength or efficiency. 'Tanks a Million' and 'Danzig with Tears in my Eyes' were two of the tasteless, unfunny slogans which were reportedly their favourite.[102] Inevitably the 'Tommies' had chalked on the sides of tanks and lorries the promise that they were going to hang out their washing on the Siegfried Line – a piece of flippancy which irritated their allies as much as the enemy. A rival version was composed by William Joyce (Lord Haw Haw), who had begun to broadcast in English on the Zeesen Radio. 'This is not a soldiers' song because soldiers do not brag,' he announced. 'It was written not in the soldiers' camps but by Jewish scribes of the

BBC. The Englishmen's washing will be very dirty before they come anywhere near the Siegfried Line.'[103] Lord Haw Haw was right in this last sentence at least. It was five years before the British Army was back within reach of the German line.

The French began to offer guided tours of their defences to prominent men from Britain and the Empire. A delegation of members of parliament were given an impressive demonstration of the Maginot Line's capabilities and were convinced enough to speak well of it to Paul Reynaud, France's Minister of Finance and future Premier. 'We've got them already, and they know it!' Reynaud told Harold Nicolson who records, 'They [the French] are convinced that if we can stick it for six months the whole German edifice will collapse.'[104]

On 10 November a delegation of Cabinet Ministers from the five major Empire countries was more critical of what was happening in France. They were briefed by Gamelin who pointed out his dispositions in front of a large-scale map. Anthony Eden was depressed by the experience: 'I was not proud of the minute British contribution represented by two small Union Jacks amid a forest of Tricolours.'[105] Eden found that in the British sector the line was thinly held and the defence generally patchy. 'The two British divisions in the line were together holding a front of 14,000 yards, about the same length as the Fifth Army had held in March 1918. This seems to me ominous,' he wrote.[106]

They found the trenches shallow, the concrete pill-boxes too far apart — about 800 yards — with only a single anti-tank rifle for each firing point. They did not like the design of the concrete domes with loopholes facing sideways. It was bad for morale, they thought, for troops not to be able to see in front of them. Deneys Reitz, a member of the South African Cabinet, writes: 'We were taken over Mont de Bouvines, an obsolete fortress dating from 1870 now held by British troops, and we watched a maze of muddy trenches and tank-traps being haphazardly scooped out by steam shovels.' Reitz says he told Chamberlain on his return to London, 'Sir, if you will pardon my saying so, the Germans will go through there like a knife through cheese.'[107] They did.

Meanwhile the German generals were planning an assault on the western front in obedience to Hitler's directive of 10 October.[108] By and large they viewed the prospect with trepidation. Guderian was frightened that the winter rains would bog down his tanks. Göring feared that November fog would ground the Luftwaffe, depriving the attacking armies of essential air support.[109] Wilhelm von Leeb, commander of the German armies on the western front, opposed the adventure on moral as well as practical grounds. He circulated a memorandum among his fellow generals prophesying that the whole world would turn against Germany if, for the second time in twenty-five years, she violated Dutch and Belgian neutrality. 'The entire nation is longing for peace,' he concluded,[110] wrongly, for there were by now many Germans sufficiently inspired by their army's victory in Poland to seek further conquests.

The generals felt that Hitler was making impossible demands upon them and once again a few of them resolved to remove him, if necessary to kill him. Their half-hearted efforts, known as the Zossen Conspiracy, have been well described elsewhere and the details of them need not be repeated here. Suffice it to say that those involved in the plot varied from the very brave to the pusillanimous. There was Kurt von Hammerstein, a general on the western front, who kept inviting Hitler to visit him in the sector he commanded. 'I would have rendered him harmless once and for all, even without judicial proceedings,' he said to Otto John. To be precise, he would have arrested and killed him.[111] There was Fabian von Schlabrendorff who actually entered the Adlon Hotel in Berlin, where all the British diplomats sat huddled on 3 September while war was being declared, and told Ogilvie Forbes about this plot. Only a man with the courage of a lion would have risked the Gestapo's violence by communicating directly with the enemy at such a moment.

Most of the generals, while they did not like Hitler and thought his policies would bring Germany harm, were less steadfast than these in their resolution to remove him at all costs. They were worried about the oath they had sworn to Hitler personally. A few said they would only act once Hitler was safely dead and they were released from their moral dilemma. Others feared that if they mounted a *coup d'état* Britain and France would take advantage of the ensuing chaos to overrun Germany and humiliate her with an imposed peace worse than Versailles.

On 27 October they were briefly galvanized into action by an instruction from Hitler to make final preparations for the western offensive. He even mentioned a date, 12 November, and confirmed this on 5 November.[112] It was this that finally moved the Commander-in-Chief, von Brauchitsch, torn between the doubts of his generals and the fanatical drive of his Nazi masters, to go to Hitler and tell him frankly that Army morale would not stand the strain of another major campaign. Brauchitsch had told his generals that if he could not talk Hitler out of the adventure he would join them in their plot to remove him. He began his sad tale and had not got very far when Hitler cut him short with a torrent of abuse and recrimination against the High Command and the Army in general. The arguments about the difficulty of military operations in wintertime Hitler simply brushed aside with the remark, 'It rains on the enemy too.'[113] The truth of the matter was, Hitler told his astonished Commander-in-Chief, that the Army had consistently sabotaged his movement and the re-emergence of Germany as a great power. It had opposed rearmament in the mid 1930s and the military advances of the late 1930s with calls to caution which he had felt bound to overrule. And each time it was he Hitler who had been proved right. The Army was not only disloyal, it was afraid, said Hitler, after which he stormed from the room in his inimitable manner leaving Brauchitsch quivering and incoherent.

'No one refers to him as if he were a man. He is a Power, a personification. No one has any down-to-earth opinion about him, but for everyone he signifies something, whether it is the essence of evil or of salvation. He is what anyone cares to make of him. I have yet to meet anyone who has overcome him so much as to reduce him to human proportions.'[114] These words, well written by a Zurich journalist on 10 November, go some way to explaining the satanic charisma Hitler possessed which enabled him to escape his enemies, to further his ends and to gain the adulation of millions. Even those who hated him were affected by it. Like rabbits confronted by a snake they were mesmerized by him into immobility.

On this occasion the Army's protests did, it seems, make some small impression on Hitler, for two days after his demolition of Brauchitsch he postponed the western offensive ostensibly on the advice of the meteorologists, but probably as a sop to the generals. The next day (8 November) another boost was given to the Führer's prestige when a bomb exploded in a Munich beerhouse a few minutes after he had left the building. The day after that two British secret service men were kidnapped and brought to Germany from Holland to be framed as perpetrators of the explosion, which killed seven innocent people and which was almost certainly organized by the Nazis themselves.

Garbled versions of these weird events reached London and, as uncoordinated intelligence is liable to do, caused more confusion than enlightenment. 'I think it is fair to say that everyone has been puzzled by Hitler's recent inactivity,' wrote Halifax to Lothian on 21 November. 'By the middle of October he had moved sufficient of his armies back from the East to enable him to attack in the West. The promised attack looked at one moment to be developing, but it was evidently a half-hearted affair and was not followed up.'[115] Cadogan wrote in his diary on 12 November, the very day of the projected offensive, 'Had fully thought Germans would be in Holland by now, but they're not.'

The British had good intelligence contacts in Germany, where there were many in high positions ready to give information as part of the fight against Hitler. But the Nazis were by now becoming expert in the art of 'disinformation'. They would make contact with a British network, gain its confidence with titbits of impressive but valueless intelligence and then feed untrue facts into the machine to confuse the picture. The British were receiving genuine approaches from generals anxious to remove Hitler and end the war, but British enthusiasm for these allies in the enemy camp was soon to be diluted, firstly, by the generals' failure to fulfil their promises and act, secondly, by the spurious machinations of Göring who pretended to be plotting against Hitler, but who in fact was keeping Hitler informed of every step he made. When in February 1940 Cadogan was yet again treated to a 'ridiculously stale story of a German opposition ready to overthrow Hitler if we guarantee we will not take advantage', he told his informant impatiently 'that this was about the hundredth time I had heard this story'.[116] He was slowly coming to the view that all his contacts in Germany, even the genuinely anti-Hitler generals, were Nazi agents. The disinformation was working well.

By mid November the excitement was over. It was the end of the campaigning season and both sides came to realize there would be no offensive during 1939. Halifax wrote, 'This pause suits us well enough, both us and the French, for we shall be a good deal stronger in the spring.' The debacle which the Allies were about to suffer was no more than a nightmare at the back of his mind. For the moment there was peace in central Europe. The action was elsewhere — in Finland which the Red Army invaded on 30 November, off Montevideo where Captain Langsdorff scuttled the *Graf Spee* on 17 December. At sea the Allies still had problems, in particular the magnetic mine which in November sank 120,958 tons of their shipping. But on land the soldiers dug and observed, watched and waited, their calm and boredom disturbed only by the occasional artillery shell.

Hitler's policy remained one of aggression. Scotched momentarily by the onset of winter and the doubts of his generals, he nevertheless planned to attack in the West at the first opportunity, and if this was not possible until the spring he was content enough to use the intervening months as a period of consolidation. In early September the German people had been unenthusiastic for the war, but he had overcome their misgivings by sheer success. He had his problems with the generals, but he overcame them by sheer force of personality, by the power of the naked eye. It would do him no harm to let the world ponder its situation for a few months. It might well come to the conclusion that its future lay not with the weak democracies but with Hitler, right or wrong.

For this was the most dangerous result of the first two months of war, that Britain's and France's decision to defeat Nazi Germany lacked all credibility. From the purely military point of view their decision to stay initially on the defensive may well have been the right one. Britain was woefully short of soldiers and supplies. France was divided and demoralized, with a paltry air force and a cumbersome, ill-prepared army. Both countries were lead by weak men, adequate perhaps to govern a democracy in peacetime but no match for the aggressive genius of a Hitler. It is interesting to note that before the decisive battles of the following summer many of the Allied leaders were dismissed: Ironside, Gamelin, Hore-Belisha, Bonnet, Daladier and Chamberlain.

But politically the effect of the Allied inaction was appalling. The Poles felt that Britain and France had broken their treaties, that their failure to act was cowardice and betrayal. The communist Russians saw their worst suspicions confirmed. They were all too ready to believe that Britain and France had no real intention of fighting Nazi Germany, and the first weeks of war did nothing to make them change this opinion. Nor would the Italians be encouraged to move further away from the German orbit and towards genuine neutrality.

Most dangerous of all was the effect of this wait-and-see policy at home. It lulled the British and French people into a sense of false security and imbued into them none of the energy and fervour which are essential if one wants to win a war. Typical of such thinking was the pamphlet called 'Assurance of Victory' which the British Ministry of Information put out just before Christmas. After harping on the usual theme that 'time is on our side' it concluded: 'We do not have to defeat the Nazis on land, but only to prevent them from defeating us.'[117] This idea was not only incorrect, as time was to prove, but also in itself defeatist. It was the sort of delusion which enabled Chamberlain to remark, 'Hitler has missed the bus,' just a few days before the brilliant German invasion of the Low Countries and his own resignation.

But, one might argue, in spite of the German defeat of France in 1940, in spite of the sufferings Britain endured as she fought Germany on her own for the next year, the policy of delay did in the end pay off. The Soviet Union and the United States of America were eventually drawn into the fight against Hitler, not perhaps in the way Chamberlain would have foreseen but certainly along the general lines of his logic which held that in the nature of things Britain and France would attract allies while Hitler attracted enemies. If without these allies Britain and France could not have defeated Germany – which most people now believe – then the general Allied policy of defence, though not the lazy way it was executed, must be seen as correct.

There are still those who feel that it was all unnecessary, that Hitler need not have won the war of 1939. Most vociferous in support of this view are the Poles. They feel that Britain and France gave them not only a general guarantee, but also specific pledges to carry out certain acts in the event of a German invasion. They based their strategy on the assumption that Britain would bomb the rear of the German Army as well as rail and road intersections, to hinder the German supply system. 'If we had had this help, we could have held out quite easily for the first two weeks of the war,' General Jaklicz told the author in 1970. The theory is that the Polish Army would then have been in position to act when Gamelin's promised offensive took place on 16 September. They would have counter-attacked and thrown the Germans back.

'On 16 September we still had possibilities. If Gamelin had attacked the Germans would have had to transfer many divisions to the western front. We could have held our Rumanian bridgehead,' says General Kopański, who was like Jaklicz a member of Marshal Rydz-Smigły's General Staff. Both men think that if Britain and France had shown a more warlike spirit in the early days of the battle, Stalin would not have sent his Red Army into Poland when he did. They agree that Stalin was committed to helping the German invaders in principle — so much is clear from the record — but they feel he would not have advanced so soon had he not been sure of a clear run against an abandoned and helpless country. The Red Army was not really ready for war, as was shown by its poor performance against Finland that winter, and Stalin would not in 1939 have risked exposing it to serious fighting in a world war.

There is one serious flaw in this Polish argument: how could they have been supplied? The corner of Poland into which they had been driven by 16 September contained little industry and none of the fuel which an army needs to maintain itself as a fighting force. The Polish generals believe that Britain and France could have supplied them through Rumania, but here they are surely wrong, for Germany had forbidden Rumania to allow any such thing and she was in a position to enforce her orders with real threats of invasion. Rumania did not even dare to allow the Polish Government to pass through the country *en route* for France. She was instructed by Germany to intern them, and she obeyed, even though she had given her word to the Poles. If she was too frightened to render her Polish allies even this small service, how much less would she have been ready to give them active help against the German giant. If Gamelin had mounted his promised offensive, and if the Red Army had held back, the Germans would simply have sealed off the Rumanian bridgehead. The trapped Polish Army could then have done little. Short of fuel, food and shelter they would surely have disintegrated before the winter was over.

But even this would have been better than nothing, better than watching passively while the Poles went down fighting. To wait and see may have been sound policy militarily, but it was just not right for an alliance trying to build up the strength to destroy a great and evil ideology. It was all very well for Churchill to say on 12 November: 'You may take it absolutely for certain that either all that Britain and France stand for in the modern world will go down, or that Hitler, the Nazi régime and the recurring German or Prussian menace to Europe will be broken and destroyed. This is the way the matter lies and everybody had better make up his mind to that solid, sombre fact.' But not many had made up their minds so decisively. Few people in Britain and France had resigned themselves to the bitter prospect of years of toil, austerity and suffering. They thought there still might be some middle-of-the-road way out which would leave both sides intact. 'War wins nothing, cures nothing, ends nothing,' wrote Chamberlain to his sister before it all began.[118] The gap between this attitude and Churchill's was wide, and the first weeks of war did little to narrow it.

Britain and France were suffering from their virtues. The parliamentary democracy which controlled their governments and the liberal tradition which influenced their ideas had prevented them from taking the necessary serious view of Nazi Germany's growing armed might. Such naivety and blindness had its origin in the First World War, in which anti-German feeling in Britain and France became so intense and so lunatic that there was bound to be a liberal backlash in favour of Germany after peace was established. The stories of German brutality in Belgium which featured so prominently in the British and French press during the First World War, and which were later shown up as gross exaggeration, so influenced Allied public opinion that when it came to Versailles the victorious leaders felt obliged to impose punitive peace terms.

It was not long before the world came to appreciate the injustice of Versailles. In Germany resentment grew and contributed to the emergence and popularity of Hitler, a man whose ideals would not in normal circumstances have come to dominate a well-educated, civilized country. In America, France and Britain reasonable opinion was for years sympathetic to German attempts to restore their national self-respect. The Allied powers felt guilty at what they had perpetrated in 1918 and when Hitler came to power they were ready to forgive him much. In his early years of power there *appeared* to be much good in his movement. Many in America and Western Europe saw the dynamism of early Nazi Germany and preferred it to their own countries' post-depression torpor. A kind schoolmaster will treat with tolerance a difficult boy who is known to have suffered cruelty in the past. It seemed natural for thinking men to view the extreme nationalism and even anti-semitism of mid 1930s Germany as a phase through which the country would have to pass, and from which she would emerge cleansed and normalized. It seemed right to treat Hitler with kindness in the belief that he would eventually respond likewise.

We now know that Hitler responded not with kindness but with a brutality which grew with the years to the climax of the mass exterminations of 1943–5, but it was another of the legacies of Versailles that reasonable, logical men in the West were unwilling to believe the full horror of the violence that was built in to the Nazi movement. The massacre of the SA on 30 June 1934, the anti-semitic laws and oppressions – these were horrors which the West was all too ready to gloss over or minimize. There was a tendency to accuse of exaggeration those who described these events in scrupulous, sober detail. The point was that the British and French had heard it all before in 1914–18 and so, they assured themselves, they were not going to be fooled a second time. The Nazis were well aware of this feeling and they exploited it cleverly. For instance, a book published by the German In-formation Center in New York in 1940 rejected any suggestion that the occupying forces in Poland were treating the population with any undue harshness. Such tales, it said, were 'garnished and magnified in London and Paris by the same inventive minds to which the world is indebted for the armless Belgian infant and crucified Canadian soldier'.[119] One can imagine how this argument may have impressed liberal Americans who remembered the false propaganda of the previous war.

These were some of the reasons why the most powerful countries of the world, which happened to be those ruled by parliamentary democracy, were unable to fight effectively in 1939 against the Nazi dictatorship. The disruption inflicted on society by the First World War, the demand for social progress which inevitably follows war, the economic depression and the sufferings of working men, the rise of Bolshevism and the fear of it on the part of Europe's and North America's traditional rulers, the universal recognition that Germany had suffered an injustice, the soul-destroying resentment this injustice caused among the German people – this was the lethal combination which made the aberration of Hitler possible and opposition to him so difficult.

Of course Britain and France should have rearmed massively years before 1939. For years Churchill was pressing for this and in retrospect it seems madness that his warnings were disregarded. But there was more to this decision than the naivety of British and French leaders like Chamberlain who thought Hitler could be appeased, or than the blindness of those other prominent men who thought Bolshevism the greater evil and Hitler a necessary bulwark against it. Standing in the way of all attempts to increase and modernize the British and French armed forces was the recent memory of the 1929 depression, the suffering it brought to the working classes of the world's richest countries, and of the economic crisis of 1931. After this Britain felt she could not afford conscription or massive rearmament. The leaders of the West feared that any such policy would make them unpopular with their working classes as well as worsening their shaky economies.

And so the path to power was made easy for Hitler. The humiliated German nation was in a mood to prefer guns to butter, to give their support to the man who had restored their self-respect, who has promised to give them a mighty empire and who ruled by a dynamic, exciting ideology. And only when it was too late did the rich parliamentary democracies wake up to a realization of how grave was the threat. They seemed strong enough, they ruled great areas in Asia and Africa, their main problems seemed internal and economic. There were tens of millions ready to fight tooth and nail against any increase in military expenditure or manpower, taking the short-sighted view that defence is a waste of money, since it provides no direct improvement in a country's living standard. They would not accept the truism that without a valid defence policy a country's wealth can be stolen from it, that without defence a country has nothing. Armed forces consume huge sums of money and most of what they do seems pointless in peacetime, but without them a rich country is like a grand house, ornate and imposing, which lacks foundations. The tiniest shift in the ground and the house will fall. Its gilded cornices will be so much lead weight as it tumbles into the dust.

The first weeks of war brought Britain, France and the United States a little closer towards understanding this truth, but many months would have to pass before the illusions were finally dispelled. It takes a major disaster to shock a nation out of complacency, to commit it to a fight to the death. The Treaty of Versailles and its consequences were reason enough for Germany to fling herself into mortal combat, and so it was that Germany entered the war in a prepared state and with due sense of urgency. But it took the fall of France to bring such resolution to Britain and Pearl Harbor to bring it to America.

This book has explained in detail some of the errors and misconceptions which caused Britain's and France's ineffectual military performance in 1939. There was the belief which lasted right up to 31 August, the eve of the outbreak, that war could be avoided. As late as March 1939 most British and French leaders apparently thought that Hitler could be bought off with concessions. After his occupation of Prague, when this theory fell to the ground, they believed that he could be deterred by loud verbal threats, that he would never dare risk war against the Allies, that he was bluffing. They thought Germany was economically on the verge of collapse. This was nonsense. They thought that Hitler's generals were opposed to war and would never allow Hitler to begin it. The generals *were* for the most part against the war, but they were too weak in character to fight Hitler's will. To oppose Hitler successfully one must be made of sterner stuff.

The Allied leaders likewise totally misinterpreted Hitler's plans for Germany and Europe. On 1 September they clung to the hope that Hitler's attack was aimed merely at securing Danzig and the German-populated areas of Poland. Their ignorance of Hitler's real aim led to the two-day delay in declaring war. Without this delay and with more active support from Britain and France, Poland might have been able to resist a little more successfully.

The Allied leaders thought that their naval blockade would bring Germany to her knees. This too was nonsense. They dismissed the idea that the Soviet Union would be able to replace much of the oil and raw material which Germany had up to then imported by sea. They were wrong, for Germany was able to make elaborate trade arrangements with Russia, and other nearby neutral countries like Sweden and Rumania, to obtain vital oil and iron ore. In spite of lurid reports in the British and French press, Germany experienced no shortages which significantly diminished her war effort.

The Allied leaders likewise dismissed Russia as a military power and made only feeble attempts to recruit her to the anti-Nazi cause. Some of them, even after the outbreak, persisted in the belief that Russian communism was a greater danger than Hitlerism. In the last month of 1939 their theory of the Red Army's uselessness seemed confirmed by its poor performance against Finland, but they had totally miscalculated its ability to withstand defeats and learn from them, to build itself up into an efficient force on the bodies of dead comrades.

Likewise they were wrong about which ideology was more dangerous to western Europe. It was not a question of which was morally the worse, Hitlerism or Stalinism. The point was that while Stalin was for the moment in a defensive mood, content to consolidate his power in his own country, albeit by viciously repressive measures, Hitler was in a thoroughly aggressive mood, resolved to march deep into eastern Europe to obtain the living-space he believed his country was entitled to seize. Whether Hitler then planned to march against France and Britain is a moot point, but what is certain is that had such a Greater Germany ever been allowed to appear, it would have dominated the European continent and become an intolerable threat to British and French independence. Churchill foresaw this danger when it was still on the horizon. He even foresaw the day when he would make an alliance with Russia to meet this danger. But his was not in 1939 the view which dominated British and French thinking.

The victim of the tragedy of 1939 is of course Neville Chamberlain, the honest man so blind in his kindly tolerance that he gave Hitler the benefit of the doubt, a man of peace so un-violent that he was almost physically incapable of making decisions necessary to conduct and win a war. He believed in the goodness of human nature so deeply that he could not understand the mesmeric hold which Hitler had over the German people. In spite of all the facts and all the advice he was given, he persisted in his faith that his radio speeches and propaganda leaflets would detach the German people from Hitler and induce them to overthrow him. He was unable to put himself in the average German's position and see the fascination of Hitler-style fascism, its dynamism and ceremony. 'Know thine enemy,' someone should have whispered in his ear at an early stage, for it appears he was not aware of the physical excitement people can derive from brute power and violence. If only he had appreciated that such people are not to be swayed by reasoned argument and liberal thought.

But even if he had, one still doubts whether he would have been able to pull himself and the country together. He was a good administrator, a good committee man. True, there was a streak of 'bitchiness' about him. He was intolerant of his political opponents in the Conservative Party. Even when the war had begun and unity was badly needed, he would not forgive them and give them their due place in his war government. At the end of his premiership he was even tempted into placing politics and personal careerism above his country's security. But this was not his most dangerous fault. The real problem was that while he was by and large a good and sensible man, he was not an inspiring man. There was no glimmer of genius about him. In the circumstances this was a fatal flaw, for the task before him was too great for just an ordinary, competent politician. By now the ultimate offence was blandness, so he should have stood down to make way for a 'bigger' man, a less reliable man perhaps but someone with a little inspiration and greatness. A leader was required who could push big ideas into the administrative machine. Some of the ideas might be foolish, some might be brilliant, it was not so much this that mattered. Good or bad, the ideas had to be pushed harder. Greater impetus from the top was needed to get the machine working more quickly. Only thus could effective war be waged against Hitler.

Churchill was of course tailor-made for the 1939 situation. His erratic, irritating behaviour was just what Britain needed to shock her out of her usual state of laziness. His grandiose schemes were ideal dishes to put before the men of Whitehall. A few of them, it turned out, could actually be watered down and made workable. Most of them were imaginative but impossible. The point was that they produced a shock to the system which was thoroughly therapeutic. Conversely Chamberlain's common-sense approach, the careful reasoning he brought to bear on every problem and the cautious way he made his decisions, were calculated to keep Britain's war machine in low gear. War makes virtue out of vice and vice out of virtue. One would have expected Chamberlain to appreciate this axiom and to make the logical decision, to wind up his government and to hand over the leadership to someone more warlike.

It is ironical to reflect that Chamberlain and Daladier were the best men the democratic world could find to stand up and fight against Hitler. No wonder he had such an easy run for the next two years, such a brilliant succession of victories. His enemies, the nations who finally destroyed him, were simply not up to his class in 1939. The two most powerful neutrals, the United States and the Soviet Union, were both implacable opponents of Hitlerism as a matter of principle, even though the principle was different, but for reasons of national interest neither of them was ready to oppose him. The Soviet Union, being closer to the danger, was bound to take more drastic measures than the Americans. 'If you can't beat 'em, join 'em,' Stalin felt, and this policy certainly paid dividends in the short term. Hitler was not able by his strength thus to recruit the United States, but his determination and success counted for much with Americans who could only compare him favourably in this respect with the torpid French and British. His conquests of 1939 frightened the Americans and were a powerful argument against providing any assistance to the Allies.

It was this bitter truth which the year 1939 taught the democratic world, that when the chips are down it is not moral rectitude or justice which impress potential allies. In vain did the British and French point to Hitler's blatant aggression of 1 September and summon the world to a crusade against fascism. The truth is that Hitler could behave with the viciousness of Satan and still not acquire enemies. His enemies would be made not by moral conviction but by power politics and military reality. So long as Hitler had the big battalions, God would support even him, and woe to the conqueror's victims or potential victims if they did not quickly increase and equip their armed forces. It is true that the success of 1939–41 went to Hitler's head, obscured his judgement and led him to take on tasks greater than he could accomplish, so that in the end he failed and was destroyed. It is true that this is usually what happens to great conquerors. But it does not alter the fact that at the end of 1939 Hitler could, had he wished, have drawn in his horns and consolidated his empire, and that in this event he could never have been defeated by France and Britain. Hitler's achievement in the real war against Poland and in the war of words against Britain and France can only be viewed as a resounding victory. He had not managed to end the war formally, but he had gained a large part of his objective at small cost and shown the world how empty was the threat to his Germany from the western Allies. A few land patrols, a few reconnaissance flights – the war on the continent of Europe amounted to no more than this. In fact it was not a war at all. The war of 1939 was won by Hitler. And there was peace.

Chronological List of Major Events

1939

1 September

4.45 a.m. German Army invades Poland. 6 a.m. Hitler's proclamation to the German Army. 10 a.m. Hitler addresses the Reichstag in Berlin. 10.30 a.m. French Council of Ministers meets, proclaims general mobilization. 11 a.m. British Government orders general mobilization. 3 p.m. Italy proclaims 'non-belligerent' status. Britain and France issue 'warning' to Germany and demand withdrawal of German troops from Poland. 6 p.m. Chamberlain addresses House of Commons. Roosevelt appeals to belligerents not to bomb civilian populations. Soviet Government mobilizes Red Army. Gauleiter Forster proclaims incorporation of Danzig into the Reich. Switzerland declares its neutrality.

2 September

Italian attempt to arrange a conference. Britain insists on German withdrawal from Poland as prior condition. Daladier announces in National Assembly that France will fulfil her obligations to Poland. Animated discussions between London and Paris about timing of declaration of war. Ten squadrons of Bomber Command begin to cross over to France. Chamberlain forms War Cabinet with Churchill's participation. Angry scene in House of Commons. British and French agree late in the evening upon a declaration of war the next day.

3 September

9 a.m. British ultimatum delivered in Berlin sets commencement of hostilities at 11 a.m. At 11.15 a.m. Chamberlain broadcasts to nation, announces declaration of war. At noon French ultimatum delivered in Berlin, to expire at 5 p.m. Australia, New Zealand and India also announce themselves at war with Germany. In London National Service

Act passed, King George VI broadcasts. Several hundred local Germans shot in Bydgoszcz (Bromberg) – the event later called 'Bloody Sunday' by Nazi propaganda. About 9 p.m. a German submarine torpedoes the passenger ship *Athenia* north-west of Ireland. Overnight leaflet raid over Germany.

4 September

Polish–French military alliance signed in Paris. Advance parties of British Expeditionary Force land in France. Ironside and Newall fly to France to meet Gamelin. During afternoon Royal Air Force raids German fleet at Wilhelmshaven. German Army captures Częstochowa.

5 September

Roosevelt declares American neutrality. General Smuts appointed Prime Minister of South Africa. Hitler visits the front, drives across the Corridor to East Prussia.

6 September

South Africa declares war on Germany. Polish Government and High Command leave Warsaw for Brześć. German Army captures Cracow and Kielce.

7 September

Surrender of Westerplatte, the Polish enclave in Danzig. The Allies grant loans to Poland: Britain £5,000,000, France 600 million francs.

8 September

German Army reaches outskirts of Warsaw. Polish Army launches counter-attack near Kutno on River Bzura.

9 September

Molotov congratulates German Government on 'entry of German troops into Warsaw'. Göring threatens reprisals if the Allies bomb Germany. Britain announces that her plans are based on probability of a three-year war. British air chief Cyril Newall suggests an extension of bomb attacks against Germany. French Army announces capture of three-mile-square Warndt Forest.

10 September

Canada declares war on Germany.

11 September

British Cabinet informed that French Army has established a line of infantry close up to the Siegfried Line. Newall changes his mind and Cabinet agrees not to bomb Germany.

12 September
Daladier, Chamberlain, Gamelin and Chatfield meet at Abbeville. German Air Force bombs diplomatic corps at Krzemieniec in eastern Poland.

13 September
Roosevelt summons special session of Congress. French Cabinet reshuffle: Daladier takes Quai d'Orsay, Bonnet moved to Ministry of Justice. German High Command announces that since civilians have participated in defence of Poland civilian targets will be bombed and shelled.

15 September
Peace treaty signed between Soviet Union, Japan and Mongolia. Soviet press alleges that Poland is violating Soviet neutrality and ill-treating the Ukrainians and Byelorussians. Some local Polish successes on the battlefield.

17 September
2 a.m. Stalin receives Ambassador Schulenburg and tells him of imminent Red Army invasion of Poland. 3 a.m. Deputy Foreign Commissar Potyomkin receives Ambassador Grzybowski and gives him the same news. Red Army invades Poland. Polish Government crosses into Rumania late that evening.

19 September
Brześć surrenders after combined German and Soviet bombardment. Hitler speaks in Danzig and implies that Germany possesses a secret weapon. First Corps of British Expeditionary Force lands in France. About 30,000 Polish soldiers reach Warsaw, having fought their way from Battle of Kutno.

21 September
Gamelin gives up his plan for an offensive against Siegfried Line. Rumanian Prime Minister Armand Calinescu assassinated. American Congress meets in extraordinary session, Roosevelt seeks repeal of Neutrality Act.

22 September
Supreme Allied Council meets at Brighton. Lwow and Białystok surrender to Red Army.

26 September
Dahlerus meets Hitler and Göring. French Communist Party dissolved by Presidential decree.

27 September
1.15 p.m. Warsaw surrender signed. 6 p.m. Ribbentrop arrives in Moscow.

28 September
Soviet Union signs Mutual Assistance Pact with Estonia. Dahlerus
arrives in London from Berlin.

29 September
5 a.m. German–Soviet agreement signed to partition Poland. Dahlerus
meets Chamberlain and Halifax. German fleet at Heligoland raided.
National Registration Day in Britain.

30 September
President Mościcki of Poland resigns, new Polish Government under
Sikorski formed in Paris. Dahlerus leaves London for Berlin.

1 October
Cordell Hull announces American recognition of Polish government-in-
exile. Hitler meets Ciano in Berlin. Churchill speaks on radio, expresses
qualified approval of Soviet invasion of Poland.

2 October
Polish garrison on Hel peninsula surrenders. General Franco speaks at
press conference, says Poland should have surrendered to avoid total
defeat.

3 October
British House of Commons debates war situation, Lloyd George calls for
secret session to discuss peace terms. Second Corps of British Expeditionary Force lands in France.

4 October
Nikita Khrushchev speaks in Lwów. .

5 October
Last Polish fighting unit surrenders in Radzyń/Kock area. Soviet Union
signs mutual assistance pact with Latvia. Halifax informs Ambassador
Corbin of negotiations being conducted through Dahlerus.

6 October
Hitler makes his peace offer.

8 October
Hitler issues his decree on 'structure and administration of Eastern
Territories' to apply from 26 October.

10 October
Hitler repeats his peace offer in a speech at Berlin's Sportpalast. Hitler
presents his generals with 'Directive No. 6' ordering an attack on France

through the Low Countries. Daladier rejects Hitler's proposals. Soviet Union signs mutual assistance pact with Lithuania.

11 October
Berlin Radio broadcasts false report of fall of Chamberlain's government. British Expeditionary Force in France reaches four divisions, 158,000 men.

12 October
Chamberlain rejects Hitler's offer. Hitler issues decree establishing the Generalgouvernement in Poland. Soviet Union offers Finland a mutual assistance pact — offer rejected.

13 October
British battleship *Royal Oak* sunk at Scapa Flow.

15 October
Mayor of Warsaw Stefan Starzyński arrested.

16 October
German bombing attack on British fleet in Firth of Forth. German Army advances between rivers Rhine and Moselle driving the French back to the Maginot Line.

17 October
German air raid on Scapa Flow, *Iron Duke* damaged.

18 October
Soviet Government returns Wilno region to Lithuania.

19 October
Britain, France and Turkey sign treaty of mutual assistance.

21 October
John Maffey sees De Valera in Dublin. German–Italian treaty signed in Rome provides for repatriation of 10,000 Italians of German origin from the Alto Adige region.

22 October
Goebbels speaks on radio, accuses Churchill of sinking the *Athenia*. Soviet-dominated elections take place in eastern Poland.

26 October
Hans Frank takes over as Governor of Poland.

27 October
Hitler orders his generals to make final preparations for western offensive. United States Senate passes new Neutrality Act.

31 October
Molotov addresses Supreme Soviet, demands territorial concessions from Finland.

2 November
United States House of Representatives passes new Neutrality Act.

5 November
Hitler announces that western offensive will begin on 12 November. Commander-in-Chief Brauchitsch visits Hitler to protest but is verbally demolished by him.

7 November
Hitler postpones offensive, ostensibly on meteorological advice – the first of many such postponements.

8 November
Bomb explodes in Munich beerhouse a few minutes after Hitler's departure.

9 November
Two British secret service men, Best and Stevens, kidnapped at Venlo on Dutch–German border.

Notes

1 THE FIRST DAY

1. Dolata and Jurga, *Walki zbrojne na ziemiach polskich* (Armed conflict in the Polish lands), p. 477.
2. Kirchmayer, p. 79.
3. *DBFP*, Vol. VII, No. 767.
4. *British Blue Book*, p. 166.
5. Dolata and Jurga, p. 99.
6. *British Blue Book*, p. 166.
7. For Canaris's talk to Keitel on this, see *Nazi Conspiracy and Aggression*, Vol. III, p. 580.
8. For Naujocks's affidavit on this, see *Nazi Conspiracy and Aggression*. Vol. VI, pp. 390–92.
9. Bonnet, *Fin d'une Europe*, p. 345.
10. Henderson, *Failure of a Mission*, p. 278.
11. Łukasiewicz's articles appeared in *Orzeł Biały* (London) under the title 'Wrzesień 1939 w Paryżu' (September 1939 in Paris), 28 August 1948.
12. Hollingworth, *The Three Weeks' War in Poland*, p. 16.
13. Szymański, *Zły Sąsiad* (Bad Neighbour), p. 175.
14. *DBFP*, Vol. VIII, Nos. 325, 333, 388, 437.
15. *DGFP*, Vol. VII, p. 561.
16. Bonnet, *Dans la Tourmente*, p. 178.
17. ibid., p. 200. See also Benoist-Méchin, *Histoire de l'Armée Allemande*, Vol. VI, p. 331.
18. *DBFP*, No. 397.
19. ibid., No. 546.
20. Bonnet, *Dans la Tourmente*, p. 179.
21. Cordell Hull, *Memoirs*, Vol. I, p. 671.

22. F.O. 371 22980.
23. F.O. 371 23091.
24. F.O. 371 22987.
25. Bonnet, *Fin d'une Europe*, p. 345.
26. Raczyński, *In Allied London*, p. 25.
27. *DGFP*, Vol. VII, No. 501.
28. ibid., No. 502.
29. Łukasiewicz's articles in *Orzeł Biały* (op. cit.).
30. *Dans la Tourmente*, p. 181.
31. Bonnet, *Quai d'Orsay*, p. 265.
32. *DBFP*, No. 639.
33. Llewellyn Woodward, *British Foreign Policy in the Second World War*, p. 2.
34. Cabinet Minutes, 1 September 1939.
35. *DBFP*, No. 638.
36. *DBFP*, No. 644.
37. Shirer, *Berlin Diary*, 1 September.
38. von Hassell, *The von Hassell Diaries 1938–44*, p. 71.
39. *Völkischer Beobachter* (Berlin), 2 September 1939.
40. *DBFP*, No. 669.
41. Shirer, *The Rise and Fall of the Third Reich*, Chapter IV.
42. Adolf Hitler, *Mein Kampf* (Boston, Houghton Mifflin, 1943), p. 643.
43. ibid., 140.
44. ibid., 654.
45. *Documents on the Events preceding the Outbreak of the War*, p. 530.
46. ibid., p. 546.
47. ibid., p. 549.
48. Fritz Hesse, *Hitler and the English*, p. 81.
49. *Documents on the Events preceding the Outbreak of the War*, p. 422.
50. *DGFP*, Vol. VIII, No. 193.
51. ibid., p. 560.
52. *DBFP*, No. 584.
53. *DBFP*, No. 472.
54. *DBFP*, No. 477.
55. *DBFP*, No. 501.
56. *DBFP*, No. 622.
57. *DBFP*, No. 574.
58. *Failure of a Mission*, p. 269.
59. *DBFP*, No. 581.

60. *DBFP*, No. 587.
61. F.O. 371 22980.
62. F.O. 371 23131.
63. *DBFP*, No. 596.
64. *DBFP*, No. 600.
65. *DBFP*, No. 618.
66. *DBFP*, No. 590.
67. Bonnet, *Dans la Tourmente*, p. 175.
68. *DBFP*, No. 590.
69. *DBFP*, No. 595.
70. *DBFP*, No. 604.
71. *DBFP*, No. 634.
72. Henryk Batowski, *Agonia pokuju i początek wojny* (The agony of peace and the beginning of the war), p. 246.
73. *DBFP*, No. 649; *Livre Jaune Français*, No. 327.
74. *DBFP*, No. 646.
75. Bonnet, *Dans la Tourmente*, p. 182.
76. Noel, p. 474.
77. *Livre Jaune Français*, No. 343.
78. *DBFP*, No. 693.
79. *DBFP*, No. 632.
80. *DBFP*, No. 631.
81. *DBFP*, Nos. 719, 725; Wheeler-Bennett, *Nemesis of Power*, p. 458.
82. *DGFP*, Vol. VI, p. 574.
83. F.O. 371 23131.
84. F.O. 371 22980.
85. *Izvestiya* (Moscow), 1 September 1939.
86. Pobóg-Malinowski, p. 37.
87. Wladyslaw Anders, *An Army in Exile*, p. 3.
88. Kirchmayer, p. 21.
89. *Robotnik* (Warsaw), 31 August 1948.
90. *DBFP*, No. 682.
91. *The Gathering Storm*, p. 346.
92. Pobóg-Malinowski, p. 47.
93. ibid., p. 38.
94. Guderian, *Panzer Leader*, p. 68.
95. *Polskie sily zbrojne w drugiej wojnie światowej*, Vol. 1, Kampania Wrześniowa 1939 (The September Campaign 1939), p. 267 (History of war published by émigré government in London in 1951).
96. Pobóg-Malinowski, p. 37.
97. *Völkischer Beobachter*, 2 September 1939.
98. Pobóg-Malinowski, p. 34

99. ibid., p. 33.
100. Rydz-Śmigły's article was written in Rumania on 24 December 1939, and published in the Jerusalem newspaper *Na Straży* of February 1947.
101. von Hassell, *The von Hassell Diaries*, p. 71.
102. Ernst Weizsaecker, *Erinnerungen* (Munich-Freiberg, 1950), p. 239; E. Kordt, *Nicht aus den Akten* (Stuttgart, 1950), p. 300.
103. *Hore-Belisha*, p. 234.
104. CAB 66 1 (Anglo-Polish Staff Conversations).
105. Bonnet, *Fin d'une Europe*, p. 375.
106. *The Gathering Storm*, p. 312.
107. *The Times*, 2 September 1939.
108. *Hansard*, 1 September 1939.
109. *The Gathering Storm*, p. 317.
110. *DBFP*, No. 655.
111. *Dans la Tourmente*, p. 183.
112. *Quai d'Orsay*, p. 263.
113. ibid.
114. *Dans la Tourmente*, p. 183.
115. *DBFP*, No. 669.
116. *DBFP*, No. 682.
117. *DGFP*, Vol. VII, No. 515.
118. *DGFP*, Vol. VII, No. 513.
119. *Failure of a Mission*, p. 278.
120. *Dans la Tourmente*, p. 184.
121. *Livre Jaune Français*, No. 347.

2 AN UNEASY LULL

1. F.O. 371 22987.
2. *DBFP*, No. 700 says incorrectly that the statement was scheduled for 3 p.m.
3. *DBFP*, No. 700.
4. *DBFP*, No. 696.
5. *DBFP*, No. 651.
6. *DBFP*, No. 652.
7. *DBFP*, No. 708.
8. *DBFP*, No. 278.
9. *Documenti diplomatici italiani*, No. 412.
10. *DGFP*, Vol. VII, No. 539.
11. *Documenti diplomatici italiani*, No. 572.
12. Paul Schmidt, *Hitler's Interpreter* (New York, 1951), p. 156.
13. *DBFP*, No. 707.

14. *DBFP*, No. 664.
15. *DGFP*, Vol. VII, No. 541.
16. *DBFP*, No. 709.
17. *DBFP*, No. 709; *Livre Jaune Français*, No. 360.
18. Bonnet, *Quai d'Orsay*, p. 266.
19. ibid.
20. *DBFP*, No. 710.
21. *DBFP*, No. 709.
22. *DBFP*, No. 710.
23. Bonnet, *Quai d'Orsay*, p. 266.
24. ibid., p. 267.
25. ibid., p. 265.
26. F.O. 371 22987.
27. Henry Channon, *Diary*, 2 September.
28. Bonnet, *Quai d'Orsay*, p. 266.
29. *DBFP*, No. 709.
30. *DBFP*, No. 716.
31. F.O. 371 22987.
32. *DBFP*, No. 716.
33. *DBFP*, No. 708.
34. Bonnet, *Dans la Tourmente*, p. 185.
35. See Łukasiewicz's *White Eagle* articles.
36. Paul Reynaud, *La France a sauvé l'Europe* (France saved Europe), p. 600.
37. *DBFP*, No. 721.
38. Bonnet, *Dans la Tourmente*, p. 189.
39. *DBFP*, No. 721.
40. R. J. Minney, *The Private Papers of Hore-Belisha*, p. 225.
41. ibid., p. 226.
42. *DBFP*, No. 718.
43. *Livre Jaune Français*, No. 327.
44. Bonnet, *Dans la Tourmente*, p. 188.
45. ibid.
46. *DBFP*, No. 727.
47. *DBFP*, No. 728.
48. Hugh Wilson (ed.), *The Ciano Diaries* (New York, 1946), p. 136.
49. *DBFP*, No. 729.
50. *DGFP*, Vol. VII, No. 554.
51. Henry Channon, *Diary*, 2 September.
52. Harold Nicolson, *Diary*, 2 September.
53. *Hansard*, 2 September, col. 280.
54. Edward Spears, *Prelude to Dunkirk*, p. 22.

55. Hugh Dalton, *The Fateful Years*, p. 265.
56. Spears, p. 21.
57. *DBFP*, No. 732.
58. *DBFP*, No. 735.
59. Dahlerus, *The Last Attempt*, p. 125.
60. *Hore-Belisha*, p. 226.
61. *Diary*, 2 September.
62. F.O. 371 22987.
63. Churchill, *The Gathering Storm*, p. 318.
64. F.O. 371 22987.
65. L. B. Namier, *Diplomatic prelude*, p. 392.
66. *Les Carnets Secrets de Jean Zay* (Paris, 1942), pp. 80–82.
67. Anatole de Monzie, *Ci-Devant*, p. 146.
68. ibid., p. 157.
69. Reynaud, p. 600.
70. Dalton, p. 271.
71. *DBFP*, No. 734.
72. Noel, *L'Agression allemande contre la Pologne* (German aggression against Poland), p. 486.
73. *DBFP*, No. 754.
74. Iwanowski, *Kampania Wrześniowa* (The September Campaign), p. 296.
75. ibid., p. 339.
76. *DBFP*, No. 734.
77. Bonnet, *Quai d'Orsay*, p. 268.
78. *DBFP*, No. 740.
79. Bonnet, *Dans la Tourmente*, p. 189.
80. *DBFP*, No. 740.
81. Bonnet, *De Munich à la Guerre* (From Munich up to the War), p. 506.
82. Namier, p. 395.
83. See Hitler's exchange of notes with Mussolini, *DGFP*, Vol. VII, No. 565, and Vol. VIII, No. 1.
84. *DBFP*, No. 741.
85. Dalton, p. 265.
86. *The Times*, 2 September 1939.
87. The *Sunday Times*, 6 September 1964.
88. Hesse, *Hitler and the English*, p. 84.
89. F.O. 371 22982.
90. *DGFP*, Vol. VII, No. 558.
91. W. L. Langer and S. E. Gleason, *The Challenge to Isolation*, p. 198.

92. Cabinet Minutes, 2 September 1939.
93. F.O. 371 22987.
94. Dalton, p. 267.
95. Keith Feiling, *The Life of Neville Chamberlain*, p. 416.
96. Samuel Hoare, *Nine Troubled Years*, p. 399.

3 A TENTATIVE BEGINNING
 1. *DBFP*, No. 741.
 2. Bonnet, *Dans la Tourmente*, p. 190.
 3. de Monzie, p. 158.
 4. *Ciano Diaries*, p. 137.
 5. Łukasiewicz's articles in *White Eagle*.
 6. F.O. 371 22982.
 7. ibid.
 8. Bonnet, *Dans la Tourmente*, p. 197.
 9. ibid., p. 200; Benoist-Méchin, *Histoire de l'armée allemande*, Vol. VI, pp. 331–2.
10. Bonnet, *Dans la Tourmente*, p. 201.
11. de Monzie, p. 150.
12. Bonnet, *Dans la Tourmente*, p. 202.
13. Feiling, p. 422.
14. F.O. 800 311.
15. de Monzie, p. 162.
16. Bonnet, *Dans la Tourmente*, p. 206.
17. *Livre Jaune Français*, No. 327.
18. F.O. 371 22982.
19. CAB 100 1.
20. F.O. 371 23904.
21. Dahlerus, *The Last Attempt*, p. 126.
22. ibid., p. 127.
23. *DBFP*, No. 762.
24. F.O. 371 23904.
25. Avon, *The Reckoning*, p. 62.
26. *The Gathering Storm*, p. 319.
27. John Slessor, *The Central Blue*, p. 234.
28. Avon, p. 62.
29. Spears, p. 25.
30. Slessor, p. 234.
31. F.O. 371 23131.
32. Hollingworth, p. 28.
33. Noel, p. 487.
34. *The Times*, 4 September 1939

35. Noel, p. 246.
36. *Berlin Diary*, 3 September.
37. Iwanowski, *Kampania Wrześniowa* (The September Campaign), p. 620.
38. Poбóg-Malinowski, *Najnowsza historia polityczna Polski* (Modern history of Poland), Vol. II, p. 112.
39. Hollingworth, p. 20.
40. A. J. P. Taylor, *English History 1914–45* (London, Oxford University Press).
41. *The Times*, 4 September 1939.
42. *The Times*, 5 October 1939.
43. Tom Harrison and Charles Madge (eds.), *War begins at Home*, p. 74.
44. ibid., p. 42.
45. ibid., p. 230.
46. Angus Calder, *The People's War*.
47. *Le Figaro*, 5 September 1939.
48. F.O. 800 311.
49. F.O. 371 22941.
50. *War Begins at Home*, p. 49.
51. Feiling, p. 422.
52. CAB 80 1.
53. Namier, *Diplomatic Prelude*, pp. 459–62.
54. Łukasiewicz's articles in *White Eagle*.
55. C. Webster and N. Frankland, *The Strategic Air Offensive against Germany 1939–1945*, Vol. I ('Preparation'), p. 135.
56. F.O. 371 22962.
57. CAB 1 65.
58. CAB 1 100.
59. *DGFP*, Vol. VII, No. 576.
60. *DBFP*, No. 766.
61. *DBFP*, No. 719.
62. *Berlin Diary*, 2 September, 23 September and 29 October 1939.
63. *New York Times*, 1 September 1939.
64. Führer Conferences on Naval Affairs, 1939, p. 13 (published by British Admiralty in mimeograph form).

4 THE FALL OF POLAND

1. *Listener*, 24 July 1969.
2. *The Times*, 12 September 1939.
3. Guderian, p. 73.
4. ibid., p. 84.

5. *The Times*, 6 September 1939.
6. F.O. 371 23131.
7. ibid.
8. Pobóg-Malinowski, p. 53.
9. *Listener*, 24 July 1969.
10. Pobóg-Malinowski, p. 55.
11. *The Times*, 24 September 1939.
12. Pobóg-Malinowski, p. 54. See also the article by Sławój-Składkowski in *Kultura* (Paris), May 1948.
13. *The Ironside Diaries*, 11 September 1939.
14. *Strategy*, p. 7.
15. Minney, p. 234.
16. *The Ironside Diaries*, p. 105.
17. Henry Channon, *Diaries*, 6 September 1939.
18. *The Gathering Storm*, p. 317.
19. F.O. 800 319.
20. *The Gathering Storm*, p. 578.
21. ibid., pp. 356–9.
22. Macleod, p. 284.
23. *The Gathering Storm*, p. 359.
24. Macleod, p. 284.
25. Feiling, p. 403.
26. *Diaries of Sir Alexander Cadogan*, 20 May 1939.
27. *The Gathering Storm*, pp. 360–62.
28. ibid., p. 382.
29. Macleod, p. 283.
30. *The Gathering Storm*, p. 355.
31. ibid., p. 388.
32. Henry Channon, *Diaries*, 26 September 1939.
33. Avon, *The Reckoning*, p. 73.
34. A. L. Rowse: *All Souls and Appeasement*, p. 107.
35. *DGFP*, Vol. VIII, No. 35.
36. The 8 September date is quoted in Raczyński, p. 33, and in *Polskie Siły Zbrojne . . .*, Part II, p. 435. Marian Staniewicz in his book *Klęska wrześniowa . . .*, published in Warsaw in 1952, writes incorrectly that Norwid-Neugebauer arrived on 3 September and was kept waiting six whole days before his interview.
37. *Przegląd Międzynarodowy* (Warsaw), Nos. 19–23, 1948.
38. Iwanowski, p. 384; Staniewicz, p. 219.
39. CAB 66 1.
40. *Le Figaro*, 10 September 1939.
41. *Polskie Siły Zbrojne . . .*, Vol. I, Part II, p. 434.

42. Iwanowski, pp. 626–7.
43. *Polskie Siły Zbrojne . . .*, Vol. I, Part I, p. 99.
44. Gamelin, *La Guerre*, p. 60.
45. ibid., pp. 60–61.
46. ibid., p. 57.
47. *The Times*, 7 October 1939.
48. Feiling, p. 416.
49. *Strategy*, pp. 567–8.
50. *Völkischer Beobachter*, 2 September 1939.
51. *DBFP*, No. 734.
52. CAB 100 1.
53. *Strategy*, p. 567.
54. *The Ironside Diaries*, p. 106.
55. Leo Amery, p. 330.
56. Spears, pp. 29–31.
57. Cabinet Minutes, 11 September 1939.
58. CAB 80 2.
59. CAB 80 1.
60. Slessor, p. 243.
61. Hollingworth, p. 66.
62. CAB 80 2.
63. *Department of State Bulletin*, Vol. I, p. 282.
64. F.O. 800 321.
65. Guderian, p. 78.
66. F.O. 371 23131.
68. *The Initial Triumph of the Axis*, p. 27.
69. *Uj Magyarzag*, 4 October 1939.
70. Pobóg-Malinowski, p. 60.
71. ibid., p. 59.
72. *The Times*, 18 September 1939.
73. Hollingworth, p. 95.
74. Józef Beck, *Dernier Rapport*, p. 238.
75. Iwanowski, p. 507.
76. F.O. 371 23131.
77. *Zeszyty Historyczne* (Kultura, Paris, 1967), No. 12, p. 144.
78. Pobóg-Malinowski, p. 50.
79. *Zeszyty Historyczne*, No. 12, p. 143.
80. Hollingworth, p. 97.
81. Iwanowski, p. 562.
82. *The Times*, 5 October 1939.
83. *Encyklopedia Współczesna* (Warsaw), No. 8/58, p. 376.
84. *DGFP*, Vol. VI, p. 574. Also Halder's diary, *DGFP*, Vol. VII, pp.

557–9 and memorandum on p. 200. Also *Trials of the Major War Criminals*, Vol. XLI, pp. 16–25.

85. International Military Tribunal, Document L-3.
86. *The Nemesis of Power*, p. 460.
87. Speer, p. 166.
88. *Mein Kampf*, Vol. I, p. 123.
89. *Völkischer Beobachter*, 9 September 1939.
90. *Berlin Diary*, 10 August 1939.
91. Canaris's diary, see *Nazi Conspiracy and Aggression*, Vol. V, p. 769.
92. International Military Tribunal, Document NO-3075.
93. International Military Tribunal, Document NO-2325.
94. International Military Tribunal, Document 3363-PS.
95. Hollingworth, p. 139.
96. *DGFP*, Vol. VIII, No. 138.
97. F.O. 800 317.
98. F.O. 371 23013.
99. *Reichsgezetzblatt* (Berlin, 1939), Vol. I, p. 2077.
100. *The Nazi 'Kultur' in Poland*, p. 4.
101. *Trials of the Major War Criminals*, Vol. I, p. 297.
102. A photograph of this document appears in W. Bartoszewski, *Warsaw Death Ring*, pp. 24–5.
103. Pobóg-Malinowski, p. 112.
104. Bartoszewski, p. 23.
105. *Nowy Kurier Warszawski*, 30 November 1939.
106. Henryk Pawlowicz, *Wawer – 27 December 1939* (Warsaw, 1962), p. 30.
107. *Nazi Conspiracy and Aggression*, Vol. IV, p. 891.
108. *The Times*, 16 October 1939.
109. Pobóg-Malinowski, p. 112.
110. *DGFP*, Vol. VIII, No. 158.
111. *The Times*, 16 October 1939.
112. *The Nazi 'Kultur' in Poland*, p. 5.
113. ibid., p. 184. See also Freiherr du Prel, *Das Deutsche General-Gouvernment Polen*, Berlin, 1940.
114. *Nowy Kurier Warszawski*, 23 August 1941.
115. F.O. 371 23131.

5 EXCHANGES OF HARSH WORDS
1. *The Times*, 4 September 1939.
2. *The Times* 5 September 1939.
3. CAB 1 65.

4. *The Gathering Storm*, p. 375.
5. John Slessor, *The Central Blue*, p. 240.
6. ibid., p. 242.
7. ibid., p. 243.
8. R. Macleod and Denis Kelly (eds.), *The Ironside Diaries*, p. 101.
9. Maurice Gamelin, *Servir: La Guerre*, p. 36.
10. ibid., p. 47.
11. *The Ironside Diaries*, p. 101.
12. Slessor, p. 243.
13. ibid., p. 239.
14. Feiling, p. 416.
15. CAB 80 1.
16. ibid.
17. S. W. Roskill, *The War at Sea*, Vol. I, p. 65.
18. CAB 80 1.
19. *The Times*, 5 September 1939.
20. Roskill, p. 66.
21. *Völkischer Beobachter*, 5 September 1939.
22. *Berlin Diary*, 10 September 1939.
23. Gomulka, *Przemówienia 1962* (Speeches, 1962), p. 17.
24. Feiling, p. 419.
25. ibid., p. 416.
26. Macleod, p. 282.
27. F.O. 371 23131.
28. Hollingworth, pp. 23–4.
29. *DGFP*, Vol. VIII, No. 45.
30. CAB 66 1.
31. Gamelin, p. 52
32. ibid., p. 50.
33. *The Polish White Book* (London, 1941), p. 187.
34. *DBFP*, No. 694.
35. Pobóg-Malinowski, p. 41.
36. *Polish White Book*, p. 188.
37. *Historiya vyelikoy otechestvennoy voyny* (History of the Great Fatherland War), Vol. 1, p. 207.
38. *Trials of the Major War Criminals* (Nuremberg), Vol. XV, p. 385.
39. *Strategy*, p. 60.
40. Gamelin, p. 15.
41. Siegfried Westphal, *Heer in Fesseln* (Bonn, 1950), p. 109.
42. CAB 80 1.
43. Gauché, *Le Deuxième Bureau au Travail* (Paris, 1953), p. 163.
44. CAB 80 1.

45. *Strategy*, p. 64
46. ibid., p. 33.
47. Ulrich Liss, *Westfront 1939–40* (Neckargemuend, 1959), p. 269.
48. Pierre Tissier, *The Riom Trial* (London, 1943), p. 51.
49. Franz Halder, *Kriegstagebuch* (War Diary), Vol. 1, p. 7.
50. H. B. Gisevius, *To the Bitter End*, p. 375.
51. Kimche: *The Unfought Battle*, p. 145.
52. *Hore-Belisha*, p. 215.
53. Liss, pp. 41 and 84.
54. Kimche, p. 89.
55. *Trials of the Major War Criminals*, Vol. XV, p. 361.
56. Westphal, p. 116.
57. *The Gathering Storm*, p. 375.
58. Figures provided by Imperial War Museum, London.
59. *War Begins at Home*, p. 35.
60. Diana Cooper, *The Light of Common Day*, p. 257.
61. Premier 1 379.
62. F.O. 800 321.
63. Premier 1 379.
64. Raczyński, p. 347.
65. *Hansard*, 3 October 1939.
66. Feiling, p. 424.
67. F.O. 371 23104.
68. Premier 1 380.
69. *DGFP*, Vol. VIII, No. 332 (note).
70. Macleod, p. 279.
71. Premier 1 380.
72. F.O. 800 317.
73. Premier 1 443.
74. Premier 1 380.
75. Macleod, p. 278.
76. Committee on Imperial Defence, paper 323A.
77. *The Times*, 13 October, 1939.
78. ibid.
79. *Daily Worker* (London), 19, 20 and 22 September 1939.
80. Hyde, *I Believed*, p. 70.
81. *Communist International* (Moscow), Nos. 8–9, 1939, pp. 23–6.
82. Mosley, p. 377.
83. ibid., p. 395.
84. ibid., p. 400.
85. *Action* (London), 2 September 1939.
86. Cabinet Minutes.

87. Mosley, p. 385.
88. *DGFP*, Vol. VI, p. 574.
89. *Action*, 23 September 1939.
90. ibid., 21 October 1939.
91. Mosley, p. 401.
92. Reynaud, p. 606.
93. ibid.
94. Feiling, p. 416.
95. Cabinet Minutes.
96. Premier 1.
97. *Hansard*, 27 September 1939, speech of Sir A. Sinclair.
98. F.O. 371 23040.
99. CAB 66 1.
100. *The Times*, 10 September 1939.
101. *The Times*, 26 September 1939.
102. Cabinet Minutes, 28 September 1939.
103. Harold Nicolson, *Diaries*, Vol. II, p. 32.
104. Shirer, *Berlin Diary*.
105. Premier 1 394.
106. F.O. 800 325.
107. ibid.
108. F.O. 371 23040.
109. *Le Figaro* (Paris), 22 September 1939.
110. F.O. 371 23040.
111. F.O. 371 22913.
112. F.O. 371 22926.
113. ibid.

6 THE EMPIRE IN PERIL

1. Ronald Storrs, p. 233.
2. ibid., p. 231.
3. Avon, *The Reckoning*, p. 67.
4. *The Times*, 6 November 1939.
5. Ronald Storrs, p. 252.
6. *The Times*, 13 January 1940.
7. Longford and O'Neill, *Eamon de Valera*, p. 347.
8. Cabinet Minutes, 1 September 1939.
9. *The Gathering Storm*, p. 583.
10. F.O. 800 310.
11. Longford and O'Neill, p. 366.
12. *The Times*, 11 September 1939.
13. *The Times*, 9 September 1939.

14. *The Gathering Storm*, p. 583.
15. ibid., p. 216.
16. *Hansard*, 5 May 1938.
17. *The Gathering Storm*, p. 577.
18. CAB 66 1.
19. Cabinet Minutes, 15 September 1939.
20. Avon, *The Reckoning*, p. 69.
21. *The Gathering Storm*, p. 583.
22. Avon, *The Reckoning*, p. 69.
23. F.O. 800 310.
24. Longford and O'Neill, *Eamon de Valera*, p. 355.
25. F.O. 800 310.
26. Harold Nicolson, *Diaries*, Vol. II, p. 142.
27. Cabinet Minutes, 23 October 1939.
28. Roskill, *The War at Sea*, p. 615.
29. Avon, *The Reckoning*, p. 70.

7 NEUTRAL – BUT ON WHOSE SIDE?

 1. F.O. 371 23743.
 2. F.O. 800 321.
 3. All quoted in *The Times*, 4 September 1939.
 4. *New York Times*, 2 September 1939.
 5. *World Telegram*, 2 September 1939.
 6. F.O. 800 321.
 7. W. L. Langer and S. E. Gleason, *The Challenge to Isolation*, p. 219.
 8. ibid., p. 220.
 9. Cordell Hull, *Memoirs*, Vol. I, p. 676.
10. Max Freedman (ed.), *Roosevelt and Frankfurter*, p. 499.
11. *New York Times*, 4 September 1939.
12. ibid.
13. ibid., 3 September 1939.
14. Robert Sherwood, *The White House Papers of Harry L. Hopkins*, Vol. I, p. 129.
15. F.O. 800 321.
16. Robert Bruce Lockhart, *Comes the Reckoning*.
17. Robert Sherwood, p. 133.
18. Alden Hatch, *Franklin D. Roosevelt* (London, 1947), p. 250.
19. Langer and Gleason, p. 203.
20. Premier 1 341.
21. ibid.

22. Letter to Halifax, F.O. 800 321.
23. Langer and Gleason, p. 203.
24. Cordell Hull, p. 693.
25. Elliott Roosevelt (ed.), *The Roosevelt Letters* (London, 1952), Vol. 1928–45, p. 273.
26. *Roosevelt and Frankfurter*, p. 499.
27. *New York Times*, 22 September 1939.
28. *The Times*, 6 November 1939.
29. Cordell Hull, p. 684.
30. *DGFP*, Vol. VIII, No. 22.
31. ibid., No. 88.
32. ibid., No. 129.
33. ibid., No. 299.
34. *The Wartime Journals of Charles A. Lindbergh*, p. 251.
35. Langer and Gleason, p. 220.
36. *New York Times*, 15 September 1939.
37. *Congressional Record*, 76th Congress, 2nd Session, Vol. 85, Part I, p. 50.
38. ibid., p. 69.
39. *The Roosevelt Letters*, p. 278.
40. F.O. 371 22842.
41. ibid.
42. F.O. 800 321.
43. F.O. 800 324.
44. F.O. 371 22913.
45. F.O. 800 321.
46. ibid.
47. F.O. 371 22842.
48. F.O. 371 22817.
49. F.O. 800 321.
50. ibid.
51. F.O. 371 22817.
52. *The Times*, 16 October 1939.
53. *The Roosevelt Letters*, p. 278.
54. *DGFP*, Vol. VIII, No. 139.
55. F.O. 371 22827.
56. ibid.
57. F.O. 371 22817.
58. Adolf Hitler, *Mein Kampf* (London, Hurst & Blackett), Vol. I, p. 123.
59. ibid., Vol. II, p. 497.
60. ibid., Epilogue, p. 560.

61. F.O. 371 22827.
62. Cordell Hull, p. 700.
63. Langer and Gleason, pp. 249–50.
64. ibid., p. 252.
65. ibid.
66. F.O. 371 22817.
67. *Daily Telegraph*, 7 December 1939.
68. *The Times*, 12 December 1939.
69. F.O. 371 22827.
70. Iain Macleod, *Neville Chamberlain*, p. 279.
71. Llewellyn Woodward, *British Foreign Policy in the Second World War*, Vol. I, p. 335.
72. *DGFP*, Vol. VIII, No. 291.
73. F.O. 371 23099.
74. F.O. 800 311.
75. F.O. 371 23099.
76. Langer and Gleason, p. 258.
77. F.O. 371 23099.
78. Langer and Gleason, p. 247.
79. ibid., p. 248.
80. F.O. 371 23099.
81. *DGFP*, Vol. VIII, No. 4.
82. *Trials of the Major War Criminals* (Nuremberg edition), Vol. XIV, p. 278.
83. *DGFP*, Vol. VII, No. 493.
84. Albert Speer, *Inside the Third Reich*, p. 165.
85. *Führer Conferences on Naval Affairs*, 1939, p. 16 (published by British Admiralty in mimeograph form).
86. *Trials of the Major War Criminals*, Vol. XXXV, p. 527.
87. *Nazi Conspiracy and Aggression*, Vol. VII, p. 114 (published by U.S. Government).
88. F.O. 371 22842.
89. ibid.
90. *The Gathering Storm*, p. 331.
91. *The Roosevelt Letters*, Vol. III, p. 288.
92. F. D. Roosevelt, *His Personal Letters*, Vol. II, p. 947.
93. *Public Papers and Addresses*, 1939, Vol. VIII, p. 556.
94. Cordell Hull, p. 695.
95. *The Times*, 6 November 1939.
96. *DGFP*, Vol. VIII, No. 323.
97. *Pravda* (Moscow), 1 November 1939.
98. F.O. 800 321.

99. F.O. 800 311.
100. *The Times*, 3 November 1939.

8   RUSSIA THE GREAT ENIGMA
1. Werth, *Russia at War 1941–1945* (London, Barrie & Rockliff, 1964).
2. *DGFP*, Vol. VII, No. 229.
3. *Pravda*, 1 September 1939.
4. F.O. 371 22980.
5. *DGFP*, Vol. VIII, No. 13.
6. *DGFP*, Vol. VII, No. 496.
7. ibid., No. 567.
8. *DGFP*, Vol. VIII, No. 5.
9. *DGFP*, Vol. VIII, No. 37.
10. *Izvestiya*, 10 September 1939.
11. *DGFP*, Vol. VIII, No. 39.
12. ibid., No. 46.
13. *Polish White Book*, p. 188.
14. Hollingworth, p. 70.
15. *DGFP*, Vol. VIII, No. 63.
16. Shirer, *Berlin Diary*.
17. *History of the Second World War*, Vol. I, No. 3 (magazine serial published by Purnell, London).
18. *DGFP*, Vol. VIII, No. 70.
19. ibid., No. 78.
20. ibid.
21. *Izvestiya*, 18 September 1939.
22. Raczyński, p. 34.
23. F.O. 371 23103.
24. CAB 80 2.
25. F.O. 371 23103.
26. Pobóg-Malinowski, p. 50.
27. *History of the Second World War* (Purnell), Vol. I, No. 3.
28. F.O. 371 23131.
29. *Zeszyty historyczne* (History Note-books), No. 12, p. 146 (Paris, 1967).
30. *Na Straży* (Jerusalem), February 1947.
31. ibid.
32. F.O. 371 23103.
33. Beck, *Dernier Rapport*, p. 240.
34. *DGFP*, Vol. VIII, No. 55.

35. *Na Straży*, February 1947.
36. Anders, p. 13.
37. Cabinet Minutes, 17 September 1939.
38. CAB 80 2.
39. *DGFP*, Vol. VIII, No. 45.
40. *Pravda*, 18 September 1939.
41. ibid.
42. *Historiya vyelikoy otechestvennoy voyny Sovyetskogo Soyuza* (History of the Great Fatherland War of the Soviet Union), Vol. I, p. 250.
43. ibid., p. 247.
44. ibid., p. 249.
45. *Pravda*, 1 November 1939.
46. *Historiya*, Vol. I, p. 249.
47. *Na Straży*, February 1947.
48. *Monitor Polski*, 25 September 1939.
49. Facsimiles of these leaflets are printed in *Biała Księga* (White Book), pp. 85–6, published by Instytut Literacki, Paris.
50. Pobóg-Malinowski, p. 51.
51. F.O. 371 23103.
52. CAB 80 2.
53. *The Times*, 18 September 1939.
54. F.O. 371 23103.
55. ibid.
56. *Hansard*, 20 September 1939.
57. F.O. 371 23103.
58. F.O. 371 23682.
59. Pobóg-Malinowski, p. 50.
60. Guderian, *Panzer Leader*, p. 83.
61. ibid. See also *Deutsche Allgemeine Zeitung*. 25 September 1939.
62. *Myezhdunarodnaya Zhizn* (Moscow), September 1969, p. 120.
63. Szymański, p. 189.
64. *Khrushchev Remembers*, p. 139.
65. *The Gathering Storm*, p. 351.
66. ibid.
67. Feiling, p. 425.
68. *Il Messagero*, 11 October 1939.
69. It was G. Mander. See *Hansard*, 26 October 1939.
70. *DGFP*, Vol. VIII, No. 90.
71. ibid., No. 103.
72. ibid., No. 109.
73. For example see *The Times*, 23 September 1939

74. *DGFP*, Vol. VIII, No. 176.
75. ibid., No. 104.
76. ibid., No. 109.
77. ibid., No. 131.
78. ibid., No. 137.
79. *Events preceding the Outbreak of War* (New York, 1940), p. 451.
80. *DGFP*, Vol. VIII, No. 137.
81. ibid., No. 115.
82. ibid., No. 124.
83. ibid., p. 940.
84. F.O. 371 23013.
85. *DGFP*, Vol. VIII, No. 159.
86. ibid., p. 941.
87. *Khrushchev Remembers*, p. 128.
88. *DGFP*, Vol. VIII, p. 942.
89. ibid., No. 158.
90. ibid., No. 162.
91. ibid., No. 160.
92. ibid., No. 157.
93. *Izvestiya* (Moscow), 1 November 1939.
94. *Khrushchev Remembers*, p. 128.
95. ibid., p. 129.
96. *Istoriya vyelikoy otechestvennoy voyny*, Vol. I, p. 247.
97. *Khrushchev Remembers*, p. 139.
98. *Istoriya vyelikoy otechestvennoy voyny*, Vol. I, p. 249.
99. ibid., p. 250.
100. Paul Reynaud, *La France a sauvé l'Europe*, Vol. I, p. 587.
101. Andrzej Werblan in *Miesięcznik Literacki* (Warsaw), June 1968, estimates that 22 to 26 per cent of the pre-war Communist Party membership was Jewish. But this figure is disputed.
102. *Polityka* (Warsaw), No. 40, 1957.
103. *Pravda*, 22 September 1939.
104. Pobóg-Malinowski, p. 121.
105. Article by Karolina Lanckorońska in *Wiadomości* (London), No. 42, 1948.
106. Pobóg-Malinowski, p. 111.
107. *Polskie siły zbrojne w drugiej wojnie światowej* (The Polish Armed Forces during the Second World War), published in London in 1950, Vol. III, p. 34.
108. S. Mora and P. Zwierniak: *Sprawiedliwość Sowiecka* (Rome, 1945), p. 66.
109. Pobóg-Malinowski, p. 111.

110. *Khrushchev Remembers*, p. 142.
111. *The Times*, 6 October 1939.
112. *Khrushchev Remembers*, p. 129.

9 THE PEACE OFFENSIVE
   1. F.O. 371 23097.
   2. F.O. 800 321.
   3. Macleod, p. 281. Letter dated 11 November 1939.
   4. Samuel Hoare, *Nine Troubled Years*, p. 405
   5. F.O. 800 321.
   6. Feiling, p. 426.
   7. Dahlerus, Introduction, p. ix.
   8. ibid., p. vii.
   9. F.O. 800 317.
  10. Dahlerus, Introduction, p. viii.
  11. Premier 1 331A.
  12. F.O. 371 23013.
  13. F.O. 800 311.
  14. F.O. 800 317.
  15. F.O. 371 23097.
  16. ibid.
  17. *DGFP*, Vol. VIII, No. 138.
  18. Giving evidence on 19 March 1946.
  19. Hitler, *Mein Kampf* (Boston, 1943), p. 674.
  20. F.O. 371 23097.
  21. Hoare, *Nine Troubled Years*, p. 405.
  22. F.O. 371 23097.
  23. von Papen, *Memoirs* (London, Deutsch, 1952), p. 456.
  24. Feiling, p. 416.
  25. Macleod, p. 281.
  26. ibid.
  27. F.O. 371 23097.
  28. F.O. 800 317.
  29. ibid.
  30. *The Diaries of Sir Alexander Cadogan*, 28 September 1939.
  31. Macleod, p. 278.
  32. F.O. 371 23097.
  33. ibid.
  34. Bonnet, *Dans la Tourmente*.
  35. *DGFP*, Vol. VII, No. 565.
  36. *DGFP*, Vol. VIII, No. 1.

37. ibid., No. 38.
38. ibid., No. 73.
39. *DGFP*, Vol. VIII, No. 176.
40. ibid., No. 131.
41. It is true that Britain knew this in advance. Ciano told Loraine on 23 August.
42. Hugh Wilson (ed.), *The Ciano Diaries 1939–43* (New York, 1946), p. 154.
43. *DGFP*, Vol. VIII, No. 97.
44. F.O. 371 23098.
45. *DGFP*, Vol. VIII, No. 186.
46. *Izvestiya*, 29 September 1939.
47. CAB 66 1.
48. F.O. 371 23102.
49. CAB 80 3.
50. CAB 66 1.
51. F.O. 371 23040.
52. F.O. 800 311.
53. Langer and Gleason, p. 251.
54. *Hansard*, 19 October 1939.
55. F.O. 800 321.
56. F.O. 371 23097.
57. ibid.
58. F.O. 371 23131.
59. ibid.
60. F.O. 800 317.
61. F.O. 371 23098.
62. *Völkischer Beobachter*, 30 September 1939.
63. *Hansard*, 3 October 1939.
64. F.O. 371 23097. Frank Osborne reporting from the Vatican.
65. *Völkischer Beobachter*, 7 October 1939.
66. Macleod, p. 279.
67. *Berlin Diary*, 6 October 1939.
68. Macleod, p. 279.
69. Llewellyn Woodward, p. 8.
70. Cabinet Minutes.
71. Macleod, p. 279.
72. F.O. 371 23040.
73. Bonnet, *Dans la Tourmente*, p. 209.
74. De Monzie, *Ci-Devant*, p. 173.
75. *Roosevelt and Frankfurter*, p. 279.
76. Langer and Gleason, p. 255.

77. *Izvestiya*, 9 October 1939.
78. Premier 1 395.
79. *British Blue Book*, No. 144.
80. *Hansard*, 12 October 1939.
81. F.O. 800 311.
82. Maxime Mourin, p. 26.
83. De Monzie, p. 168.
84. *DGFP*, Vol. VIII, No. 222.
85. *Berlin Diary*, 11 October 1939.
86. *Hansard*, 12 October 1939.
87. *DGFP*, Vol. VIII, No. 246.
88. F.O. 800 317.
89. F.O. 371 23099.
90. *DGFP*, Vol. VIII, No. 337.
91. *The Diaries of Sir Alexander Cadogan*, 28 December 1939.
92. F.O. 371 23099.
93. Dahlerus, *The Last Attempt*, p. 19.
94. Feiling, p. 416.
95. A. J. P. Taylor, *English History 1914–45*.
96. Liddell Hart, *The Defence of Britain*, p. 41.
97. CAB 80 1.
98. Macleod, p. 281.
99. Feiling, p. 424.
100. *Berlin Diary*, 14 September 1939.
101. *The Times*, 30 September 1939.
102. *The Times*, 2 October 1939.
103. *Daily Telegraph*, 6 October 1939.
104. Harold Nicolson, *Diaries*, 31 October 1939.
105. Avon, *The Reckoning*, p. 77.
106. ibid., p. 78.
107. Deneys Reitz, *No Outspan*.
108. *DGFP*, Vol. VIII, No. 224.
109. Wheeler-Bennett, *The Nemesis of Power*, p. 465.
110. *Trials of War Criminals* (Washington, 1951–2), Vol. X, pp. 864–72.
111. *The John Memorandum*, quoted by Wheeler-Bennett, p. 459.
112. Halder, *Diary*, 27 October 1939.
113. ibid., 5 November 1939. See Halder, *Kriegstagebuch*, edited by Hans-Adolf Jacobsen, Stuttgart, 1962.
114. *Die Weltwoche* (Zurich), 10 November 1939.
115. F.O. 800 311.
116. *The Diaries of Sir Alexander Cadogan*, 28 February 1940.

117. *War Begins at Home*, p. 417.
118. Feiling, p. 404.
119. *Polish Acts of Cruelty against the German Minority*, p. 13 (New York, German Information Center, 1940).

Source Materials

The main unpublished source used in this book is the British official papers for 1939, which were opened to historians in 1970 and are kept in the Public Record Office, London. These are the original papers compiled by the Administration and each Government department has its own collection of volumes. In the reference notes to this book the term 'Premier 1' denotes the files of Chamberlain's private office, 'F.O. 371' denotes the 1939 Foreign Office papers, 'F.O. 800' denotes papers from Foreign Office private collections, 'CAB' denotes Cabinet Papers. I am grateful to the Public Record Office for their help in my researches and for permission to quote from the documents, copyright of which rests with the Crown.

PUBLISHED DOCUMENTARY SOURCES

Documents on British Foreign Policy, 1919–39, Her Majesty's Stationery Office, 1947– (Marked in the notes as '*DBFP*')

Documents on German Foreign Policy, 1918–45, Her Majesty's Stationery Office (Marked in the notes as '*DGFP*')

I Documenti diplomatici italiani, 1935–39, Libreria dello Stato, Rome, 1952

Livre Jaune Français, documents diplomatiques, 1938–39, Ministry of Foreign Affairs, Paris, 1940

Nazi Conspiracy and Aggression, 10 volumes, U.S. Government Printing Office, Washington, 1946

Trial of the Major War Criminals before the International Military Tribunal, 42 volumes, Nuremberg

Trials of War Criminals before the Nuremberg Military Tribunals, 15 volumes, U.S. Government Printing Office, Washington, 1951

Select Bibliography

Amery, Leopold, *My Political Life*, Vol. III, 'Unforgiving Years, 1929–40', Hutchinson, 1955

Anders, Władysław, *An Army in Exile*, Macmillan, 1949

Avon, Earl of (Anthony Eden), *The Reckoning*, Cassell, 1965

Batowski, Henryk, *Agonia pokoju i początek wojny* (*The Agony of Peace and the Beginning of the War*), Wydawnictwo Poznańskie, Poznań, 1969

Beck, Józef, *Dernier Rapport: Politique polonaise 1926–39*, Neuchâtel, 1951

Birkenhead, Lord, *Life of Lord Halifax*, Hamish Hamilton, 1965.

Bonnet, Georges, *De Munich à la Guerre*, Plon, Paris, 1967; *Quai d'Orsay*, Times Press, Isle of Man, 1965; *Dans la Tourmente*, Paris, 1971

Borisov, Yu V., *Sovyetsko-frantsuzski otnoshenia 1924–45 (Soviet-French Relations 1924–45)*, Moscow, 1964

Bullock, Alan, *Hitler – A Study in Tyranny*, Odhams, 1952

The Diaries of Sir Alexander Cadogan, Ed. David Dilks, Cassell, 1971

Chips: the Diaries of Sir Henry Channon, Ed. Robert Rhodes James, Penguin, 1970

Churchill, Winston S., *The Second World War*, Vol. I, 'The Gathering Storm', Cassell, 1948

Coulondre, Robert, *De Staline à Hitler: Souvenirs de deux ambassades 1936–39*, Hachette, Paris, 1950

Dalton, Hugh, *The Fateful Years*, Muller, 1957

Documents on the Events Preceding the Outbreak of War, German Library of Information, New York, 1940

Ellis, L. F., *The War in France and Flanders*, Her Majesty's Stationery Office, 1953

Feiling, Keith, *The Life of Neville Chamberlain*, Macmillan, 1946

Flandin, P. E., *Politique française 1919–40*, Paris, 1940

Frankland, Noble and Webster, Charles, *The Strategic Air Offensive Against Germany, 1939–45*, Vol. I, 'Preparation', Her Majesty's Stationery Office, 1961

Fuller, J. F. C., *The Second World War 1939–45*, Eyre & Spottiswoode, 1948

Gamelin, Maurice, *Servir: La Guerre (septembre 1939–19 mai 1940)*, Plon, Paris, 1947

Gilbert, Martin and Gott, Richard, *The Appeasers*, Weidenfeld & Nicolson, 1963

Gisevius, Hans, *To the Bitter End*, Cape, 1948

Guderian, Heinz, *Panzer Leader*, Michael Joseph, 1952

Halder, Franz, *Kriegstagebuch (War Diary)*, Ed. Hans-Adolf Jacobsen, Stuttgart, 1962

Halifax, Earl of, *Fullness of Days*, Collins, 1957

von Hassell, Ulrich, *The von Hassell Diaries 1938–44*, Hamish Hamilton, 1948

Henderson, Nevile, *Failure of a Mission*, Hodder & Stoughton, 1940

Henriot, Philippe, *Les carnets de Jean Zay*, Editions de France, Paris, 1942

Hitler, Adolf, *Mein Kampf (My Struggle)*, Hurst & Blackett, 1939

Hoare, Samuel (Viscount Templewood), *Nine Troubled Years*, Collins, 1954

Hollingworth, Clare, *The Three Weeks' War in Poland*, Duckworth, 1940

Hull, Cordell, *Memoirs*, Vol. I, Macmillan, New York, 1948

The Ironside Diaries, Ed. R. Macleod and Denis Kelly, Constable, 1962

Istoriya Diplomatii, Vol. III, Izpollit, Moscow, 1965

Iwanowski, Wincenty, *Kampania Wrześniowa 1939 (The September Campaign 1939)*, PAX, Warsaw, 1961

Khrushchev Remembers, Trans. Strobe Talbott, Deutsch, 1971

Kimche, Jon, *The Unfought Battle*, Weidenfeld & Nicolson, 1968

Kirchmayer, Jerzy, *Kampania Wrześniowa 1939 (The September Campaign 1939)*, Lodz, 1946

Knatchbull-Hugessen, Hughe, *Diplomat in Peace and War*, John Murray, 1951

Kordt, E., *Nicht aus den Akten: Die Wilhelmstrasse in Frieden und Krieg*, Stuttgart, 1950

Kowalski, Włodzimierz, *Walka dyplomatyczna dla miejsca Polski w Europie (The Diplomatic Struggle for the Place of Poland in Europe)*, Książka i Wiedza, Warsaw, 1967

Langer, William L. and Gleason, S. Everett, *The Challenge to Isolation 1937–40*, Royal Institute of International Affairs, 1952

The Wartime Journals of Charles A. Lindbergh, Harcourt Brace Jovanovich, New York, 1970

Longford, Earl of and O'Neill, T. S., *Eamon de Valera*, Hutchinson, 1970

Mackiewicz, S., *Polityka Józefa Becka*, Paris, 1960

Macleod, Iain, *Neville Chamberlain*, Muller, 1961

Malinowski, Marian, *W obronie stolicy (Defending the Capital)*, Warsaw, 1960

Minney, R. J., *The Private Papers of Hore-Belisha*, Collins, 1960

de Monzie, Anatole, *Ci-Devant*, Flammarion, Paris, 1942

Mourin, Maxime, *Les tentatives de paix dans la deuxième guerre mondiale*, Payot, Paris, 1949

Namier, Lewis B., *Diplomatic Prelude 1938–39*, Macmillan, 1948

The Nazi 'Kultur' in Poland, His Majesty's Stationery Office, for the Polish Ministry of Information, 1945

Harold Nicolson Diaries and Letters, Vols. I and II, Ed. Nigel Nicolson, Collins, 1967

Noel, Léon, *L'Agression allemande contre la Pologne*, Flammarion, Paris, 1946

Norwid-Neugebauer, M., *The Defence of Poland*, Kolin, 1942

Papen, Franz von, *Memoirs*, Deutsch, 1952

Pobóg-Malinowski, Władysław, *Najnowsza historia polityczna Polski (A Modern Political History of Poland)*, Vol. III (1939–45), London, 1960

Polish Acts of Cruelty against the German Minority, German Information Center, New York, 1940

The Polish White Book, Documents on Polish–German and Polish–Soviet Relations, 1933–9, London, 1941

Polskie siły zbrojne w drugiej wojnie światowej (Polish Armed Forces During the Second World War), Vol. I, 'Kampania Wrześniowa 1939' (The September Campaign 1939), Sikorski Institute, London, 1951

Raczyński, E., *In Allied London*, Weidenfeld & Nicolson, 1962

Reynaud, Paul, *La France a sauvé l'Europe*, Vol. I, Flammarion, Paris, 1947

Ribet, Maurice, *Le Procès de Riom*, Paris, 1945

Roos, Hans, *Geschichte der polnischen Nation 1916–60*, Stuttgart, 1961

Roosevelt and Frankfurter: Their Correspondence 1928–45, Bodley Head, 1967

The Roosevelt Letters, Ed. Elliott Roosevelt, Vol. III (1928–45), Harrap, 1952

Roskill, S. W., *The War at Sea*, Vol. I, Her Majesty's Stationery Office, 1954

Schmidt, Paul, *Hitler's Interpreter*, Heinemann, 1951

Sherwood, R., *The White House Papers of Harry L. Hopkins*, Eyre & Spottiswoode, 1948

Shirer, William, *Berlin Diary*, Sphere, 1970.

Shirer, William, *The Rise and Fall of the Third Reich*, Simon & Schuster, New York, 1959

Slessor, John, *The Central Blue*, Cassell, 1956

Spears, Edward, *Assignment to Catastrophe*, Vol. I, 'Prelude to Dunkirk', Heinemann, 1954

Speer, Albert, *Inside the Third Reich*, Macmillan, 1970

Staniewicz, Marian, *Klęska wrześniowa na tle stosunków międzynarodowych 1918–39*, Ministry of Defence, Warsaw, 1952

Strang, William, *At Home and Abroad*, Deutsch, 1956

Szembek, J., *Journal 1933–9*, Plon, Paris, 1952

Szymański, Antoni, *Zły sasiad (Bad Neighbour)*, Veritas, London, 1959

Taylor, A. J. P., *The Origins of the Second World War*, Penguin, 1971

Taylor, Telford, *Sword and Swastika*, Simon & Schuster, New York, 1952

War Begins at Home, a 'Mass Observation' study, Ed. Tom Harrison and Charles Madge, Chatto & Windus, 1940

The Memoirs of Ernst von Weizsäcker, Gollancz, 1951

Werth, Alexander, *Russia at War 1941–45*, Barrie & Rockliff, 1964

Whalen, Richard J., *The Founding Father – The Story of Joseph P. Kennedy*, New American Library, New York, 1964

Wheeler-Bennet, J. W., *The Nemesis of Power*, Macmillan, 1967

Woodward, Llewellyn, *British Foreign Policy in the Second World War*, Her Majesty's Stationery Office, 1962

Index